CHAINING DOWN LEVIATHAN

ISBN: 978-1-7334075-1-9

By the Abbeville Institute Press
P.O. Box 10
McClellanville, SC 29458

Cover by Michela Rusconi
Creative director - photography and illustration in Milan, Italy

CHAINING DOWN LEVIATHAN

The American Dream of Self-Government 1776-1865

LUIGI MARCO BASSANI

Abbeville Institute Press

This book is dedicated to Joshua Wong, Oscar Lai, Derek Lam, Nathan Law and Agnes Chow. In our world, these brave youths fighting against the most powerful dystopia on earth are the only political combatants who can be considered the heirs of America's founding fathers.

Contents

America is ... the land of the future, where, in the ages that lie before us, the burden of the World's History shall reveal itself.

-GWF Hegel, Lectures on the Philosophy of History

Foreword

As a distinguished historian of political thought at the University of Milan, Italy, Professor Marco Bassani brings a cosmopolitan perspective to the study of American political thought unencumbered by such self-congratulatory myths as the "city on a hill," and "American exceptionalism." In the present work, he views America as an extension of European civilization. But in doing so, he reveals an American exceptionalism unknown to most Americans. The story begins with seventeenth-century European monarchs who worked out a unique form of political association known by scholars as "the modern European state" or simply "the state." Its goal was to bring independent social authorities such as cities, provinces, the church, the law, banking, money, and business corporation—all of which were potential centers of resistance to royal authority—under control of the crown to the extent possible.

This brought forth violent resistance, and the monarchs were eventually overthrown. They were replaced by mass democracies in the name of various forms of liberalism or socialism. These regimes, however, did not dismantle the king's coercive instruments of centralization; rather, they were expanded in the name of the people to a degree the monarchs could not have imagined. Indeed, a new word was later invented—totalitarianism—to describe what a modern state would become if not checked in its disposition to centralize power. Modern totalitarian regimes and their mass murders were not possible under European monarchies because the kings were hedged in by powerful independent social authorities who could resist. These were gradually hollowed out or weakened by the centralization needed to create mass liberal democracies. Hitler did not create the massive concentration of political power he put to such evil use; that was the work of over a century of German liberalism which destroyed the rich mosaic of over a hundred small principalities and free cities in Germany that limited centralization of power.

Having unleashed the modern state upon the world, Europeans now had the problem of how to control its inherent disposition to centralize power. In this they failed. Power would ebb and flow, but it inevitably moved toward increasing centralization. This was not the case, however, with the founding America that Bassani explores. The colonies were planted in the seventeenth century when Britain was not a fully developed modern state and still had one foot in the medieval world. A century and a half later, Britain spoke as a modern state, telling the colonists in the Declaratory Act (1766) that it had the authority to bind the colonies "in all cases whatsoever." The colonies, however, had not changed much since their *pre-modern* founding, and this enabled them to step outside the logic of the modern state and to view it critically. Professor Bassani shows how during their first 90 years (1776-1865), Americans theorized *and* put into practice, constitutional rules that were able not only to check the growth of centralization but also to reverse it.

Here was the form of government the Europeans had failed to produce. America's central government did not possess plenary power. It had only a few well-defined powers delegated to it by a compact between sovereign states. In a constitution of this kind, the states had the right to check unauthorized acts of central power and even to secede. The right of secession was affirmed by New York, Virginia, and Rhode Island in their ordinances of ratification. And elsewhere power was widely distributed through competing jurisdictions and a prevailing ethic that conflicts should be settled by institutions of deliberation and consent. When states grew too large for self-government, counties seceded and negotiated a state of their own. People formed political societies in the vast stretches of federal territory, seceded and then negotiated with the Union to become a state. Jefferson believed as Americans moved westward states would negotiate secessions and form new Unions of states. He imagined three countries in the future united by trade and defense treaties: a federation along the Atlantic coast, one along the Mississippi River, and one along the Pacific.

Whereas Europeans were burdened with heavy taxation, debt, and stood in fear of a standing army, Americans, after 1800, paid no inland federal taxes. By the 1830s the federal government was free of debt and pretty much remained so until the Civil War. The sword was in the hands of state militias. The states were equally frugal with taxes and debt, and as of 1860 the central government had actually diminished in size. This is not the description of a libertarian utopia but of how America actually worked, until it was derailed by the Lincolnian revolution.

It was a *revolution* because Lincoln had no constitutional authority to use military force against states that had seceded from the Union. So said President James Buchanan and his attorney general. Whatever the Constitution is today, an American state had as much right to secede from the Union in 1860 as Britain had to secede from the European Union in 2016, or as 15 states had to secede from the Soviet Union in 1991. Every southern state that seceded exercised the proper legal procedures, and Confederate commissioners were sent to Washington to negotiate an amicable political divorce.[1] Lincoln, however, refused to receive them on the grounds that secession was treason against central authority. In so acting, he falsely presupposed that America was founded as a modern unitary state; whereas the Constitution, as amended in 1791, was formed in opposition to such a state.

Lincoln's invasion to prevent secession and his use of total war to transform America into a would-be modern state cost around a million lives, if one counts civilians and the tens of thousands of slaves that died from the dislocations of war and the disease and epidemics that sprang from the fetid "contraband camps" hastily built to control them. If adjusted for today's population, that would be some 10 million deaths. Today this should be a moral outrage, and not only because secession does not have the connotations of anarchy that Lincoln gave it in his first inaugural and which persisted up to the end of the Cold War.

So today, it is fashionable to justify the War by preaching that it was about slavery, that the South seceded to protect slavery and the North invaded to abolish it. But that is special pleading. First, Lincoln and Congress insisted that the invasion was intended to

1 Cf. H. Newcomb Morse, "The Foundations and Meaning of Secession," *Stetson University Law Review*, Vol. XV, No.2 (1986), pp. 419-436.

prevent secession and did not touch the question of slavery. Second, three states did not publish their reasons for secession. Four states did publish reasons and mentioned agitation over the demand for immediate and uncompensated emancipation backed by John Brown-style terrorism, as well as other reasons. Four other states, however, initially voted *not to secede,* namely Virginia, North Carolina, Tennessee, and Arkansas. Slavery was not an issue for them. They reversed their vote only when Lincoln requested troops to invade the seceding states. This, they thought, was opposed to everything America stood for. If successful, Lincoln's invasion would draw the teeth of state sovereignty by consolidating the states into a unitary state. Those four states, at least, were fighting against the imposition of a modern European state in America just as their fathers had done when the British tried the same in 1775. And this was arguably a large part of why the other states seceded, as can be seen in the Confederate Constitution which retained the founder's Constitution, almost word for word, except for some strategic reforms that made it more difficult ever to form a modern European state in the Confederacy.

Lincoln's would-be modern American state built by war out of the ruins of the founders' federative polity has had an illustrious career and, despite its origins, is not to be despised. But it is coming apart because it is too large, too centralized, and has lost social trust. Despite having pledged allegiance, from childhood on, to the flag of a modern state (one and indivisible), 39 percent of Americans, according to a 2018 Zogby poll, favor secession of their state and 29 percent were not sure. That means 68 percent are open to thinking about a restructuring of the Union, if not actual secession. So, Bassani's study is not of mere historical interest, for it brings to light the only period in the American tradition that can provide insight on how to disengage from a modern state that has lost the knowledge of how to stop growing.

Donald Livingston

July 2020

Preface

More than thirty years ago, Robert Higgs published a book which became a classic on government growth. Analyzing the staggering evolution of American political power in the twentieth century, Higgs emphasized the role of both crises and ideology. "For more than a century ... the United States had a government that [was] ... strong but limited." And during that time America became "the world's richest and freest society."[1] In his study, ideology in the American context is presented as a "somewhat coherent, rather comprehensive belief system that, in the 1900s, invariably called for the expansion of federal power rather than its retreat. All the good crises that the century produced were never let "go to waste" but were used to build a highway for the centralization and extension of power.

This book should be read as a prequel to that story. It would be impossible, in fact, to understand such a federal power grab as the one discussed by Higgs, without the knowledge of what happened after the Civil War, when America was already under the spell of the most potent instrument for the growth of power ever produced in Western history, the very modern, modern state.

This book is not part of the 1619 project. It is an intellectual history that barely mentions the problem of slavery. If you believe that American history is nothing but a cover up for inhuman

1 Robert Higgs, Crisis and Leviathan. Critical Episodes in the Growth of American Government (New York: Oxford University Press, 1987), pp. 3-4.

bondage, for white supremacy, Anglo-Saxonism, and so on, you will find little here to interest you or to support that view. In this book what the protagonists say is taken at face value.

Despite this, the present writer is not so naïve as to believe that the first eighty years of the American Republic were the "golden age of liberty." I perfectly understand that for some people such an age lies in a post-capitalist future, for others it may be nowadays. Nonetheless, many things that are deemed rights and freedoms today were not even conceivable at the Founding.

This book is about the golden age of federalism and federal liberty. It is about an era in which every political issue in America revolved around the federal system of government. Federalism was a success because it mirrored premodern contractual and consensual institutions. In the golden age of communal liberty merchants and citizens formed their own statutes in everything related to self-government. During these times there was no clear-cut definition of power over a given territory, as there were no borders in the modern sense. An institutionalized power always found an antagonistic counter-power claiming allegiance from the same subjects. The result was that every command was nothing more than a claim, subject to be opposed and contained in a web of competing counterclaims. This book analyses the intellectual endeavor of federalism as the most important bastion of resistance to the modern state in the Western world.

The demise of federalism after the Civil War opened the door to the largest growth of government activity in American history. By contrast, the federal government shrank in the years between the Revolution and the Civil War, when federalism was at the heart of all political and constitutional debates. U.S. history shows conclusively that federalism, as an "institutional fact," produced the only effective barrier to governmental growth.

Much of the research for this book was done over the course of several years. I was lucky to be invited as a visiting scholar several times (2011-2012, 2018-2019) at Florida Atlantic University, and I thank Marshall L. DeRosa and Ilaria Serra for the opportunity. The manuscript was discussed during a splendid Jefferson Seminar organized in June 2019 by Donald Livingston. Scholars and friends were present and precious suggestions were provided by Ethan Alexander-Davey, Bill Craver, Vince Graham, Brad Green, Alex Habighorst, Gyuhwan Han, Jonathan Harris, Ivan Jankovic, Marjorie Jeffrey, Patrick Reasonover, Carey Roberts, Jake Starbuck and Joe Stromberg. I am also very grateful to Kevin C. Gutzman, Howard Lee Cheek and Tom Woods who read and commented on this book prior to publication.

My friend Jason Jewell invited me to Faulkner University in Montgomery as a visiting scholar from February to June 2020. He and his wonderful family kept me exceptionally good company in the trying times of coronavirus. By a stroke of good luck, I dodged the lockdown in my hometown of Milan, Italy, and got a moderate stay-at-home in Alabama in its stead, so I was able to complete this work in the beautiful surroundings of Lake Martin.

Marco Bassani, August 2020

Introduction

This book is an analysis of American political thought between the Revolution and the Civil War. It is grounded in "conceptual history" and, though based on solid historical research, will not be aimed at finding new evidence, but rather at providing a quite different interpretation of the period. During this period (1776-1860) America was in no way an appendix to Europe, particularly from an institutional point of view. Yet it later became just that during the second half of the nineteenth century, following a process of osmosis that, as it succeeded, eventually placed Europe itself (after the two World Wars) on the periphery of America.

Europe certainly cannot be omitted in any history of American political thought. The generation that fought the Revolution was nagged by fear that America could become a second Europe. What the revolutionary generation worried about the most, although at times in no crystal-clear terms, was the creation of a fully-fledged modern state in the new world. The modern state, from the European monarchies of the early modern era onward, has become the sole model of political organization of free and non-free peoples. But as far as American institutional reality is concerned, it took the whole epoch from the Revolution to the Civil War for such a model to solidify (and the case could additionally be made that it was never fully transplanted).

Whether consciously or not, the politicians who won the Civil War (and Abraham Lincoln in particular) laid out the premises for transforming America into a second, strengthened Europe. The importation of the idea of the modern state into America was central to this transformation. American "exceptionalism"—the belief that there are distinct historical, social and cultural aspects that make America a nation unto itself, and therefore impossible to compare to European societies[1]—can perhaps be glimpsed in its prolonged resistance to the allure and rationalistic simplifications of the modern state. However, the tension between the powerful forces of centralization and those of the territorial division of power (federalism)—the topic of this book—created a country that cannot be investigated, using European political categories, at least until the Civil War. As one historian put it, "it is the absence of a sense of the state that has been the great hallmark of American political culture."[2]

It is interesting to observe in this regard what Georg W. F. Hegel said about the "new Free States of North America":

> In general, the [North American] state is only in a process of becoming. ... [It] is a still-forming state, a state in the making, which does not yet have need of a monarchy because it has not yet developed to this point. It is a federation of states. Such states are the worst when it comes to foreign relations. Only its peculiar location has saved the federation from total destruction. ... But when all the land has been occupied so that there are internal social

---

1 See Charles Lockhart, *The Roots of American Exceptionalism: History, Institutions, and Culture* (New York: Macmillan, 2003); Seymour Martin Lipset, *American Exceptionalism: A Double-Edged Sword* (New York: Norton, 1996); Ellis Sandoz, *Republicanism, Religion, and the Soul of America* (Columbia: University of Missouri Press, 2006).

2 Stephen Skowronek, *Building a New American State. The Expansion of National Administrative Capacities, 1877-1920* (New York: Cambridge University Press, 1982), p. 3.

> pressures and the need for trade arises, the state must necessarily develop to the point of having to maintain a different system of government.[3]

Despite having given to the early republic only an apparently distracted glance, Hegel had seen quite correctly into the future. The United States of his time was clearly not a modern state, though within a few decades it would turn into one, albeit of a peculiar type. This would not happen due to societal forces driving toward industrialization, as Hegel predicted, but rather because of the efforts of Lincoln, whose determination to preserve the Union, at whatever human sacrifice, finally rendered the United States a country governed in a European fashion.

Hegel's most important disciple held a quite different view. In 1845 Karl Marx stated that "the most perfect example of the modern state is North America." However, this was due in Marx's view to the fact that property in America was well safeguarded; in fact, "the state has become a separate entity, alongside and outside civil society; but it is nothing more than the form of organization which the bourgeois are compelled to adopt, both for internal and external purposes, for the mutual guarantee of their property and interests."[4]

The twentieth century drew the two sides of the Atlantic together, not because the century of the masses, of socialism, and of totalitarianism created the same problems in the two regions, but because American and European institutions were already drawn in principle toward convergence. The *societies* did not resemble each other as much as their political institutions did; and, having become almost indistinguishable, the latter provided similar

---

3 Georg W. F. Hegel, *Lectures on the Philosophy of World History*, vol. 1, 1822-1823, ed. and trans. Robert F. Brown and Peter C. Hodgson, with the assistance of G. Geuss (Oxford: Oxford University Press, 2011), pp. 193-194. It is the translation Vorlesungen über die Philosophie der Weltgeschichte, Berlin 1822-1823 .... Seelmann, eds. (Hamburg: Felix Meiner, 1996).

4 Marx portrays his own outlook as a general consensus: "The modern French, English and American writers all express the opinion that the state exists only for the sake of private property." Karl Marx and Friedrich Engels, *German Ideology*, in *Collected Works* (London: Lawrence and Wishart, 1976), vol. 5, p. 90.

responses to different problems. In both America and Europe, the twentieth century was the age of the triumph of the state, of centralization, of government intervention in the free market, and, naturally, of wars. This happened more "softly" between the Atlantic and Pacific, and in, the final analysis, the advent of the "imperial presidency" was, in terms of the loss of freedom, just a pale *simulacrum* of the charismatic leaders and the dictatorships that plagued Europe. It may not be just another fortunate American exception, and if not, the secret of why America remained relatively freer than Europe, and not just in the 1800s, must be found in prior history. The declaration of Madame de Staël that "liberty is ancient, and tyranny is modern" is no truer of any country in the world than it is of America.

In this work continental Europe serves as the hidden touchstone: The motherland of the state represents a political universe that was in the beginning America's "other," and, over the long run, it insinuated itself into the very fabric of the American republic. The European solution of the problem of political order, i.e. the state, was not easily imported into America; but eventually, after many crises of rejection, it finally took hold, though never quite fully. This work will focus on a period during which American political thought and institutions were relatively separate from those of Europe. The heart of the entire experience of the American republic from the Revolution to the Civil War is summed up by the term "federalism." In the same period in which Europe passed from the French Revolution to the Napoleonic era, and then became obsessed by the myth of the nation, America lived out a golden age of freedom from government control. In fact, we should not forget that the federal government (the object of apprehension of nearly all the political thinkers we will consider, from George Washington's presidency until the beginning of Lincoln's) not only did not grow proportionally, but was scaled back. Here was a unique case in modern history.

A comparative history, whether of ideas or of facts, has a unique perspective that a history focused only on one country cannot have: It raises questions that we would otherwise never consider. Thus, for example, taking continental Europe as a benchmark of "normality" for developed countries (in truth, a norm rather questionable), European historians have extracted from the tumbler of facts and ideas a frequently confronted problem such as "why is there no socialism in the United States?"[5] Yet this would never have leaped to the attention of an American historian. It is interesting to note that Theodore Lowi explains the negligible influence of socialism on the American labor movement by the presence of a federal system of government.[6] By the same token, studies of American political parties and their supposed "lightness" (taking the heavy European party as the universal norm of various party forms) always highlight the organization of the parties at the state level, since they endured as allied coalitions of large state parties until the 1970s, if not to the present day. In short, what is increasingly evident from the study of the academic literature is the enormous importance that the federal system of government plays in American politics and culture even today. Federalism represents the permanent structure, changes to which can explain many political phenomena.

However, the American political system today, in which the government in Washington is an absolute and nearly undisputed actor, is not federalist. If anything, the current system is but a pallid reverse image of the one constructed by the Founding Fathers, which survived with varying fortunes until the Civil War. The states' rights school of thought, whose authentic federal vision provided the backdrop for the debates on the nature of the Union until the War, represented an intellectual universe in which the outlook of the modern state not only was inoperative but was directly attacked. The unifying theme of the political battle waged by the most prominent Antifederalists, Thomas Jefferson, and then John C. Calhoun, is precisely the rejection of the modern state as the solution to the problem of political order.

5 See Werner Sombart, *Warum gibt es in den Vereinigten Staaten keinen Sozialismus?* (Tübingen: Mohr, 1906), *Why is there no Socialism in the United States*, translated and edited with an Introductory essay by C.T. Husbands, foreword by Michael Harrington (White Plains, NY: Sharpe, 1976).

6 See Theodore J. Lowi, "Why Is There No Socialism in the United States?" *International Political Science Review* 5, no. 4 (1984), pp. 369-380.

By now we fully understand the modern state—its theological roots,[7] its legal doctrines and its "natural history—that originated in Europe and then spread all over the world, rendering Westphalia the only conceivable norm. Since this is the only form of state that has ever existed in human history, we should really erase the word "modern." The origin, the development, and the "great saga" of the creation of the *jus publicum europaeum* (to use the famous Schmittian expression) are by now well-ploughed ground for anyone who has the time and desire to study them. But does a model of political organization exist apart from the state? Is there a concept of political relationships and obligations that might be divorced from a fictitious person acting through bureaucrats, agencies, taxation, and prohibitions?

Cultural anthropologists find the state even among the most remote African tribes. Historians of antiquity speak with confidence of the state in Mesopotamia five thousand years ago. The concept of the state influences—often obscures—how we see distant realities. We shall see that America, which was already the most modern society on the planet by the mid-1800s, for most of its history as an independent country did not know, either in theory or practice, the modern state, its categories, or its task to reduce all politics to juridical relationships.

The wagon trains of pioneers that drove westward were not the only ones to inhabit a stateless geographical and political space, in which the rifle was the only government they needed. Indeed, the very core of American life in the 1800s developed with relatively few ties to European concepts of the state. The American difference, however, did not directly rest on the system of government constructed by the framers in 1787 in the longest-enduring constitution in the world. It is found rather in the reaction against the centralization of power that was the outcome of the Constitutional Convention in Philadelphia. The heart of this vision

7 Cf. Bernard Bourdin, *The Theological-Political Origins of the Modern State: The Controversy Between James I of England and Cardinal Bellarmine* (2004) trans. Susan Pickford (Washington, DC: Catholic University of America Press, 2010); cf. also Hans Blumenberg, *The Legitimacy of the Modern Age*, trans. Robert M. Wallace (Cambridge, MA: MIT Press, 1983).

is to be found in a purely American political tradition, which is the object of this work: states' rights. To translate this into continental terms: While in Europe the dominant tradition has followed along the Machiavelli-Bodin-Hobbes path, America, for a long time, pursued the course anticipated by Johannes Althusius, the long forgotten forerunner of federal theory.

America, by now the West *tout court*, suddenly appeared on the scene during the World Wars, carving out the leading role in the field of international relations. The result was an explosion of power and "modernity" that is without precedent in history. Yet this happened largely without acknowledging the "presence of the past"—the history that made America a non-Europe. So, on the one hand, the American past blends into Western history; on the other it really stands apart from it. The American genesis was, in fact, a battle against the triumph of the modern state. This poses a problem which is not merely one of philosophical or historical perspective. The American past is always narrated in terms of limited government v. democracy, Lockean liberalism v. republicanism, sometimes liberty v. empire.

From the consensus historians of a century ago to the present day, and particularly during the Cold War, there has been a veritable suppression of the most important American political tradition. It is a political tradition that unfolded from the early battles of the first Continental Congress through the fight for ratification, then through the key figures of Thomas Jefferson, John Taylor of Caroline, and John Caldwell Calhoun. The states' rights tradition dominated the panorama of political thought until at least the Civil War, and then became a "sinking stream" that resurfaced in critical moments of twentieth century American history, from the New Deal through desegregation, and again in the Reagan era.

Did the thirteen colonies separate collectively or singularly from Great Britain in 1776? Prior to 1787, did the Union concern just the States or the American people as well? Is the Constitution that was ratified in 1789 simply a compact between sovereign States or a Union of the entire American population? These are perennial questions in American history, briefly encapsulating the entire political debate that developed prior to the twentieth century, after which the main question became the extension of the powers of the federal government not over the States, but into the free market. It should be emphasized, however, that a division had already briefly arisen over the role of government in the economy during the struggle between the early advocates of centralization and the defenders of state sovereignty. The original *laissez-faire* doctrine, taken up by states' rights champions such as Jefferson and Calhoun, is indissolubly tied to the antifederalist position regarding the contractual and voluntary nature of the American compact. By contrast, those who favored a robust and energetic federal government largely preferred an interventionist policy from the dawn of the republic. In any case, the fundamental genetic questions about the birth of the United States always tend to re-emerge during times of crisis or of sharp political polarization.

During the first century of American independent history, the Civil War and the Supreme Court solved the controversies arising from these questions, and the response was unambiguous: The Constitution established a perpetual union of the people and not of the States, whose sovereignty was by then demolished, since they had been denied the possibility of "authentically" interpreting the Constitution. The States were no longer the framers of the Constitution; over them there was a metaphysical and meta-constitutional entity never mentioned in any founding document: the "People of the United States"; and its will was whatever the Supreme Court determined it to be. If the doctrinal dispute over the nature of the Union engaged American scholars and politicians for the first ninety years and beyond, it should be noted that the controversy was not resolved by interpretation, scientific consensus, or even popular support, much less by Thomas Kuhn's logic of scientific paradigms that follow in succession, each displacing the previous ones without expressly refuting them. Rather, the outcome was decided only by the might of Lincoln's army.

For a long time in America, at least during the period from its founding down to the Civil War—that is, the period when federalism was the cornerstone of political thought and government—the vision was that of citizenship granted by a State, each one separate and distinct within the federation. Indeed, both Thomas Jefferson and James Madison believed that the Constitution implicitly affirmed the non-existence of a federal common law. According to the American constitutional design—as reinforced by the Tenth Amendment—the States held all powers not expressly delegated to the federation, and no law conferred on the central government the power to involve itself in any way with the individual rights of American citizens.

However, an enormous problem is presented by the fact that, even from the beginning, American political thought was loaded, if not overloaded, with the "legal mythologies of modernity"[8] that had accompanied the modern state as it took root in Europe. "State of nature," "social contract," and later even "sovereignty"—as I will show in the chapter devoted to Calhoun—populated the vocabulary of the young republic and, even earlier, the colonies. But—and this is the ultimate thesis of this volume—we are dealing with conceptual "false friends." Though the vocabulary is that of the *jus publicum europaeum* of the late eighteenth century, such terms were utilized quite loosely in the colonies and did not in any way imply a search for political unity. The jargon that in Europe helped to build the conceptualization of a political community that had to coalesce around a given center (King or Parliament) must be reinterpreted in the American context.

The result in Europe under the pressure of the "natural law project" was that of a "historical stage reduced to two actors, the individual and the state, each the consequence of the same process, each allied with the other in the same life and death war against old ideologies and organizational practices."[9] The outcome in America

8 See Paolo Grossi, *Mitologie giuridiche della modernità* (Milan: Giuffrè, 2007).

9 Paolo Grossi, "Modernità politica e ordine giuridico," *Quaderni fiorentini* 28 (1998), p. 32. Grossi, eminent historian of medieval law, concludes: "The free-spirited itinerary of political modernity evolved over the history of law into the confines of legal positivism, thanks to the intensification of politics by the deceptive but effective means of natural law strategy, of which, despite the passage of time, we are still victims," p. 39. In his view, "eighteenth century natural law theory" presented itself as "the most intelligent, the most aware, the most able foundry of legal myths ever encountered over the long history of Western legal thought; from it emerged a complex of integrally imagined and ordered myths that gave rise to a true legal mythology" ("Oltre le mitologie giuridiche della modernità," *Quaderni fiorentini* 29 (2000), p. 218).

was quite different. For the period we are considering, the doctrines of natural law and the contractual conceptions of the origin of political community (in short, the Lockean heritage), and even the concept of sovereignty, were without a nucleus capable of drawing everything into the orbit of a state. Rather, these were always used against the formation of such a center—inevitably identified with the federal government. In the famous analysis of Louis Hartz,[10] America was bred in a Lockean liberal consensus since it had no feudal social forms; even more crucial was the absence of a Prince, the pivotal, and in certain respects irreplaceable, figure in the formation of the modern state. As with every "national" legislative assembly, Congress became the heir of the "sovereign," though of a sovereign that never existed—and the difference is not trivial. If in Europe the doctrine of natural law can appear as the true theoretical bulwark of a project of individual emancipation within the state (not from the state), such a vision should not be exported across the Atlantic. Although the US is now governed by the second body of the king, to use Ernst Kantorowicz famous metaphor,[11] it is not irrelevant that the *corpus naturale* was never here, and even in colonial times the king was as distant as he was immaterial.

The first chapter will focus on the concept of the state and its absolute modernity. It will show just how much the conceptual categories that dominated its formation and its logic were non-operative in America during the period under consideration. Subsequent chapters analyze the critical political debates of the American republic, from the one over the ratification to the Jeffersonian doctrine of 1798, to New England's bid for secession, to the re-emergence of states' rights due to the central theorist of that time, John Calhoun. The final chapter will be devoted to the figure of Abraham Lincoln as the defender of the Union, the maker of the nation and, through this, of the American state.

10 Louis Hartz, *The Liberal Tradition in America* (New York: Harcourt, Brace, 1955).

11 Ernst Kantorowicz, *The King's Two Bodies: A Study in Medieval Political Theology* (Princeton: Princeton University Press, 1957).

Chapter 1

State and/or Federation: A Framework of Analysis

> The state is not an eternal and unchanging element in human affairs. For most of its history, humanity got by (whether more happily or not) without a state. For all its universality in our times, the state is a *contingent* (and comparatively recent) historical development. Its predominance may also prove to be quite *transitory*. Once we have recognized that there were societies *before* the state, we may also want to consider the possibility that there could be societies *after* the state.[1]

The primary task of this book is to offer a realistic view of the state and apply it to the American experience. Our analysis will show that neither the organized reality nor the conceptual arsenal of the modern state was enthroned in America until the era of Abraham Lincoln. Thus it is of paramount importance to have a clear view of what was missing.

To that end we must begin with a scientific and historical description of the state. The state nourishes itself with powerful myths, chief among which are its own eternity, inescapability, and ubiquity. The construction of *jus publicum europaeum,* a process that took at least five centuries, is an ideological undertaking that produced an intellectual political world in which all too often scholars call *state* any form of political association, *jurist* any political

1 Christopher Pierson, *The Modern State* (New York: Routledge, 1996), p. 35.

thinker, and tend to pigeonhole in the paradigm of *sovereignty* every political community. As we shall see, this misunderstanding has brought an unparalleled array of confusion, particularly in the United States. This chapter will discuss prevailing definitions of the state, many of them erroneous, and then show that Jacksonian America during the first half of the nineteenth century managed pretty well *without* a modern state.

1.1) The State is Modern

For nearly a century, the historiography of the state has addressed two major issues: 1) whether this organization of political power is perennial or transient; and 2) the problem of its origins. The two questions can essentially be stated as follows: "Has the state always existed?" and, if not, "when did it begin?" The most significant question is whether the state is new or old.

The expression *modern state*, analogous in European languages (e.g. *moderne Staat*, *État moderne*, *Stato moderno*, *Estado moderno*), is, as noted in the Introduction, quite misleading. The term suggests evolution. It implies that there was an ancient, a medieval, and maybe a contemporary (or postmodern) state. It suggests that, while it became "modern" in the modern era, the state had always existed. That the state is simply a natural development of power, and that such an institution has accompanied human societies from their earliest beginnings, is a myth, as false as it is persistent and difficult to eradicate.

In fact, the state is modern. Indeed, the term "modernity" itself makes very little sense politically except in relation to the state. As the Spanish historian José Maravall noted many years ago: "The modern mindset is projected onto the state, and such a mindset is in turn largely determined by the state."[2] And, he continues, "the state becomes the symbol of all changes ... that occurred in Europe during the historical crisis that ushered in modern times."[3] Gianfranco Miglio, a prominent scholar of

2 José Antonio Maravall, *Stato moderno e mentalità sociale* (Bologna: il Mulino, 1991) [1972], vol. 1, p. 17.

3 *Ibid.*, pp. 40-41.

European political institutions, proposed altering the written form of the inherited expression into "(modern) State." That is to say, the state, in the view of Miglio and of a long tradition of scholarship, is *only* modern. The medieval and ancient eras did not have state-like forms of political power, as their institutions were not even remotely comparable to that of the modern era.[4] As Miglio states, "[T]oday's political order, far from being the sole and inevitable product of universal reason, is rather the random result of a series of historical junctures."[5] Whether we see its cradle in the Italian system of states after the Peace of Lodi (1454), or later in Western Europe (Spain, France and England), the state "[g]radually emerged in the course of the fifteenth and sixteenth centuries and found its first mature form in the seventeenth."[6]

The state is European in the sense that it originated and developed in Europe (though it then became highly exportable). It is modern because it began its history during a period which more or less coincides with the modern age. And it is an "invention," not a "discovery." Leopold von Ranke notoriously believed states to be "thoughts of God," but we should consider them as man-made artifacts. The modern state appears as an artificially engineered "institutional complex rather than as one that has developed spontaneously by accretion. ... [It] is not bestowed upon a people as a gift by God, its own *Geist*, or blind historical forces; it is a 'made' reality."[7]

There is no doubt about the European origin of state institutions. The American author of a well-known booklet on the medieval roots of statehood clarified the point: "The European model of the state

4 Among scholars the absence of the concept of the state during the Middle Ages is widely accepted, so much so that what a rather well-known Italian academic, Roberto de Mattei, states seems inexplicable: "Since its formation at the dawn of the Middle Ages, European civilization has known the sovereignty of the state," *La sovranità necessaria* (Rome: Il Minotauro, 2001), p. 13.

5 Gianfranco Miglio, "Genesi e trasformazioni del termine-concetto 'Stato'" (1981), in *Le regolarità della politica* (Milan: Giuffrè, 1988), vol. 2, p. 803.

6 Heinz Lubasz, Introduction, *The Development of the Modern State*, ed. Heinz Lubasz (New York: Macmillan, 1964), p. 1.

7 Gianfranco Poggi, *The Development of the Modern State: A Sociological Introduction* (Stanford: Stanford University Press, 1978), p. 95.

became the fashionable model. No European state imitated a non-European model, but the non-European states either imitated the European model in order to survive or else went through a colonial experience which introduced large elements of the European system."[8] This flow followed a one-way path, from Europe toward the rest of the world, and never vice-versa. Wolfgang Reinhard stated: "Europe invented the state. ... The state and the power of the state so clearly have a European origin that even indicating its provenance is superfluous."[9] In short, the adjective "European" is superfluous, while "modern" is simply redundant: The state is intimately European and modern.

For additional support of this view, one need only look to medievalist scholar Paolo Grossi, who defines the state as "the ordering scheme of a precise historical and political reality ... an historical category arising from an intense interpretive value ... loaded with a highly intense historicity."[10] Miglio also paid homage, though always blended with "realism," to this grand construct of the European tradition: "It is not an exaggeration to consider the abstract and 'personalized' idea of the 'state' as the masterpiece of western political thought, and, at the same time, the most sophisticated 'pretense' behind which those who make up the political class are always forced to hide."[11] And Hans Kelsen, arguably the jurist who most fully believed in the possibility of cloaking the raw reality of power in legal garb both elegant and functional, was well aware of the fictitious nature of such a construction. Anyone still seeking an answer to the eternal problem of what lies behind positive law "will find neither an absolute truth of a metaphysical entity nor the absolute justice of a natural law. Anyone who lifts that veil without eyes closed will be fixed in the full gaze of the Medusa of power."[12]

8 Joseph R. Strayer, *On the Medieval Origins of the Modern State* (Princeton: Princeton University Press, 1970), p. 12.

9 Wolfgang Reinhard, *Geschichte der Staatsgewalt: Eine vergleichende Verfassungsgeschichte Europas von den Anfängen bis zur Gegenwart* (München: C.H. Beck, 1999), p. 11.

10 Paolo Grossi, "Un diritto senza Stato," *Quaderni fiorentini* 25 (1996), p. 270.

11 Gianfranco Miglio, *Genesi e trasformazioni del termine-concetto 'Stato,'* p. 825.

12 Hans Kelsen, *Die Gleichheit vor dem Gesetz* (Berlin: de Gruyter, 1927), vol. 3, p. 55.

However, this consensus among scholars is relatively recent (and it is still far from being as comprehensive as it ought to be).

1.2) Treitschke's View of the State

To glimpse the view of the state that was prevalent in western Europe in the nineteenth century, Heinrich von Treitschke's works are extremely valuable, because they perpetuate misconceptions, while also getting parts of the definition right. A professor at the University of Berlin for almost thirty years until his death in 1896, Treitschke has been studied mostly for his aggressive nationalism (very famous is his definition of the essence of the state: "*Macht, Macht und wieder Macht,*" —"power, power, and more power") as well as for his virulent anti-Semitism. But, in his time, he was also called the Machiavelli of the century and was considered an authority on politics and the state. "[A]s an indefatigable and brilliant writer and as an inspired lecturer he exercised a tremendous influence on the young academic generation who later as teachers and public officials helped spread Treitschke's ideas and evaluations," wrote his editor, Hans Kohn.[13] For the moment, we are solely interested in his view of the state, which is "the people, legally united as an independent entity. By the word 'people' we understand briefly a number of families permanently living side by side. This definition implies that the state is *primordial* and *necessary*, that it is as enduring as history, and no less *essential* to mankind than speech. ... We, on the other hand, must deal here with man as an historical being, and we can only say that creative political genius is inherent in him, and that the state, like him, subsists from the beginning."[14]

In his view, it is the state that makes men fully human. Human communities are made of speech, written records, and the state. Through this institution, mankind emerges from prehistory. The savage becomes a human being and part of a political body. In Treitschke's perspective, it is the state that brings mankind into

13 Hans Kohn, *Introduction* to Heinrich von Treitschke, *Politics* (New York: Macmillan Company, 1963), p. ix. The original German edition was published in 1898-1900 in Leipzig; for a good biography see Andreas Dorpalen, *Heinrich von Treitschke* (New Haven, CT: Yale University Press, 1957).

14 Heinrich von Treitschke, *Politics*, p. 3 (italics added).

history, and not mankind, at a peculiar stage and in a peculiar place, that invented the state. The phenomenon "state" is essentially meta-historical: It has an eternal nucleus that defies any attempt to corner it in contingency. In this, Treitschke was merely echoing the lesson of Immanuel Kant in *Conjectures on the Beginning of Human History* (1786).[15]

However, as one goes on reading Treitschke's writing about the state, a more accurate analysis of modern politics emerges. Comparison with political power in antiquity, and most importantly with the Middle Ages, makes crystal clear that the state cannot be what he would like it to be (*i.e.*, perennial). The state was not just one institution among many others. It originated *after* the breakup of the medieval political order. Of such a break, according to Treitschke, it was Luther and Machiavelli who were the best interpreters.

Treitschke is trying to come to terms with an institutional and political entity, the state, which he proclaimed to be perennial at its core and responding to a human necessity. However, as Treitschke very well knows, the details of the historical drama do not fit the state into the categories that he (and a long tradition before him) crafted. He is caught between forces: his own historical investigation of the state, the great philosophical tradition, and his own passion. The latter pushes Treitschke to link the state to a human vital need, rather than to an historical period. The modern state project—the search for political unity in human communities—appears to him so noble that it has to become a categorical good for all humanity at all times. Devoid of any contingent meaning, it becomes the ultimate conceptual test of any human political aggregate.

Thus, for Treitschke, the state is both modern *and* eternal. The state is as inevitable as language: "We can imagine humanity without a number of important attributes. But humanity without government is simply unthinkable, for it would then be humanity without reason. Man is driven by his political instinct to construct

15 Cf. Immanuel Kant, "Conjectures on the Beginning of Human History," in *Political Writings*, ed. Hans Reiss, trans. H. B. Nisbet (Cambridge, UK: Cambridge University Press, 1970), pp. 221-234.

a constitution as inevitably as he constructs a language."[16] But for all its inexorability, the state of which he talks is firmly rooted in modern Europe.

Treitschke's analysis of the right of resistance to the state is likewise enlightening. Such a right presupposes a point of view that is *external* to the political power. Since the birth of the state, there has been no external order that could be invoked *vis-à-vis* the sovereign power, to check it or to shed a different light on it. As in Kantian political philosophy, the people cannot be in conflict with the sovereign for two reasons: 1) they cannot have a will of their own, and 2) there cannot be a point of view which is outside of the state. The very idea of justice is produced by the state.

Treistchke's reflections on the state follow the winding path of his grand ideological construct of western *Geist* (spirit). Historically placed between the mythical image of the state produced by Kant and Hegel, and the total disenchantment brought about by Weber and Schmitt later on, his *Politics* has been overlooked by students of the state. But if the state had a personality (not only from the legal point of view, but also in reality), it would probably pick Treitschke as its herald *par excellence*.

Modern, European, unique in its traits, the state appears eternal in its self-positioning as the only possible and reasonable technique for reconstructing political relations. Born from individual (not social) needs, the state renders man an historical animal and creates a civil society in its own image. However, it does not tolerate any different outlook: Otherness is not an option, as all the tools for evaluation are produced by the state itself. The impossibility of such an outlook on the state renders its relationship with society a peculiar one, as society cannot interact with a reality that unassailably leads it ethically and normatively.[17]

16 Heinrich von Treitschke, *Politics*, p. 5.

17 On this topic see also William T. Cavanaugh, "Killing for the Phone Company: Why the Nation-State Is Not the Keeper of the Common Good," *Modern Theology* 20, ... (April 2004), pp. 246-260.

1.3) Weber, Schmitt, Brunner: Modernity Unmasked

Until Germany's defeat in World War I, the German historical and legal schools generally contended that medieval forms of power were fully-achieved statehood.[18] This was the case even though nineteenth-century German scholars, as briefly shown above, had already laid out an analysis of the modernity of the state. A step of no small importance was still necessary in order to break the myth of the perennial existence of the state.[19]

---

18 Georg von Below, in his *Der Deutsche Staat des Mittelalters: ein Grundriss der Deutschen Verfassungsgeschichte* (Lepzig: Quelle und Meyer, 1914), attempted to prove the uninterrupted statehood of the Germanic territories.

19 If the contributions of the Marxist school are not even mentioned in this partial overview, it is owing to the fact that, although some contributions are quite notable, that academic tradition cannot emancipate itself from "historical materialism." The immense body of research on the state amounts, on the other hand, to a "checkmate" to Marx, since it clearly shows that at the emergence of the modern age all the major political changes precede economic changes, and not vice-versa. Jean Baechler summarized the point: "Capitalism is the transcription of a principle into the economic order, that, transcribed into the political order, is called 'democracy', and ... political actions determine economic actions" (*Le capitalisme, Les origins* [Paris: Gallimard, 1995] vol. 1, pp. 35-36.) The reversal of the Marxist interpretative rule resulting from the history of the state is by now such an undisputed fact as to render entire libraries obsolete, to put it mildly. Even the well-known debate of forty years ago on the nature of the state in which Ralph Miliband and Nicos Poulantzas opposed each other "left many Marxists with the uncomfortable reality of a still unresolved dichotomy at the core of Marxian political theory, and for many it brought an end to the idea that there is something called *the* Marxist theory of the state" (Clyde W. Barrow, "The Miliband-Poulantzas Debate: An Intellectual History," in *Paradigm Lost. State Theory Reconsidered*, Stanley Aronowitz and Peter Bratsis, eds. [Minneapolis: University of Minnesota Press, 2002], p. 43. The two key volumes in the debate are: Ralph Miliband, *The State in Capitalist Society* (New York: Basic Books, 1969), and Nicos Poulantzas, *Pouvoir politique et classes sociales de l'état capitaliste* (Paris: Maspéro, 1968). Cf. also Clyde W. Barrow, *Critical Theories of the State: Marxist, Neo-Marxist, Post-Marxist* (Madison: University of Wisconsin Press, 1993). Martin Oppenheimer in his *The State in Modern Society* (Amherst, NY: Humanity Books, 2000) is, on the contrary, pretty sure that the Marxist theory of the state is alive and kicking. One of the very few Marxist studies of the growth of the state and on international relations is Benno Teschke, *The Myth of 1648. Class, Geopolitics, and the Making of Modern International Relations* (London: Verso, 2003).The author wants the readers to understand immediately that the work is "rooted in dialectical historical–materialist approach," p. 4. He poses a question that is the most difficult to answer for a Marxist: "What was the connection between the development of the modern state ... and Capitalism?" p. 5. The answer is quite unequivocal: none. At the dawn of modernity,

Since most studies on the modernity of the state began right after the First World War, the sense of estrangement following the war must have played a role. Twelve million dead—and futilely dead—were an indictment of the state, or at least they must have provoked an immense sense of uneasiness. Thus, there was an effort to pin the institution to its history.[20] After the investigations of European scholars after World War I, the state looks more and more like the product of a "process of rationalization" (Weber), born in a specific historical period (Schmitt), and following the progressive disarmament of the populace in favor of an armed bureaucratic caste (Brunner).

Max Weber's definition of the state is one of the best known in the history of the social sciences.[21] While "the state is a relation of men dominating men, a relation supported by means of legitimate (*i.e.*, considered to be legitimate) violence ... [it] is a human community that (successfully) claims the *monopoly of the legitimate use of physical* force within a given territory."[22] Weber was well aware that this creature was a totally novel one in the European political panorama. "The basic functions of the 'state' ... the enactment of law (legislative function); the protection of personal safety and public order (police); the protection of vested rights (administration of justice) ... [were] either totally lacking under primitive conditions,

---

and this is a given in the historiography of the state, every major political development preceded any economic adjustment.

20 For some of the costs, see Gabriel Kolko, *Century of War* (New York: New Press, 1994).

21 John Hoffman, to give one example, affirms that in this definition "we can grasp the ambiguous and elusive notion of the state," in *Beyond the State: An Introductory Critique* (Cambridge, UK: Polity Press, 1995), p. 3.

22 Max Weber, *Essays in Sociology* (1919), trans. and ed. H. H. Gerth and C. Wright Mills (New York: Oxford University Press, 1958), pp. 77-78. Yoram Barzel, among many, provides a definition: "The state consists of (1) a set of individuals who are subject to a single ultimate third party who uses violence for enforcement and (2) a territory where these individuals reside, demarcated by the reach of the enforcer power," in *A Theory of the State* (New York: Cambridge University Press, 2002), p. 4. Here the state seems to be neither the set of individuals (people) nor the land they inhabit (territory), as in the legal definitions of the early 1900s, but rather "a single ultimate third party" that has control over population and territory. That is, the state is the king, the Parliament, or simply the ruling class. Cf. also Leonard Brewster, "The Impossibility of the State," *Journal of Libertarian Studies* 16, (Summer 2002), pp. 19-34.

or they lacked any form of rational order," he wrote.[23] Modernity is thus characterized by monopoly of violence and rationalization of rules.[24] These two features place the state and its political scheme apart from any other prior political aggregate.

The definition in textbooks is still the "monopoly on legitimate force." For Weber the notion of legitimacy was indeed very important, yet given the complexity of the term "legitimate," scholars today speak with few scruples of the "monopoly of violence." Charles Tilly pointed out that "the distinction between 'legitimate' and 'illegitimate' force ... makes no difference. ... If we take legitimacy to depend on conformity to an abstract principle or on the assent of the governed (or both at once), these conditions may serve to justify, perhaps even to explain, the tendency to monopol[ize] force; they do not contradict the fact." And in turn, "legitimacy is the probability that other authorities will act to confirm the decisions of a given authority ... [as they] are much more likely to confirm the decisions of a challenged authority that controls substantial force." In short, it is the monopoly of the "the means of violence [that] makes a government's claim to provide protection ... more credible and more difficult to resist."[25] The state must first disarm the populace, after which its protection becomes an offer they cannot refuse. Such a unilateral agreement becomes binding as the populace is disarmed *vis-à-vis* well-armed state officials.[26]

The idea that the state must disarm its people was well-investigated, albeit in a small geographical area, Austria, by Otto Brunner in his *Land und Herrschaft*. He identified the gradual abolition of the feudal right of vengeance of the Germanic peoples in the Austrian regions as a partial explanation for the emergence

---

23 Max Weber, *Economy and Society*, eds. Guenther Roth and Claus Wittich (New York: Bedminster Press, 1968), vol. 2, p. 905.

24 *Ibid.*, p. 909.

25 Charles Tilly, "War Making and State Making as Organized Crime," in Bringing the State Back In, ed. Peter B. Evans, Dietrich Rueschemeyer, and Theda Skocpol (Cambridge, UK: Cambridge University Press, 1985), pp. 171-172.

26 The Second Amendment is still one of the main factors that make America a rather *imperfect* modern state.

of the state. The modern legal and political order was built by disarming the citizenry and creating a caste of armed servants of the state. All the traditional functions of the state, beginning with the monopoly over legislation, emerge squarely from the requirement to lay down arms in deference to society.[27] The annihilation of the feud, as Brunner shows, played a crucial role. The disarming of individuals and the abolition of their capacity to act in defense of their own rights paved the way for the creation of a monopoly of legislation, which in turn led to the submission of the entire society. While the modern state mentality considers the feud barbaric and arbitrary, it was not an illegitimate practice. It was premised on a juridical foundation, a mode of righting a wrong. Without such a foundation there was no feudal system of vengeance, but simply violence between individuals. The ancient "feud" was seen as a right. Its "legitimacy ... depended above all on a just claim; for feud and enmity were at heart a struggle for right that aimed at retribution and reparation for a violation of one's right."[28] Lords and subjects declared war and concluded peace with each other "as if" each were subject to international law. On the other hand, Brunner shows that "in a 'legitimate' feud the parties were required to 'offer justice' in some sort of preliminary negotiations." In many cases, a feud was also a duty that took priority over "an individual's obligation to a third party,"[29] a creditor in particular. As Brunner noted, "prohibiting feuds was not a matter of a simple act of state; it entailed a fundamental change in the structure of law and politics."[30] The abolition of the feud and the pacification of society together

27 Otto Brunner had more than loose ties to the Nazi regime. The 1939 edition of *Land und Herrschaft*, Brunner's magnum opus, is overloaded with "Volksgeschichte, Volksordnung" and Nazi jargon in general; but after the war, the volume reappeared cleaned up and ready to make its debut into the scholarly world outside the German context. Pierangelo Schiera edited a very fine Italian translation: *Terra e potere. Strutture pre-statuali e pre-moderne nella storia costituzionale dell'Austria medievale* (Milan: Giuffrè, 1983), and ten years later an American partial translation appeared: *Land and Lordship: Structures of Governance in Medieval Austria*, introduction by Howard Kaminsky and James Van Horn Melton, eds. (Philadelphia: University of Pennsylvania Press, 1992).

28 Otto Brunner, *Land and Lordship*, p. 36.

29 *Ibid.*, pp. 41-42.

30 *Ibid.*, p. 29.

were the crucial step that changed the structure of the provision of law and order. Pierangelo Schiera nicely summarized the meaning of Brunner's long research on the imposition of modern statehood:

> The state finally absorbed into itself and came to 'dominate' the historically determined 'mode' of the organization of power in the modern West; this came about when it controlled social discipline and the forms and rules of the new civil society were so well fused that they could be managed from outside society in the formalized and bureaucratic manner that is characteristic of the modern 'administrative' experience, that is, of the (modern) state.[31]

Similarly, Charles Tilly saw the established organization of violence over a territory as the linchpin of the entire organization of the state.[32] Janice Thomson also shows that the centralized control of violence marks the emergence of state institutions: "The contemporary organization of global violence is neither timeless nor natural. It is distinctively modern. In the six centuries leading up to 1900, global violence was democratized, marketized, and internationalized."[33]

It is with Carl Schmitt, probably the foremost investigator of relations between the political and legal components in the formation of the state, that the full modernity of the state emerges with crystal clarity. In a 1941 text, Schmitt's unease with the prevailing conceptual confusion was accompanied by the awareness that this mess was the product of state institutions and their ideological power:

> We still hear today the Greek *polis* or the Roman republic spoken of as the "ancient Greek and Roman states," and instead of the Reich we hear discussion of

31 Pierangelo Schiera, Introduction to the Italian edition of Otto Brunner's *Land und Herrschaft*, p. xxxv.

32 Cf. Charles Tilly, "War Making and State Making as Organized Crime."

33 Janice E. Thomson, *Mercenaries, Pirates, and Sovereigns: State-Building and Extraterritorial Violence in Early Modern Europe* (Princeton: Princeton University Press, 1994), p. 3.

> the German medieval "state" and even about the Arab, Turkish and Chinese states. A historically conditioned organizational form absolutely tied to specific periods, as well as specific to each political entity, thus loses it historical placement and its typical content; by erroneous abstraction it is transferred to times and peoples to which it is utterly foreign and projected on frameworks and organizations which were completely different. This elevation of the concept of the state to a general and normal concept of political organization of all times and peoples soon terminated with the era of statehood.[34]

Schmitt not only points out the absurdity of the way concepts tied to a political and legal organization that is well-anchored in time and place have migrated elsewhere, but also claims that such a mistake is rather consistent with the state's self-representation. Only the decline or twilight of statehood itself will put an end to the narrative of the state's timelessness.

The modern state represents a political order that is both domestic and international in character. The project of the state implies the creation of a sovereign power destined increasingly to monopolize public life and to dissolve any other center. And the concept of sovereignty is both an internal and an external coordinator.[35] In order for the state to thrive, succeed, and assert itself universally as the model of order, it must become the sole acceptable "political synthesis." That is, the state must be able to survive among its peers in a world made of states. The state was born with a global and universal vocation. The ascent of the sovereign state relegated its competitors (the Hanseatic League, the Italian city-states, the Swiss confederation) to the margins of history, condemning them to certain death.

---

34 Carl Schmitt, "Staatliche Souveränität und freies Meer: Über den Gegensatz von Land und See im Völkerrecht der Neuzeit," in *Das Reich und Europa*, ed. Fritz Hartung (Leipzig: Köhler und Ameland, 1941), pp. 98-99.

35 Cf. Anthony Giddens, *The Nation State and Violence* (Cambridge, UK: Polity, 1985), p. 281.

Hendrik Spruyt analyzes the internal victory of the state as a function of the development of a system of states: "Actors intentionally created a system of sovereign territorial states. They preferred a system that divided the sphere of cultural and economic interaction into territorial parcels with clear hierarchical authorities." The relationship between the several sovereign states is a system of political interdependence that was first European and then global. As Schmitt noted, even the modern international political order, the system of sovereign territorial states, is so undergirded as to become erroneously the classic and timeless model of relations between political communities.

In short, the first item on the agenda of the modern state was the centralization of power. At the dawn of the modern era the state began its long journey when absolute monarchs created a single decision-making center of command, which gradually imposed itself on all other decision makers. The centers that constituted the "medieval cosmos" were obliterated. The state asserted itself as the sole, overriding and exclusive focus: In due time no other political power remained. Hence, "state sovereignty" became "the prevailing idea of political and legal authority of the modern era."[36]

Centralizing power also meant, *à la* Weber, forming a rational basis for it. This happened through the creation of the increasingly bloated bureaucratic apparatus. While all states in the seventeenth and eighteenth centuries moved to attack any sort of intermediate body between themselves and individuals, "by the mid-eighteenth century, the European states had for the most part won ... their 'war of annihilation' against the major intermediate institutions that had survived since the Middle Ages."[37] Only a few associations between individuals were tolerated, so long as they did not pose any threat to the new political order. It was the state that sanctioned them, granted them legitimacy and the simple right to exist. The state became the master and creator of all other forms of association between the people. "For both state administrators and the early theorists of the state ... virtually all associations of any consequence

36 Robert Jackson, *Sovereignty. The Evolution of an Idea* (Cambridge, UK: Polity Pres, 2007), p. 7.

37 David Gross, "Temporality and the Modern State," *Theory and Society* 4, 1 (1985), p. 63.

were treated as if they were gratuitous concessions of sovereign authority, if not administrative extensions of the state itself."[38]

The outcome of this process was the construction of a regulatory machine based on a proposition: to regulate politics in a legal manner. In the end, such a general concurrence of legal and political rules brought about an institution that moved autonomously and that represented neither rulers nor the ruled. In this, territorial boundaries played a crucial role. The state is, by definition, territorial (and every time we pronounce the heavily ideological word "state," we imply sovereign, territorial, European-born, solely modern). The boundaries establish a "within" and a "without" that are the precondition for even the conceivability of the "state." Boundaries are the line of discrimination between "being" and "non-being," between the state's wholeness and its nothingness. The state is construed as a legal person, and it must occupy a definite space. Its existence takes place only within certain geographical lines that trace its "corporeity." Within its boundaries, the state created good citizens through public education, made citizens into soldiers, and taxed them at will. But, to do this, the state had to deprive citizens of any other loyalty. The citizen of the modern state, in fact, has no other real membership or identity than being part of the mystical body of the nation.

Another controversial issue among historians is the age of the state. Should state-like characteristics be attributed to some power structures in the late Middle Ages? According to the Italian constitutional historian Maurizio Fioravanti, for example, the state had a sort of medieval "prehistory" that was essentially non-sovereign, but no less a "state." The existence of a precise "governmental" relationship between the "lords" and the territory, despite the absence of "any monopolistic pretenses," leads the Florentine scholar to assert that in the waning years of the Middle Ages there was "a state because there was already a government and a territory, though yet without the assertion of sovereignty."[39] Gianfranco Miglio indicated the period of 1250-1350 as "the great

38 *Id.*

39 Maurizio Fioravanti, "Stato e costituzione," in *Lo Stato moderno in Europa: Istituzioni e diritto* (2002), ed. Maurizio Fioravanti (Rome: Laterza, 2004), p. 6. I

century in which the state was founded."[40] Historian James Collins names the seventeenth century the age of the state in the most important European country. At that time, "Bourbon kings ... made the state a part of everyone's daily existence ... [and] sought to make the state itself be the political community."[41] Wolfgang Reinhard contends that "the modern state [as described by nineteenth century jurists] existed only between the late eighteenth century and the first two thirds of the twentieth century."[42]

For the purposes of this work, the problem of precise dating is of peripheral concern. The intent is to show that *American* political discourse from the Revolution to the Civil War was free from both the mindset and the institutional operations of the modern state. In the nineteenth century, America beat an institutional and doctrinal path without taking its bearings from the categories of the modern state, and this at the very time when the sovereign, abstract state enjoyed matchless success in Europe.

1.4) Sociologists, Anthropologists, and Archeologists: The Ubiquitous State

The agreement reached by historians of political thought on the state has not been well-heeded by scholars in other fields, who have generally overlooked the link between the state and modernity. In fact, sociological and anthropological approaches to the problem of the state have created no small amount of confusion.[43] Anthropology

---

doubt I am alone in being quite perplexed, as it is difficult to conceive a non-sovereign, yet territorial state.

40 Gianfranco Miglio, *Genesi e trasformazioni del termine-concetto 'Stato,'* p. 809. See also Jan Dumolyn, "The Political and Symbolic Economy of State Feudalism: The Case of Late-Medieval Flanders," *Historical Materialism* 15 (2007), pp. 105-131.

41 James B. Collins, *The State in Early Modern France* (1995) (New York: Cambridge University Press, 2009) p. 6. Cf. Frederick D. Wilhelmsen, "Donoso Cortés and the Meaning of Political Power," *Intercollegiate Review* 3 (January-February 1967), pp. 115-116.

42 Wolfgang Reinhard, *Storia del potere politico in Europa*, p. 12.

43 This is not to pronounce judgment on the intrinsic importance of the contributions of sociologists or anthropologists, but only to clarify that the immense body of literature they produced on political issues has really nothing to do with the problem of the origins of the state.

is a field of research firmly committed to reversing centuries of Eurocentrism. Anthropologists believe that "the state was developed in many places and times and under varying conditions."[44] Assuming that the state is not a peculiarly European creation, they have concentrated on other areas of the world and on different times: "Traditionally anthropologists studied pre-capitalist, preindustrial, non-Western states from their origins five to six thousand years ago up to the present,"[45] writes Donald Kurtz. That is to say, they have studied the state exactly where it could not possibly be found! According to these scholars, however, the state emerged and consolidated itself in successive stages within all human communities.[46]

An "evolutionary theory" of the emergence of the state is the result of the confluence of archeology and cultural anthropology. According to this tradition,[47] the political development of humanity is a continuum that progressed in "stages" and without interruptions. Band, tribe, chiefdom, and state are the steps that all human communities are bound to follow. The era of the state, at which all peoples must naturally and inevitably arrive, lends itself in turn to being analyzed in various periods, such as proto-state, primordial state, mature state, and so forth. As one author put it, "early states" are "distinctive not only from modern states, but also from the ancient states ... where the latter marked the next higher stage of development."[48]

---

44 Lawrence Krader, *Formation of the State* (Englewood Cliffs, NJ: Prentice Hall, 1968), p. 3.

45 Donald V. Kurtz, *Political Anthropology: Power and Paradigms* (Boulder, CO: Westview, 2001) p. 169.

46 A book that could be of some help in the conundrum of the evolutionary theories on the state advanced by scholars of antiquity–a political institution that simply did not exist in ancient times–is Vicente Lull and Rafael Micó, *Archaeology of the Origin of the State: The Theories* (New York: Oxford University Press, 2011), translated by Peter Smith. In this book, the authors, professional archaeologists, seem to be nevertheless quite aware of the fact that the western political tradition and practice has something to do with the formation of the state, thus they feel the urge to let us know more or less what they think of every single political thinker of some consequence, from Plato to Marx.

47 Cf. some criticism in Norman Yoffee, *Myths of the Archaic State. Evolution of the Earliest Cities, States, and Civilizations* (Cambridge: Cambridge University Press, 2005), and Robert A. Nisbet, *Social Change and History: Aspects of the Western Theory of Development* (New York: Oxford University Press, 1969).

48 Anatolii M. Khazanov, "Some Theoretical Problems of the Study of the Early State," in *The Early State*, Henri J. M. Claessen and Peter Skalník eds. (The Hague: Mouton, 1978), p. 77.

To Eli Sagan, "the state may be defined as that form of society in which non-kinship forms of social cohesion are as important as kinship forms."[49] In fact, "state building was the process of kingship triumphing over kinship."[50] Here, the author is clearly looking for a model, a pattern that could explain the birth of the state in any possible social and human setting. The complete absence of historical perception underlining such a postulate must be noted. While it may be true that tribal and blood relations must be overcome in order to approach a system of command, this simple truth has little to do with the state. The timeless nature of the anthropological analysis may help to understand some perennial features of human societies. It is unsuccessful, however, when applied to transient, peculiarly European institutions such as the state. The whole construction of the anthropological school follows the same line of reasoning laid out by Ludwig Gumplowicz more than a century ago. He gave the following account of the origins of the state:

> The state is a social phenomenon consisting of social elements behaving according to social laws. The first step is the subjection of one social group by another and the establishment of sovereignty; and the sovereign body is always the less numerous. But numerical inferiority is supplemented by mental superiority and greater military discipline.[51]

One element of this definition, the idea that the disorganized mass will always be ruled by an organized elite, is convincing, but it almost entirely ignores the complexity of the different institutional orders and political cultures that have periodically emerged. It implies the existence of a process of subjugation going on since the beginnings of time. However, let us notice that Gumplowicz employs a word, "sovereignty," which was a concept only "discovered" by Jean Bodin in 1576. This school speaks of organizations, power politics, and domination, but what the scholars always have in

49 *Ibid.*, p. xx.

50 *Ibid.*, p. 261.

51 Ludwig Gumplowicz, *The Outlines of Sociology* (Philadelphia: American Academy of Political and Social Science, 1899), p. 116.

mind is the state. There is both a projection of a semi-barbaric and timeless condition onto western institutions and the casting of the state image back onto the hordes and tribes of all continents.

A book on the state that has had a significant impact on the American political tradition is *Der Staat* by Franz Oppenheimer, which exactly replicates the great misreading of the rise of the state that we have just discussed.[52] Oppenheimer is so chaotic and confused in his inspiration that he is perhaps of no use at all. Nonetheless, the author of *Der Staat* must be judged for what he has to say on this very topic. According to Oppenheimer, the state, completely in its genesis, essentially and almost completely during the first stages of its existence, is a social institution, forced by a victorious group of men on a defeated group, with the sole purpose of regulating the dominion of the victorious group over the vanquished, and securing itself against revolt from within and attacks from abroad. Teleologically, this dominion had no other purpose than the economic exploitation of the vanquished by the victors.[53] The claim is that the state came out of conquest and brutal force. Appealing as this may sound, this claim is entirely false.

In another passage Oppenheimer hints that the dawn of the state must be recognized in the division of labor—the simple fact that some people were endowed by nature with a warrior character and physical ability. "The peasants become accustomed, when danger threatens, to call on the herdsmen, whom they no longer regard as robbers and murders, but as protectors and saviors. ... The herdsman has learned to capitalize."[54] In other words, it was not only direct conquest, but also failed assaults that gave birth to the state.[55] The best defenders discovered that they could do nothing and yet be nurtured by the population until the next wave of assailants came by. The warriors were thus the soul of the rising

52 Franz Oppenheimer, *The State* (1908), trans. John Gitterman (San Francisco: Fox & Wilkes, 1997).

53 *Ibid.*, p. 9.

54 *Ibid.*, p. 32 and p. 31.

55 Cf. Morton H. Fried, "Tribe to State or State to Tribe in Ancient China?" in *The Origins of Chinese Civilization,* ed. David N. Keightley (Berkeley: University of California Press, 1983), p. 479, on the emergence of states from defense.

state. Needless to say, to defend and protect other people is a perfectly legitimate function, and, if some people are very good at it, they deserve all the idleness they may get. But the birth of the state, in Oppenheimer's enthusiastic conjecture, is quite contradictory: plunder on the one side (definitely illegitimate) and the division of labor (clearly legitimate) on the other. Nation and state, as well as economy and laws, were born together and quite indistinguishably, or so this German scholar imagined:

> The moment when first the conqueror spared his victim in order permanently to exploit him in productive work, was of incomparable historical importance. It gave birth to nation and State, to right and the higher economics, with all the developments and ramifications which have grown and which will hereafter grow out of them.[56]

At the heart of the anthropological tradition lies Karl Wittfogel's well-known 1957 work on Oriental despotism.[57] Based on the "hydraulic hypothesis," this massive study proposed a voluntary and cooperative vision of the birth of the "state" in the East (except that he then outlined a history of degeneration of power that led to tyranny). The original problem was the management of scarce water resources. The natural characteristics of this precious asset ("the distinctive quality of water—its tendency to gather in bulk—becomes institutionally decisive")[58] are the key to the emergence of cooperation between farmers, *i.e.*, the "midwife" of the state in the ancient East. Such a "hydraulic" emergence of the state involves various consequences for society. It was never strong enough to counter-balance and control the political machine.[59] The state apparatus became so heavy and pervasive that, in the end, a state

56 Franz Oppenheimer, *The State*, p. 32.

57 Karl A. Wittfogel, *Oriental Despotism: A Comparative Study of Total Power* (New Haven, CT: Yale University Press, 1957). For an application of Wittfogel's themes to the United States, see Donald Worster, *Rivers of Empire: Water, Aridity and the Growth of the American West* (New York: Pantheon, 1985).

58 Karl A. Wittfogel, *Oriental Despotism*, p. 18.

59 *Ibid.*, pp. 72-86.

was constituted that was stronger than society.[60] Whatever the merits of this approach might be (which would apply to an Orient centered in China, but then was used to analyze pre-Columbian Mexico, and any society in which "hydraulic" characteristics could be discerned), it is clear that continual references to machines, bureaucracies, apparatuses, and society *versus* the state, reveal a theoretical structure.[61]

In a famous 1970 article first published in *Science*, the New York anthropologist Robert Carneiro advanced a theory of the origin of the state that had some success.

> For the first 2 million years of his existence, man lived in bands or villages which, as far as we can tell, were completely autonomous. Not until perhaps 5000 B.C. did villages begin to aggregate into larger political units. But, once this process of aggregation began, it continued at a progressively faster pace and led, around 4000 B.C., to the formation of the first state in history.[62]

Of course, one is tempted to solve this puzzle by postulating that the writer is not actually talking about the state. However, Carneiro

60 Reading Wittfogel's work, one finds that Providence should be thanked for giving Europe a "rain-based" agriculture, with abundant water resources that required few water sharing arrangements.

61 His thesis was subject to numerous criticisms. Jean Baechler spoke of "Wittfogel's Marxist-inspired thesis ... [according to which] despotic states and bureaucracies are established in order to ensure that maintenance and repair work, indispensable for agriculture production, are maintained. An inverse thesis seems to me to conform to the facts better; it is because a centralized political power has been created by war that maintenance and repair work could be conducted properly," Jean Baechler, *The Origins of Capitalism* [1971] (Oxford: Basil Blackwell, 1975), p. 40. Diamond concurs: "Detailed archaeological studies have shown that complex irrigation systems did not *accompany* the rise of centralized bureaucracies but *followed* after a considerable lag. That is, political centralization arose from some other reason and then permitted construction of complex irrigation systems," Jared Diamond, *Guns, Germs and Steel: The Fates of Human Societies* (New York: Norton, 1997), p. 23.

62 Robert L. Carneiro, "A Theory of the Origin of the State: Traditional Theories of State Origins Are Considered and Rejected in Favor of a New Ecological Hypothesis" (1970), in *The State: Critical Concepts*, ed. John A. Hall (New York: Routledge, 1994), p. 433.

immediately provides a definition of what he means when he uses the term: "When I speak of a state I mean an autonomous political unit, encompassing many communities within its territory and having a centralized government with the power to collect taxes, draft men for work or war, and decree and enforce laws."[63] It seems thus clear that the author, in line with the socio-anthropological school on the origins of the state, is simply fantasizing about ancient forms of power. The three characteristics that he holds to be the crux of a definition of a state—recruiting men, making laws, and taxation—became in fact the rarely achieved objectives of monarchies in modern Europe. No other political community ever dreamed of doing anything of that sort. Though it may seem counterintuitive (so accustomed have we become to the anthropological view of the "state"), prior to the rise of the modern state in the seventeeth century, it was not "law" that regulated conduct but *custom*. As for taxation, it was sporadic and difficult to obtain; nor were men "drafted" for the purposes of labor or war.

Many traces of such an approach can still be seen in the current mania for projecting the thoughts and concepts of the modern European state onto the ancient world, from Mesopotamia to Egypt. In fact, there exists a ponderous *corpus* of studies on the ancient world that glibly uses the term "state," at times modified by "ancient," at other times without any qualification.[64] One example is the work of Marcella Frangipane[65] on the birth of the state in ancient Mesopotamia. Jan Assmann, analyzing the ancient Egyptian political forms, writes at length on the "invention of the state" in that part of the world. According to the German scholar,

63 *Idem.*

64 Cf. Mario Liverani, *Uruk: La prima città* (Bari-Rome, Laterza, 1998). Liverani is an important scholar and my criticism is marginal. Cf. a collection articles written between 1973 and 1983, *Myth and Politics in Ancient Near Eastern Historiography*, edited and introduced by Zainab Bahrani and Marc Van De Mieroop (Ithaca: Cornell University Press, 2004). Liverani's work is well documented, carefully researched, and prudent in the areas in which the author, an archaeologist, is an expert. I have trouble only with his political analyses and his use of the term *state*. Like so many of his colleagues, both in Europe and America, he seems not to be particularly aware of the ideological implications of the term.

65 Marcella Frangipane, *La nascita dello Stato nel vicino Oriente* (Rome: Laterza, 1996).

"Egypt is the earliest territorial state in the history of humanity."[66] In the final analysis, the anthropological school seems to be in total denial of what has been aptly called the 'scientific testament' of Max Weber, who asked, "Why did not the scientific, the artistic, the political, or the economic development ... in China or India ... enter upon that path of rationalization which is peculiar to the Occident?"[67]

In summary, even if we concede that it was "the common experience of humanity throughout recorded history, from remote antiquity to the present, and in every part of the world, to gather in associations for different purposes, both general and specific,"[68] there is an historical and methodological leap from this to speak of "state," "statehood," of "constitution" and "sovereign community."

1.5) How Far Back Does the State Go?

Another school of thought acknowledges the state as a creation of modernity, but only as a "finished product." The state supposedly existed as a *work in progress* in the ancient and medieval worlds. Such a thesis is generally coupled with the highly authoritative name of the Italian scholar Norberto Bobbio.[69] Pier Paolo Portinaro, a disciple of his, published a few years ago a work that based its analysis precisely on this "hypothesis," which he defined as "moderately and ... critically" in favor of continuity.[70] His central conviction is that the Greek, Roman and, even the medieval political worlds, while not knowing modern political vocabulary, did distinguish the "essence of things." So, although "sovereignty" is undeniably

66 Jan Assmann, *The Mind of Egypt: History and Meaning in the Time of the Pharaohs* (1996), trans. Andrew Jenkins (Cambridge, MA-London: Harvard University Press, 2003), p. 73. One may wonder which state was the first non-territorial one, or the last, for that matter.

67 Max Weber, *The Protestant Ethic and the Spirit of Capitalism* (1905), trans. Talcott Parsons (New York: Scribner's, 1930), p. 25.

68 Martin Sicker, *The Genesis of the State* (New York: Praeger, 1991), p. 1.

69 Cf. Norberto Bobbio, *Stato, governo, società. Per una teoria generale della politica* (1978) (Turin: Einaudi, 1985).

70 Pier Paolo Portinaro, *Il labirinto delle istituzioni nella storia europea* (Bologna: il Mulino, 2007), p. 65.

a modern term, "one cannot deny that the ancient world already knew an organization of sovereign powers in both fact and law."[71] The author is sure that once we set aside the formulations and the words used by moderns to describe their political communities, the similarities between the ancient world and the modern one will be clear. In his opinion, "the ancient world" discerned "the existence of a normative concept of a constitution (not understood formalistically)" and also had the "idea of the rule of law (also not understood formalistically)."[72]

If sovereignty were fully operational, *de facto*, in the ancient world,[73] if the Greeks had really considered a constitution the safeguard of the rights of individuals against abuses of power, then there would be nothing incorrect or even problematic in this thesis. Moderns would have just created a new vocabulary in which to enshroud an essentially constant reality of political power that can be traced back to Plato and beyond. But sovereignty is not an operational concept that can describe a reality in which the term does not exist. It is a self-constructing reality. As we shall discuss further, the term, the notion, and the debates on sovereignty are what created sovereignty, which in turn has no real existence outside the realm of thought. It never was an operational reality looking to be conceptualized by Jean Bodin. Rather, it became operational only when theorized and disseminated. Rooks and pawns exist only on a chessboard. One cannot look around everywhere to see if there is an operational pawn or something behaving like a rook. This seems to me to be the chief error of those who consider sovereignty a *living* concept. That is, some historians seem to believe that kings exercised "sovereignty" long before Bodin was even born.

---

71 *Ibid.*, p. 61.

72 *Ibid.*, p. 60. "The ancient political world—continues Portinaro on the same page—had an understanding of 'constitution' as the limit and boundary to the arbitrary exercise of power (for which reason the discontinuity between ancient, medieval and modern is far less marked than is usually assumed)."

73 But on this point cf. the lucid analysis of John K. Davies, "On the Non-Usability of the Concept of 'Sovereignty' in an Ancient Greek Context," in *Federazioni e federalismo nell'Europa antica* (Milan: Vita e Pensiero, 1994), vol. 1, pp. 51-65.

Bobbio, one of the leading Italian professors of the past century, disputed the modernity of the state, arguing that Aristotle spoke the language of the state. He warned against "let[ting] oneself be dazzled by the appearance [with Machiavelli] of a new term," since everything depends "on a broader or narrower definition of the term" state, which depends, ultimately, on the preferences of the observer.[74] Bobbio even stated that "a political treatise like that of Aristotle ... has lost none of its descriptive and explanatory effectiveness regarding successive political systems to date."[75] The ancients and their institutions taught much to moderns, a thing which could not be explained "were there a rift at a certain moment in historical development which gave rise to a social and political organization incomparable with those of the past."[76] If Aristotle's *Politics* has something to say to contemporary political observers, then it means that our political institutions are not so completely at odds with those of the Greeks. And, in fact, as soon as one opens a translation of Aristotle's one finds immediately the language of the state:

> Every state is a community of some kind, and every community is established with a view to some good; ... if all communities aim at some good, the state or political community, which is the highest of all, and which embraces all the rest, aims at good in a greater degree than any other, and at the highest good.[77]

However, the editor of this Italian translation claims it is difficult to translate the term *polis* (considered "complex and ambiguous," though it is quite doubtful that it was so for the Greeks), deciding to render it as "state" where there is a *political significance* and as

74 Norberto Bobbio, *Stato, governo, società*, p. 59.

75 *Ibid.*, p. 60.

76 *Ibid.*, p. 61.

77 Aristotle, *Politics,* trans. Benjamin Jowett, Introduction by Max Lerner (New York: Random House, 1943), p. 51. In his *Intellectual History of Europe* (1953) (New York: World Publishing, 1966), p. 498, Friedrich Heer refers to that eminent Christian Aristotelian—St. Thomas Aquinas—and "Thomas's war against hypostatization of society and state, which he sees not as beings in their own right ('Holy Empires') with a necessary tendency towards self-deification, but simply as *relations*."

"city" where the *political sense is absent.*[78] The idea that *polis* for the Greeks could have two meanings, one "political" and the other empty of political import, seems truly baseless. The *Constitution of the Athenians* appears at the end of the work, and the editor does not even pose the question of how to translate *politeia* (*πολιτεία*). Following a longstanding tradition, he used the term "constitution," which is intimately connected to a precise phase of modern statehood.

A scholar of Aristotle, Curtis Johnson, poses the ultimate question: "What do we mean when we say that Aristotle has produced a theory of the state?"[79] Although he remarks in a rather casual manner that "Aristotle's theory of the state ... will ... be found in *certain respects* to be pitched to a different world than our own,"[80] the author soon forgets his warning and discusses *Politics* using the entire arsenal of the modern political jargon. We are thus brought into a discussion in which state, constitution, and sovereignty are supposed to enlighten a political world that was totally ignorant of such concepts and terms.

In sum, the moderns make Aristotle's *Politics* speak with their own language, using it to support the real political hallucination of omnipotence of the state. The state is thus not only a re-founding of politics using the categories of public law, but it is projecting its entire reconstruction all over the political world. Aristotle then becomes simply a puppet through which his ventriloquist, the state, speaks of itself. So, in the end, the paradox lies in the fact that Bobbio is absolutely right: Aristotle—or for that matter Cicero, Aquinas, Marsilius and even savages—all speak the language of the state. That is because we have lost the capacity to speak any other political language but that of the state. Aristotle is thus overdubbed by writers entrapped in the state reconstruction of politics.[81]

78 Aristotele, *Politica*, trans. and ed. Renato Laurenti (Bari: Laterza, 1972), p. 21.

79 Curtis N. Johnson, *Aristotle's Theory of the State* (New York: St. Martin, 1990), p. 1.

80 *Ibid.*, p. 2 (italics added).

81 Dwelling further on the paradox, the real question to resolve the issue would have to be stated in quite the opposite terms: Could a work by Max von Seydel or Paul Laband, perfectly translated by an ancient Greek who knew modern German, say anything to the Greeks about their *poleis*? By this, I certainly do not mean to say that

The fact is that anyone who espouses the view of the continuity of western political experience believes that he or she can distinguish clearly between the state and its ideological construct, that is, between the reality of power and the construction that accompanies it. That in itself is equivalent to believing that the state is a peculiar organization of political power of the modern era, but that the underlying permanent phenomenon is more relevant than the new garbs and guises in which power is outfitted. This is an error.

The search for the state's "*modus operandi*," in the absence of concepts, vocabulary, and category defies logic. It is historically and methodologically flawed. In order to act as a state, the political creature must *be* a state. It is a fact, however, that the thesis of the strict modernity of the state is not yet fully accepted. Several decades ago, Ernst-Wolfgang Böckenförde, an important historian of law, stated that "it [was] ... no longer possible to speak of the 'state of the Greeks', of the Incas, of the Middle Ages and of the 'state' of Plato, Aristotle and Thomas Aquinas, as generations of scholars in the nineteenth century did glibly and intrepidly."[82] He proved to be too optimistic. Paolo Grossi was more accurate when he noted the opposite, *i.e.*, that "the uncritical use of 'state' and 'sovereignty' ... applied to the middle ages is frequent and almost uncontroversial." Such an approach "plunges us into a quagmire of equivocations from which it is difficult to extract ourselves."[83]

This work takes instead a strong position on the matter of the state as founded on several key points widely shared in twentieth century thought, though, as we have seen, not without important critics. In the first place, the state is a strictly modern and European invention. It follows that any transposition of the categories that emerged from a state environment onto systems that are not similar to those of modern Europe is unwarranted and will cause confusion. Exactly this sort of transposition—ideological in nature—is the cause

Aristotle's *Politics* has nothing to say to contemporary humanity, only that it is mute with respect to the matter of the state.

82 Ernst-Wolfgang Böckenförde, "La nascita dello Stato come processo di secolarizzazione" (1967), in *Diritto e secolarizzazione. Dallo Stato moderno all'Europa unita*, ed. Geminello Preterossi (Rome, Laterza, 2007), p. 33.

83 Paolo Grossi, "Un diritto senza Stato," pp. 268-270.

of endless misunderstandings. The historical emergence of the state can be validly understood and investigated only if one keeps in mind that the (modern) state is at once a specific institutional framework and an equally indisputable ideological construct. The multi-century evolution of the (modern) state goes hand in hand with the self-narrative produced by the advocates of the state. The construction of the dogmas that presided over its development is of paramount importance, as the state is indeed a narration that makes sense only in a specific context. The historian and the scholar should not take everything in this story at face value.

The notion of the continuity between the various forms of power in the West is not a neutral historiographical thesis. This continuity has been craftily articulated by the key authors of the state dogmas. In fact, these authors never present such a creation as unique or as an historical novelty without precedent. Even Jean Bodin, the inventor of the new and unprecedented concept of sovereignty (which is the real theoretical prop of the state),[84] masked the fracture of modernity in the very wording of the notion itself: "Sovereignty is the absolute and perpetual power of a commonwealth, which the Latins called *maiestas*; the Greeks *akra exousia, kurion arche*, and *kurion politeuma*; and the Italians *segnioria* ... while the Hebrews call it *tomech shévet*—that is, the highest power of command."[85]

Bodin offered the gift of a totally new concept: that of the absolute authority over a monarch's kingdom, subject only to the divinely ordained laws. But such an innovation had to be garbed in old clothes: Bodin pretended to be simply defining more

84 Nicola Matteucci summed things up nicely: "The concept of sovereignty is a powerful theoretical tool for the affirmation of the state; it is the finest weapon to overcome any possible resistance from below, and it sanctions the separation of the state from society, which is no longer master of its own law," Nicola Matteucci, *Lo Stato moderno. Lessico e percorsi* (Bologna: il Mulino, 1993), p. 30. As Charles H. McIlwain noted: "The full development of the idea of sovereignty belongs to the historian of modern, not medieval, political thought, "*The Growth of Political Thought in the West* (New York: McMillan, 1932), p. 392. Olivier Beaud is one author who emphasizes the "Bodinian fracture"—that is, the enormous weight of the invention of sovereignty—in *La puissance de l'Etat* (Paris: PUF, 1994).

85 Jean Bodin, *On Sovereignty: Four Chapters from the Six Books of the Commonwealth* (1576), ed. and trans. Julian H. Franklin (New York: Cambridge University Press, 1992), p. 1.

precisely a universally recognized fact of politics. But instead, he declared something totally new, and, in so doing, he became one of the greatest theorists of the disjuncture between the modern and medieval political worlds. The state categories, in order to triumph, had to be seen as a mere rationalization of power, not as a revolution: The state must be thought of as universal reason applied to politics. Even though we now know that sovereignty was a revolution, it had to be presented as a slight systematization of political power.

The birth of the state through a monarchic absolutism centered in the "sovereign" person emphasizes a continuity that was in fact only presumed. The monarch had every incentive to present himself as heir to a glorious dynasty that is planted firmly in history, certainly not as a political innovator. Niklas Luhmann's subtle comment immediately comes to mind: "With the proclamation of the sovereign state, particularly in France in the second half of the sixteenth century, historians went to work. The present needed a past that conformed to it."[86]

The state has a dual function that is at the very heart of its ambiguity. On the one hand it is seen exactly for what it is, an historically defined concept that marks an era ranging from the time of the absolute monarchies to the present-day democracies. On the other hand, state advocates produced a narrative that put it as the highest and only possible reconstruction of politics. It is an historical contingency dressed up as a universal necessity. The true calling of the state is to enfold all existing political relations between individuals in a given community. The "political" cannot be conceived outside the state and its paradigms. Encompassing and stifling politics within the "synthesis of the state" becomes one of the "sub-projects" of modern power. As Hedley Bull put it many years ago: "One reason for the vitality of the state's system is the tyranny of the concepts and normative principles associated with it."[87]

---

86 Niklas Luhmann and Raffaele De Giorgi, *Teoria della Società* (Milan: Angeli, 1992), p. 183.

87 Hedley Bull, *The Anarchical Society: A Study of Order in World Politics* (London: Macmillan, 1977), p. 275.

The idea of the twilight of the sovereign state, once associated with Carl Schmitt, has been around for so long that it now seems to be an endless sunset. While Schmitt had already declared by 1932 the end of the era of statehood and of the whole superstructure of concepts relating to the state, caused by an irreversible crisis of its legal construction (what he called the *jus publicum europaeum*),[88] today the argument for decline is typically related to the process of market globalization. While, up to a certain point in its historical path, the state, given national unification, succeeded in using the market as an instrument of order and approval within its boundaries, "capital" today seems to follow its own stateless logic to its own ends, feeding fears old and new. One can certainly agree with Jens Bartelson that there is now a widespread conviction that the sovereign state is unlikely to remain the main source of political authority in the future. It is challenged by new forms of authority and community which transcend the inherited divide between the domestic and the international, and it will, therefore, ultimately be replaced by new forms of political life which know nothing of this distinction and what once followed from it. As a result of the corrosive effects of globalization, the state will eventually enjoy a fate similar to that of the tribe, the city republic and the empire.[89]

Similarly, Martin van Creveld's view is that the state is no longer threatened by groups or individuals within its boundaries, as happened before 1648. The real threat "comes from other corporations: in other words, from such 'artificial men' as share its own nature but differ from it both in respect to their control over territory and in regard to the exercise of sovereignty"[90]—that is to say, the large corporations that thrive in a world of porous borders and weak sovereignty, in which goods and people can move about freely. In short, scholars see the gravedigger and cemetery, but no one can even remotely imagine a political order without the state.

---

88 Cf. Carl Schmitt, *The Concept of the Political*, (1932) George Schwab trans., ed. (Chicago: University of Chicago Press, 1996), pp. 19-80.

89 Jens Bartelson, *The Critique of the State (Cambridge*: Cambridge University Press, 2001), p. 1.

90 Martin Van Creveld, *The Rise and Decline of the State* (Cambridge: Cambridge University Press), 2004, p. 416.

Even so refined a scholar as Charles Tilly—who deeply studied the reality of the modern state without yielding to the temptation of reading such a history as a violent march toward progress—fails to come up with plausible alternatives. "Destroy the state and create Lebanon. Fortify it, and create Korea." Concluding with some wishful thinking, which is hardly in tune with the realism that characterizes his scholarship, he writes: "The only real answer is to turn the immense power of national states away from war and toward the creation of justice, personal security and democracy."[91] The dilemma is lucidly presented by Bartelson: "Within large parts of our legacy of political theorizing, the state is both posited as an object of analysis *and* presupposed as the foundation of such analysis." Such ambiguity of the state "makes it inherently difficult to take political theorizing out of its statist predispositions."[92]

Yet another historiographic myth accompanies the track of the state, and even the most attentive scholars frequently fall for it. I am referring to the relationship between the state and "progress." Even when the "grand novel of the state," as Gianfranco Miglio liked to call it, is properly narrated, an ideological statist prejudice often creeps in. The long course of the state, uprooting individuals from their natural communities and "liberating" them from their burdensome relationships (*i.e.*, destroying the power of corporations and churches), appears to be a grandiose attempt to create only two entities: the "sovereign power" and the individual subject. Thus, Bertrand de Jouvenel's analysis is that "the *plenitudo potestatis* became the goal toward which monarchs deliberately moved. To reach that, a long road lay ahead of them, since it was necessary to destroy all authority other than their own. That meant the complete overthrow of the existing social order. This slow revolution established what we call 'sovereignty.'"[93]

---

91 Charles Tilly, *Coercion, Capital, and European States, AD 990-1990* (Oxford: Basil Blackwell, 1990), p. 225.

92 Bartelson, *The Critique of the State*, p. 5.

93 Bertrand de Jouvenel, *Sovereignty: An Inquiry into the Political Good* (1955), trans. J. F. Huntington, Preface by Daniel J. Mahoney and David Des Rosiers (Indianapolis: Liberty Fund, 1997), p. 208.

However, others claim that there was a purpose quite distinct from that of subjugating society and individuals: the creation of a single legal subject and the affirmation of the principle of "equality of everyone before the law." The path of sovereignty was through the "unstoppable, destructive force of all individuality in the territory." But precisely through this force "the society of individual rights, based on the principle of equality, or the uniqueness of the subject before the law" finally emerged.[94] Another Italian professor believes that "the modernization of Europe depended ... on the growth of the state,"[95] and this summarizes a very common feeling among scholars who favor "modernity" and all its derivatives. More generally, a large majority would subscribe to (or assume the truth of) Stephen Krasner's naïve statement: "Over the last five hundred years, the sovereign state has been a powerful instrument of human progress."[96] Yet there are reasons for holding—with a disenchanted look at the state and its logic—that the idea of equality before the law as well as the noble concept of the "impersonality of command"[97] (that government of laws, not of men, which in some ways seems to be the ultimate essence of the state) were no more than ideological trade goods to win the favor of the intellectual classes whose political sensitivities were changing in the transition from absolutism to the Enlightenment.

94 Maurizio Fioravanti, *Stato e costituzione*, p. 17.

95 Nicola Matteucci, *Lo Stato moderno*, p. 22.

96 Stephen D. Krasner, "Sovereignty: An Institutional Perspective," in *The Elusive State: International and Comparative Perspectives*, ed. James A. Caporaso (Newbury Park, CA: Sage, 1989), p. 69.

97 In an inaugural lecture of 1957, Gianfranco Miglio had good reason to "indicate the genuinely permanent place in European political history of the constant aspiration for impersonality in command. ... It seems to me that Western political history is united and has set itself apart in virtue of a stubborn fight against exactly these most genuine and natural aspects of political obligation [the personality of power]: ... as the depersonalization of command and poignant longing for a system in which only impersonal precepts reign, removed from the arbitration of all human will," Gianfranco Miglio, "L'unità fondamentale di svolgimento dell'esperienza politica occidentale" (1957), in *Le regolarità della politica*, vol. 1, pp. 329-330. Here I would only point out the difficulty of seeing the state as the natural repository and the "fulfillment" of such a multi-millennial longing of the European educated classes.

In any case, it is undeniable that the attribution of some higher political purpose to the state is part of a broad and deep tradition of thought that finds its high philosophical ground in Immanuel Kant, and particularly in the notorious eighth thesis of *Idea for a Universal History with a Cosmopolitan Purpose* (1784): "The history of the human race as a whole can be regarded as the realization of a hidden plan of nature to bring about an internally—and for this purpose also externally—perfect political constitution as the only possible state within which all natural capacities of mankind can be developed completely."[98] Although scholars have long since abandoned the faith in nature that underpins Kant's thesis, the notion remains. An historical movement such as that of the state will have a positive goal as its objective. And the indestructible link between state and progress is a rather simplified Hegelian legacy.

The desire to announce the fulfillment, however noble, of a movement such as that of political power in Europe in the last few centuries reveals the persistence of categories such as "progress," which seem indefensible. Max Weber, as we mentioned, held that the state could not be understood by taking its proclaimed goals as an heuristic tool. Indeed, goals come and go; what holds is the real characteristic of the state as a successful pursuer of a monopoly on violence. The idea that the emergence of the state has contributed to the general cause of human freedom is as widespread a notion as it is a questionable one. The logic of the state movement is the acquisition of *plenitudo potestatis*, and its relationship to human freedom is at least open to debate. If there is one characteristic that distinguishes states from all other political arrangements in human history, it is their ability to request and easily obtain "blood and money" from their subjects. Only modern states, and only in a very recent phase of their development, have been able to force nearly all their healthy young citizens into the army and seize nearly half of the resources produced in their territories. Perhaps one day, many centuries from now, someone might reasonably conclude that, in terms of individual freedom, the balance is still favorable. But such a conclusion seems premature today, to say the least.

98 Immanuel Kant, *Idea for a Universal History with a Cosmopolitan Purpose*, in *Political Writings*, p. 50.

The rise of the state was a true revolution that destroyed the medieval world, created a new political order, guaranteed privileges, immunity, and outcomes to some groups, while forever denying them to others. "The European State-makers engaged in the work of combining, consolidating, neutralizing, manipulating a tough, complicated, and well-set web of political relations. ... They had to tear or dissolve large parts of the web, and to face furious resistance as they did so," writes Tilly.[99] The history of freedom cannot be analyzed as a development connected to the rise of the state, as the sole driving center from which everything emanates and which legitimizes everything, but rather in resistance to that emergence. The slow march of freedom is found in the attempts to restrict and contain the state, in the small surviving pockets of immunity, guarantees, and medieval legacies in Europe, and not their eradication. Freedom proceeds as a "karst river" underneath and frequently running counter to the major institutional changes of the modern and contemporary era.

1.6) American Sovereignty and the State

Of course, not all Europeans have lived under the banner of the state in modern times. Just to give a few examples, the Netherlands (from 1579 to 1798), the Republic of Venice, the Swiss Confederation, and the Germanic Hansa were institutions that cannot in any way be construed according to the categories of *jus publicum europaeum*. The secret of the long duration of the Hanseatic League (from the twelfth to the seventeenth centuries, founded as an association of merchants that developed into a confederation of cities) was that it was an economic and peaceful arrangement for providing western products to the East and vice versa.[100] As the French historian Philippe Dollinger points out, the secret of its success was common interest, correctly understood:

99 Charles Tilly, "Reflections on the History of European State-making," in *The Formation of National States in Western Europe* (Princeton: Princeton University Press, 1975), pp. 24-25.

100 Cf. Philippe Dollinger, *The German Hansa* (Stanford: Stanford University Press, 1970), p. 8.

> The Hansa ... [was] an anomalous institution which puzzled contemporary jurists. ... It was not a sovereign power. ... In spite of these structural weaknesses ... [it] was able to hold its own for nearly five hundred years. The secret of its long life is to be found not in coercion, which played no appreciable role, but in the realization that common interests bound the members of the community together.[101]

The hollowness of its institutions (the *Hansetag* [diet] rarely met and had no power of coercion against its own members, as it had no finances, army or independent navy) is disconcerting to the modern mind. The Hansa "was inspired by a spirit which, though based on material self-interest, is nonetheless worthy of admiration and respect." It provided an example of peace through commerce that seems to confirm the well-known classical liberal doctrine of Constant, Cobden, and Bastiat. "Indifferent to nationalistic prejudices, and even, to a large extent, to religious differences, the Hanseatics were deeply pacific and had recourse to war only when all else failed. They always did their utmost, both among themselves and in their dealings with foreign countries, to settle their quarrels and remove their grievances by arbitration and negotiation."[102]

In short, even though the privileged research thread of the modern era follows the development of the state and fixes the historian's vigilance in particular on France as the country of political modernity—and things could not be otherwise—important areas were outside the dominant paradigms. Across the Atlantic the colonies were building a society that would long prove to be one of the most recalcitrant against importing the categories and the institutional factuality of the modern state.

Frederic William Maitland (1850-1906) warned against using "our modern 'State-concept'" to describe the medieval past.[103] What holds for the Middle Ages should guide investigation into countries

101 *Ibid.*, p. xvii.

102 *Ibid.*, pp. 375-76.

103 Frederic W. Maitland, Introduction to Otto F. von Gierke, *Political Theories of the Middle Ages* (Cambridge-New York: Cambridge University Press, 1900) p. ix.

like the United States or Switzerland. They are outside the privileged areas of scholarly study on state-building: the "prince-assembly-nation" process. There is, however, one non-trivial difference: While Switzerland and the Hansa were content to live in free confederations that made negotiated, contractual decisions without bothering much to reflect on their institutional structure, in America the debate on politics and institutions was the most popular pastime, at least from the Revolution to the Civil War.

Compared to European statehood, America at its origins represents a doctrinal counterpart of vast theoretical relevance, in some ways in spite of what America has become. While pockets of resistance to the modern state were common in the West, none of them produced either a doctrinal reflection or an institutional arrangement as articulated and complex as that of the early United States. The modern state is understood today as the sole institution capable of "governing complexity" (as if the creation of a single command room were the only way to respond to the requests of "complex societies"). It is thus interesting to analyze the example of Jacksonian America, one of the most modern and composite societies of the first half of the nineteenth century, which existed without a modern state. During that time in America, it is not only that "a 'State' in the European metaphysical sense—or at least continental Europe—[could] not have developed,"[104] but that the compelling need for such an entity was simply not felt.

The American political vocabulary of the time, however, was punctuated by conceptual "false friends." From the passage of the Constitution onwards, the political debate unfolded and illuminated a strongly "institutionalized" territory, in which the founding document of the newborn Republic was the center of attention and the focus of the controversy. The political vocabulary arrived from the other side of the Atlantic, long before the state was ushered in. Use of this vocabulary fluctuated within the American political discourse; many heavy terms were resemanticized and adapted to different circumstances. For many decades, for example, Americans

104 Jürgen Heideking, "The Pattern of American Modernity from the Revolution to the Civil War," *Daedalus* 129, 1 (2000), p. 232.

used the word "sovereignty"—as we shall soon see—naively and unwittingly to mean primarily the power to make laws.

Some years ago, Daniel Deudney proposed the name "Philadelphia System" for the relational world that differed from the Westphalian logic of sovereign states.[105] Although the political model produced by the Peace of Westphalia in 1648 was the most successful of the modern age, Deudney argues that the United States before the Civil War, when the Philadelphian system was fully-operative, represented "an alternative to the European Westphalian system rather than an oddly constituted state within it."[106] This did not happen by chance, as the "institutions of the United States were designed to avoid the Europeanization of North American politics."[107] The alienation of the young Republic from the territorial European sovereign system of states is revealed by the fact that "it had elaborate institutions that went beyond confederation, but stopped short of being an internally sovereign state."[108] In short, federalism was the single most important element that separated the American republic from the European political world—and it determined the nation's radical diversity (and still determines whatever degree of political variance might still separate the two sides of the Atlantic).

And yet scholars trained in the world of *jus publicum* have proceeded, from the beginning, toward a normalization (that is to say, *Europeanization*) of America. They do this by radically denying any autonomy to federation, whether as a political discourse or institutional reality. The use of *jus publicum europaeum* to bring clarity to the federal phenomenon is simply unfounded, and the source of many theoretical errors. We see again the "ancient vice of overlaying the patterns and concepts typical of political modernity

---

105 Cf. Daniel Deudney, "Binding Sovereigns: Authorities, Structures, and Geopolitics in the Philadelphian System," in *State Sovereignty as Social Construct*, ed. Thomas J. Biersteker and Cynthia Weber (Cambridge, Melbourne: Cambridge University Press, 1996), pp. 190-239.

106 *Ibid.*, p. 191.

107 *Ibid.*, p.192.

108 *Ibid.*, p. 191.

and codified law onto an age that was profoundly different in terms of its conceptual structures well prior to its constitutional structures."[109]

For many European scholars, the principal means of the conceptual normalization of federation (and with it of the entire American political experience) is to differentiate between federation and confederation. It is worth remembering that the core of the ill-conceived federation-confederation distinction is about a simple sovereignty domicile question. If the locus of sovereignty is to be found in the federation, then it is a state, maybe oddly construed, but a state. If it is in the constituent units, then the political construction is confederal.

In this dichotomy all the classic defects of state-centered analysis (which for the continental jurist are merits) are not only extant but enhanced.[110] Not only that, but as we have already remarked, the state thrives and prospers only in a world made of states. Its successes, primarily military, have created a drive toward its systemic emulation—while its very nature induces observers to see mainly similarities and analogies. Anyone who uses the confederation-federation scheme, or terms that are only apparently neutral, such as "federal State," erroneously applies legal concepts surrounding the modern state onto a federal reality. Each time we use the distinction between confederation and federation, we use a

109 Diego Quaglioni, *La sovranità* (Rome: Laterza, 2004), p. 17.

110 The best-known critiques of such a dichotomy are found in Carl J. Friedrich, *Trends of Federalism in Theory and Practice* (New York: Praeger, 1968). For a critique on different grounds, see the lucid analysis of Preston King, *Federalism and Federation* (Baltimore: Johns Hopkins University Press, 1982), pp. 133-145. Even the constitutional scholar Giovanni Bognetti, addressing himself directly to Friedrich, devoted attention to the problem of the distinction between a "federal State" and a "Confederation of States," concluding that "the science of law has largely tried to base the distinction between those various classificatory figures primarily by using a dogmatic concept of sovereignty as primary power that is absolute and unlimited in command, which would be characteristic of a State entity and on the basis of which, in seeking its proper place, one could identify in the system of each figure its precise qualitative and differentiating traits. ... In terms of a realistic description of the historical and legal phenomenon of 'State' and the subtypes of 'federal State', 'regional state', 'confederation' and 'supranational organization of states', the [dogmatic] concept [of sovereignty] cannot serve as an intellectual treatment of the matter," Giovanni Bognetti, "Federalismo," *Digesto* (Turin: UTET, 1991), vol. 6, p. 274.

set of juridical concepts that are extraneous to either concept and wholly within the construction of the modern state. It lends new knowledge neither about the *phenomenon* of federation, nor about federalism. Furthermore, the distinction, in the terms in which it has crystallized, was unknown to classical American juridical and political thought in the period from the Declaration of Independence (1776) to the Civil War (1861-1865). And since no one seriously disputes that America is the birthplace of "modern federalism," this simple observation should at least raise some doubts about the heuristic value of separating confederation and federation.[111] For the Americans, the two were largely the same.

American and European thinkers were working with two different concepts of sovereignty, which in turn underlay two different conceptions of the relationship between the political community and society, between power and freedom, and so forth. While Americans used terms similar to those of the common European political vocabulary, there was no comparable analogous reality, nor a corresponding system of political thought. The terms of the modern European political vocabulary create the reality of the modern state. They were used by the Americans, but did not mean the same to them.

The boldest definition of sovereignty found in American reflections is the "supreme legislative authority" used by John C. Calhoun (1782-1850) to defend the sovereignty of each American state in the first half of the nineteenth century. Such a notion would be considered absolutely restrictive as compared to "sovereignty's necessary attributes" used by almost all European jurists. This is a substantial point: The constitutional doctrine of sovereignty as developed in Europe from the sixteenth century up to the present time is eminently juridical and implies the idea of an unlimited and illimitable concentration of power at a given

111 A simple glance at the founding documents and the political discourses of America of the late eighteenth century shows us that the terms are used as pure synonyms rather than as words that merely sound alike but have different meanings. In the *Federalist* the terms "federation" and "confederation" are used interchangeably, although it remains an open question whether Hamilton or Madison had in mind some sort of distinction. According to some, in the *Federalist* no. 15 Hamilton already seems to foreshadow such a distinction.

center, quite the opposite of federalism. So, if sovereignty requires potentially unlimited concentrations of power in a territory, how can that term be used for federalism? In other words, behind the gilded cage of sovereignty, do we not risk losing sight of the crucial theme of federalism, the check against the consolidation of power? Sovereignty in a European sense is *ipso facto* in a very different sphere from federal political theory. The centralization of power is the permanent, ineradicable characteristic that has accompanied the historical development of the state and that favored the emergence of the model that could be called the "reified State."[112] Centralization is the opposite of federalism.

In a federation sovereignty resides in the so called "federal state." In a confederation it lies in the constituent units, the "confederated states." The first is a state in any sense of the word, while the second is nothing more than a compact between sovereign states.[113] In the case of a federation, the answer should be that sovereignty is "partly in the federation, partly in the constitutive entities," according to the political and constitutional doctrine worked out in the United States and described as "divided sovereignty." James Madison is the leading enthusiast of such a constitutional theory. The phrase *partly federal, partly national* with which Madison defined the document produced by the Philadelphia convention referred to the

112 See Daniel J. Elazar, *Exploring Federalism* (Tuscaloosa: University of Alabama Press, 1987).

113 Carl Schmitt argued that the concept and characteristics of a federation must be developed without regard to this distinction: "The theoretical treatment that the problem has had until now in Germany suffers from the fact that it is completely dominated by self-interest when comparing a federation of States ... and a federal State; regarding this distinction it searches as much as possible for simple antitheses. German public law books ... present alternatives that seem clear and convincing, but they are actually logically unusual or impossible. A confederation of States should be a relationship of pure international law, in contrast to a federal State, which is a subject of pure public law; the former is based is an international treaty, and the latter has a constitution of public law; the former is a legal relationship, while the latter is a legal subject, etc. It is historically understandable and explainable that after 1871 the publicist of the German Reich would minimize the difference of this Reich with respect to the previous German Federation of 1815 to similar simple slogans; with that the general problem of the federation seemed resolved." Carl Schmitt,*Verfassungslehere* (1928) (Berlin: Dunker & Humbolt, 2017), p. 385. See the flawless translation of this classic by Jeffrey Seitzer, *Constitutional Theory* (Durham, NC: Duke University Press. 2008).

fact that the settlement had, in his view, produced a plan in which two parallel worlds, each sovereign in its respective sphere, had been designed: the federal government and the federated State. However, European jurists have turned what might appear at first sight to be a unitary-federal-confederal division into a sharp alternative between confederation and federation. Thus, the federation-confederation distinction supports the goal often attributed to federalism: the achievement of that "more perfect union" which cannot be reached outside the modern political community *par excellence*: the state, possibly national, undoubtedly unitary. In this model, sovereignty—one and indivisible just like the republic of the French Jacobins, representing the essence of every state, is the premise of the argument placing the "federal state" at a higher stage of perfection than the confederation. And perfection is understood in achieving *unity*, the ultimate goal of any political community. Confederation is a first and immature stage of development, as fully developed political order is achieved only within a unified State that recognizes nothing above itself, nor any sort of *imperium in imperio* within its boundaries. Within this very logic the Austrian jurist Hans Kelsen argued in 1934 that international law is an elementary legal system, and that the process of development of international law would very much parallel that which the legal system of the individual state has already traversed.[114]

It used to be a sort of commonplace that existing federations represented nothing but a stage in historical development toward either disaggregation or a unitary nation-state. In the late nineteenth century, Henry Sidgwick (1838-1900) stated that federalism "arising from historical causes is likely to be in many cases a transitional stage through which a composite society passes on its way to a completer union. ... A confederation of states, if it holds together, has a tendency to pass into a federal state."[115] The late nineteenth century is precisely the period in which the final version of this theoretical and conceptual distinction was crystallized and

114 Cf. Hans Kelsen, *Reine Rechtslehere* (1934) *Introduction to the Problems of Legal Theory,* trans. Bonnie L. Paulson and Stanley L. Paulson (Oxford: Clarendon Press, 1992), pp. 107-125.

115 H. Sidgwick, *The Elements of Politics* (London-New York: Macmillan, 1891) p. 544.

still hangs over the entire study of federalism in Europe, as well as in some academic quarters of America.[116]

The conclusive works are those of Justus Bernhard Westerkamp, *Staatenbund und Bundesstaat*, 1892, and Louis Le Fur, *État fédéral et Confédération d'états*, 1896.[117] The doctrinal issue is solely and obsessively that of perfect statehood. As Le Fur put it, "Only the federal state constitutes a state and it is essentially different from a confederation, because in the latter only the confederated states possess the features of a state."[118] Therefore, in the federal state there would be an irrevocable transfer of sovereignty from the federated entities to the federal "center" (clearly an oxymoron). To this is conjoined the classic discourse on the legitimacy of secession, an act which is acknowledged implicitly or explicitly in a confederation, while it is allegedly repudiated at the outset of every federation. Retracing this misconception, Dusan Sidjanski held that a federation is founded on a constitutional base "that excludes any possibility of secession.[119]

The American Constitution, however, is silent on the subject of secession. Historians have wondered why at the Philadelphia Convention men of great wisdom, like Madison, Hamilton, and Wilson did not discuss or even mention the possibility that a State

116 In America, to be sure, the distinction revealed more than a moderate resistance. From the legal perspective this was due to the influence of the German school. From the viewpoint of political theory this was due to the fact that the nature of the distinction was completely altered: "The American experience shows federation and confederation to be two species of the same genus, federalism," Daniel J. Elazar, "Confederation and Federal Liberty," *Publius* 12, no. 4 (1982), p. 1 (cf. also *Ibid.*, p. 5, for a definition that takes no account of the concept of sovereignty). It is obvious that if these categories are reconstructed within the same genus, such a distinction loses any similarity to the rigid dichotomy that emerged in Europe, which was based on the sharpest contrast between the two terms.

117 Cf. Justus B. Westerkamp, *Staatenbund und Bundesstaat: Untersuchungen über die Praxis und das Recht der mordenen Bunde* (Leipzig: Brockhaus, 1892) and Louis Le Fur, *État fédéral et Confédération d'états*, (Paris: Marchanal et Billard, 1896).

118 Le Fur, *État fédéral*, p. 728.

119 Dusan Sidjanski, *Fédéralisme Amphictyonique: éléments de système et tendance international* (Lausanne: Rouge, 1956), p. 48.

could dissolve its ties with the union.[120] The answer is that in 1787 there was no entity, not even imaginary one, from which to secede. In 1860-61, however, secession was the word of the day because its dialectical opposite, the modern state, was finally taking shape. Secession is in a dialectically close relationship with the idea of the state: What sense could secession ever have, except in a fully state context? The very term "secession" began to gain ground in the United States when politicians in the South started to consider that the security of living within a free federation of States was pretty much a thing of the past. And the issue of secession is precisely the litmus test for understanding the profound changes that had occurred with respect to the original republic: There finally existed an institutional reality from which to secede.

The problem of where sovereignty lies in a federal system—the crux of the matter in the struggle between the southern and northern sections of America—was reworked in Germany. On the basis of a particular reading of the historical experience of the American republic, Georg Waitz, Max von Seydel, and their pupils erected both the categories that would direct the formation of the federation-confederation distinction as well as crucial elements of the doctrine of the state.

Georg Waitz (1813-1886), partially harking back to the ideas expressed in the *Federalist* and even more so in the works of Alexis De Tocqueville (1805-1859), worked out an original theory of "divided sovereignty." In *Das Wesen des Bundesstaates*[121] he identifies an intermediate form between the unitary state (*Staatenreich*) and a confederation of states (*Staatenbund*), or the federal state (*Bundesstaat*). According to Waitz, sovereignty, or independence from any outside power, is the essential prerequisite for statehood, and in the federal state this is shared by the "collective state" and the "member states," each fully independent within its proper sphere.

120 See Frank Donovan, *Mr. Madison's Constitution: The Story Behind the Constitutional Convention* (New York: Dodd, Mead, 1965), p. 123.

121 Georg Waitz, "Das Wesen des Bundesstaates," in *Allgemeine Kieler Monatsschrift für Wissenschaft und Literatur* (Berlin, 1853) pp. 495-530.

The conceptual patterns in which the legal analysis of the federal phenomenon is still debated today—moving from the distinction between federation and confederation of states (fruitless because polarized around the obsessive European notion of sovereignty)—derived from the birth of modern federalism. Federalism was born as a compromise over where sovereignty lies: "partly federal, partly national," to use again Madison's famous characterization.

Although it uses the European notion of sovereignty, Waitz's theory is historically important, insofar as it follows the *Federalist*'s framework, which attributes a three-dimensional unitary-federal-confederate aspect to statehood. In other words, statehood is rethought in the fashion of a "hybrid" system, which could be called "modern federalism," presented in its most classical form by James Madison. Waitz and a score of European legal scholars focused attention only on one political side of the constitutional debate. The greatest risk is failing to grasp the nature of the compromise which was at the base of the Philadelphia constitutional convention, as it is by now a well-established fact that the Constitution was "as national as the Federalists could make it and as confederate as the Anti-federalists could keep it."[122]

Max von Seydel based the concept of the exclusivity of sovereign power explicitly on John Calhoun's theory, which we will discuss in depth later.[123] Sovereignty is illimitable and indivisible: It is only the various rights of sovereignty that can be exercised by several bodies expressly delegated by the "sovereign" power. However, none of these rights, nor their sum, may coincide with sovereignty which, rather, must be recognized in the superior will, which concedes individual rights, determines their exercise, and transfers and subtracts them as it deems fit.

Seydel denied the logical coherency of the concept of *Bundesstaat*, arguing that any intermediate form between the

122 Gary L. McDowell, "Federalism and Civic Virtue: The Antifederalists and the Constitution," in *How Federal is the Constitution?*, eds. R.A. Goldwin and W.A. Schambra (Washington: American Enterprise Institute, 1986) p. 123.

123 Cf. Max von Seydel, *Staatsrechtliche und politische Abhandlungen* (Freiburg-Leipzig: Mohr, 1893), pp. 41-44, and *Commentar zur Verfassungs-Urkunde für das Deusche Reich* (Freiburg-Leipzig: Mohr, 1897), pp. 3-18.

unitary state and a confederation of states could not exist due to the impossibility of dividing sovereignty. He thus traced with linear consistency the theoretical positions that put such a tripartite division on the ropes, and remodeled it as a clear dichotomy.[124] In this instance Seydel appears to be truly paradigmatic regarding the transposition of conceptual "false friends" from America. In fact, he adopted Calhoun's theories almost *verbatim*, so much so that the Italian scholar Guido Lucatello stated many years ago that the thesis of the full sovereignty of member states "bears the name of the Calhoun-Seydel Theory ... [and exhibits] greater consistency than any other theory."[125] And yet Seydel never even reflected on the real meaning of the term "sovereignty" in the American context, taking for granted that it meant *exactly* what it did in the European continent.

---

124 Otto von Gierke clarified that the distinction between federation and confederation is formed in the legal development of the concept of sovereignty: "Without exception, the theory developed the concept of sovereignty so as to exclude any possibility of a state over the states. Thus when in practice federal systems (unions, really) were evident, the view was that the only alternative was either to consider a federal relationship (or a unified relationship) between several fully sovereign States, or a unitary State composed of various members. Thus even those communities formally ordered in a federalist manner, and the Swiss Confederation and the United Provinces of the Netherlands in particular, were simply considered as a collection of federalist relationships. On this basis the concept of a confederation of states, formed by an 'foedus arctissimum' and organized as a 'corpus confoederatorum' or 'systema civitatum,' alongside—and more or less distinct from—various equal and unequal pacts, was introduced into the traditional doctrine of the 'foedera'; however, it is of the utmost importance to stress that such a close union left the sovereignty of the individual states intact, and therefore these alone could qualify as such, while the collection had at most the appearance of a State. Conversely, whenever one could not or would not deny the nature of a State to a union—and especially for the German Empire—it was generally held to be a unitary State," Otto von Gierke, *Johannes Althusius und die entwicklung der naturrechtlichen staatstheorien: zugleich ein beitrag zur geschichte der rechtssystematik* (Breslau: Verlag von Wilhem Koebner, 1880), pp. 237-238. See the English translation, *The Development of Political Theory*, by Bernard Freyd (New York: W. W. Norton, 1939).

125 Guido Lucatello, *Lo Stato federale* (Padua: Cedam, 1939), p. 117. According to Lucatello, the Calhoun-Seydel construction can be reduced to two propositions: "1) The federal State is a creation of the 'member states,' which, uniting themselves by an accord called the 'federal constitution,' have not relinquished their own sovereignty; 2) the structure of the organizations of the true federal states confirms their nature as a union of states," *Ibid.*, p. 118.

There is no need to ransack further the entire libraries that these questions have generated: The concept of sovereignty lies at the heart of all such inquiry. As previously noted, however, the very idea of sovereignty in a federal system is complex. Federalism presupposes the exercise of power subordinated only to the very common goals that led to the federal agreement (*pactum* and *casus foederis*). Reconstructing politics into "federation" and "confederation" denies any conceptual autonomy to "federation" as a form of association and of the doctrinal elaborations on federalism. The traditional point of view of continental jurists on this theme was capably summarized by the Italian constitutional scholar Antonio La Pergola: "Either a federal framework is recognized as having the nature of a state system safeguarded by an effective coercive apparatus ... or the federal constitution is rigorously understood as a contract, giving rise to consensus among the members as the base of the system."[126] In his view, "it is the prevailing opinion in America, and here as well, that for the jurist, the phenomenon of federalism cannot be surveyed except under one or the other of the two forms traditionally considered by scholars: the confederation or the federal state. It would then be up to the interpreter to classify the specimen under examination in the international framework of confederate union, or in the statehood one of federation."[127]

The difference, then, is between the domestic jurisdiction and the international arena. Federalism, commonly considered the greatest contribution to the art of government rising out of American political theory and experience, simply does not exist: All that is necessary is the European system from Westphalia onwards (with the transition from *jus gentium* to international law) to build the two worlds in which to pigeon-hole the phenomena of "federal state" and "confederation of states" (domestic jurisdiction and international law).

When a dogmatic European legal view extends its gaze beyond its "natural boundaries" (the border inscribed theoretically by the German scholars of the last century and practically framed by

126 Antonio La Pergola, *Residui "contrattualistici" e struttura federale nell'ordinamento degli Stati Uniti* (Milan: Giuffrè, 1969) p. 92.

127 *Ibid.*, p. 109.

the French model predicated on the "King-Assembly" historical succession) it cannot help seeing exactly what it perceives at home. The European jurist reproduces schemes and grand designs patterned around the notion of "internal" and "external," which are typical of the inter-state community and the multi-century evolution of the modern state and its obsessive notion of "boundary" as well as of "sovereignty."

The Jacobin motto ("the republic, one and indivisible") and the confederation-federation model respond to the same question on sovereignty, the former in a peculiarly prescriptive manner—remember that the accusation of "federalism" during the months of the Great Terror (1794) could mean serious risk of a death sentence and further diminution of defense rights—and the latter in a way that is only apparently descriptive.

"Who is the sovereign?" is the standard question of monist constitutions. Pluralist, or federal, constitutions cannot provide an answer to this question since they opt for establishing the boundaries between overlapping powers, for establishing (rather tentatively) to whom the exercise of this or that prerogative belongs. The federation as a constitutional fact and federalism as the sum of political and doctrinaire reflections do not conform to the theories of sovereignty worked out by European thinkers along the lines of Bodin and Hobbes.[128] The theory of sovereignty is helpful if one pictures a federal system simply as a step which politically immature societies adopt in transition to a total concentration of power. While it can be argued that this was the ultimate fate of the American experiment of self-government and limited government, it would be very hard to prove that, with the possible exception of Alexander Hamilton, anyone in the early republic ever thought of the federal system as a state-building step. The federal arrangement was never considered as a mere

128 Bodin-Hobbes is a sort of genetic conceptual pattern, useful to grasp the immediate meaning of the concept of sovereignty. Clearly, I do not intend to hint at any substantial proximity between the theories of the French and the British thinkers. See H. Hinsley, *Sovereignty* (1966) (Cambridge, UK-New York-Melbourne: Cambridge University Press: 1986) pp. 136-150, and Massimo Terni, *La pianta della sovranità: teologia e politica tra Medioevo ed età moderna* (Rome-Bari: Laterza, 1995).

stage that politically immature societies temporarily go through on the way to a full concentration of powers.

Arbitrarily viewing the fact of federation through the lenses of the modern state, scholars "squeezed" federalism until it fitted within the most rigid legal design, which crystallized during the golden age of juridical positivism. In the realm of federalism, the conceptual distinction between federation and confederation has been the medium through which the reconstruction of politics from the starting point of the modern state has taken place: Politics must be thought of as a state-building process, in any time and in any place. European jurists completed the work of other scholars already committed to recounting the timelessness of the state. All the categories of the modern state—already used to illustrate the Greek, Roman and medieval political worlds—had to make quick landfall on the other shore of the Atlantic.

This is a well-known and very successful history of cultural imperialism. And such was also the dream (and the illusion) of *Jus Publicum*: to call "state" any form of political association; *Ordnung* every set of political rules; "doctrine of the state" every form of political thought; and "jurist" every political thinker. The *Gestalten* inherited as a sediment during this grand intellectual enterprise are the ultimate impediments to the historical and institutional comprehension of the phenomenon "federalism," the most important American political innovation.

But let us return to the issue of "sovereignty." If the concept of sovereignty that dominated the multi-century development of the modern state in Europe had had any circulation and success in America, then the same cradle of federalism ("the empty cradle of a great nation," in Tocqueville's well-known expression) would confer a certain legitimacy to the European process of extension of "*jus publicum.*" However, this is not the case. In the course of this work we will analyze the most important constitutional reflections of the states' rights school of thought, which were prevalent in the American debate until the Civil War, the better to clarify just how early American political thought was hostile to European categories. In a subsequent period, things changed significantly. One consequence of the meta-constitutional theory of the Union as an "end in itself," advanced with adamantine coherence by Abraham Lincoln and even more so by his armies, resulted in making the American political panorama more receptive to the European doctrine of sovereignty. This, however, does not change the problem in the slightest (since federalism in America took shape and it was the dominant political theme *prior* to the Civil War) and historians in a free society are not required to write the winners' history, or to sanction what was obtained at the point of a bayonet.

In summary, the two great minds of the South, Thomas Jefferson and John Calhoun, constructed a formidable defense of the federal model of government and, at the same time, produced a wide-ranging reflection on the contractual and voluntary nature of the American Union. For the former, a Lockean natural law model, transposed from individuals to the states, was sufficient to declare the characteristics of the Union. In fact, Jefferson did not draw from the theory of sovereignty (which term is absent from the crucial document, the Kentucky Resolutions of 1798) to declare that the States are "free and independent." It is the nature of the bond between them (and, we should note, not in relation to the federal government) that makes them thus, without any need for the States to assert themselves as autonomous political communities.

From the end of the 1820s, for nearly two decades, it fell to John Calhoun to update the conceptual armory of the states' rights school. In his political structure, however, he proceeded in a very different manner from Jefferson. While for Jefferson the States held a set of rights (expressly declared "natural") that derived from the very nature of the Union, Calhoun started from the playbook of the theory of "indivisible sovereignty." According to Calhoun, the divided sovereignty theory defended by Madison in the *Federalist*, the outcome and the heart of the constitutional compromise in Philadelphia, was the root of all error. There can be no doubts regarding the *locus* of sovereignty, because sovereignty is indivisible: "Sovereignty is an entire thing;—to divide is to destroy it."[129] Sovereignty belongs either to the States or to the Union,

129 John C. Calhoun, *A Discourse on the Government and Constitution of the United States*, in *The Works of John C. Calhoun*, ed. Richard K. Crallé, (New York: Appleton, 1851-1855), vol. 1, p. 146.

but it could not belong to both. Calhoun considered the States self-governing political communities, and he always maintained that the people of the States, and not their governments, were the sovereign authority. He even attempted to distinguish between sovereignty and the exercise of sovereign powers. In his view, the Madisonian "divided sovereignty" theory was fallacious precisely because it did not take into consideration this political distinction. Thus, the States had delegated to the central government only some "powers of sovereignty" that were to be used for the benefit of all, but they had never delegated any portion of sovereignty itself, simply because they could not do it in as much as sovereignty is a *oneness*. This meant that the delegated powers could be retracted by the States at any time.[130] To confuse the exercise of sovereign powers with sovereignty itself was, in Calhoun's opinion, the fundamental defect of Madison's view. Those delegating powers can always reclaim them. As one of the refrains of the states' rights school goes: "in no instance can the creation overcome the creator."

A crucial distinction, according to Calhoun, was that the violation of the Constitution and not "sovereign caprice" should warrant the re-appropriation of those powers. However, as in every agreement between parties that do not have a common judge, every agent could decide the nature of the infraction and the adequate methods to mend it. In Calhoun's vision, the Constitution is not a "higher law" open to any type of evolution according to the spirit of the times prevailing among the majority of the people or the new class in power, but rather a "compact" between the sovereign States that can be renegotiated only by means of amendments. If the federal government is nothing but "a great joint-stock company, which comprehends every interest,"[131] then the typical relation between States and federation is that of commander and agent. It was a simple and efficient way of clarifying to the American people that the creature (the federal government) cannot become superior to its creator (the States). The problem of the nature of the

130 See August O. Spain, *The Political Theory of John C. Calhoun* (New York: Octagon Books, 1951), pp. 174-8.

131 John C. Calhoun, "South Carolina Exposition and Protest" (1828), Calhoun, *Works*, vol. 6, p. 33

US government could be reduced to a single question: "whether the act of ratification, of itself, or the constitution, by someone, or all of its provisions, did, or did not, divest the several States of their character of separate, independent, and sovereign communities, and merge them all in one great community or nation called the American people."[132] According to Calhoun, the United States were not a nation, but an "assemblage of nations" or of the member peoples of their respective political communities, the States. The fact that these States entered into a relation with other States to form a compact using a common agent did not change their status as sovereign political communities. But as hastily concluded by many theorists of confederation, there is no place at all for such a view. Calhoun in fact argues for the distinction between federation and confederation on totally different grounds from those already presented, and certainly in harmony with American political tradition:

> Ours is a union, not of individuals, united by what is called a social compact—for that would make it a nation; nor of governments—for that would have formed a confederacy, like the one superseded by the present Constitution; but a union of States, founded on a written, positive compact, forming a Federal Republic, with the same equality of rights among the States composing the Union, as among the citizens composing the States themselves.[133]

Calhoun did not deny the changes that had taken place in relation to the system set out by the Articles of Confederation. Under the Constitution, the federal government could act directly on individuals, while prior to that it acted only through the mediation of the States. But the point of Calhoun's entire analysis is that, when the States and the federal government exercise their own "governmental powers," they operate like agents of the sovereign States, meaning the people of each individual State,

132 John C. Calhoun, *A Discourse*, Calhoun, *Works*, vol. 1, p. 121.

133 John C. Calhoun, "Speech on the Veto Power" (Senate, February 28, 1842), Calhoun, *Works*, vol. 4, pp. 80-81.

who are the genuine and authentic sovereign of the Constitution. Thus, in relation to each other, the federal and state governments might be "equal and coordinates," but from the viewpoint of the sovereign they "both stood in the same relations," simple agents, that could be "ordered, changed or abolished at will."[134] As Calhoun stated: "Sovereignty is not in the Government, it is in the people. Any other conception is utterly abhorrent to the ideas of every American." Naturally, he was referring to the people of the several States and certainly not to the people of the Union, given that "no such community ever existed, as the people of the United States, forming a collective body of individuals in one nation."[135]

Although his conceptual framework was unbound by arguments based on either natural law or the contractual model that were used by Jefferson, a central question for Calhoun was the same one posed by the third president. It concerned the absence of a common judge between the sovereign parties to a contract. In both Jefferson's and Calhoun's versions of states' rights, what matters is that the Constitution is not considered open to any form of evolution according to either the spirit of the times, the moods of the majority instructed by the political class in power, or some Supreme Court justice. The Constitution is a compact between the States, which can be renegotiated only by amendments and with strict procedures.

The right of a state to declare an authoritative interpretation of the constitutional compact of the federation and make it binding on its citizens, that is, the doctrine of nullification—on which we will later dwell at length—is the central theme of the constitutional interpretation of this school of thought. As will become clear, it is also the most important formulation of the right of resistance within the federal community. The right of resistance shifts from an "appeal to heaven," to an appeal to one's own state, and then from one's own state to the "supermajority" that has the power to

134 Spain, *The Political Theory of John C. Calhoun,* p. 187.

135 John C. Calhoun, "Speech Introducing Resolutions Declaratory of the Nature and Power of the Federal Government" (Senate, January 22, 1833) in *The Papers of John C. Calhoun,* ed. Clyde N. Wilson (Columbia: South Carolina University Press, 1979), vol. 12, p. 21 [Calhoun, *Papers*].

modify the constitution. The Declaration of Independence adopted the radical Lockean doctrine of the appeal to heaven in its entirety, and considered it an extra-constitutional rectification. On the other hand, the legal hooks for a legitimate rebellion against despotic governments are provided, according to states' righters, by a Constitution with as many "sovereigns" as there are states and one, and only one, potential despot, the federal government.

In the final analysis, two profoundly different conceptions of power in America and Europe are concealed under the term "sovereignty." In the United States, the concept of sovereignty has an eminently anti-statist function (*i.e.*, the sovereignty of the primary political communities as a limit on the consolidation of the Union), while in Europe sovereignty is the bulwark of the construct of the state (that is, it claims the absolute political synthesis of the "state").

If Calhoun's interpretation of "American sovereignty" involves the power to enact laws, indivisibly residing in the people of the individual States, it is however totally devoid of the elements that dominated the formation of the modern state in Europe. Sovereignty, for American political theorists, is not given as a specific and reified attribute of statehood, but is instead derived from the interpretation of the Constitution. More precisely, state sovereignty and the contractual nature of the federal bond are deduced from—and are not instruments of—Constitutional hermeneutics. Essentially, the States are not sovereign political communities in spite of the Constitution but, on the contrary, they are such precisely by virtue of it.

Contemporary scholars, accustomed to regarding the federal government as the principal actor of the American system, can easily maintain that the entire construction of this tradition was merely an attempt to build a rationale in defense of white privileges in the South. But that is not the case. As Carl Schmitt put it, Calhoun's theses "remain theoretically crucial for a constitutional theory of federation and are not made irrelevant by the fact that the Southern states were defeated. ... Calhoun's ... doctrines deal with key concepts in the constitutional theory of federation. The task here is not to prove that ... the U.S. ... today is a 'federation,' but rather to pose the question (without preconceived notions and phraseology) whether today there is some sense in which ... [it] can still be called a federation or whether only the remnants of an earlier federation have been deployed organizationally in the construction of a unitary state or whether true federal elements have been transformed gradually into the organizational elements of a unitary state."[136]

This is the crucial point. Calhoun and the entire South became obstinate in their belief that the United States was an authentic federation, that the Constitution was a tool that gave amending powers to three-fourths of the States, and that ascribing governmental functions to a superstructure established to administer common matters did not substantially change the contractual and voluntary character of the association between the States. But history was moving in another direction.[137]

136 Carl Schmitt, "The Constitutional Theory of Federation," in *Telos* 91 (Spring 1992), pp. 35-36, a partial translation of Schmitt's *Verfassungslehere*.

137 Calhoun was aware of this. Thus, from the mid-1840s to his death, he abandoned the doctrine he had defended in the previous decade in order to elaborate (in *Disquisition on Government,* published posthumously) the theory of the "concurrent majority," which is one of the most important critiques of the tyranny of the majority ever written. However, it must be noted that he was much more appreciated by his contemporaries as the brilliant champion of the constitutional cause of the "South as a conscious minority." His "remedies" to unrestrained majority rule, such as the peculiar consent theory presented in the *Disquisition,* became matters of scholarly interest much later, in the mid-twentieth century.

Chapter 2

THE ORIGINAL AMERICAN DEBATE: FEDERALISTS AND ANTIFEDERALISTS

> Europe seemed incapable of becoming the home of free States. It was from America that the plain ideas that men ought to mind their own business, and that the nation is responsible to Heaven for the acts of the State,—ideas long locked in the breast of solitary thinkers, and hidden among Latin folios,—burst forth like a conqueror upon the world they were destined to transform.[1]
>
> -Lord Acton

2.1) The "Construction" Period (1776-1791)

The more one analyzes the causes of the American Revolution, the greater is the sense of frustration. The event has been examined from so many perspectives, but a summary, however broad, seems impossible. The American Revolution was caused primarily by the intransigent rigidity of England toward the colonies (one only need consider the fact that Edmund Burke delivered his parliamentary appeal for conciliation to a nearly deserted house).[2] Between 1763 and July 4, 1776, the date the Declaration of Independence was signed, a political course played out in which the language of the

1 Lord Acton, *History of Freedom and Other Essays* (London: McMillan, 1907) p. 52.

2 Over the course of time Burke's speeches favoring the colonies were numerous and consistent, beginning with an address to the House of Commons on November 18, 1768. See Edmund Burke, *On the American Revolution: Selected Speeches and Letters*, ed. Elliott R. Barkan (New York: Harper, 1966). While Burke is the most famous, the Americans had a number of other British sympathizers, cf. Jerome R. Reich, *British Friends of the American Revolution* (Armonk, NY: M.E Sharpe, 1998).

British subjects in the colonies and the ruling class in London followed such divergent reasoning that an unbridgeable chasm opened between them.

By now nearly all historians agree that to find the force that drove the colonies to challenge one of the world's greatest powers one must research the "American ideology."[3] Even among the protagonists themselves the ideological roots of the Revolution are quite clear. As John Mercer stated, "we rather combatted the theory of tyranny than the practice."[4]

The doctrinal shift of the revolutionary spirit is evidenced in the long trail of pamphlets from James Otis's 1764 *The Rights of the British Colonies Asserted and Proved* to the first American best-seller, *Common Sense*, by Thomas Paine in 1776. The fundamental features of the revolutionary rift are found in the adoption of a political theory linked to the doctrinal radicalization of natural law, and, above all, to the "federal" vision of the British Empire.

In fact, the American colonists were convinced that the London parliament had no power over them, and therefore its actions were totally arbitrary. They recognized, however, at least during the decade prior to 1776, a certain authority in the Crown. It was necessary to sever ties with the king, as the revolutionaries held that a link between the colonies and the English political class, the English "people," and the English Parliament had never existed.[5] Thus, the formidable indictment in the Declaration of Independence targets only George III.

3 Bernard Bailyn's work, *The Ideological Origins of the American Revolution* (Cambridge, MA: Harvard University Press, 1967), has become a classic not only for its undoubted merits, but also because it identified ideology as the real driving force of the Revolution.

4 A Farmer VII (Part 5), *Baltimore Maryland Gazette*, 22 April 1788, in *Documentary History of the Ratification of the Constitution*, Jensen Merrill, John P. Kaminski, Gaspare J. Saladino eds., 29 vols. (Madison: State Historical Society of Wisconsin, 1976–2017) [DHRC], Vol. 12, p. 525.

5 For a detailed analysis of the vision of the British Empire on both sides of the Atlantic, Richard Koebner's work is still important: *Empire* (Cambridge, UK: Cambridge University Press, 1961). See also Alfred F. Young and Gregory H. Nobles, *Whose American Revolution Was It? Historians Interpret the Founding* (New York: New York University Press, 2011), and *The American Revolution Reborn*, eds. Patrick Spero and Michael Zuckerman (Philadelphia: University of Pennsylvania Press, 2016).

The reason for this relationship of the colonies with the king rather than the English political class is that the Americans were convinced that the British Empire was a free association of independent political communities, with the Crown as the guarantor of the various autonomies. While the issue of representation was the litmus test used to counter Parliamentary aggression in London, the basis of the tax revolt was the federal theory of the Empire, a doctrine that London did not accept. It was more a product of the new political winds blowing through the colonies than a calm analysis of the reality of imperial relations.[6]

The most famous grand debate on sovereignty preceding independence took place in Massachusetts in 1773 between Governor Thomas Hutchinson and the General Court (the colonial legislature). In the response of the future Bay Staters we can see "an important break with the metropolitan conception of authority and an early instance in which colonists begun to grope toward a conception of multilayered sovereignty in reaction to the theory of unitary sovereignty that they saw gaining ground among British officials."[7]

While it was clearly a rather perilous undertaking, Hutchinson decided that he wanted to openly clarify to the people of the colony (or plantation, as he called it) the idea that sovereignty is indivisible and belongs entirely to the British authorities. While he "was not

6 There is a so-called "imperial" historical school of thought, formed mainly by Herbert L. Osgood, George L. Beer, and Charles McLean Andrews, that tended to oppose the nineteenth-century simplifications of George Bancroft, who considered the Revolution a logical and irrepressible consequence of English oppression. This assessment took account of the points of view of the mother country and considered "imperial relations" the real matter of the dispute. This school, especially in the monumental works of Lawrence H. Gipson since the 1930s, produced an interpretation of the Revolution that emphasized the role of the American environment in creating interests and ideals that differed from those in England. See especially Charles M. Andrews' *Colonial Background of the American Revolution: Four Essays in American Colonial History* (1924) (New Haven, Yale University Press, 1958) and Lawrence H. Gipson, *The British Empire before the American Revolution*, 15 volumes (New York: Knopf, 1936-1970).

7 Allison L. LaCroix, *The Ideological Origins of American Federalism* (Cambridge, MA: Harvard University Press, 2010), p. 70.

a political theorist ... his thought was nevertheless systematic."[8] The Governor wanted to silence once and forever the writers who denied "the authority of the Parliament of Great Britain to make and establish laws for the inhabitants of this province."[9] After a defense of the notion of "one sovereignty," indivisible and equally binding in any part of the British dominions, stemming from King, Commons and Lords, Thomas Hutchinson ventured to put forward clearly the options:

> I know of no line that can be drawn between the supreme authority of Parliament and the total independence of the colonies: it is impossible there should be two independent Legislatures in one and the same state; for, although there may be but one head, the King, yet the two Legislative bodies will make two governments as distinct as the kingdoms of England and Scotland before the union.

The inhabitants of the plantation, on their part, were convinced that the existing state of affairs "was occasioned ... by the British House of Commons assuming and exercising a power inconsistent with the freedom of the constitution."[10] The colonists were portraying themselves as British subjects, but a quite different people from the residents of the mother country: "Nothing is more evident ... that any people, who are subject

---

8 Bernard Baylin, *The Ordeal of Thomas Hutchinson* (Cambridge, MA: Harvard University Press, 1974), p. 76. According to Baylin one of the major sources of the Governor's political creed was a pamphlet written by Allan Ramsay, which the former "saluted ... as 'the best thing I have ever seen on the subject'," p. 77. Ramsay believed that popular consent was not a sine qua non for taxation as in the colonies, like everywhere else, sovereignty was sufficient. "*Sovereignty* admits of no degrees, it is always *supreme*, and to level it, is, in effect, to destroy it." While he clearly conceived of natural law as the sole legitimate limitation of government, he argued that the rights of the colonists had not been violated. [Allan Ramsay], *Thoughts on the Origin and Nature of Government: Occasioned by the late Disputes Between Great Britain and her American Colonies, written in the year 1766* (London: T. Becket & P.A. de Hondt, 1769), pp. 52-55.

9 *Speeches of the Governors of Massachusetts from 1765 to 1775* ... (Boston: Russell & Gardner, 1818), p. 338.

10 *Ibid.*, p. 352.

to the unlimited power of another, must be in a state of abject slavery."[11] Parliament had no authority whatsoever in America, as it was "constitutionally confined within the limits of the realm, and the nation collectively, of which alone it is the representing and Legislative Assembly."[12] Their bond with the motherland was only through the Crown, and they acknowledged the "just sense of allegiance which we owe to the King of Great Britain, our rightful Sovereign".[13] And somehow in the colonists' mind such a sovereign had granted them all the liberties they needed as he "stipulated with them ... that they should enjoy and exercise this most essential right, which discriminates freemen from vassals, uninterruptedly, in its full sense and meaning; and they did, and ought still to exercise it, without the necessity of returning, for the sake of exercising it, to the nation or state of England."[14] So if no line could be drawn between independence and submission—as the Governor boldly stated—then "the consequence is, either that the colonies are the vassals of the Parliament, or that they are totally independent." Since the state of servitude was logically and historically unthinkable, "we were thus independent"[15] from the beginning, proclaimed the legislature. Allison L. LaCroix sees this debate "a crucial moment of productive conflict between the British vision of indivisible governmental authority and the emerging American vision of authority apportioned among different levels of government according to specific, substantively defined principles."[16] The least that one can say is that American federalism had profound roots in the colonial experience and in the ideological conception of the British Empire entertained by the Americans.

A year later, Thomas Jefferson clearly stated that Parliament had no power to pass laws, either good or bad, for the colonies; that the colonies were members of the British Empire on an equal

11 *Ibid.*, p. 357.

12 *Ibid.*, p. 358.

13 *Ibid.*, p. 364.

14 *Ibid.*, p. 358

15 *Ibid.*, p. 363.

16 Allison L. LaCroix, *The Ideological Origins of American Federalism*, p. 76.

footing with England; that every political community had its own sovereign organs to which supreme legislative power belonged; that any relationship of an imperial nature between the various communities happened through the figure of a common monarch, the supreme magistrate of the people and subject to the law.[17] It is worth quoting a passage from *A Summary View of the Rights of British America* (1774), the essay in which Jefferson best expressed these theories.

> Not only the principles of common sense, but the common feelings of human nature, must be surrendered up before his majesty's subjects here can be persuaded to believe that they hold their political existence at the will of a British parliament. ... Let them name their terms, but let them be just. Accept of every commercial preference it is in our power to give for such things as we can raise for their use, or they make for ours. But let them not think to exclude us from going to other markets to dispose of those commodities which they cannot use, or to supply those wants which they cannot supply. Still less let it be proposed that our properties within our own territories shall be taxed or regulated by any power on earth but our own. The God who gave us life gave us liberty at the same time; the hand of force may destroy, but cannot disjoin them.[18]

The entire Constitutional phase was an integral part of the Revolution and lasted until the passage of the Bill of Rights (1791). In 1815 John Adams described "the last twenty-five years of the last century, and the first fifteen years of this" as "the age of revolutions

17 The bibliography on Jefferson is almost boundless, see Luigi Marco Bassani, *Liberty, State & Union: The Political Theory of Thomas Jefferson* (Macon, GA: Mercer University Press, 2010). The most comprehensive biography is still Dumas Malone, *Jefferson and His Time*, 6 volumes (Boston: Little, Brown, 1948–1981); the best in a single volume is by Merrill D. Peterson, *Thomas Jefferson and the New Nation: A Biography* (New York: Oxford University Press, 1970).

18 Thomas Jefferson, *A Summary View of the Rights of British America,* with an Introduction by Thomas P. Abernethy (New York: Park Av., 1943), pp. 12 and 23.

and constitutions."[19] America had the revolutionary birthright, and in 1787 constitutions, in the modern sense, existed only on the Atlantic coast of the United States.[20]

American political thought took the specific form of constitutionalism. American polity was conceived as a system founded on a document, the interpretation of which determines the nature of the system. All political problems are reconfigured and reconsidered on the basis of this document which, over time, has become increasingly authoritative. If the great constitutional phase took place at the dawn of the Republic, the debate on the Constitution has engaged Americans throughout their history. The interpretations of the relationship between the States and the federation dominate all discourse on individual rights, prerogatives, and liberty, and they are the threads that connect the crucial moments in the life of the country to its founding years.

The Constitutional Convention in Philadelphia during the summer of 1787 was something rather novel, but America at the time did not live in any "institutional vacuum." During the session in which the Second Continental Congress approved the Declaration of Independence, the delegates initiated a "plan of the Union" for the colonies to become free and independent states. The resulting document, the *Articles of Confederation and Perpetual Union,* was the first American Constitution. Squarely placed in the by-then solid constitutional tradition—from the Mayflower Compact of 1620 to the long series of State Constitutions—the Articles were little more than an alliance between thirteen states.[21]

---

19 John Adams to J. Lloyd, March 29, 1815, *The Works of John Adams,* ed. Charles F. Adams (Boston: Little, Brown, 1860–1865), vol. 10, pp. 148-149.

20 Cf. Donald S. Lutz, *The Origins of American Constitutionalism* (Baton Rouge: Louisiana State University Press, 1988).

21 Cf. Merrill Jensen, *The Articles of Confederation: An Interpretation of the Social-Constitutional History of the American Revolution, 1774–1781* (Madison: University of Wisconsin Press, 1940), pp. 164-167. See also Jack Rakove, "The Legacy of the Articles of Confederation," *Publius* 12, no. 4 (1982), pp. 45-66, and Donald S. Lutz, "The Articles of Confederation as the Background to the Federal Republic," *Publius* 20, no. 1 (1990), pp. 55-70.

Today we know almost everything about the Philadelphia Convention, but for decades Americans were unaware of the most important facts. The secrecy surrounding the work lasted at least until the 1820s, when publications appeared that began to shed light on the assembly. In 1818 Congress decided to make public the *Journal of the Convention* (largely incomplete), and three years later the journal of New York delegate Robert Yates (*Secret Proceedings and Debates of the Convention*, which ends on July 5, the day he left the Convention) was published in Albany. It was not until 1840 that Americans had available the most complete memoir compiled by James Madison, as he wanted it to be published posthumously.[22] The most important documentary source of the Convention was not published until 1911, when Max Farrand compiled the four-volume *Records of the Federal Convention of 1787*.[23] In essence, for several decades, Americans (and most importantly, the Supreme Court justices)[24] interpreted a sparse set of texts, frequently referring to the "will of the Framers," with nothing in hand to back it up.

---

22 During the 1830s Jonathan Elliot published four volumes of documents that are still essential for the study of that period: *The Debates in the Several State Conventions on the Adoption of the Federal Constitution* (Philadelphia: Lippincott, 1836). In 1840 a fifth volume containing James Madison's *Notes* was added. Yates' work was republished in 1821 in the first volume of Elliot, pp. 389-479. The report by the Maryland delegate, Luther Martin, known as *Genuine Information*, is on pages 344-388 of the same volume. Luther, one of the most famous Antifederalists, had presented the Report to his State Assembly in 1788. The most comprehensive collection is the already mentioned *Documentary History of the Ratification of the Constitution*. It must be kept in mind that, as Mary Bilder has shown conclusively, James Madison revised his *Notes* before they were published, so that the major source of contemporary knowledge "altered the depiction of the Convention and the Constitution." Mary S. Bilder, *Madison's Hand: Revising the Constitutional Convention* (Cambridge, Harvard University Press, 2015), p. 15.

23 *The Records of the Federal Convention of 1787*, ed. Max Farrand (New Haven: Yale University Press, 1911); the revised and final edition appeared in 1937. In addition to the foundational and nearly complete notes by Madison, the first two volumes contain the daily notes taken by the delegates Yates, Rufus King, James McHenry, William Pierce, William Paterson, Alexander Hamilton, Charles Pinckney and George Mason. The third volume presents letters, diaries, and official documents that complete the framework of the Convention.

24 For instance, the decisive constitutional opinions of John Marshall, chief justice of the Supreme Court from 1801 to his death in 1835, were written without any reference text on what had really happened in Philadelphia.

In a well-known essay John Fiske called the years between the Revolutionary War to the passage of the Constitution the "critical period."[25] Fiske, and with him countless later historians, took at face value the complaints against the *Articles of Confederation* that the federalists had raised both before and after the Constitutional Convention. The old document was considered the cause of the ills that plagued the Union because it did not give actual "sovereignty" to the federal government, which was unable to tax, conscript men, and enforce international treaties. In the words of one early-twentieth-century historian: "Weak and disorderly, inefficient and unsatisfactory, was the government under the Articles of Confederation, and simply because the people in the new States could not appreciate fully the necessity of surrendering sovereignty and putting force behind laws."[26] No need to delve further, as a supermajority of historians hummed the same tune for more than two centuries. These historians, to be sure, echoed many protagonists of the Convention itself, like James Wilson: "Every act of Congress, and the proceedings of every State ... all point to the weakness and imbecility of the existing confederation; while the loud and concurrent voice of the people proclaims an efficient national government to be the only cure."[27]

Despite this consensus, the era of the *Articles of Confederation* should not be considered a failure, either from an economic or an institutional point of view. It is generally held that a society without a strong political center and leadership cannot prosper, but the Americans of that time were demonstrating the exact opposite. Robust economic growth was not impeded by the weakness of the constitutional document. "Objectively, the first decade of the history of the United States was a whopping success.... Despite certain postwar economic dislocations, most Americans were

25 Cf. John Fiske, *The Critical Period of American History*, 1783–1789 (Boston: Houghton, Mifflin, 1888).

26 Henry Litchfield West, *Federal Power: Its Growth and Necessity* (New York: George Doran, 1918), p. 25.

27 James Wilson in the Pennsylvania Convention, November 24, 1787, Farrand, vol. 3, p. 142.

prospering,"[28] states Forrest McDonald. Moreover, most of the *Articles* were incorporated in the federal Constitution that was ratified in 1789 (from half to two-thirds of the old text was "saved" in Philadelphia, although of course the system of governance was wholly redesigned).[29]

2.2) The Philadelphia Project

The Convention certainly went beyond its own limits, but many had understood by then that an advisory committee that would propose a few minor modifications to the States was not what was convened in Philadelphia. The newspapers in all the States declared that the political destiny of the United States would be decided at that meeting. Michael J. Klarman has recently written a massive study on how the Federalists staged a veritable coup d'état in Philadelphia. He is one of the very last advocates of the Beardian thesis—that is, the quite common belief that the convention was in fact a coup in which a faction forced "a system of government very different from the one that most Americans would have expected or desired."[30] The classic 1913 work of Charles Beard, *An Economic Interpretation of the Constitution*, has been revisited in so many ways, and has produced so much secondary literature, that it cannot be discussed here.[31]

The delegates decided that the Constitution would be ratified by the populace gathered in conventions and not by state governments, which had been the signatories of the *Articles of Confederation*. State authorities were circumvented (and tricked) by Federalists seeking a direct agreement with the people of the various states.

28 Forrest McDonald, *Novus Ordo Seclorum* (Lawrence: University Press of Kansas, 1985), p. 143.

29 Regarding the first American constitutional experiment see also Richard B. Morris, *Forging the Union*, 1781–1789 (New York: Harper & Row, 1987) and Robert W. Hoffert, *A Politics of Tensions: The Articles of Confederation and American Political Ideas* (Niwot: University Press of Colorado), 1992.

30 Michael J. Klarman, *The Framers' Coup: The Making of the United States Constitution* (New York: Oxford University Press, 2016), p. 616.

31 See Charles Beard, *An Economic Interpretation of the Constitution of the United States* (New York: Macmillan, 1913).

From then on, and in particular for Madison, Jefferson and Calhoun, "State" was used to designate the people and never the governmental authorities.

European history leads us to consider the drive toward centralization of powers as "political realism." To understand the debate that developed in the United States it is necessary to avoid that European idea, if for no other reason than the institutional fact of the existence of the States and not the Union. The American territory, far from being the Lockean *tabula rasa* imagined by some, by 1787 was already heavily in debt due to its colonial past, the revolutionary uprising, wars, and the States' institutions. In the frank public debate, no leader of the time clearly espoused the "European solution" to the problem of political order. Although the British model was a clear demonstration that such a solution could be attractive, especially in Alexander Hamilton's view, politicians were well aware that the American public showed a high preference for "federalism." Yet during the debates and secret deliberations[32] of the Constitutional Convention an authentically national (or extremely centrist) position emerged. It was relegated to the margins of the dispute, considered simply impractical in the American context.[33] This "nationalist" interpretation—as it was called from the beginning—of the birth of the United States always held that the Union emerged prior to the States, which received their legal status from the Union. But all the historical documents and the phrases used prove exactly the opposite. The real champion of the "nationalist" interpretation, as we will see better in the final chapter, was Abraham Lincoln, who, confronted with the secession

32 On May 29, that is, the second day of work, it was established that "nothing spoken in the House be printed, or otherwise published or communicated without leave." James Madison, *Notes of Debates in the Federal Convention of 1787* (1840), ed. Adrienne Koch (Athens: Ohio University Press, 1966), p. 28.

33 The use of the term "national" during the convention was made crystal clear by Madison in 1828 in a letter to Andrew Stevenson: "The term, national applied to the contemplated Government, in the early stage of the Convention, particularly in the propositions of Mr. Randolph, was equivalent to unlimited or consolidated. This was not the case. The term was used, not in contradistinction to a limited, but to a federal Government." Farrand, *Records*, Vol. 3, p. 473. In essence, it implied the centralization of *not* unlimited powers. See also Richard Beeman, *Plain, Honest Men: The Making of the American Constitution* (New York: Random House, 2009).

of the Southern states, declared: "The Union, and not themselves separately, procured their independence and their liberty. By conquest or purchase the Union gave each of them whatever of independence and liberty it has. The Union is older than any of the States, and, in fact, it created them as States."[34] Donald Livingston calls this Lincoln's spectacular lie, as it is crystal clear that States formed the Union and not vice versa. The *Declaration*, the *Articles of Confederation*, and the *Treaty of Paris of 1783* leave no doubt in this regard,[35] so much so that the nationalist interpretation was described as simply "unsustainable" by a leading American

---

34 Abraham Lincoln, "Special Message to Congress," July 4, 1861, in *The Life and Writings of Abraham Lincoln*, ed. P. Van Doren (New York: Modern Library, 1940), p. 671. While the military and political intent of the president is clear and must be assessed as such, the reformulations of the same argument advanced by contemporary scholars are more difficult to understand. See as one example, Samuel H. Beer, *To Make a Nation: The Rediscovery of American Freedom* (Cambridge, MA: Harvard University Press, 1993).

35 It is worth noting that from a linguistic point of view the United States became a "singular" entity only after the Civil War. The transition from "the United States *are*" to "the United States *is*" was slow and troubled (to the ears of many, and not just to those nostalgic for the Old South, the expression grates still). Originally the name of the "non-country" was "united States," with the capital sometimes used for States but never for united, thus indicating that a characteristic of the States was to be united, and yet that fact did not alter their nature as independent and sovereign states. The subsequent use of the capital letter had no ideological implications, as was the case in the previously cited shift from plural to singular. It is common to note the good fortune in American history to have an acronym for the country, US, that appeals directly to us. This may be so, but this *us* is completely outside the founding American documents. While European constitutions proclaim the unity of the people and parliamentary and national sovereignty well before nations existed, in America the documents from the Declaration to the Constitution give no place to the American people, whose existence can be an empirical fact or a matter of faith, but never a legal truth. Even thirty years after the Civil War a Southern author expressed himself thusly regarding the Constitution and the existence of an American people: the Constitution "was voted for by States in the Convention, submitted to the people of each State separately, and became the constitution only of the States adopting it. 'The people of the United States' as a political organism, never had an existence; in the aggregate, never performed a single political act, never was entrusted with any civil function, never was appealed to for sanction to any proceeding, and never can do what a National Government might do, without an entire, radical revolution of our system of constitutional, representative, confederated republics," J. L. M. Curry, *The Southern States of The American Union Considered in Their Relations to the Constitution of the United States and to the Resulting Union* (Richmond, VA: Johnson, 1895), p. 100.

historian.[36] Even Robert Nagel acknowledged that the idea "that the Constitution gained its legal authority as an act of the undifferentiated people of the whole nation—is simply at odds with the history of ratification and with the ongoing practice of formal amendment."[37]

In any case, the divisions that were later to take hold throughout the country were already revealed within the Convention. Delegate Luther Martin's view was that there were three clear factions "of very different sentiments and views": the absolute "centralizers," those who were there to protect their own states, and the true federalists who wanted to save the previous system of American government by amending it.[38] The first was a "party, whose object and wish it was to abolish and annihilate all State governments, and to bring forward one general government, over this extensive continent, of a monarchical nature, under certain restrictions and limitations."[39] Though this first group had few known adherents, in Martin's view many delegates had similar opinions but lacked the courage to express them openly. "The second party ... wished to establish such a system, as could give their own States undue power and influence in the government over the other States."[40] Against these first two factions stood a "third party ... truly federal and republican" [and] "nearly equal in number with the other two."[41]

The positions were quite distinct. One faction led by Alexander Hamilton, Charles Pinckney, Governor Morris, and James Madison intended to secure the passage of a strongly centralized plan of

---

36 Forrest McDonald, *States' Rights and the Union: Imperium in Imperio 1776-1876* (Lawrence: University Press of Kansas, 2000), p. 9.

37 Robert F. Nagel, *The Implosion of American Federalism* (New York: Oxford University Press, 2002), p. 52.

38 Luther Martin, "Genuine Information II," *Baltimore Maryland Gazette*, 1 [January 1788], DHRC, Vol. 15, p. 205.

39 *Ibid.*

40 *Ibid.*

41 *Ibid.* The political divisions that Martin described were accepted by all later authors. To give just one example, Thomas Cooper, a leading theorist in South Carolina, adopted Martin's categories in his pamphlet *Consolidation*. Cf. Thomas Cooper, *Consolidation: An Account of Parties in the United States, from the Convention of 1787 to the Present Period* (Columbia: Black & Sweeny, 1824), pp. 2-3.

the Union, within which the role of the states would have been essentially that of provinces granted some autonomy. This group—which actually convened the Convention—immediately went on the offensive, even taking advantage of the absence of some delegations, and already by the end of May had put its own views on the table. But the opposition, formed by all those who wanted to maintain the federal nature of the government of the Union—that is, to derive its legitimacy from the States alone—was slowly taking shape around John Dickinson and William Paterson.[42]

The Virginia Plan, presented by Edmund Randolph on May 29th, but whose principal author was James Madison, was a project of political centralization. It outlined a bicameral national parliament, with one elected chamber and the second chosen from the first, in which voting rights were proportional either to property or to the number of inhabitants (excluding slaves). This national parliament would "legislate in all cases to which the separate States are incompetent, or in which the harmony of the United States may be interrupted by the exercise of individual Legislation."[43] The national legislative power would have had veto rights over all state legislation it held to be inconsistent with the Constitution; and it would have had the right to use the full force of the Union against a state that failed to comply with its Constitutional duties. Furthermore, Randolph's project provided for a very strong national executive linked to the legislature by a relationship of trust. The national judiciary was composed of one or more supreme courts, whose justices, selected from among the national assembly, would serve "during good behavior,"[44] that is, for life. The plan embodied a categorical imperative around which the debate centered: "The Style of this Government shall be The United States of America & the Government shall consist of

42 In the New York delegation, for example, next to Hamilton the most committed advocates of a strong national government were John Lansing and Robert Yates, two supporters of states' rights.

43 James Madison, *Notes*, p. 31.

44 Madison, *Notes*, p. 32.

supreme legislative Executive & Judicial Powers."[45] The question posed by the Virginia delegation, particularly regarding just how "national" the government should be, became the object of debate not only by the Convention, but for all subsequent American political history.

The most comprehensive project of centralization, introduced by Alexander Hamilton,[46] was quite similar to the Virginia Plan. However, the Virginia Plan conceded too much ground, for Hamilton's liking, to the States as autonomous political communities. On June 18 the New York delegation proposed its plan,[47] more as a symbolic act than as a real contribution to the debate taking shape, as it had no influence on the constitutional project approved later. Had the project had been accepted the United States would have immediately become a single, administratively decentralized republic, if not outright "one and indivisible." As Russell Kirk rightly observed, "a similar centralization would have been impossible to obtain even by force of arms"[48]According to historian Robert Nagel:

> The most extreme version of radical nationalism proposed eliminating the states. ... A fallback proposal [was] to transform the existing states into administrative units of the national government. ... Still, the idea in one form or another has had advocates

45 Madison, *Notes,* p. 34. The term governance in American political terminology, as will become clear, does not mean just the executive, but rather indicates the entire body of executive, legislative, and judicial political powers.

46 On the political thought of this complex figure see Forrest McDonald, *Alexander Hamilton: A Biography* (New York, Norton, 1979); Richard Brookhiser, *Alexander Hamilton, American* (New York: Free Press, 1999); Harvey Flaumenhaft, *The Effective Republic: Administration and Constitution in the Thought of Alexander Hamilton* (Durham, NC: Duke University Press), 1992.

47 The plan is summarized in Alexander Hamilton, "The Plan presented by Alexander Hamilton, June 18, 1787," in *The Origins of the American Constitution,* ed. Michael Kammena (New York: Penguin, 1986), pp. 36-38. See also James Madison, *Notes,* pp. 129-139.

48 Russell Kirk, *Le radici dell'ordine americano,* ed. Marco Respinti (Milan: Mondadori, 1996), p. 442.

> as far back as Alexander Hamilton. ... Such proposals are important mainly in indicating how wide the range of permissible discourse is among nationalists.[49]

After the ratification of the Constitution, Louis Guillaume Otto, the French ambassador, showed concerns of a Hamiltonian nature when he stated that "the individual legislatures, so jealous of their independence and even their sovereignty, will stop the [federal] government from making the progress, that without them, she would not fail to make in a few years."[50] From the standpoint of federal representation, the Connecticut Compromise reached on July 16 was crucial: in the House the "federal strength" of each state was determined by the percentage of the white population, with each slave counting as three fifths,[51] while representation in the Senate was on equal footing, without regard to the number of inhabitants. With this problem resolved, the work proceeded expeditiously. During the rest of July, the text of the Constitution was prepared for discussion, which took place in the hall from August 6 to September 10. On September 17 the draft Constitution was approved and signed by thirty-nine of the forty-two delegates.

"Modern federalism," the complex system of fluid balance between the States and the federation, of collective management of goods in common, and of self-government regarding the internal affairs of the States, was actually created in Philadelphia, although it has clear doctrinal and institutional precedents both in antiquity

49 Robert F. Nagel, *The Implosion of American Federalism*, p. 51.

50 Louis G. Otto to Montmorin, New York, June 1790, cited in Jürgen Heideking, "The Pattern of American Modernity from the Revolution to the Civil War," *Daedalus* 129, no. 1 (2000), pp. 226-227.

51 This rule was created to favor the adoption of the Constitution by the Southern states, where the vast majority of slaves was concentrated. In fact, though they had a white population that was clearly a minority with respect to that of the North, the Southern states could count on a substantial equilibrium in the House of Representatives that lasted almost until the Civil War. On the other hand, it represented a mortal *vulnus* (wound) to the generally libertarian politics of the Founding Fathers: The link between slavery and the Constitution of the United States created what the great abolitionist William Lloyd Garrison called a "pact with the devil."

and in the modern era.[52] The distribution of powers between the States and the federal government, each exercising perfect political power within their spheres of competency, is the heart of the Constitutional pact. It is the distinctive characteristic of the entire structure of American governance. The Constitution establishes a simple and clear separation of powers: the States have overall political power, while the federation is a government with delegated and limited, enumerated powers. This means that the States need not seek permission in the Constitution to implement political action, but need only to be certain that there are no prohibitions against the specific action. The federal government must find a specific mandate in the Constitutional provisions in order to take action. Furthermore, the federal areas of competence are listed in detail and separated from each other. From this love of detail it is evident that the Framers sought analytically to limit the federal power to the written text.

However, presenting the work of the Convention as the result of a conscious design, of a predetermined plan, of a battle to shape the government and society, is not consistent with reality, even though, as Michael Lienisch writes, "Constitutional historians have rewritten the history of the Convention, depicting the Constitution not as the product of fortuitous events and compromises, but rather as the result of philosophical and theoretical elaboration."[53]

The final form of the Constitution was a negotiated compromise—and the only one possible—between centrists and supporters of the rights of the States. If either of the parties had fully prevailed, the

52 The question whether or not the ancient world knew instances of a "federal" sort has long been debated. See the classic work by J.A.O. Larsen, *Greek Federal States* (Oxford: Clarendon Press, 1968).

53 Michael Lienisch, *New Order of the Ages. Time, the Constitution, and the Making of Modern American Political Thought* (Princeton: Princeton University Press, 1988), p. 170. Levi Lucio insists on the constitutional battle as conscious design, particularly by Alexander Hamilton, in "La Federazione: costituzionalismo e democrazia oltre i confini nazionali," in his introduction to an Italian edition of *The Federalist*, pp. 9-110. In his view, "the federal government was not the product of historical evolution, but the result of a political design intended to overcome division and anarchy among states. The Federalist is the book which presents the fundamental lines of this political design," *Ibid.*, p. 10.

United States would have either remained a free association of states or would have immediately become a politically centralized country. In fact, "the Constitution was as national as the Federalists could make it and as confederal as the Antifederalists could keep it."[54]

James Madison, considered the patient inspiration behind the "agreements" in Philadelphia, lived longer than any other major figure of his generation[55] and spent his old age surrounded by the myth of being the "father of the Constitution."[56] It must be noted that Madisonian constitutional preferences were far from seconded by his contemporaries. According to Forrest McDonald, "of the seventy-one specific proposals that Madison ... [supported] he was on the losing side forty times."[57] This does not look like an astounding record.

However, the Constitutional compromise indeed owes much to Little Jimmy, not so much in its final wording, but because the spirit of accommodating seemingly irreconcilable positions characterizes all his thought. Madison was certain that a middle ground must be found on the locus of sovereignty, that more than two possible solutions were possible regarding the core of the American political dilemma. Already, shortly before leaving for Philadelphia, he explained in a letter to Edmund Randolph both the theoretical and practical impossibilities facing the political class:

54 Gary L. McDowell, "Federalism and Civic Virtue: The Antifederalists and the Constitution," in *How Federal is the Constitution?* eds. Robert A. Goldwin and William A. Schambra (Washington, American Enterprise Institute, 1987), p. 123.

55 His enemies always accused him of having avoided the Revolutionary War when he was twenty years old, citing poor health, when he subsequently lived into old age. See Drew R. McCoy, *The Last of the Fathers: James Madison and the Republican Legacy* (New York: Cambridge University Press, 1989), p. xi.

56 John Quincy Adams was first to confer upon him this epithet. For a detailed analysis of Madison as politician and theoretician, as well as of his legacy, see Drew R. McCoy, *The Last of the Fathers,* and Lance Banning, *The Sacred Fire of Liberty: James Madison and the Founding of the Federal Republic* (Ithaca: Cornell University Press, 1995). Madison was a constant point of reference as well for Robert Dahl in the fifty years from his *A Preface to Democratic Theory* (Chicago: University of Chicago Press, 1956) until "James Madison: Republican or Democrat?" *Perspectives on Politics* 3, no. 3 (2005), pp. 439-448. See also the review by Alan Gibson, "The Madisonian Madison and the Question of Consistency: The Significance and Challenge of Recent Research," *Review of Politics* 64, no. 2 (2002), pp. 311-338.

57 Forrest McDonald, *Novus Ordo Seclorum*, pp. 208-209.

> I hold it for a fundamental point, that an individual independence of the States is utterly irreconcilable with the idea of an aggregate sovereignty. I think, at the same time, that a consolidation of the States into one simple republic is not less unattainable than it would be inexpedient. Let it be tried, then, whether any middle ground can be taken, which will at once support a due supremacy of the national authority, and leave in force the local authorities so far as they can be subordinately useful.[58]

And yet, the compromises of the "Philadelphia System" did not satisfy all the protagonists in the newly formed Republic. A battle that endured for about a year and a half was unleashed during the ratification of the Constitution, which the Federalists, the proponents of the new project, won. Their opponents, the Antifederalists,[59] frightened by the process of centralization taking place in the political life of the country, gave battle from their strongholds of North Carolina and Georgia and lost by a narrow margin in key states such as Virginia (89 to 79) and New York (30 to 27). The Federalists in turn, partly to ensure the success of the Constitution, promised to consider seriously the objections of their opponents, so that the first task of the first American Congress was the approval of a bill of rights. The Bill of Rights emerged as the final point of compromise in the fierce battle for ratification and became over time the heart of the defense of Americans' individual

58 James Madison to Edmund Randolph, April 8, 1787, *The Papers of James Madison*, eds. William Hutchinson, et al. (Chicago: University of Chicago Press, 1962-1991), Vol. 9, p. 369.

59 The rediscovery of Antifederalist thought is a relatively recent phenomenon. Cecelia M. Kenyon with her work "Men of Little Faith: The Anti-Federalists on the Nature of Representative Government," *William and Mary Quarterly*, 3rd series, 12, no. 1 (1955), pp. 3-46, changed the course of studies on the Constitution, restoring the Antifederalists to their rightful place of a lead role in the American political tradition. The most succinct and still useful monograph on the subject is that of Jackson Turner Main, *The Antifederalists: Critics of the Constitution, 1781-1788* (New York: Norton, 1961). See also, *The Antifederalist Papers and the Constitutional Debates*, ed. Ralph Ketcham (New York: Mentor, 1986); Saul Cornell, T*he Other Founders: Anti-federalism and the Dissenting Tradition in America, 1788-1828* (Chapel Hill: University of North Carolina Press, 1999); and David J. Siemers, *The Antifederalists: Men of Great Faith and Forbearance* (Lanham, MD: Rowman & Littlefield, 2003).

rights.[60] The rights to free expression of thought, of citizens to bear arms, the guarantees of individual freedom from arbitrary arrests and searches, the right to a jury trial, the right to due process, the right to defense, and many others, are specified in the first through the Eighth amendments, while the ninth asserts that the rights listed are in addition to those that citizens already enjoy. The Tenth amendment summarily closed the system by specifying that the powers not expressly delegated to the federal government belong to the states or the people.

One side of the Constitutional debate—that of the Federalists—has enjoyed an unprecedented historiographical advantage. Until nearly a half century ago the collection that Alexander Hamilton, John Jay, and James Madison wrote under the *nom de plume* "Publius" in defense of the Philadelphia Constitutional project had an absolute authority and stood out alone. It was viewed as the authentic interpretation of the Constitution, almost the only reference text for the study of "modern federalism."

Yet a simple reflection on the origins of the volume should have driven historians to dig deeper. The defenders' articles first appeared in New York newspapers and were later collected under the title *The Federalist or, The New Constitution* (1788).[61] The primary objective was to convince New York voters to elect delegates to the state ratification convention. New York had been a bastion of resistance to the constitutional project, and two of its three

60 See *The Bill of Rights: Government Proscribed*, eds. Ronald Hoffman and Peter J. Albert (Charlottesville: University Press of Virginia, 1997) and *The Bill of Rights: Original Meaning and Current Understanding* (1990), ed. Eugene W. Hickok Jr. (Charlottesville: University Press of Virginia, 1991).

61 A good American edition, among the many that have been reprinted over time, is *The Federalist Papers*, ed. Clinton Rossiter (New York: New American Library, 1961); the first Italian translation is *The Federalist*, Gaspare Ambrosini, Guglielmo Negri and Mario D'Addio eds. (Pisa: Nistri-Lischi, 1955). The enormous popularity of the *Federalist* has obscured a long series of writings, including those by other federalists, which at the time had equal or perhaps greater influence (despite not being collected together) in the battle over ratification. Their authors, George Washington, Noah Webster, Benjamin Rush, and Fisher Ames, among others, were as well known or more so than Madison, Hamilton and Jay. See *Friends of the Constitution: Writings of the "Other" Federalists, 1787–1788*, eds. C. A. Sheenan and G. L. McDowell (Indianapolis: Liberty Fund, 1998). Federalist political thought has been the subject of extensive historical studies.

delegates had refused to sign the draft. Neither Robert Yates nor John Lansing Jr. participated much in the Convention and refused to endorse the project, so that Hamilton, the third representative of New York, actually signed it on a personal basis.

The goal of the essays, the ratification by the State of New York, was assured on July 26, 1788, more by the practical ability of Hamilton the politician than by his and Madison's theoretical efforts. Hamilton succeeded in obtaining repeated postponements of the state convention in the well-founded hope that the news of ratification by the other states might reverse the result. Elsewhere, however, the circulation of the essays by Publius "was too limited to influence the debate."[62]

The *Federalist* was structured according to a specific editorial plan, one that divided the work among the authors (Madison and Hamilton did the lion's share, while Jay wrote no more than five essays in a total of eighty-five). In the first fourteen articles, the theory of the federal Union was set forth, how it should be and the advantages to which it would lead. In particular, the authors held the view that a strong federal government would be the best guarantee of freedom in America.

In the famous *Federalist* 10, Madison argued that the scheme of representative democracy in an extended republic such as the one designed by the Constitutional Convention would tend to blunt and hold special interests in check. Hamilton concentrated on the commercial advantages of the Union (in 11-13), while Jay explained the external dangers to which the United States were exposed (in 2-5). The essays from 15 to 36, largely the work of Hamilton, attacked the *Articles of Confederation* and showed their inadequacy, drawing also on ancient history to show the failings of past confederations. In particular, Hamilton insisted that the federal power to tax was an essential requirement for an effective government (23-36). The essays from 37 to 51, all attributed to

62 Larry D. Kramer, "Madison's Audience," *Harvard Law Review* 112, no. 3 (1999), p. 665. For an "essay [that] outlines the traditional case for the immediate historical importance of Madison's theory and the argument of the challengers to this standard interpretations," see Alan Gibson, "Inventing the Extended Republic: The Debate over the Role of Madison's Theory in the Creation of the Constitution," in *James Madison: Philosopher, Founder, and Statesman*, eds. John R. Vile, William D. Pederson, and Frank J. Williams (Athens: Ohio University Press, 2008), pp. 63-87, p. 66.

Madison, illustrated the general principles of the new system of government designed in Philadelphia. *Federalist* 51 was of primary importance. After extensively laying out the theory of sovereignty, which Madison thought should be divided between the states and the federation (41-50), it illustrated the principles of the separation of powers within the federal government. The technical explanation of the new government structure at the federal level was the object of much effort, largely by Hamilton (the essays from 52 to 58, plus 62 and 63 were by Madison, 64 by Jay, and the rest, to 85, by Hamilton), directed toward defining all the Constitutional mechanisms that were obscure, even to educated citizens, and which were the object of close criticism by opponents. Essays 84 and 85 were a final impassioned peroration by Hamilton urging his fellow citizens to elect delegates favorable to the approval of the new Constitution.

To the careful observer the *Federalist* is not at all a theoretical defense of "modern federalism," but rather a (highly authoritative) part of a much wider debate on the worthiness of the Constitutional project. The collection of essays brilliantly constructs the arguments against the previous confederal system of government while also eviscerating the principles of the centralization of power in the American political community. Yet it cannot be, nor was it so perceived by its contemporaries, as the final word on American political and legal thought over time. Moreover, and this cannot be stressed enough, the essays are situational, written in the immediacy of what can be considered the first political campaign of the modern age. According to William Riker, the *Federalist* provided key propaganda in favor of the Constitution.[63] Furthermore, Madison and Hamilton, who in the Convention wanted to annihilate the States, adopted in the essays the "language of co-ordinate, co-equal and co-sovereign, and this can certainly seem 'suspect'."[64]

63 William Riker, *Federalism: Origin, Operation, and Significance* (Boston: Little Brown, 1964), p. 19.

64 S. Rufus Davis, *The Federal Principle: A Journey through Time in Quest of a Meaning* (Berkeley: University of California Press, 1978), p. 100.

Well beyond just a suspicion, rather a veritable fact, is that the two principal authors held views in the essays that were contrary to one other, as well as to their preceding or successive political views.[65]

The history of political thought is a complex subject, but it would become an inextricable tangle if historians were even brushed by the suspicion that thinkers had "retro thoughts." If, for example, we were to discover that John Locke did not hold that property is a natural right, but that he had so stated, although anonymously, only to prevail in a controversy; or if it were to come to light that Rousseau held that society was real progress and had maintained the opposite only to win a political battle (or the competition at the Academy of Dijon); if so, the textbooks in circulation would need to be destroyed. The *Federalist* is a repository of only slightly less striking paradoxes. In essays 26 and 28, for example, Hamilton extolled the role of state governments as guardians of liberty against the national government. This was a position contrary to his entire preceding and successive political visions—in short, a simple nod to the opposition. Madison, explaining the clause "necessary and proper," formulated a veritable doctrine of implied powers. When, shortly afterward, Hamilton used just such a Constitutional argument to propose the creation of a central bank to George Washington, Madison strenuously opposed him and together with Jefferson developed the strict constructionist doctrine of the Constitution.

And yet the myth of the *Federalist* grew slowly through the nineteenth century to become an obsession in the twentieth century in both America and Europe, particularly in the aftermath of World War II. A German scholar began a monograph on the *Federalist*, as follows: "It is a treatise on free government in peace and security. It is the magnificent American contribution to the literature on constitutional democracy and federalism, a classic of Western

65 For the constitutional scholar Giovanni Bognetti neither the problem of the different voices of Publius (its split personality) nor the fact that "one can hypothesize" that Hamilton and Madison "did not fully express their most intimate thoughts" are particularly relevant when speaking of the work, which should rather be evaluated for what it "objectively" states. Giovanni Bognetti, "Il Federalist e lo Stato federale liberale," *Il Federalista: 200 anni dopo*, ed. Guglielmo Negri (Bologna: il Mulino, 1988), p. 174.

political thought."[66] And the praises grew more lavish. For example, Vincent Ostrom thought it "the single most important American contribution to the world of discourse on political theory."[67] Clinton Rossiter spoke of it as "the most important work of political science ever written in the United States."[68]

Yet the belief that the secret of the American federal system of government is found in those essays is a mirage, extremely unproductive from a scientific perspective. In a 1990 work on the *Federalist*, Edward Millican indicated the profound ambiguity of the text: "It is venerated as a guide to the mysteries of American government and as a fount of political wisdom in general, but the content of that wisdom is a subject of considerable debate."[69] He came to the conclusion that it

> has [been] shown that the *Federalist* exhibits a clearly nationalist outlook and that the other prominent themes of the essays—federalism, separation of powers, checks and balances, and the interest-group theory of No. 10—are less central to Publius's purpose. From the text of the work we can assert without difficulty what we know from other sources, that is, that Hamilton and Jay desired above all else to situate well the resources of the American nation, and that they actually did not like the federal aspects of the new Constitution.[70]

66 Gottfried Dietze, *The Federalist: A Classic of Federalism and Free Government* (Baltimore: Johns Hopkins Press, 1960), p. 3.

67 Vincent Ostrom, *The Political Theory of a Compound Republic: Designing the American Experiment* (Lincoln: University of Nebraska Press, 1987), p. 3.

68 Clinton Rossiter, Introduction, *The Federalist Papers*, p. vii.

69 Edward Millican, *One United People: The Federalist Papers and the National Idea* (Lexington: University Press of Kentucky, 1990), p. 1.

70 *Ibid.* p. 209.

As Preston King pointed out, the *"Federalist* ... appears to be a footnote to the theory of sovereignty of Hobbes."[71] He also firmly states what many have always suspected: "Basically, the argument of The Federalist is a centralist one," as the work is marked by the doctrine of sovereignty. Regarding the objects allotted to the center, these are only less extensive than those attributed by Bodin and Hobbes.[72] In view of these considerations, one notes a tragic historical irony in the fact that "Brissot and many other Jacobins, among them [Charles M.] Trudaine de la Sablière, the French translator of the *Federalist*, paid with their lives the proposal to the members of the Convention to use this book as a constitutional textbook."[73]

Naturally, in some ways the admiration by historians is entirely understandable, since "what the Federalists had to do, and what they did, in the debate over ratification was to develop a conceptual framework that made it possible to accommodate the creation of a powerful national government to the strong anti-statist current in the American political tradition."[74] The fact that the *Federalist* was greatly appreciated in Europe and in twentieth-century America, becoming the ultimate and only authority on modern federalism, is in point of fact a sign of the decline of federalism, and certainly not of its (re)discovery. European and American scholars oriented toward a favorable evaluation of a central power can anchor their deeply rooted political preferences in a propaganda text that became a conventional reading.

---

71 Preston King, *Federalism and Federation* (Baltimore: Johns Hopkins University Press, 1982), p. 24.

72 *Ibid*, p. 26.

73 Corrado Malandrino, *Federalismo: Storia, idee, modelli* (Rome: Carocci, 1998), p. 50. "Instead of the Federalist ... the anonymous text was preferred (perhaps by the radical William Livingston) *Examen du gouvernement d'Angleterre, comparé aux Constitutions des États-Unis*, [Paris: Froullé, 1789] an indictment against liberal constitutionalism, guilty of having ignored that on reason alone, and not on history, can a legislative system be founded on the liberty of humanity," Dino Cofrancesco, *La democrazia liberale (e le altre)* (Soveria Mannelli: Rubbettino) 2003, p. xxi.

74 Max M. Edling, *A Revolution in Favor of Government: Origins of the U.S. Constitution and the Making of the American State* (New York: Oxford University Press, 2003), p. 219.

2.3). The Political Ideas of the Antifederalists

In sum, the Federalists and their most famous writings cannot be held to be either the sole party in the origins of the constitutional controversy (since there was a debate)[75] or to be those who showed the attractiveness of the federal system of government. The true defenders of the federal system were those who opposed the draft constitution, and they are fully entitled to be on an equal footing in the history of American political thought. Research in recent decades has demonstrated that the Antifederalists "were an articulate and formidable group who not only offered a searching, intelligent, and coherent criticism of the proposed new government but also spoke the views of a substantial portion of the population, perhaps even a majority of Americans."[76] Presented until recently as "narrow-minded local politicians, unwilling to face the utter inadequacy of the Articles of Confederation or incapable of seeing beyond the boundaries of their own states,"[77] the Antifederalists have begun to gain a prominent place in the history of the founding of America.[78] In essence, Donald Lutz was right when he stated that they were simply one of the "two political cultures fighting for supremacy" in the young Republic. [79]

---

75 The Antifederalists "compel us to consider the Constitution and its principal justifications (including *The Federalist Papers*) as emerging from a hard-fought debate," Joel A. Johnson, "Disposed to Seek Their True Interests: Representation and Responsibility in Anti-Federalist Thought," *Review of Politics* 64, no. 4 (2004), pp. 650.

76 Richard E. Ellis, "The Persistence of Antifederalism after 1789," in *Beyond Confederation: Origins of the Constitution and American National Identity*, eds. Richard Beeman, Stephen Botein and Edward C. Carter (Chapel Hill: North Carolina University Press, 1987), p. 295.

77 Herbert J. Storing, *What the Anti-Federalists Were For, The Complete Anti-Federalist*, vol. 1, p. 3.

78 During recent discussions on the constitutional debate, the citations of Antifederalist positions—although only about half those of their opponents—are increasing considerably, including in American textbooks. See Anthony J. Eksterowicz and Paul C. Cline, "Ratification of the Constitution: The Great Debate as Portrayed in American Government Textbooks," *PS: Political Science and Politics* 24, no. 2 (1991), pp. 211-215.

79 Donald S. Lutz, *Popular Consent and Popular Control* (Baton Rouge: Louisiana State University Press, 1980), p. 202.

A succession of works, at their apex in the 1950s but perhaps traceable further back, held that the generation that carried out the Revolution and participated in the construction of American institutions shared a general consensus about basic political issues.[80] Since the times of Richard Hofstadter, Louis Hartz and Daniel J. Boorstin,[81] the fairy-tale of a US history almost deprived of any conflict has become quite common. What started as a Cold War ideological instrument, and a way to mark the discontinuity with Marxism of many historians, became an article of faith. "The cold war brought a certain closing of the ranks, a disposition to stress common objectives, a revulsion from Marxism and its tendency to think of social conflict as carried *à outrance*. ... While Daniel Bell was writing about the end of ideology in the West, historians were returning to the idea that in the United States it had hardly ever begun."[82] However, "a theory of consensus must face the fact of the

---

80 John Higham rechristened it as "consensus history." See "The Cult of the 'American Consensus': Homogenizing Our History," *Commentary*, XXVII, February 1959, pp. 93-100. The manifesto is perhaps found in Richard Hofstadter's introduction to his classic *The American Political Tradition and the Men Who Made It* (New York: Knopf, 1948). See also Daniel J. Boorstin, *The Genius of American Politics* (Chicago: University of Chicago Press, 1953). By all the evidence, this was a broadly "conservative" reaction to the Marxist school of historiography (mostly carried out by former Marxists, of course) and its vision of a process of modernization based on class conflict. The question of conflict and/or consensus became fundamental since "the consensus-conflict dichotomy clearly expressed a simple and fundamental truth, and it proved so helpful in organizing the massive body of American historical writing since World War II that it developed great staying power." Michael Kraus and Davis D. Joyce, *The Writing of American History* (1953) (Norman: University of Oklahoma Press, 1990), p. 313.

81 A rather bizarre trio, at least from the ideological point of view. While, "all moved during their careers from left to right on an intellectual-political track," Hofstadter ended his journey as a pragmatic liberal, Boorstin became a "cultural protectionist" suspicious of foreign influences, and Hartz spent his life at the margin of the Marxist camp, disconsolately perceiving no conflict in American history. Bernard Sternsher, *Consensus, Conflict, and American Historians*, (Bloomington: Indiana University Press, 1975), p. 14. Cfr. Richard Hofstadter, *The American Political Tradition and the Men Who Made It* (New York: Norto, 1948); Daniel J. Boorstin, *The Genius of American Politics* (Chicago: University of Chicago Press, 1953); Louis Hartz, *The Liberal Tradition in America. An Interpretation of American Political Thought since the Revolution* (New York: Harcourt Brace, 1955).

82 Richard Hofstadter, *The Progressive Historians. Turner, Beard, Parrington* (New York: Knopf, 1968), p. 439.

ubiquity of conflict in American history. There are severe limits to a model that offers a consensual interpretation of the history of a nation, when the central event of that history is a civil war."[83]

From the consensus perspective, the Antifederalists' objections to the Constitution were considered a nuance incapable of making inroads into the general political agreement that characterized the dawn of the Republic. This vision is hard to dispel. Richard Sinopoli notes that "Disagreements between Federalists and Anti-Federalists hinged largely on empirical expectations regarding the ability of the system of government proposed in the U.S. Constitution to foster allegiance rather than on deep differences in political first principles."[84] Quite the contrary. The two blocs offered political visions for America that were radically distinct, and each centered on the most critical controversy in modern history: the centralization of power.

Herbert Storing, for his part, took the view that "the nation was born in consensus," but he adds that it "lives in controversy, and the main lines of that controversy are well-worn paths leading back to the founding debate."[85] However much the two sides of the debate were in agreement about "the fundamental political principles derived from the liberal contractarian tradition," Storing continued, there was a clear boundary between the views of the two groups: "Federalists and Anti-federalists differed—often profoundly—over the proper role of citizens in a just state. Much of this difference hinged on empirical arguments, for example, supposed relations between the size of government and one's loyalty to it. But some of its elements were more theoretical, and the Anti-federalists did indeed call upon republican values."[86]

---

83 James P. Young, *Reconsidering American Liberalism: The Troubled Odyssey of the Liberal Idea* (Boulder, CO: Westview Press, 1996) p. 4.

84 Richard C. Sinopoli, "Liberalism and Political Allegiance in Anti-Federalist Political Thought," *Publius*, vol. 22, No. 2, (Spring 1992), pp. 123-124.

85 Herbert J. Storing, *What the Anti-Federalists Were For*, p. 6.

86 Richard C. Sinopoli, *The Foundations of American Citizenship: Liberalism, the Constitution, and Civic Virtue* (New York: Oxford University Press, 1992), p. 131.

The first fracture between the supporters of a "modern" solution to the problem of political order—that is, creating a single command center—and those who opposed them follows the general lines of demarcation of the Constitutional debate. The Antifederalists were the first conscious champions of American resistance to the modern state and to importing the European model. According to Christopher Duncan, the Federalist project of building America as a national and commercial republic meant a reduction of "state sovereignty," which corresponded to a general removal of individual responsibility in politics. Deprived of an authentically participative element, local politics, people were driven to privacy.[87] Such a flight from politics is essential for the construction of the *déraciné* individual, without community bonds, subject only to the law, which is the human construction most conducive to the modern state, and which went hand in hand in America with the attempt to build a single center of power. In "Men of a Different Faith," Duncan finds a key difference between Federalist and Anti-Federalist political theory. In the Federalist hierarchy, the community is replaced by the nation through an act of Reason and Will. The problem, however, with such a shift is that it is ultimately a-theoretical or impossible within the context of republicanism, because of the latter's emphasis both on extensive citizen participation in the construction and care of the public sphere and on the shared values and mores that enable such an endeavor in the first place. In other words, the Federalist nation-state cannot hope to produce republican sentiments or manners because it is historically ancillary to, and conceptually separate from, the concept of community that functions as the social and political prerequisite of republican government.

He adds: "This is the theoretical thread that ties Anti-Federalist thought together. It is the notion that the Constitution as a centralizing, ultimately disempowering, document will leave them bereft of their power to 'save' themselves, that it will ultimately, in

87 Cf. Christopher M. Duncan, *The Antifederalists and Early American Political Thought* (DeKalb: Northern Illinois University Press, 1995), pp. 177-178.

the words of Hannah Arendt, 'banish the citizens from the public realm into the privacy of their households, and demand of them that they mind their own private business'"[88]

Morton Borden grasped an essential aspect of the polemic against the Constitution when he stated that the "Antifederalists believed adoption of this Constitution, based on European experience and political philosophy and only slightly modified to the American environment, would condemn America to repeat the sad history and unhappy fate of European nations."[89]

It should be clear that the Antifederalists were not opposed to "federalism." As early as 1794 the French ambassador to America wrote that there was "a bizarre contrast between the names and the actual opinions of the parties, a contradiction little understood in Europe so far." While the Federalists "tried by every means to destroy federalism," the Antifederalists "have always wanted to preserve it."[90] The Federalists were in fact in favor of a strong national government (*energetic government* was the mantra of the day), while the Antifederalists held that the only way to defend American liberty was for state governments to act vigorously together to keep rigid limits on the powers of the federal government.

According to Herbert Storing, the Antifederalists "usually denied, in fact, that the name was either apt or just, and seldom used it themselves. They were, they often claimed, the true federalists. ... Unquestionably the Federalists saw the advantage of a label that would suggest that those who opposed the Constitution also opposed such a manifestly good thing as federalism."[91] Luther Martin, one of the Philadelphia delegates, urged the Maryland Assembly not to approve the federal Constitution. He asserted in his *Genuine Information* that the label swap had happened only after

88 Christopher M. Duncan, "Men of a Different Faith: The Anti-Federalist Ideal in Early American Political Thought," *Polity* 26, no. 3 (Spring 1994), p. 397 and p. 414; Hannah Arendt, *On Revolution* (New York: Viking Press, 1965), p. 127.

89 Morton Borden, Introduction, *The Antifederalist Papers* (East Lansing: Michigan State University Press, 1965), p. xii.

90 Diplomatic Correspondence of Jean Antoine Joseph Fauchet, cited in Jackson Turner Main, *The Antifederalists*, p. xii.

91 Herbert J. Storing, *What the Anti-Federalists Were For*, p. 9.

the convention. "[A]lthough, *now*, they who *advocate* the system pretend to call themselves *federalists,* in convention the distinction was quite the reverse; those who *opposed* the system were *there* considered and styled the *federal party,* those who advocated it, the *antifederal.*"[92]

In the New York State ratification convention, Melancton Smith demanded an immediate change of names. Given that it was widely accepted that the Federalists' goal was "not a confederacy, but a reduction of all the states into a consolidated government," it was necessary for the Federalists "to exchange names with those who disliked the Constitution," he said, since by then it was clear that the latter "were Federalists, and those who advocated it were Anti-Federalists."[93] And yet, as Storing noted, the very ambiguity of the term "federal" made such a name reversal possible. Strengthening the institutions of the federation was essentially a type of federal operation, while on the contrary, a preference for the State governments indicated an antifederalist sentiment.

The term "federal" had by then acquired such an ambiguous meaning that not only could the Federalists adopt the name, but they succeeded in keeping it. One of the most debated issues during the era of the *Articles of Confederation* was if and how much the general government—or the federation as such—should work through the States or whether it had the ability to act on its own capacity. In this context, politicians positioned themselves as "federal" or "antifederal" depending on their view of the locus of power: the States or the federation. This is what James Wilson meant when he spoke of the "fœderal disposition and character" of Pennsylvania. Patrick Henry understood it similarly when he stated that, in rejecting the Constitution, New Hampshire and Rhode Island "have refused to become federal."[94]

---

92 Luther Martin, "Genuine Information IV," *Baltimore Maryland Gazette*, 8 January 1788, DHRC, vol. 11, p. 160.

93 Melancton Smith, New York Convention Debates, 20 June 1788, DHRC, vol. 22, p. 1714.

94 Herbert J. Storing, *What the Anti-Federalists Were For*, p. 9.

The first point of controversy of the Constitutional project appeared to be the phrase *We, the people,* which opened the preamble. It seemed that the Convention could give birth to a people of the United States, that the underlying pact, though subject to the approval of the individual States, called into play a mythical organism which had never been heard of previously, precisely the "people of the United States." A minority of the ratification convention in Philadelphia saw the prologue as an insurmountable barrier: "The preamble begins with the words, 'We the people of the United States,' which is the style of a compact between individuals entering into a state of society, and not that of a confederation of states."[95] Patrick Henry attacked the Federalists on this point during the ratification convention in Virginia: "Who authorized them to speak the language of *We, the People*, instead of *We, the States*? States are the characteristics, and the soul of a confederation. If the States be not the agents of this compact, it must be one great consolidated National Government, of the people of all the States."[96] In the New York newspapers, Cincinnatus (probably Richard Henry Lee) complained: "When the whole people of America shall be thus recognized by their own solemn act, as the people of the United States, I beseech you Sir, to tell us over whom the sovereignty, you say you leave to the several states, is to operate."[97]

Actually, the Antifederalists were aiming at the wrong target. The change in the preamble from *We, the people of the States of*, followed by the complete list of the States was decided by the "Committee on Style," paradoxically due to their regard for the States. It was feared that the list of all the States could be considered an undue pressure against their freedom of ratification. It was thus an act of diplomacy but subject to later misunderstanding.[98] In any

95 "The Dissent of the Minority of the Pennsylvania Convention," *Pennsylvania Packet*, 18 December 1787, DHRC, vol. 15, p. 25.

96 Patrick Henry, Debates, 4 June 1788, DHRC, vol. 9, p. 930.

97 Cincinnatus V, "To James Wilson," *Esquire New York Journal*, 29 November 1787, DHRC, vol. 19, p. 324. The target of the controversy was James Wilson and his famous speech in Philadelphia on October 6, 1787.

98 It seems definite that the change was the work of the Committee on Style and was not discussed further by the assembly. The committee, in fact, had no power to change the substance of the document, and, as Abel Upshur recalled: "The presumption is,

case, the next "states' rights school" did not object to the preamble in such a manner. Rather, in what is probably the single most important volume of the entire states' rights tradition, *New Views on the Constitution of the United States*, published in 1823, John Taylor overturned the Antifederalist arguments. In his view, "We, the people of the United States" guaranteed that the States, and not the American people, were the real parties to the Constitutional pact. Taylor, who while writing finally had available a series of previously unknown works on the Philadelphia Convention (and in particular the previously mentioned diary of Robert Yates), discovered that the substitution of *United States* for *national* was approved on June 25.

> The government was no longer national, but by the United States. Thus we see an opinion expressed by the Convention that the phrase 'United States' did not mean 'a consolidated American people or nation.' Thus, all inferences in favor of a national government from the style in 'We, the people of the United States' are overthrown, as that style was adopted, not to establish the idea of an American people, but to defeat it.[99]

Summarizing Antifederalist political thought turns out to be rather complex. Antifederalists did not defend a specific government plan, but rather attacked the work of the Convention, and thus proceeded somewhat in disarray. The disadvantage of having never produced a complete text comparable to their opponents' *Federalist*

therefore, that the two were considered substantially the same, particularly as the committee had no authority to make any change, except in the style." Abel P. Upshur, *A Brief Enquiry Into the True Nature and Character of our Federal Government: Being a Review of Judge Story's Commentaries on the Constitution of the United States* (1840) (Philadelphia: John Campbell, 1863) p. 51. The essay by Upshur, a judge who died tragically in 1844, is considered a brilliant counterpoint to Story's commentaries, whose "great effort throughout his entire work, is to establish the doctrine that the Constitution of the United States is a government of 'the people of the United States' as contradistinguished from the people of the several States; or, in other words, that it is a consolidated, and not a federative system," *Ibid.*, p. 13.

99 John Taylor, *New Views on the Constitution of the United States* (Washington City: Way and Gideon, 1823), p. 29.

explains why their political arguments and reflections fell into oblivion for a long time. Fortunately, reconstruction of some essential lines of their doctrinal development is made easier by many works that have appeared on the subject in recent years and by the efforts to document their positions by republishing newspaper articles and forgotten speeches.

The Antifederalist leaders—George Mason, Patrick Henry, George Clinton, Elbridge Gerry, Richard Henry Lee and Melancton Smith, just to mention a few of the most well-known—had a few common traits: Because they held that democracy was only possible in "small republics," the traditional political doctrine from the Greeks to Montesquieu,[100] they were convinced that the government design proposed in Philadelphia would consolidate power in the federal government, with an imbalance in favor of the executive branch. Every battle cry of the emerging Antifederalist movement had an implicit message: Over time, a strong national government would weaken and eventually destroy local governments. A corollary was that local governments would preserve democratic institutions, while a national government would become a large aristocracy.[101]

The Antifederalist position was in fact conservative in the strict sense: their fight was to defend the existing *Articles of Confederation*, which they considered an excellent text that needed amendments, but not the substantial distortion that was proposed. According to Patrick Henry,

100 Naturally one could add the highly authoritative name of Rousseau, yet evoking his name could create confusion. While the Antifederalists were under the spell of Montesquieu's *Spirit of the Laws*, the same cannot be said of Rousseau's *Social Contract*. See Abraham Kupersmith, "Montesquieu and the Ideological Strain in Antifederalist Thought," in *The Federalists, the Antifederalists, and the American Political Tradition*, eds. Wilson Carey McWilliams and Michael T. Gibbons (New York: Greenwood Press, 1992), pp. 47-75. There is only one very vague reference to Rousseau in all of the Antifederalist literature; see A Newport Man, *Newport Mercury*, 17 March 1788, DHRC, vol. 24, p. 116.

101 Robert A. Rutland, *The Ordeal of the Constitution: The Antifederalists and the Ratification Struggle of 1787–1788* (1966) (Boston: Northeastern University Press, 1983), p. 5.

> The Confederation; this same despised Government, merits, in my opinion, the highest encomium: It carried us through a long and dangerous war: It rendered us victorious in that bloody conflict with a powerful nation: It has secured us a territory greater than any European Monarch possesses: And shall a Government which has been thus strong and Vigorous, be accused of imbecility and abandoned for want of energy?[102]

The Antifederalists showed great admiration for the first American constitution, but "they unitedly believed that the Articles needed to be amended to give Congress more power."[103]

However, it was necessary to understand why changes were needed, and, above all, which ones would be acceptable. The pseudonymous Impartial Examiner wondered if the change was dictated by intrinsic flaws in the Confederation: "Does it flow from certain vicious properties, which reside in the old system and form the essential parts of it?"[104] The response was negative: The only real shortcoming in the Articles appeared to be that the federal power lacked the ability to provide for the common needs: "[In] the present system of union the Congress are not invested with sufficient powers for *regulating commerce*, and procuring the *requisite contributions* for all expenses, that may be incurred for the *common defence* or *general welfare*."[105] As the Federal Farmer lamented, "The defects of the confederation are extravagantly

102 Patrick Henry, Debates, 5 June 1788, DHRC, vol. 9, pp. 952-953.

103 Ralph Ketcham, "Antifederalist Essays and Speeches, 1787–1788," in *Roots of the Republic: American Founding Documents Interpreted,* ed. Stephen Schechter (Lanham, MD: Madison House, 1990), p. 384.

104 The Impartial Examiner V, *Virginia Independent Chronicle*, 18 June 1788 (Extraordinary), DHRC, vol. 10, pp. 1645-1648.

105 *Ibid.*

magnified, and every species of pain we feel imputed to them ... and hence it is inferred, there must be a total change of the principles, as well as forms of government."[106]

The Antifederalists agreed that the Confederation was flawed in that the Confederation Congress was "not able to raise a revenue by taxation, and they have not a complete regulation of the intercourse between us and foreigners"; but they were generally in favor of the *Articles* because they made America "in the strictest sense of the terms, a federal republic." That meant that "[e]ach part has within its own limits the sovereignty over its citizens, while some of the general concerns are committed to Congress."[107]

Thomas Jefferson expressed the same sentiment regarding the American Constitution: by 1786 he already held that "the Confederation is a wonderfully perfect instrument, considering the circumstances under which it was formed."[108] In any case, the opponents of the Constitutional project maintained that the claims of the troubles that would arise if the Constitution were not adopted were elaborately inflated. The Antifederalists did not accept the idea of a "state of emergency." Such a step, extremely dangerous in and of itself, should be carefully thought out, as should every political innovation, they thought. It was necessary to avoid the Federalist traps, and the Federal Farmer urged his fellow citizens not to dramatize the situation:

> We are in state of perfect peace, and in no danger of invasions; the state governments are in the full exercise of their powers; and our governments answer all present exigencies ... and whether we adopt a change three or nine months hence, can

106 Federal Farmer, *An Additional Number of Letters to the Republican*, New York, 2 May 1788, DHRC, vol. XVII, p. 355.The author here may have been Richard Henry Lee.

107 Agrippa VIII, *Massachusetts Gazette*, 25 December 1787, DHRC, vol. 5, p. 516.

108 Thomas Jefferson, "Answers to Démeunier's First Queries," January 24, 1786, *The Papers of Thomas Jefferson*, eds. Julian P. Boyd et al., (Princeton: Princeton University Press), vol. 10, p. 14.

> make but little odds with the private circumstances of individuals; their happiness and prosperity, after all, depend principally upon their own exertions.[109]

Opponents of the Constitution often expressed the classical liberal idea of a society that directs itself without the need for a stable political guide. Their comments highlight the distance not only between them and their rivals, but their opposition to the whole doctrine of the state. A few examples will suffice.

Fear of a vast parasitic apparatus that would weigh heavily on the shoulders of the entire country was widespread. A Friend to the Rights of the People complained of the pageantry and pomp that would necessarily surround Congress, as Congress would soon share the habits of European courts.[110] Philadelphiensis, reflecting a common attitude of the Antifederalists, said that, despite much talk about government efficiency and energy (consider again how often the expression "energetic government" appears in the Federalist),

> The only thing in which the government should be efficient, is to protect the liberties, lives, and property of the people governed from foreign and domestic violence. This, and this only is what every government should do effectually. For any government to do more than this is impossible and every one that falls short of this is defective.[111]

Agrippa held in 1787 that "when business is unshackled, it will find out that channel which is most friendly to its course," and the way to resolve economic problems was to safeguard the sanctity of private contracts in the courts, "and thus to encourage a mutual confidence among the citizens, which increases the resources of them all, and renders easy the payment of debts. By this means

---

109 Federal Farmer, *Letters to the Republican*, 8 November 1787, DHRC, vol. 19, p. 208..

110 A Friend to the Rights of the People, "Anti-Fœderalist, No. I," *Exeter Freeman's Oracle*, 8 February 1788, DHRC, vol. XXVIII, pp. 109-118. The "Friend" quote here may have been Thomas Cogswell.

111 Philadelphiensis, 5 December 1787, DHRC, vol. 14, p. 351.

one does not grow rich at the expense of another, but all are benefited."[112] In other words, the economic difficulties of the time were not due to the weakness of the federal government, but to the decline in private industriousness, which certainly would not have flourished again simply by instituting a stronger government or adopting a new Constitution.[113]

Regarding the issue of debt and public deficit that gripped the American economy after the war, Patrick Henry confidently declared that the market alone, and not only the political process, could produce enough wealth to alleviate the debt. "No nation ever paid its debts by a change of Government, without the aid of industry. You will never pay your debts but by a radical change of domestic economy. ... The evils that attend us, lie in extravagance and want of industry, and only can be removed by assiduity and economy."[114]

The public debt was seen as a Trojan horse that would serve to erode the powers of the state governments. The worry was about the enormous power conferred on Congress to find money in any possible way, as well as to contract debit.[115] And Brutus prophetically declared that Congress "may create a national debt, so large, as to exceed the ability of the country ever to sink.... [I]t is unwise and improvident to vest in the general government, a power to borrow at discretion, without any limitation or restriction."[116] The supermajority required by the Articles of Confederation to contract public debts (nine states out of thirteen) seemed to him a guarantee of financial prudence, one that the new Constitution should have confirmed.[117]

---

112 Agrippa VII, *Massachusetts Gazette*, 18 December 1787, DHRC, vol. 5, p. 483.

113 See (Samuel Adams or Benjamin Austin Jr.) Candidus I, *Independent Chronicle*, 6 December 1787, DHRC, vol. 4, pp. 392-399.

114 Patrick Henry, June 9 1788, *Debates in the Virginia Convention*, DHRC, vol. 9, pp. 1055-1056.

115 Cf. A Federal Republican, "A Review of the Constitution," October 28, 1787, DHRC, vol. 14, p. 269.

116 Brutus (probably Robert Yates), January 10, 1788, *Documentary History*, vol. 15, p. 335.

117 See Brutus, pp. 335-336.

In short, the Antifederalists were ready to recognize the existence of government as a necessary evil, in the famous words of Tom Paine, one that should be as limited as possible. Instead, the new design frightened them because of the enormous bureaucratization of politics that it would inevitably entail. Their fears of a strong central power and the abuses that would unfailingly follow can be understood from numerous passages. Prudence would counsel entrusting little power to rulers, since taking it away is always more difficult than granting it. Ultimately, as Morton Borden noted, among the Antifederalists "there remained the belief that the American character had not been fully tested and might yet prove capable of exercising maximum individual freedom with a minimum of government restraints."[118]

The crucial rallying point of the opponents of the Constitutional project was the very idea of consolidation, that is, the concentration of power and the creation of a sole command center, which in their view permeated the proposed document. Americans of that time were quite clear about the difference between a consolidated and a federal government. In short, the consolidation of power, which was the constant fear of the enemies of the Constitutional plan, meant the annihilation of the distinction between federal and state power. A consolidated republic would have made the states into simple administrative provinces of the federation and amassed the American people into a single, undifferentiated political community. By contrast, in a federal republic, the source of political power would have remained firmly in the hands of the States, or the peoples of the various States, and the latter could have delegated the management of common affairs to a single agent, the federal government. The Antifederalists saw the strengthening of the Union and the centralization of power that it entailed as the chief danger of the proposed Constitution. That would have been a first and irreversible step toward a new political entity which would have laid the foundations of a modern state.

The Antifederalist minority at the ratification convention in Pennsylvania produced a document, in all probability written by Samuel Bryan, that circulated widely and clarified the reasons

118 Morton Borden, Introduction, *Antifederalist Papers*, p. xii.

for their aversion to the Constitution. There were essentially three reasons for their dissent, all reducible to the theme of the concentration of power. The first problem was the size of the Republic, perhaps the argument the Antifederalists used most.

> [I]t is the opinion of the most celebrated writers on government, and confirmed by uniform experience, that a very extensive territory cannot be governed on the principles of freedom, otherwise than by a confederation of republics, possessing all the powers of internal government; but united in the management of their general, and foreign concerns.[119]

The other two reasons were closely related to the first, referring to the consolidation of power in the federal government that the new Constitution would have required.

> The powers vested in Congress by this constitution, must necessarily annihilate and absorb the legislative, executive, and judicial powers of the several states, and produce from their ruins one consolidated government, which from the nature of things will be *an iron banded despotism*, as nothing short of the supremacy of despotic sway could connect and govern these United States under one government.[120]

This is because "The powers of Congress under the new constitution, are complete and unlimited over the purse and the sword, and are perfectly independent of, and supreme over, the state governments."[121]

The third objection is that, even if it were possible to govern such a vast territory according to the principles of liberty and happiness of the people, the proposed Constitution absolutely did not intend to attempt this path, and "would of itself, necessarily

119 "The Dissent of the Minority of the Pennsylvania Convention," *Pennsylvania Packet*, 18 December 1787, DHRC, vol. 15, p. 21.

120 *Ibid.*

121 *Ibid.*, p. 22.

produce a despotism, and that not by the usual gradations, but with the celerity that has hitherto only attended revolutions effected by the sword."[122] "In short, consolidation pervades the whole constitution."[123] In essence, in the opinion of the Pennsylvania Antifederalists, "this government will not enjoy the confidence of the people, but be executed by force, it will be a very expensive and burthensome government."[124] The federal bureaucracy and the army "will swarm over the land, devouring the hard earnings of the industrious. Like the locusts of old, impoverishing and desolating all before them."[125] Even Agrippa had no serious doubts about the ultimate goal of the Constitution:

> This new system is, therefore, a consolidation of all the states into one large mass, however diverse the parts may be of which it is to be composed. The idea of an uncompounded republick, on an average, one thousand miles in length, and eight hundred in breadth, and containing six millions of white inhabitants all reduced to the same standard of morals, or habits, and of laws, is in itself an absurdity, and contrary to the whole experience of mankind.[126]

And after a few days the same author stated that "the direct tendency of the proposed system, is to consolidate the whole empire into one mass, and, like the tyrant's bed, to reduce all to one standard."[127] Again, in Agrippa's view,

> One consolidated government is inapplicable to a great extent of country; is unfriendly to the rights both of persons and property, which rights always adhere together; and that being contrary to the interest of

122 *Ibid.*, p. 25.

123 *Ibid.*

124 *Ibid.*, p. 33.

125 *Ibid.*

126 Agrippa IV, *Massachusetts Gazette*, 4 December 1787, DHRC, vol. 4, p. 383.

127 Agrippa V, *Massachusetts Gazette*, 11 December 1787, DHRC, vol. 4, p. 407.

> the extreme of an empire, such a government can be supported only by power, and that commerce is the true bond of union for a free state.[128]

Thus the new government would inevitably become "*dirigiste*," that is, an opponent of commerce and private property, the natural complements to human freedom.

2.4) The Dimensions of the Republic: Madison and his Critics

James Madison is considered today a classic thinker on democracy, who, according to a prominent writer, "by his creative leadership at the American Constitutional Convention in 1787 and his persuasive contributions to the Federalist immediately thereafter, ... helped to inaugurate one of the most fundamental changes in democratic ideas and practices that has occurred over the entire history of this ancient form of government."[129] The reference is clearly to his contribution to *Federalist* 10 (which should be read in contrast to and together with 51), considered the true "center of gravity" of the work and praised as "the greatest paper in that greatest of all works of American political thought."[130] According to another author, "the essay enjoys a quasi-constitutional status."[131]

Russell Hardin is certainly not the only one to commit the error of projecting his own infatuation with Madison on the generation that debated the Constitution: "But of all the great liberal thinkers, Madison was the most effective. When he went head-to-head with the Antifederalist exponents of Montesquieu's views during the

128 Agrippa X, *Massachusetts Gazette*, 1 January 1788, DHRC, vol. 5, p. 576.

129 Robert A. Dahl, "James Madison: Republican or Democrat?" *Perspectives on Politics* 3, no. 3 (2005), p. 439 (see also pp. 439-448,).

130 Theodore Draper, "Hume & Madison: The Secrets of Federalist Paper N. 10," *Encounter* 58 (1982), p. 34.

131 George W. Carey, *In Defense of the Constitution*, revised and expanded edition (Indianapolis: Liberty Fund, 1995), p. 32.

ratification debates, he won the day. He won the intellectual debate overwhelmingly and he and the Federalists won the political debate by sometimes narrow margins but still with finality."[132]

Oddly enough, it was not until Charles Beard published his most famous work in 1913 that *Federalist* 10 became popular.[133] Until the early twentieth century, no one had noticed the greatness of Madison's theory. Moreover, this was not due to an eclipse of attention to the constitutional dispute, since, as Larry Kramer has demonstrated, "in all the torrent of pamphlets and essays and articles that streamed from the presses—enough to fill many volumes—there are only the Federalist Papers and ... two other essayists to suggest that Madison's theory of the extended republic was part of the debate at all."[134] While the Antifederalists simply ignored Madison's argumentation, his own friends were not well acquainted with it either: The great majority of those who discussed the Constitution were unacquainted with Madison's doctrine.

Madison himself gained a peculiar status at the time of the progressive revision of the founding. Vernon Parrington, author of *Main Currents in American Thought*, the classic work on American thought for many years, portrayed the Declaration of Independence as a "classical statement of French humanitarian democracy," whereas the Constitution was "an organic law designed to safeguard the minority under republican rule." For Parrington, it was incontestable that the two documents formed part of a "conflict between the man and the dollar" that had characterized American history ever since its origins.[135]

---

132 Russell Hardin, *Liberalism, Constitutionalism, and Democracy* (Oxford: Oxford University Press, 1999), p. 61.

133 See Douglass Adair, "The Tenth Federalist Revisited" (1951) in *Fame and the Founding Father: Essays by Douglass Adair*, ed. Trevor Colbourn (Indianapolis: Liberty Press, 1998).

134 Larry D. Kramer, "Madison's Audience," p. 667.

135 Vernon L. Parrington, *Main Currents in American Political Thought: An Interpretation of American Literature from the Beginnings to 1920: The Beginnings of Critical Realism in America, 1860–1920* (New York: Harcourt Brace, 1930) 3:410–11

Abraham Lincoln himself believed there was quite a conflict between the man and the dollar. "The Jefferson party formed upon the supposed superior devotion to the personal rights of men, holding the rights of property to be secondary only and greatly inferior.... Republicans ... are for both the man and the dollar, but in case of conflict the man before the dollar."[136]

This quite bizarre notion of a struggle a struggle between man and the dollar was taken up repeatedly by Parrington, who transformed Jefferson into one of the great champions of this titanic and far-fetched clash. In this, the Harvard scholar was unquestionably influenced by the works of J. Allen Smith, Frederick Jackson Turner, and the leading figure of the progressive school, Charles Beard. These early twentieth-century historians developed what has come to be known as the "conflict" interpretation of American history. Not only did they view the history of the republic as torn by bitter clashes, they also pointed to the feature that formed a constant element of these tensions: an unceasing struggle between persons and property, between democracy and aristocracy. Charles E. Merriam launched an attack on the Constitution, as early as 1903, arguing that it ran counter to the revolution; while the latter was authentically democratic, the Constitution was a conservative, if not outright reactionary document.[137] Charles Beard presented the most comprehensive indictment of the Constitution. Beard's fame springs precisely from having cast the conflictual element in American history in terms of "rights of persons" versus "rights of property," which he believed were incorporated in the Declaration and the Constitution, respectively.[138]

James Madison became the villain of this historiography, as there was not much of a chance to make him a founding father unaware of the importance of property rights. Jennifer Nedelsky,

---

136 Abraham Lincoln to H. L. Pierce *et al.*, April 6, 1859, *The Collected Works of Abraham Lincoln*, ed. R. P. Basler (New Brunswick, NJ: Rutgers University Press, 1953) vol. 2, pp. 374–376.

137 See Charles E. Merriam, *History of American Political Theories* (New York: Macmillan, 1903).

138 See Charles A. Beard, *An Economic Interpretation of the Constitution of the United States* (New York: Macmillan, 1913) and *Economic Origins of Jeffersonian Democracy* (New York: Macmillan, 1915).

just to cite a more recent scholar, in her *Private Property and the Limits of American Constitutionalism,* does not conceal her radically democratic vision and declares herself convinced that the preoccupation of the drafters of the American Constitution "with protecting property from democratic incursions ... led to the greatest weakness of our system: its failure to realize its democratic potential."[139] Nedelsky's criticism of Madison is based on her assumption that a greater protection awarded to property rights necessarily entails a decrease in the right of political participation. Thus, her fundamental tenet is that the Founding Fathers, when contemplating the bifurcation between property and equality, opted for defense of the former. It matters little that they never genuinely faced a political dilemma of this type. The scholar's imagination is by nature much broader than reality.

At any rate, that well known case for a non-democratic Madison has been at least overstated in the past century and a half. A more objective view can be found in the assessment of Jeff Broadwater, who believes that "as much as he loathed intemperate and self-interested majorities, Madison believed that a republican government had to rest on popular consent. While he favored the "filtration" of public participation through an elaborate system of checks and balances, both formal in the case of the separation of powers and informal in the case of the multiplicity of factions in an extended republic, Madison assumed the people would participate in their government."[140]

This being noted, what Madison argued in *Federalist* 10 has in itself and for itself a precise theoretical relevance in the debate, completely apart from its quite imaginary contemporaneous influence. Madison's arguments opposed the Antifederalists on a crucial point, their clear preference for small republics, by overturning established convictions of the Western political

---

139 Jennifer Nedelsky, *Private Property and the Limits of American Constitutionalism. The Madisonian Framework and Its Legacy* (Chicago–London, The University of Chicago Press, 1990), p. 1.

140 Jeff Broadwater, *Jefferson, Madison, and the Making of the Constitution* (Chapel Hill, NC: University of North Carolina Press, 2019), p. 149.

tradition in favor of the extended republic.[141] A large republic founded on the principle of representation would in fact have the "tendency to break and control the violence of faction."[142] For Madison, the states could possibly be democracies in the classic sense, while the federation, founded on political representation, should be a large, extended republic. But the latter form of government enjoys the decisive advantage of limiting the damage caused by factions and self-interested coalitions acting against the public interest. While it could be argued that Madison was so fixated on the defense of property that "both the extended sphere and the Constitution's restrictions on the States were intended to protect property against popular excesses,"[143] it is to the matter of representation that Little Jimmy owes his reputation as a political thinker. No political philosopher would acknowledge that he produced essential reflections property rights.

The government's actions are either the result of "reason" and "judgment," aimed at achieving the "public good," or they originate from the "conflicts of rival parties," from a "factious spirit" that tends to satisfy private interests. According to Madison, one faction is "a number of citizens, whether amounting to a majority or minority of the whole, who are united and actuated by some common impulse of passion, or of interest, adverse to the rights of other citizens, or to the permanent and aggregate interests of the community." In politics and in the government the presence of factions is inevitable, but "there are two methods of curing the mischiefs of faction: The one, by removing its causes; the other, by controlling its effects." In what are probably the most quoted words of the *Federalist*, Madison summarized the dilemma of a republican government:

141 In truth, Madison maintained that "pure, unmediated democracy" could work only on a small scale. What he did say is that the optimal dimensions of a republic are a large populace and a large territory. The distinction between "democracy" and "republic" referred to the design of political representation, which was applicable only to the latter.

142 James Madison, *Federalist* no. 10, Nov 22, 1787, in Alexander Hamilton, James Madison, and John Jay, *The Federalist: With the Letters of "Brutus,"* Terence Ball ed. (New York: Cambridge University Press, 2003), pp. 40-46.

143 Gary Rosen, *American Compact: James Madison and the Problem of Founding* (Lawrence: University Press of Kansas, 1999), p. 67.

> Liberty is to faction, what air is to fire, an aliment, without which it instantly expires. But it could not be a less folly to abolish liberty, which is essential to political life, because it nourishes faction, than it would be to wish the annihilation of air, which is essential to animal life, because it imparts to fire its destructive agency.[144]

Thus, the effects of factions can only be controlled and limited, never eliminated; otherwise, a loss of freedom would result. The key position in *Federalist* 10 consists first in comparing how a democracy and a republic operate in controlling the actions of special interests, and second in applying the same comparison to "small" and "extended" republics.

A pure democracy, "by which I mean, a society consisting of a small number of citizens, who assemble and administer the government in person, can admit of no cure for the mischiefs of faction," wrote Madison. "A common passion or interest will, in almost every case, be felt by a majority of the whole; a communication and concert, results from the form of government itself; and there is nothing to check the inducements to sacrifice the weaker party, or an obnoxious individual." On the contrary, a republic, founded on the principle of representation, promises to heal the damage caused by factions.

In fact, Madison showed great faith in the ability of representative government "to refine and enlarge the public views, by passing them through the medium of a chosen body of citizens, whose wisdom may best discern the true interest of their country, and whose patriotism and love of justice, will be least likely to sacrifice it to temporary or partial considerations." But he thought this process might not be sufficient, because "men of factious tempers, of local prejudices, or of sinister designs, may by intrigue, by corruption, or by other means, first obtain the suffrages, and then betray the interests of the people." In any case, republics are better equipped than democracies due precisely to their large size: "The other point of difference is, the greater number of citizens, and extent of territory, which may

144 *Ibid.*, p. 41.

be brought within the compass of republican, than of democratic government; and it is this circumstance principally which renders factious combinations less to be dreaded in the former, than in the latter." Madison wanted to convince the citizens of the rightness of the proposed Constitution, that is, the comparative advantages of the extended republic, the Union, compared to small democracies, the States. "Hence it clearly appears, that the same advantage, which a republic has over a democracy, in controlling the effects of faction, is enjoyed by a large over a small republic ... is enjoyed by the union over the states composing it."[145]

In *Federalist* 51, Madison sounded as optimistic as one could be about the future of the American political community and developed even further the theory of the superiority of large republics.

> In the extended republic of the United States, and among the great variety of interests, parties and sects which it embraces, a coalition of a majority of the whole society could seldom take place on any other principles than those of justice and the general good; and there being thus less danger to a minor from the will of the major party, there must be less pretext also, to provide for the security of the former, by introducing into the government a will not dependent on the latter; or in other words, a will independent of the society itself. It is no less certain than it is important, notwithstanding the contrary opinions which have been entertained, that the larger the society, provided it lie within a practicable sphere, the more duly capable it will be of self government. And happily for the *republican cause*, the practicable sphere may be carried to a very great extent, by a judicious modification and mixture of the *federal principle* [146]

145 *Ibid.*, p. 45.

146 James Madison, Federalist 51, February 6, 1788, and Federalist 10, Nov 22, 1787, in Alexander Hamilton, James Madison, and John Jay, The Federalist, p. 255.

Madison's argument was essentially based on the fact that in large republics it is more difficult to construct solid majorities. Majorities must be constructed from minorities; in the smallest political communities there are few such minorities, and they carry great weight, while in extended political communities the minorities are decentralized, smaller and more numerous. The free interaction of the parties would thus result in a zero-sum game in which special interests cancel each other out, without ever being able to come together to seize control of the government. Douglass Adair well summarized Madison's theory: "Compound various economic interests of a large territory with a federal system of thirteen semi-sovereign political units, establish a scheme of indirect elections which will functionally bind the extensive area into a unit while 'refining' the voice of the people, and you will have a stable republican state."[147]

Madison's arguments, even had they been known, would not have stirred up much interest among the opponents of the Constitution, who would have rejected the whole line of reasoning as unrealistic. A single government over such a vast territory could never be "republican," that is, controlled by the people and based on common consent. Freedom could only exist in small and homogeneous republics. According to the Virginian George Mason, "there never was a Government, over a very extensive territory, without destroying the liberties of the people."[148] There was something deeply corrupt in trying to hold together such a vast territory; if the desire was to standardize laws and customs, the fact that it was becoming so overbearing was a clear signal that the Constitution was about creating an empire, not a republic. Patrick Henry reminded his countrymen that the countries that "have gone in search of grandeur, power and splendor ... and [have] been the

147 Douglass Adair, "'That Politics May Be Reduced to a Science': David Hume, James Madison, and the Tenth Federalist" (1957) in *Fame and the Founding Fathers*, p. 151. In this well-known essay Adair showed the decisive influence that a few pages from David Hume's *Essays, Moral, Political, and Literary* (1758) had on Madison's thought.

148 George Mason, Debates, 4 June 1788, DHRC, vol. 9, p. 937.

victims of their own folly: While they acquired those visionary blessings, they lost their freedom."[149] Concerning the proposed new government, he added:

> If we admit this Consolidated Government it will be because we like a great splendid one. Some way or other we must be a great and mighty empire; we must have an army, and a navy, and a number of things: When the American spirit was in its youth, the language of America was different: Liberty, Sir, was then the primary object.[150]

The Antifederalist suspicion about a large-scale republic was corroborated by a series of Federalist arguments on political representation and popular control over laws and those elected. These arguments were anticipated by Edmund Burke. In his famous 1774 Bristol address, Burke stated that the British Parliament "is not a Congress of Ambassadors from different and hostile interests; which interests each must maintain, as an Agent and Advocate, against other Agents and Advocates," but rather "a deliberative Assembly of one Nation, with one Interest, that of the whole." He continued, explaining the meaning of their action to his constituents: "You chuse a Member indeed; but when you have chosen him, he is not Member of Bristol, but he is a Member of Parliament."[151] In essence, each member's judgment on public policy decisions should be free of constraint, particularly from that of his constituents.

Burke's line of argument was the one followed by the two main authors of the *Federalist*, who ascribed to the representatives an autonomous and guiding role over the public debate. In the *Federalist* Madison stated that it would be a good thing for the

149 Patrick Henry, Debates, 5 June 1788, DHRC, vol. 9, p. 954.

150 *Ibid.*, p. 959. On June 24, Henry, as a final attempt, used the argument of the defense of slavery in Virginia to defeat the Constitution; see Robin L. Einhorn, "Patrick Henry's Case against the Constitution: The Structural Problem with Slavery," *Journal of the Early Republic* 22, no. 4 (2002), pp. 549-573.

151 Edmund Burke, "Speech at Mr. Burke's Arrival in Bristol, 1774," *The Portable Burke*, ed. Isaac Kramnik, (London: Penguin, 1999), p. 156.

representatives to remain faithful to their constituents to some extent, but the relationship between voters and elected officials, though strongly advocated, remained very generic. In fact, the latter were not in any way bound by the choices of their constituents; they were leaders who must "refine and enlarge the public views" and not bow to their constituents' positions, who would be little inclined to sacrifice their particular interests to pursue the "great and national objects."[152]

This view of political representation was challenged by the Antifederalists on multiple occasions, both directly and indirectly. The representatives were not elected to do what most pleases them. Rather, they were there to solve a technical inconvenience: it was impossible to constitute an assembly that was coextensive with the population. For obvious reasons direct participation by the citizenry in the formation of laws was not possible, but that did not alter the nature of political representation According to Brutus, representation is "the only practicable mode in which the people of any country can exercise this right" to participate in the formation of laws.[153] In any case, for representation to be compatible with liberty it must be "an equal, full and fair representation," and this is possible only in small republics. In fact, representatives should not only be accountable to the citizens, but "collect the views and wishes of the whole people in that of their rulers."[154] If the electoral base is too broad—such as that of the federal House of Representatives—"the choice of members would commonly fall upon the rich and great, while the middling class of the community would be excluded." [155] The existence of fewer interests within a small republic would naturally make conflicts easier to resolve. If the plan is to create "a free [government] ... it should be so framed

152 Madison, *Federalist* 10, p. 45.

153 Brutus IV, *New York Journal*, 29 November 1787, DHRC, vol. 19, p. 313. See also Patrick Henry, Debates, 7 June 1788, DHRC, vol. 9, pp. 1035-1047. As previously noted, the pseudonymous "Brutus" is presumed to have been Robert Yates of Albany, New York.

154 *Ibid.*

155 *Ibid*, p. 314. Cf. Melancton Smith, who saw "the first class in the community ... the *natural aristocracy* of the country" as taking control of the House. Convention Debates, 21 June 1788, DHRC, vol. 22, p. 1751.

as to secure the liberty of the citizens of America, and such a one has to admit of a full, fair, and equal representation of the people." Brutus asked, skeptically, whether "a government thus constituted ... [could] be exercised over the whole United States, reduced into one state"?[156]

Having cited both Montesquieu and Beccaria among the authorities who deny the possibility of a free government "over a country of such immense extent," Brutus claimed to be able to present other "reasons [that] may be drawn from the reason and nature of things, against it."[157] Brutus's idea of representation was that of an extremely rigid mandate: "In a free republic ... the people do not declare their consent by themselves in person, but by representatives, chosen by them, who are supposed to know the minds of their constituents, and to be possessed of integrity to declare this mind." In short, the problem is one of knowing and implementing the popular will, which becomes absolutely impossible in a large republic. This is because "[t]he confidence which the people have in their rulers, in a free republic, arises from their knowing them, from their being responsible to them for their conduct, and from the power they have of displacing them when they misbehave."[158]

The "scientific" aspect—which was subjective to say the least—of the Antifederalist predictions and criticisms is correctly underscored by Abraham Kupersmith. The Antifederalist ideology was organized so that "when the Antifederalists claimed that the Articles of Confederation protected the republican nature of American government, they felt they were stating a scientific fact. When they argued that the proposed constitution would eliminate the right to shape laws to fit the needs of local communities, their argument had an ideological foundation. When the Antifederalists

156 Brutus, I, *Complete Anti-Federalist*, 2.9.16. While in Europe the first victims of the French Revolution were precisely the small states, the American constitutional debate was dominated instead by the positive theorization of the "small state."

157 Brutus I, *New York Journal*, 18 October 1787, DHRC, vol. 19, p. 110.

158 *Ibid.*, p. 113.

argued that America had to retain a confederation of small, sovereign republics, they were as sure of this position as were those who made predictions based on the laws of gravity."[159]

For the Antifederalists, choosing freedom coincided with a clear idea of a simple "good life." Their opponents, and especially Hamilton, had painted a bleak picture not only of the current American situation, but also of the future risks of wars between states and of weakness on the international front. Patrick Henry's response to all that was this:

> Sir, we are not feared by foreigners; we do not make nations tremble: Would this, Sir, constitute happiness, or secure liberty? ... Go to the poor man, ask him what he does; he will inform you, that he enjoys the fruits of his labour, under his own fig-tree with his wife and children around him, in peace and security. Go to every other member of the society, you will find the same tranquil ease and content; you will find no alarms or disturbances: Why then tell us of dangers to terrify us into an adoption of this new Government?[160]

The private individual was not the only fortunate one, but entire peoples as well, who could peacefully live their lives far from the fracas of history. Maryland Farmer stated that "*the silence of historians is the surest record of the happiness of a people.* The Swiss have been four hundred years the envy of mankind, and there is scarcely a history of their nation."[161]

And it was certainly no accident that the first real American opponents of the idea of a national state were fascinated by Switzerland, which was the antithesis of that model. The same author, after having asserted that "where the government resides in the body of the people," as in Switzerland, "they can never be

159 Abraham Kupersmith "Montesquieu and the Ideological Strain in Antifederalist Thought," p. 48.

160 Patrick Henry, Debates, 5 June 1788, DHRC, vol. 9, pp. 959-960.

161 A Farmer III (Part 1), *Baltimore Maryland Gazette*, 7 March 1788, DHRC, vol. 11, p. 366.

corrupted by the artifice or the wealth of the *few*," added that the Swiss are "the only part of the human species that sustain the dignity of character, belonging to the divine resemblance we bear. ... " This is because they are a free people, whose confederation "comprehends one hundred perhaps two hundred, independent governments and States."[162]

Patrick Henry also paid highest honors to Switzerland and the indomitable spirit of its people: "The Swiss spirit ... has kept them together: They have encountered and overcome immense difficulties with patience and fortitude. In this vicinity of powerful and ambitious monarchs, they have retained their independence, republican simplicity and valour."[163]

More generally, while there are still historians who consider them simply as the losing side, as a minority faction of would-be founders of what would have been a very different country,[164] the influence of the Antifederalists on the origins of the American republic were enormous. And yet, as Lance Banning recalled, it is true that "no anti-constitutional party emerged in the new United States." He notes also that "as early as the spring of 1791 the Constitution was accepted on all sides as the starting point for further debates. Within four years of ratification, the Republican opponents of the new administration—a party that probably included a majority of the old Antifederalists—insisted that they stood together to defend the Constitution against a threat that originated within the government itself. While interest in fundamental amendments persisted for years, determined opposition to the new plan of government disappeared almost as quickly as it arose."[165] But this should not cause us to neglect the profound continuity that links later events

162 A Farmer V (Part 2), *Baltimore Maryland Gazette*, 25 March 1788, DHRC, vol. 12, p. 453.

163 Patrick Henry, Debates, 5 June 1788, DHRC, vol. 9, p. 966.

164 Cf. Paul Finkelman, "Turning Losers into Winners: What Can We Learn, If Anything, From the Antifederalists?" *Texas Law Review* 79 (2001), p. 854.

165 Lance Banning, "Republican Ideology and the Triumph of the Constitution, 1789 to 1793," *William & Mary Quarterly*, 3rd series, 31, no. 2 (1974), pp. 167-168. On the decline of the Antifederalists, already clear by the end of the ratification process, see Steven R. Boyd, *The Politics of Opposition: Antifederalists and the Acceptance of the Constitution* (Millwood, NY: KTO, 1979), pp. 121-138.

in the political debate back to the dispute over the Constitution. In effect, "there were significant continuities in national politics between the controversies surrounding ratification and those of the first few Congresses."[166] The Antifederalists absolutely did not disappear from the American political scene; rather, they simply became less visible for a few years.

The divisions over the Constitutional project also shed light on the nature of early American political thought, and they represent the embryonic American party system. Thomas Jefferson found himself profiting by that political divide just a few years later. Though the Antifederalists seemed satisfied with the compromise reached in the Bill of Rights, shortly thereafter they began to swell the ranks of Jefferson's party. Moreover, as we'll discuss in the next chapter, the 1798 Kentucky Resolutions can be seen, in part, as an Antifederalist interpretation of the Constitution.

The divergent views of society—essentially, whether it directs itself or must be directed by the paternal iron fist of a national government—were at the heart of the divisions over power between the newly emerged Jeffersonian party and the Federalists in power. And these rifts in turn were but the further development and the ideological crystallization of the political issues raised during the ratification debate. The Democratic-Republican Party of Jefferson and Madison formed by taking advantage of the opposition to the Hamiltonian system in the early 1790s.[167] But it could not have had the success that it did in later years had it not appealed, first and foremost, to the antifederalist forces already rooted in the country. As two prominent historians have expressed it: "The Democratic-Republicans elaborated many of the same themes opponents of the Constitution had invoked during the ratification debates."[168]

---

166 John H. Aldrich and Ruth W. Grant, "The Antifederalists, the First Congress, and the First Parties," *Journal of Politics* 55, no. 2 (1993), p. 296.

167 John F. Hoadley, *Origins of American Political Parties, 1789-1803* (Lexington: University Press of Kentucky, 1986).

168 Cathy D. Matson and Peter S. Onuf, *A Union of Interest: Political and Economic Thought in Revolutionary America* (Lawrence: University Press of Kansas, 1990), p. 168.

Jefferson agreed profoundly with all of the classic themes of the Antifederalists: the superiority of local interests over "national" interests, self-government, the close link between localism and liberty, the direct responsibility of elected officials, and the physical proximity to the voters by those elected. The Antifederalists were mostly Jeffersonian in their acclamation of *laissez-faire*, and for a government restricted to the protection of life, liberty, and property. Classic Lockean liberalism, linking up with the American experience of self-government, became a new political ideology that was the glue of the coalition that opposed the Federalist party in power. The central *leitmotiv* of that coalition, uniting the Antifederalists to the Democratic-Republicans, was the fight against consolidation, the concentration of power in a single center, the "project of projects" of modern politics, or the state.

Chapter 3

Thomas Jefferson and the Revision of the American Constitutional Order

> Were we directed from Washington when to sow, and when to reap, we should soon want bread.
>
> -Thomas Jefferson

3.1) States and Federation: The Collision Course

The Philadelphia convention had given rise to a plan that fostered wishful thinking. As Madison described it, two parallel worlds had been designed—the federal government and the federated State, each one sovereign in its sphere. They were never supposed to come into conflict. Under the name of "dual federalism," this theory survived until the 1930s as a quasi-legal definition of the American system of government. But far from traveling in neatly defined and distinct orbits, the States and the federal government immediately collided on just about every topic. The adoption of the Constitution had not resolved the relationship between the States and the federal government. It merely opened up new grounds for conflict, which in the 1790s took the form of how to interpret the Constitution itself.

Prior to the Philadelphia convention, American political divisions had followed the Old Whig pattern: On one side were the supporters of natural rights, limited government, and popular sovereignty; on the other the enemies. Following the doctrinal realignment imposed by the Constitution, the Whigs and Tories in America found a new battleground: the States and the federation. A strong federal power, potentially the arbiter of its own powers (as in Hamilton's interpretation), became the new Tory standard.

Opposing this was a political order based no longer just on human rights, but on the rights of the States as well, on the grounds that the States had created the federal government as their agent for the management of common affairs. By the 1790s, the field was already divided between the proponents of a free and voluntary constitutional pact revolving around the States, and the supporters of the gradual consolidation of federal power.

This dilemma, unresolved by the Philadelphia convention, and the clustering of political forces which fed on it, was rapidly ushering in a novel canon of tyranny. European political doctrine had produced the idea of tyranny as the concentration of power in a single entity, basically the king, not as a single, overarching political center, which had become a permanent fixture in European modernity. In the European context, checks, balances, division, and separation were deemed sufficient controls, because problems arose only when power was concentrated in a single set of hands, not in a single center. In short, from the time of the emergence of the state, the European debate has revolved around two risks: one, dividing sovereignty and thus "breaking up the ship" we are sailing, to use the well-known Bodinian metaphor;[1] or, two, the opposite risk that too tight a grip on the helm by a single individual might reduce the freedom of the passengers. But there is still just one ship in European doctrine.

The redefinition of this old problem, first by the Antifederalists and then by Thomas Jefferson and his followers, saw tyranny emerging from the concentration of powers, not simply from a single person with too much power. This Jeffersonian view, which had already surfaced during the first sessions of the Continental Congress and which continued with greater intensity in the constitutional fight, became a permanent fixture in American politics. And the rift between the two viewpoints was a geographical divide, with the New England States openly federalist and the southern States increasingly aligning with Jefferson's and Madison's party. It was easy to foresee the possible implications of such a fight: the creation of two different confederations.

1 See Jean Bodin, *The Six Books of a Commonwealth* (1576), ed. K.D. MacRae (Cambridge: Harvard University Press, 1962).

As Jefferson wrote in May 1792 to President Washington, "The division of sentiment & interest happens unfortunately to be so geographical, that no mortal can say that what is most wise & temperate would prevail against what is most easy & obvious." He added, "I can scarcely contemplate a more incalculable evil than the breaking of the union into two or more parts."[2]

Although Alexander Hamilton supported the constitutional project, he had played no role in the drafting of the constitutional document. In Jefferson's judgment, Hamilton's support of the Constitution was not due to its positive elements but because it was a "stepping-stone to monarchy."[3] Karl-Friedrich Walling says, "because he was more concerned with unleashing than restraining national power [in the 1790s, Hamilton] came close to establishing by legal construction [by the courts] what he had failed to obtain at the federal Convention: congressional authority to make all laws whatsoever for the safety and welfare of the Union."[4]

As discussed in the previous chapter, Hamilton represented the state of New York at the Philadelphia convention, which he had strongly supported as a means of mending the flaws of the confederation. The other two New York delegates, Robert Yates and John Lansing Jr., did not vote the same way as Hamilton. Hamilton's "active participation" at the Philadelphia convention was essentially limited to a memorable, almost six-hour-long speech he delivered on the morning of 18 June 1787, amid the dismay and admiration of his peers: dismay at the audacity of his statements and admiration that he had spoken from the heart and stated his true beliefs. Discussion had been in progress for almost a week on the amended plans put forward by New Jersey (small state plan) and Virginia (big state plan), both of which Hamilton regarded as totally inadequate. He proposed his own plan for

2 Jefferson to the President of the United States, May 23, 1792, *The Papers of Thomas Jefferson*, eds. Julian P. Boyd et al. (Princeton: Princeton University Press, 1990), vol. 23, p. 537.

3 *Ibid.*, p. 538.

4 Karl-Friedrich Walling, *Republican Empire: Alexander Hamilton on War and Free Government* (Lawrence: University Press of Kansas, 1999), p. 162.

a national government,[5] which, however, had no effect on the constitutional project. His plan would have given the executive authority wide-ranging powers, vested in a governor elected for life. Most governmental powers would be divided between the governor and the Senate, all of whose members, like the governor, would be chosen for life by indirect election. A supreme judicial authority would have both original and appeal jurisdiction, and the governor of each state was to be appointed by the U. S. government, which would have a right of veto over all state laws. No state would be allowed to have an armed militia.

As Russell Kirk rightly observed, "such centralization would [at that time] have been impossible to attain except by force of arms," [6] but had Hamilton's plan been approved, the United States would have become a semi-centralized Republic, "one and indivisible," right away.

Hamilton's emphasis on executive power was deliberate. He believed that a strong government would lead the country toward rapid industrialization on the lines of the British model. He had very little trust either in the invisible hand of the market—his polemic against Adam Smith is well-known—or in man's capacity for self-government, and he was inclined toward a commercial and oligarchic republic. Consequently, the executive logically became the center and the engine of the system. As John Koritansky has pointed out, "For Hamilton ... only the executive had the requisite degree of unity that could generate the energy and the rationality ... that is necessary for sound public policy."[7] For this reason, Daniel Elazar is quite justified in depicting Hamilton as a solitary figure against the backdrop of the political doctrines of the Founding Fathers, one who in many ways prefigured the "managerialist"

5 The plan is sketched in Alexander Hamilton, "The Plan Presented by Alexander Hamilton, June 18, 1787" in The Origins of the American Constitution, ed. Michael Kammen (New York: Penguin, 1986) pp. 36–38. A larger version is to be found in The Records of the Federal Convention, ed. M. Farrand (New Haven: Yale University Press, 1911) vol. 1, pp. 281–93.

6 Russell Kirk, The Roots of American Order, 3rd ed. (Washington, DC: Regnery 1991), p. 424.

7 John C. Koritansky, "Alexander Hamilton's Philosophy of Government and Administration," Publius 9, no. 2 (Spring 1979), p. 111.

school that became popular in America during the twentieth century.

But let us return to Hamilton's speech at the convention. One can hardly fail to share the judgment expressed by the popular historian Catherine Drinker Bowen:

> That Hamilton was not interrupted seems extraordinary, considering the tenor of his remarks, their boldness, and the growing unpopularity of this "British example." *Annihilate state distinctions and state operations?* In the whole gathering, perhaps only Read of Delaware and Butler of South Carolina would have agreed. *A single executive, elected for life?* It came closer to monarchy. Paradoxically, Hamilton's idea of a lower house elected directly by the people went beyond what most delegates were ready to concede to "democracy." Even Madison was against it. *A general and national government, completely sovereign?* Nothing less, Hamilton had argued, could establish American power at home and American prestige abroad.[8]

Shortly after such a revelation of his opinions on "federalism," Hamilton abandoned the convention, reasonably convinced that the climate was not propitious for such a far-reaching project. However, unlike his co-delegates from New York (who left the convention because they feared it would culminate in an excessively centralist plan), Hamilton returned to Independence Hall from time to time, and in September he signed the constitutional proposal against the opinion of his own state.

3.2) The Hamiltonian Legacy

In 1791, during Washington's first term of presidency, Hamilton and Jefferson were the most popular politicians in America, both members of the administration. Hamilton, a sort of "shadow prime minister," was the powerful secretary of the treasury, as well as

8 Catherine D. Bowen, *Miracle at Philadelphia* (Boston: Little, Brown, 1966), p. 113.

the leader of the majority party in Congress, the Federalist Party. Jefferson was the secretary of state and was beginning to organize opposition to the centralist plan. The inevitable conflict between the two men dominated the political scene. Despite conciliatory overtures by George Washington, it turned into an irreconcilable rivalry once Hamilton's bill to institute a federal bank obtained the majority of votes in Congress. Jefferson hoped to convince the president to reject it on the basis of its blatant unconstitutionality, but after considering the opinions of the two contenders, Washington yielded to Hamilton's arguments and signed the Bank Bill.

As early as 1780, Hamilton had begun to mull over the establishment of a federal central bank, which would be funded by mixed private and public capital and able to issue bonds to finance the federal debt and fund the country's needs, both at war and in peacetime. In 1781, the Continental Congress had created the Bank of North America, vesting it with fairly limited powers, but its statutes were repealed by the Pennsylvania assembly in 1785. The bank was reestablished in 1788, with even more limited capital, prestige, and duration.[9]

Once the federal constitution had been approved, creating a bank depended on constitutional interpretation. In the Hamiltonian proposal, the Bank of the United States was intended to serve as a means of repaying the debt. Hamilton proposed to forge a close connection between the lifetime of the bank and that of the public debt. He saw the latter as the driving thrust of economic growth and wanted both the bank and the debt to be perpetual. However, awarding federal power such a sweeping mandate over the debt and over the methods of its financing, let alone a tendency to a monopoly over the issuing of money, might be regarded as overstepping the boundaries of the Constitution and undermining its rigorous demarcation of spheres of authority between the States and the federation.

Jefferson had realized that only a strict construction of the Constitution could save the States from having to submit to the federal power. Hamilton, by the same token, was well aware that

9 See Bray Hammond, *Banks and Politics in America from the Revolution to the Civil War* (Princeton: Princeton University Press, 1957).

only by allowing an elastic interpretation of the constitutional provisions could the powers of the federal government be reinforced. He wished to introduce to the very heart of the national political life the controversial clause referring to the absolute supremacy of federal power—the clause the States were so reluctant to accept (and on which they could not reach an agreement in Philadelphia).[10]

The two antagonists' opinions on the question of the central bank, expressed in their report to the president, were to have momentous importance. First, they revealed the rift between those who believed the Constitution could be modified only through amendments (strict construction) and those who argued it could be modified through interpretation (loose construction). This division was to surface again and again, in each and every American constitutional debate. Second, they emphasized that the political struggle in America was centered on the issue of centralization versus states' rights.

Very briefly, the two statesmen offered President Washington the following views: Jefferson started out from the Tenth Amendment ("The powers not delegated to the United States by the Constitution, nor prohibited by it to the States, are reserved to the States respectively, or to the people") to assert that "to take a single step beyond the boundaries thus specially drawn around the powers of Congress, is to take possession of a boundless field of power, no longer susceptible of any definition."[11]

Hamilton, in contrast, aware that he had fewer textual footholds with which to prop himself up,[12] prepared his report with the most painstaking attention to every minute detail and, for the first time in American history, set forth the so-called "implied powers" theory:

10 On the issue of constitutional interpretation and the congressional debates on the establishment of the First National Bank, see Benjamin B. Klubes, "The First Federal Congress and the First National Bank: A Case Study in Constitutional Interpretation," Journal of the Early Republic 10, no. 1 (Spring 1990), pp. 19–41.

11 Jefferson to G. Washington, "Opinion on the Constitutionality of the Bank," 15 February 1791, The Writings of Thomas Jefferson, eds. Andrew A. Lipscomb and Albert E. Bergh (Washington, DC: Thomas Jefferson Memorial Association, 1904–1907), vol. 3, p. 146.

12 "Hamilton spent most of his career trying to reconcile the necessity of empire with the moral authority of consent, a problem that was perhaps most acute in his discussion of the federal courts and broad construction of the Constitution," writes

"Every power vested in a Government is in its nature *sovereign*, and includes by *force* of the *term*, a right to employ all the *means* requisite, and fairly *applicable* to the attainment of the *ends* of such power; ... there are *implied*, as well as *express* powers, and that the former are as effectually delegated as the latter."[13] As Hamilton saw it, the constitutionality of a law should not be judged simply by looking at the specific powers vested in the federal government by the Constitution. Rather, the assessment should be conducted on the basis of a clearly specified question, namely, "Does the proposed measure abridge a preexisting right of any State, or of any individual? If it does not, there is a strong presumption in favour of its constitutionality."[14]

The constitutional text on this point seems clearly to support Jefferson's view. In order to act, the federal government must be able to point to something in the letter of the Constitution that permits it to do so. This differs sharply from the situation of the States, which have a sort of general political competence, even though some of their actions may encounter prohibitions. For Hamilton, on the contrary, a general presumption of constitutionality existed in actions of the federal government. The powers of the federal government, in his understanding, were substantial: those expressly stated by the constitutional text, those implicitly derived from the granting of the aforementioned powers, and those that did not abridge the rights of the States or of the individuals. Within such a framework, the boundaries established by the Constitution became so blurred as to make it almost impossible to define *a priori* where the federal sphere of authority ended and where that of the States began.

Karl-Friedrich Walling, *Republican Empire: Alexander Hamilton on War and Free Government* (Lawrence: University Press of Kansas, 1999), p. 154.

13 Alexander Hamilton, "Final Version of an Opinion on the Constitutionality of An Act to Establish a Bank" (February 23, 1791) in The Papers of Alexander Hamilton, eds. H. C. Syrett et al. (New York: Columbia University Press, 1961–1987), vol. 8, pp. 98 and 100. Hamilton was also availing himself of a decisive advantage; he had already read Jefferson's report to the president.

14 *Ibid.*, 107.

As early as his contribution to the *Federalist*, Hamilton had shown himself loath to accept limitations on federal government activity. In his own words, "These powers ought to exist without limitation, *because it is impossible to foresee or define the extent and variety of national exigencies, or the correspondent extent and variety of the means which may be necessary to satisfy them.*"[15] Shortly afterward, he added, in words that anticipate the doctrine of implied powers: "The *means* ought to be proportioned to the *end*; the persons, from whose agency the attainment of any *end* is expected, ought to possess the *means* by which it is to be attained."[16]

The doctrine of implied powers was subsequently embraced and perfected by the chief justice of the Supreme Court, the Federalist John Marshall, who headed the court during the crucial first thirty years of the nineteenth century, from 1801 to his death, and who was the real *dominus* of the legal system of the young republic.[17] With Marshall, the Supreme Court became the center of the Federalist resurgence after Jefferson's victory in the 1800 presidential election. In *Fletcher v. Peck* (1810), Marshall annulled an act approved by the assembly of Georgia, informing the state that Georgia was only "a part of a larger empire ... a member of the American union ... which opposes limits to the legislatures of the several States."[18] This was followed by the decision *McCullough v. Maryland*, 1819, in which the Chief Justice crushed the attempt by a state to tax an agency of the federal government. The same year saw the Dartmouth College case, in which Marshall declared a law of the New Hampshire assembly to be null and void, thereby breaching the statutes guaranteed to the university under English

---

15 Alexander Hamilton, Federalist 23, in Alexander Hamilton, James Madison, John Jay, The Federalist Papers, with an introduction by Clinton Rossiter (New York: New American Library, 1961), p. 274.

16 *Ibid.*

17 A work on the clash by the two Virginians, Marshall and Jefferson, summarizes thus the difference: "Marshall believed in an ordered society. Jefferson, more a philosopher and a romantic, was interested in ideas rather than order; John Marshall was interested in doing whatever it would take to make the United States successful," Ronald C. Zellar, *A Brave Man Stands Firm: The Historic Battles between Chief Justice John Marshall and President Thomas Jefferson* (New York: Algora, 2011), p. 8

18 Quoted in Felix Morley, *Freedom and Federalism* (Chicago: Regnery, 1959), p. 54.

rule. The centralist-Hamiltonian interpretation had found its most powerful ally in the Supreme Court—and precisely during the years of republican-Jeffersonian ascendancy. In the future, there would no longer be any need to seek arguments to persuade the president or Congress of the constitutionality of a federal law at odds with the Tenth Amendment.

Here lay the real core of dispute, the deepest roots of the hostility between Jefferson and Hamilton. Their dispute ran the entire gamut of issues: from foreign policy (Jefferson was a Francophile while Hamilton was an Anglophile) to the overall political vision of the just society and of the "good life" (wary of governmental coercion and agrarian in Jefferson's position, interventionist and commercial for Hamilton). But the central point was always the institutionalization of power and of states' rights. To Hamilton, states' rights were a veritable juridical monstrosity (in which each state became an *imperium in imperio*), while in Jefferson's perspective these constituted the one and only true barrier against the concentration of power.[19]

Thus, in September 1787, Hamilton began supporting a constitution about which he harbored more than a few doubts. His support was motivated by the fact that he felt it represented a step—the only step that appeared at all feasible at that moment—toward the centralization of power in America. At the same time, however, he immediately set about bringing the power and political arrangements in America closer to the vision he had extolled in his speech on 18 June 1787.

In a letter to Gouverneur Morris dated 1802, Hamilton confessed he had never had confidence in the Constitution. He had only signed it hoping to mend it, "and contrary to all my anticipations of its fate, as you know from the very beginning, I am still laboring to prop the frail and worthless fabric."[20] Hamilton then appended a

---

19 The rivalry had a very well-known and unlikely ending; see Arnold A. Rogow, *A Fatal Friendship: Alexander Hamilton and Aaron Burr* (New York: Hill & Wang, 1999).

20 Alexander Hamilton to G. Morris, February 27, 1802, *The Works of Alexander Hamilton* (1904), ed. H. C. Lodge (New York: Haskell House, 1971), vol. 10, p. 425.

disconsolate remark: "every day proves to me more and more, that this American world was not made for me."[21]

Jefferson bequeathed to posterity a *post-mortem* judgment on Hamilton that is a tribute to the New Yorker's personal qualities, and he attributes most of his flaws to a single cause, his preference for the English model: "Hamilton was indeed a singular character. Of acute understanding, disinterested, honest, and honorable in all private transactions, amiable in society, and duly valuing virtue in private life, yet so bewitched & perverted by the British example, as to be under thoro' conviction that corruption was essential to the government of a nation."[22] George Will's remark certainly has the sound of truth: "There is an elegant memorial in Washington to Jefferson, but none to Hamilton. However, if you seek Hamilton's monument, look around. You are living in it. We honor Jefferson, but live in Hamilton's country."[23]

Some scholars are quite passionate about the endeavors of the New Yorker. While finances of the Union were in their infancy, "in the first seventeen months that Hamilton served as Secretary of the Treasury, the credit of the United States rose from essentially non-existent to roughly equal to that of the most stable and long established countries in the world. Through his proposal that the federal government assume the debts of the States and that the federal government be given the sole right of taxation of imports, major obstacles to the unity of the country were removed. ... The financial plan proposed by Hamilton and enacted by Congress not only strengthened the central government but dramatically improved the popular support of the government."[24]

---

21 *Ibid.*, pp. 425-426.

22 *Ibid.*, p. 279.

23 George F. Will, *Restoration: Congress, Term Limits, and the Recovery of Deliberative Democracy* (New York: Free Press, 1992), p. 167.

24 Joseph A. Murray, *Alexander Hamilton: America's Forgotten Founder* (New York: Algora, 2007), p. 150. With all due respect for the scholars enamored of Hamilton's character, a tendency to veer into hagiography is very common among them.

3.3) The Jeffersonian Legacy

Jefferson's criticism of the Constitution was not much different from that of the Anti-federalists. He had liked the old instrument, the Articles of Confederation. Already in November 1787, as he confessed his qualms to John Adams, he did not fail to refer yet again to that ancient and venerable frame of government.

> There are things in it [the new constitution] which stagger all my disposition to subscribe to what such an assembly has proposed. The house of federal representatives will not be adequate to the management of affairs either foreign or federal. *Their* President seems a bad edition of a Polish king. ... All the good of this new constitution might have been couched in three or four new articles to be added to the good, old and venerable fabrick, which should have been preserved even as a religious relique.[25]

Well informed in France about the most recent developments back at home thanks to the news conveyed by his trusted friends, Jefferson confided to a Virginian friend in the summer of 1787, "I confess, I do not go as far in the reforms thought necessary as some of my correspondents in America." Further, expressing in a nutshell what would become the core of the Anti-Federalist position, "My general plan would be, to make the States one as to everything connected with foreign nations, and several as to everything purely domestic."[26]

Before the Philadelphia convention, Jefferson wrote to Madison, "To make us one nation as to foreign concerns, and keep us distinct in domestic ones, gives the outline of the proper division of powers between the general and particular governments."[27] The

25 Jefferson to J. Adams, November 13, 1787, *The Adams-Jefferson Letters: The Complete Correspondence Between Thomas Jefferson and Abigail and John Adams*, ed. Lester J. Cappon (Chapel Hill: University of North Carolina Press, 1988), p. 212 (italics mine).

26 Jefferson to E. Carrington, August 4, 1787, *The Papers of Thomas Jefferson*, vol. 11, p. 678.

27 Jefferson to J. Madison, December 16, 1786, *The Papers of Thomas Jefferson*, vol. 10, p. 603.

concept was reiterated over and over again, to each and every correspondent. "My idea is that we should be made one nation in every case concerning foreign affairs, and separate ones in whatever is merely domestic."[28] During his presidential campaign in 1800, he wrote:

> The true theory of our constitution is surely the wisest and best, that the States are independent as to everything within themselves, and united as to everything respecting foreign nations. Let the general government be reduced to foreign concerns only, and let our affairs be disentangled from those of all other nations, except as to commerce, which the merchants will manage the better, the more they are left free to manage for themselves, and our general government may be reduced to a very simple organization, and a very inexpensive one; a few plain duties to be performed by a few servants.[29]

This passage also embodies the core of Jefferson's theory of limited government, which is based on the federal division of powers. Many years later, when contesting the statement made by John Melish, who argued that both factions were faithful to the Constitution, Jefferson claimed that the division between the two parties resided in "a real and radical difference of political principle."[30] In his view, the "question of preference between monarchy and republicanism, which has so long divided mankind elsewhere, threatens [to become] a permanent division here."[31] The faction headed by Alexander Hamilton was essentially working toward one major goal, importing the English system of government into America, "and only accepted and held fast, at first, to the present constitution, as a stepping-stone

28 Jefferson to J. Blair, August 13, 1787, *The Papers of Thomas Jefferson*, vol. 12, p. 28.

29 Jefferson to G. Granger, August 13, 1800, *The Papers of Thomas Jefferson*, vol. 32, p. 96.

30 Jefferson to J. Melish, January 13, 1813, *The Writings of Thomas Jefferson*, vol. 13, p. 208.

31 *Ibid.*, p. 209.

to the final establishment of their favorite model."[32] On the other hand, "The party called republican is steadily for the support of the present constitution [since] they obtained at its commencement, all the amendments to it they desired."[33]

3.4) The Kentucky Resolutions

Thomas Jefferson produced a document of about three thousand words that, if read carefully between the lines, contained his entire theory of the restraint on the federal government. In American political history, the Kentucky Resolutions of 1798 were destined long to remain the fountainhead of states' rights doctrine. This document is also a deeply embarrassing piece of evidence for those scholars keen on creating the image of a Jefferson who loved the union just as much as or even more than Abraham Lincoln. The major Jeffersonian biographers tend to pass the Kentucky Resolutions off as worthy of no more than a few pages among thousands; as, perhaps, a jarring note of marginal importance in the work of an otherwise clear lifetime, to be brushed aside like a bothersome fly that threatens to light on a tasty morsel.

For example, the most significant biographer of Jefferson, Dumas Malone, allocates to the Kentucky Resolutions only six pages of his monumental six-volume work on the life and times of the author of the Declaration. Likewise, Merrill Peterson, the author of the best single-volume Jeffersonian biography, deems this "business" to be only worth four or five pages in more than 1,000.[34] More recently, it seems quite amazing that a legal scholar such as Richard Bernstein, in what is said to be "the best short biography" on Jefferson, devotes only about a quarter of a page to the Kentucky Resolutions.[35] Conflicting as they are with his portrait of a Jefferson single-mindedly

---

32 *Ibid.*

33 *Ibid.*, 210-211.

34 See Dumas Malone, *Jefferson and the Ordeal of Liberty* (Boston: Little, Brown, 1962), pp. 402-406 and 419-420 and Merrill Peterson, Thomas Jefferson and the New Nation: A Biography (New York: Oxford University Press, 1970), pp. 613-614 and 622-624.

35 See Richard B. Bernstein, *Thomas Jefferson* (New York: Oxford University Press, 2003), pp. 125-126.

striving to achieve an ever stronger and solid union, the Kentucky Resolutions are mentioned only in passing also by Peter Onuf in a book that collects a decade of the distinguished professor's research on the works and thought of the third president of the Unites States.[36]

Nevertheless, the resolutions are the core of Jefferson's federal idea, and they embody, in a nutshell, the whole of his constitutional doctrine.[37] The influence of the resolutions and of the writings published to explain and defend the principles that underpinned them (foremost among them, Madison's *Virginia Report* of 1800) is paramount. William J. Watkins Jr. writes:

> The Resolutions ... were not the first American statement of the compact theory, the locus of ultimate sovereignty, or the division of legislative sovereignty. But the Resolutions were perhaps the most lucid and succinct statements of first principles ever penned. Though originally condemned by nine States in the late 1790s, the Resolutions' cogent reasoning won acceptance in the marketplace of ideas.[38]

The Kentucky Resolutions represent Jefferson's greatest contribution to a constitution that may well have been the offspring of "an assembly of demi-gods,"[39] but in which he had been unable to take part since he was minister to France at the time.[40]

---

36 See Peter S. Onuf, *Jefferson's Empire: The Language of American Nationhood* (Charlottesville: University Press of Virginia, 2000), p. 72.

37 Quite properly, the best book on this subject, David N. Mayer's *The Constitutional Thought of Thomas Jefferson* (Charlottesville: University Press of Virginia, 1994), gives much space to the Resolutions.

38 William J. Watkins Jr., *Reclaiming the American Revolution: The Kentucky and Virginia Resolutions and Their Legacy* (New York: Palgrave, 2004), pp. 116-117.

39 After lamenting the secrecy surrounding the meetings of the convention in Philadelphia, Jefferson stated that "it is really an assembly of demi-gods" (Jefferson to J. Adams, August 30, 1787, Adams-Jefferson Letters, p. 196), and while it is not difficult to imagine a note of sarcasm in this remark, the common opinion among students is that he actually meant it.

40 For a detailed analysis of the constitutional principles of '98 cf. H. Jefferson Powell, "The Principles of '98: An Essay in Historical Retrieval," *Virginia Law Review*, vol. 80, No. 3 (April 1994), pp. 689-743.

Madison drafted resolutions for Virginia and Jefferson drafted them for Kentucky (although he initially intended to give them to North Carolina). They were both responses to the Alien and Sedition Acts. Although Madison had been a close associate of Hamilton in 1783–1788, he changed his political stance, becoming a fervent supporter of states' rights to the point where his interpreters must distinguish between a "Hamiltonian" and a "Jeffersonian" Madison. "The Kentucky and Virginia resolutions were the opening guns of the campaign of 1800," writes Noble E. Cunningham Jr.[41] This is not to say that the election of Jefferson was a referendum on the constitutional doctrine expounded by the resolutions, although in 1821 a subcommittee of the Ohio state assembly did suggest that the victory of the Jeffersonian party in 1800 should be considered a popular endorsement of the Kentucky and Virginia resolutions.[42]

Jefferson was vice president when the Alien and Sedition laws were passed, and they occasioned the final break between Jefferson and the Federalist Party. By this time, political strife and partisan anger had reached fever pitch. As Jefferson wrote to a correspondent, "The passions are too high at present, to be cooled in our day. ... Men who have been intimate all their lives, cross the street to avoid meeting, and turn their heads another way, lest they should be obliged to touch their hats."[43] There can be little doubt as to the illiberal character of the laws. The law on aliens increased from five to fourteen years the period of residence required for naturalization and imposed compulsory registration on all aliens present in the country.[44] It granted the president of the United States the power to order any alien citizen to be expelled from American soil or interned without trial. And it allowed the president to deport

41 Noble E. Cunningham Jr., *The Jeffersonian Republicans: The Formation of Party Organization 1789-1801* (Chapel Hill: University of North Carolina Press, 1957), p. 129.

42 See State Documents on Federal Relations, ed. H. V. Ames (Philadelphia: University of Pennsylvania Press, 1900), pp. 95-96.

43 Jefferson to E. Rutledge, June 24, 1797, The Papers of Thomas Jefferson, vol. 29, pp. 456-457.

44 In fact, at the time the States were empowered to naturalize aliens—Pennsylvania, for instance, required two years of residence in the country, while Maryland only requested one—and this measure had thus very little practical effect.

any alien in time of war or threat of war. Any alien refusing prompt compliance would face three years in prison.[45]

The Federalists' aversion to aliens was political, for immigrants were drawn *en masse* toward Thomas Jefferson's Democratic-Republican Party. Although generally "not in search of a Republic, but of bread,"[46] the number of English, Scottish, and Irish immigrants who arrived in America during the 1790s was significant, and among their ranks were more than a few political firebrands. As one historian has put it, at least 74 of these had been militants back in their home country. Half of these were Irish, three-fifths of the remainder were English, and the rest were Scottish.[47] Thus, the Alien Laws were also intended to depict Jefferson's party, the first genuine organized opposition in the country, as a den of spies in the pay of Paris.

The law on aliens, although extremely severe, basically remained a paper tiger, but the law on sedition was quite a different matter. The law made it an offense, punishable with a fine of 5,000 dollars and five years in jail, to act in a manner that prevented the full implementation of a United States law. Further, it was an offense to intimidate anyone who sought to obtain a federal office or, more generally, to participate in any sort of seditious assembly. And anyone found to be the author or publisher of scandalous or defamatory material that offended the president or Congress could be punished by a fine of 2,000 dollars and imprisonment for two

45 See Wendell Bird, *Criminal Dissent: Prosecutions Under the Alien and Sedition Acts of 1798* (Cambridge: Harvard University Press, 2020) for a complete analysis of the incredible amount of people who were targeted under those laws.

46 James T. Callender, *A Short History of the Nature and Consequences of the Excise Laws...* (Philadelphia, 1795), p. 450, quoted in Michael Durey, "Thomas Paine's Apostles: Radical Emigres and the Triumph of Jeffersonian Republicanism," William and Mary Quarterly 3rd series, vol. 44, no 4 (October 1987), pp. 666. On the political ideology of the Jeffersonian party and the many contributions from across the Atlantic, see particularly Richard J. Twomey, *Jacobins and Jeffersonians: Anglo-American Radicalism in the United States, 1790–1820* (New York: Garland, 1989). This investigation of the radicalism of the Jeffersonians shows to advantage the variegated social and ethnic composition of the activists of this party.

47 See Durey, "Thomas Paine's Apostles," p. 666.

years.[48] As has been pointed out by Frederick Allis, "The key words in the act were vague[;] ...'defaming' the government of the United States and 'bringing it into contempt or disrepute' had been a favorite sport of Americans ever since the birth of the republic."[49] The basic result was that the First Amendment, which established the right of every citizen to absolute and incoercible freedom of manifesting his or her own thought, had been superseded by a mere act of Congress. Thomas Paine noted a few years later, "the plan of the leaders of the faction was to overthrow the liberties of the New World."[50] The Sedition Law became the basic issue in a number of lawsuits against journalists and politicians, although the number actually convicted is difficult to determine. One of the purposes of this law was to restore the old common law action against seditious libel, which was widely invoked in the convictions despite the fact that it was held to have been superseded by the First Amendment.[51]

The dispute over the constitutionality of the Federalist acts was probably the most significant of the day:

> The stakes in the controversy ... included whether Americans had a right to publish opposition newspapers and to establish an opposition party, and the outcome of the nation's first effort to suppress that opposition. They included the growth of the nascent political parties toward maturity, the Federalist loss of power to the Republicans in the election of 1800,

---

48 The text of the two acts can be found in *The Virginia Report of 1799–1800: Touching the Alien and Sedition Laws; Together with the Virginia Resolutions of December 21, 1798, The Debate And Proceedings Thereon in the House of Delegates of Virginia, and Several Other Documents Illustrative of the Report and Resolutions*, ed. J. W. Randolph (Richmond: J. W. Randolph, 1850), pp. 17–21.

49 Frederick S. Allis Jr., Government Through Opposition, Party Politics in the 1790s (New York: Macmillan, 1963), p. 63.

50 Thomas Paine, [The National Intelligencer (November 22, 1802)] in *The Complete Writings of Thomas Paine*, ed. Philip S. Foner (New York: Citadel Press, 1945) vol. 2, p. 917.

51 For a brilliant and accurate historical investigation of the fact that the First Amendment was really intended to abolish the ancient common law action against "seditious libel," see Leonard W. Levy, *Freedom of Speech and Press in Early American History: Legacy of Suppression* (New York: Harper & Row, 1963), pp. 1–18.

> and America's first peaceful transfer of political power between parties. The stakes in the controversy also included provoking Republican thought to articulate a liberal view of First Amendment freedoms, and stimulating thought about the proper response to an administration's violation of the Constitution.[52]

We shall focus solely on the constitutional gloss that it produced. "For Jefferson, the Sedition Act's unconstitutionality was a matter of federalism rather than of free speech and press. Republican efforts to punish Federalist critics of the administration failed, especially after *People of New York v. Harry Croswell* (1804), in which Alexander Hamilton, in his last court appearance before his death in a duel with Aaron Burr, argued that publishing the truth for good motives was not sedition. The New York court accepted his argument, launching a nationwide abandonment of seditious libel."[53]

Jefferson did not overtly take sides during the debate in the Senate when he was vice president. While as a consummate politician, he may have secretly gloated over what he considered to be the political suicide of his adversaries, he took great care to organize the opposition behind the scenes, since his rivals would have had no qualms about impeaching him. Nevertheless, Jefferson stated in a letter that these laws should be considered "as merely an experiment on the American mind, to see how far it will bear an avowed violation of the Constitution. If this goes down, we shall immediately see attempted another act of Congress, declaring that the President shall continue in office during life, reserving to another occasion the transfer of the succession to his heirs, and the establishment of the Senate for life."[54]

---

52 Wendell Bird, "New Light on the Sedition Act of 1798: The Missing Half of the Prosecutions," *Law and History Review*, vol. 34, no. 3 (August 2016), p. 543.

53 R.B. Bernstein, "Thomas Jefferson and Constitutionalism," in *A Companion to Thomas Jefferson*, ed. Francis D. Cogliano (Malden, MA: Wiley-Blackwell, 2012), p. 432. See Kate E. Brown, "Rethinking 'People v. Croswell': Alexander Hamilton and the Nature and Scope of 'Common Law' in the Early Republic," *Law and History Review*, vol. 32, no. 3 (August 2014), pp. 611-645.

54 Jefferson to S. T. Mason, October 11, 1798, *The Papers of Thomas Jefferson*, vol. 30, p. 560.

The Jeffersonian resolutions were delivered to Wilson Cary Nicholas, the fellow Virginian who acted as Jefferson's substitute in the House of Representatives, with the understanding that the North Carolina assembly would discuss and approve them. Jefferson had chosen the North Carolina assembly because his party was building strength there. John Breckinridge from Kentucky happened to be on a visit to Virginia, and Nicholas proposed, instead, that Breckinridge should present them in his own state. This decision turned out to be extremely effective. On 10 November 1798, the House of Representatives of Kentucky approved the nine resolutions with only one vote against the first, two against the second, third, fourth, fifth, sixth, seventh, and eighth, and three against the ninth.[55] However, Kentucky, which had been admitted to the union only a few years earlier, turned out to be a controversial choice in terms of political impact. Breckinridge was a useful ally—and above all extremely discreet, since secrecy about the authorship of the resolutions was essential for the success of the plan—despite the fact that the version of the Jeffersonian document he presented to his state had been watered down on several crucial points. Breckinridge added an appeal to the other states to unite and repeal the Alien and Sedition laws. Ironically, such an appeal greatly weakened the Jeffersonian view of state's rights, which originally envisaged that every single state was entitled to declare null and void in its own territory any federal law exceeding the delegated powers, without the need for other states to join. Moreover, the Kentuckians deleted entirely the passage on nullification.[56]

In the Kentucky Resolutions, Jefferson for the first time clearly expounded the political and juridical foundations of the states' rights school of thought, which soon become the mainstream position in the American constitutional thought, retaining its

55 See *The Virginia and Kentucky Resolutions of 1798 and '99;...with other documents in support of the Jeffersonian doctrine of '98*, ed. J. Elliot (Washington, DC: 1832), p. 15.

56 See Cunningham, *Jeffersonian Republicans*, p. 127.

primacy right up until the Civil War.[57] Formulated in greater detail by John Caldwell Calhoun, this doctrine and its underlying assumptions became the true bone of contention between the states of the North and the South.

The controversy presents two aspects which, although historically linked, can be kept logically distinct. The first relates to the struggle to preserve the rights and civil liberties enjoyed by Americans, so brazenly jeopardized by the actions of the Federalists.[58] The second pertains to the political/juridical debate on the nature of the American union. Today, mainstream political and constitutional thought holds that federal citizenship is unthinkable without common and uniform juridical protection of individual freedoms. That is to say, contemporary scholars almost unanimously agree that individual rights enjoy a greater protection under federal than state power and that, in any case, there should be no disparity of treatment among the various states on this sensitive issue. Indeed, in the eyes of many contemporary scholars, the essence of a federation resides specifically in the equality of its citizens before the law, and this cannot but be guaranteed at the federal level.

Thomas Jefferson declared exactly the opposite: It was not the federacy but the States—the buffers against the Federalists' attempt to lump the American population into a single polity—that were the true safeguard of the freedom of the citizens. As Charles Wiltse has observed, the battle shifted American political discourse from the paradigm of natural rights to that of states'

57 "The Virginia and Kentucky Resolutions, Madison's 1799 Report, and the oratory that accompanied them became known as the Principles of Ninety-eight and would for decades be regarded as almost sacred to the adherents of the states' rights faith," Forrest McDonald in *States' Rights and the Union,* p. 43.

58 See Adrienne Koch and Harry Ammon, "The Virginia and Kentucky Resolutions: An Episode in Jefferson's and Madison's Defense of Civil Liberties," *William and Mary Quarterly,* 3rd series, vol. 5, no. 2 (April 1948), pp. 145-76. This otherwise valuable essay is slightly affected by contemporary concerns. In 1948, the loyalties of American citizens were already subject to governmental scrutiny (a harbinger of the witch-hunt to come), and, understandably, the authors preferred to emphasize the defense of civil liberties over constitutional construction. For a discussion of what triggered the interest of the two scholars, cf. Kevin R. C. Gutzman, *Thomas Jefferson, Revolutionary: A Radical's Struggle to Remake America* (New York: St. Martin's Press, 2017), pp. 53-54.

rights: "It was the *Alien and Sedition Acts* that led to the first gloss upon the Constitution, made the States rather than the courts the defenders of individual liberty, and completed the transformation of the natural rights dogma into the far more powerful and effective doctrine of State rights."[59]

The Kentucky Resolutions are, first and foremost, an acknowledgment of the irreplaceable role played by the States in safeguarding the constitutional balance against the risk of consolidation of federal power. Hamilton immediately grasped the potential implicit in the theory embodied in the resolutions and complained of "the tendency of the doctrines advanced by Virginia and Kentucke [*sic*] to destroy the Constitution of the U[nited] States."[60] Hamilton went as far as advocating recourse to a mobilization of the militia: "In the mean time the measures for raising the Military force should proceed with activity. ... When a clever force has been collected let them be drawn toward Virginia for which there is an obvious pretext—& then let measures be taken to act upon the laws & put Virginia to the Test of resistance."[61] A recent scholar writes, "What Jefferson had proposed [in the Kentucky Resolutions] was nothing less than the overthrow of the constitutional settlement of 1787–88, for nullification would have emasculated the national government and restored the States to the predominant position they had occupied under the Articles of Confederation."[62] Ironically perhaps, Hamilton had earlier (in the Federalist nos. 23, 26 and 28) made clear the means available to the States when the federal government overstepped its powers. [63]

---

59 Charles M. Wiltse, "From Compact to National State in American Political Thought" in *Essays in Political Theory. Presented to George H. Sabine*, eds. M. R. Konvitz and A. E. Murphy (Ithaca, NY: Cornell University Press, 1948), p. 156.

60 Alexander Hamilton to T. Sedgewick, 2 February 1799, *The Papers of Alexander Hamilton*, vol. 12, p. 452.

61 *Ibid.*, p. 453.

62 John Ferling, *Adams v. Jefferson: The Tumultuous Election of 1800* (New York: Oxford University Press, 2004), p. 115.

63 While needing elaboration, and undeniably hard to reconcile with the spirit of centralization that pervades the entire body of Hamiltonian thought, these reflections may appear as a forerunner of Jeffersonian doctrine. Cf. Madison, Hamilton, Jay, *The Federalist Papers*, especially nos. 23, and 26.

It is now appropriate to quote the core of the arguments set forth in the resolutions:

> The several States composing the U.S. of America are not united on the principle of unlimited submission to their general government; but that by a compact under the style and title of a Constitution for the United States, and of amendments thereto, they constituted a general government for special purposes—delegated to that government certain definite powers, reserving, each State to itself, the residuary mass of right to their own self-government; and that whenever the general government assumes undelegated powers, its acts are unauthoritative, void and of no force: that to this compact each State acceded as a State, and is an integral party, its co-States forming, as to itself, the other party: that the government created by this compact was not made the exclusive or final judge of the extent of the powers delegated to itself; since that would have made its discretion, and not the Constitution, the measure of its powers; but that, as in all other cases of compact among powers having no common judge, each party has an equal right to judge for itself, as well of infractions as of the mode and measure of redress.[64]

Jefferson asserted that the States, inasmuch as they were sovereign parties entering into the constitutional compact, had created the federal government simply as their agent, subordinate to their own power, and designed to carry out limited and well-defined functions. As a result, the federal government had no right to expand its own sphere of authority without the agreement of the contracting parties.

In Jefferson's original formulation of the Resolutions, each individual state, when dealing with controversies that concerned the Constitution, had the right to establish two things: 1) whether

64 Jefferson, "Draft of the Kentucky Resolutions of 1798," *The Papers of Thomas Jefferson*, vol. 30, p. 536.

the pact had been breached and, if such a breach had occurred, 2) whether the measures required to restore the order had been disrupted. Jefferson argued in favor of the existence of a "natural right" of each state to declare the illegitimacy of an act of Congress deemed to be contrary to the constitutional contract. Furthermore, in the draft submitted to the Kentucky assembly, he had used the term *nullification* to refer specifically to that particular right.[65] This term would prove to be of crucial importance in American history. The nullification crisis of the early 1830s, which saw the state of South Carolina pitted alone and defiantly against the government of the United States and President Andrew Jackson, is generally considered to be one of the landmark stages on the path toward the great crisis that eventually culminated in the Civil War.

That Jefferson was the author of the document had always been strongly suspected, but when in 1832 the original version of the Resolutions was found among his papers, complete with the word "nullification" in his unmistakable handwriting, the nullifiers scored a decisive point in their favor and began to regard the Virginia and Kentucky resolutions as part of the Constitution of the country. Jefferson's authorship was revealed by the *Richmond Enquirer* on 16 March 1832. The debate on the right of a state to nullify on its own territory a federal law was of such moment that the paper engaged in a veritable philological exercise, comparing the document approved by the Virginian assembly (written by Madison) with the Jeffersonian original.

The crucial passage was contained in the eighth Kentucky resolution, which addresses the issue of how to set things right in the case of a constitutional infringement.

> In cases of an abuse of the delegated powers, the members of the General Government, being chosen by the people, a change by the People would be the Constitutional Remedy; but, where powers are assumed which have not been delegated, a nullification of the act is the rightful remedy: that

65 *Ibid.*, p. 539.

> every State has a natural right in cases not within the compact (*casus non foederis,*) to nullify of their own authority all assumptions of power by others.[66]

Essentially, then, in the case of "ordinary abuses," those occurring within the scope of the powers that the Constitution firmly vests in the federal government, the remedy would lie in the free succession of political majorities and minorities (in a nutshell, democracy), without the States acting in their own right. But when the federal government reached for powers that had not been delegated, each state would become the champion of its own citizens and the guarantor of the original constitutional compact. This function, whereby a state protects its own citizens against the encroachments of the federal government—effectively shielding them from unconstitutional laws—would later be called also the power of "interposition," a term favored by James Madison.[67] As Kevin Gutzman points out, "whatever Jefferson's and Madison's intentions, the compact theory of the Constitution enunciated in Virginia and Kentucky Resolutions had this in common with the tree of knowledge: the forbidden fruit (nullification or secession) likely would be eaten sometime."[68]

---

66 Jefferson, "Drafts of the Kentucky Resolutions of 1798," *The Papers of Thomas Jefferson*, vol. 30, p. 539. The one significant addition to the second Kentucky Resolution of 1799 was the sentence: "That the several States, who formed that instrument, being sovereign and independent, have the unquestionable right to judge of its infraction; and that a nullification by those sovereignities of all unauthorized acts done under the color of that instrument, is the rightful remedy," quoted in Warfield, *The Kentucky Resolutions*, pp. 125–26.

67 Interestingly, about thirty years before, Edmund Burke had sketched a similar notion, albeit, of course, in a different context: "Indeed, in the situation in which we stand, with an immense revenue, an enormous debt, mighty establishments, government itself a great banker and a great merchant, I see no other way for the preservation of a decent attention to public interest in the representatives, but *the interposition of the body of the people itself*, whenever it shall appear, by some flagrant and notorious act, by some capital innovation, that these representatives are going to overlap the fences of the law" ("Thoughts on the Present Discontents, 1765," *The Portable Burke*, ed. Isaac Kramnik [London-New York: Penguin, 1999], pp. 141–42.)

68 Kevin R. Gutzman, "A Troublesome Legacy: James Madison and The Principles of '98," *Journal of the Early Republic*, vol. 15, No. 4 (Winter, 1995), p 581.

Both the Kentucky and Virginia resolutions ended with an appeal to the *co-States*, urging them to orchestrate common actions to banish from the legal system the horrors brought about by the 1798 acts. In the southern states, Jefferson's party was gaining strength, while the whole of the North was firmly in the hands of the Federalists. In the North, the states debated and passed documents stating their formal disapproval of the resolutions, while in the South the strength of the Jeffersonians was sufficient to forestall any action of this kind, but not enough to pass motions of approval of the Kentucky and Virginia doctrines.

The tone of the states' responses varied widely, but the leading theme seems to have been that the States were not empowered to judge federal laws, for which there already existed an arbiter: the Supreme Court. Only Vermont actually questioned the premise that the union originated in a contract entered into by the parties, and this is a clear indication that the notion of the union advanced by Jefferson and Madison was not a truly contentious issue.[69]

The propositions voted on by the assemblies of Kentucky ("to this compact each State acceded as a State, and is an integral part, its co-States forming, as to itself, the other party") and Vermont ("the people of the United States formed the federal Constitution, and not the States, or their Legislatures") embody the whole of the controversy that would trouble the union during its first decades of life. The subsequent doctrinal reflections of John C. Calhoun and Daniel Webster in the 1830s embellished the arguments with erudite and sophisticated analyses, adding historical, logical, and philosophical rigor to a controversy born in this simple opposition. And even though in 1798 slavery had nothing to do with the issue at hand, it is interesting to note that the notion of the Constitution being a compact, founded on the States and entered into voluntarily, was championed by the South, while the centralizing and "consolidating" credo—summarized in the quite bizarre notion that the American people were to be considered as a whole—was expounded by a northern state.

69 See Frank M. Anderson, "Contemporary Opinion of the Virginia and Kentucky Resolutions. Part II," *American Historical Review* 5, no. 2 (December 1899), pp. 225-252. It is the second of a two-part essay by the same title. The first part was published in the preceding issue of the same journal (5, no. 1, October 1899, pp. 45–63).

In a letter written to Madison dated August 1799, Jefferson proposed that Virginia and Kentucky should proceed side by side and in a very resolute manner. Having taken note of the responses from the other states, he was now convinced that it was necessary to "answer the reasoning of such of the States that have ventured in the field of reason ... they have given us all the advantage we could wish." Further, it was necessary to strongly reiterate the principles laid down a few months earlier, and to "express in affectionate & conciliatory language our warm attachment to the union with our sister-States" but at the same time to make it clear that "[we are] determined, were we to be disappointed in this, to sever ourselves from that union we so much value, rather than give up the rights of self-government which we have reserved, and in which alone we see liberty, safety & happiness."[70] Rarely do we find a clearer expression of the view that a preference for freedom and limited government can imply the relative decrease of the significance of the union. From that moment on, this was to become one of the classic Jeffersonian themes: Freedom and self-government cannot be subordinated to the union. Adrienne Koch and Harry Ammon state it very clearly: "By his willingness to consider the grave possibility of separation from the union, Jefferson showed that he placed no absolute value upon 'union.' Compared to the *extreme* evil of ruthless violation of liberty, a destruction of the compact which bound the States together was the *lesser* evil."[71]

For Jefferson, as for many political thinkers of the period prior to the Civil War, the union was an experiment in liberty and in no way constituted an end in its own right. During his presidency, Jefferson wrote to Joseph Priestley that it was ultimately of little relevance to the happiness of Americans whether the union was preserved or abandoned in favor of Atlantic and Mississippi confederacies. In Jefferson's words, if an upheaval of this kind occurred, the people "of the western confederacy will be as much our children & descendants as those of the eastern, and I feel myself

70 Jefferson to J. Madison, 23 August 1799, ed. Adrienne Koch, published in the *Library of Congress Information Bulletin* (August 1947), pp. 4-11.

71 Koch and Ammon, "The Virginia and Kentucky Resolutions," p. 167.

as much identified with that country, in future time, as with this."[72] It was the right of self-government, and not necessarily the union, that guaranteed the safety and happiness of citizens.

The resolutions also include also the assertion of a classical postulate of liberal constitutionalism. "Confidence is everywhere the parent of despotism—free government is founded in jealousy, and not in confidence. ... In questions of power, then, let no more be heard of confidence in man, but bind him down from mischief by the chains of the Constitution."[73] According to David Mayer, this embodies "the most succinct expression of ... Jefferson's constitutionalism."[74] As can be seen, although the author of the Declaration was known for his boundless trust in man's unlimited potential to improve himself through education and the use of reason, when it was a matter of political power, and thus of the authority some men exert over others of their kind, then he was not inclined to embrace a meaningless and generic "anthropological optimism." The Jeffersonian construction of the Constitution is an attempt to build up an impregnable bulwark against the doctrine of implicit powers formulated by Alexander Hamilton. Such a defense centered on the Tenth Amendment to the Constitution as the keystone of the whole American federal system. Notably, the amendment is cited twice and at full length in the resolutions.

To grasp the reasons supporting an unbiased assessment of Jeffersonian thought on the nature of the union, we must debunk the myth that the Constitution contains some sort of "federal supremacy" clause, a notion dear to twentieth century jurists. The Tenth Amendment summarizes the partitioning of spheres of authority between the federal government and State governments—powers not delegated to the United States remain with the States or the people. However, many scholars hold this to be in sharp contradiction to Article VI of the Constitution, which they understand to establish a federal supremacy clause because it

72 Jefferson to J. Priestley, 29 January 29, 1804, *The Writings of Thomas Jefferson*, vol. 10, p. 447.

73 Jefferson, "Drafts of the Kentucky Resolutions of 1798," *The Papers of Thomas Jefferson*, vol. 30, p. 540.

74 Mayer, *The Constitutional Thought of Thomas Jefferson*, p. 205.

establishes the "supreme law of the land." In any case, the articles would not resolve the problem of the antinomies within the United States legal system. We are faced here with an exclusive alternative. Either the federal supremacy clause applies, in which case any State law contrary to the federal law "disappears," or the point of view is inverted, and a court can judge whether the federal law oversteps the powers that have been delegated to it, in which case it falls into abeyance.

John C. Calhoun objected to this castle of cards. His objection, to my mind, is decisive and worth considering here because it seems to be fully in line with the Jeffersonian analysis. "The clause [within Article 6] is declaratory; ... it vests no new power whatever in the government, or in any of its departments;" in effect, the article does not establish anything at all, much less a supremacy of the federal order, which "results from the nature of the relation between the federal government, and those of the several States, and their respective constitutions and laws." For when a common constitution and government are set up, "the authority of these, *within the limits of the delegated powers*, must, of necessity, be supreme. ... Without this, there would be neither a common constitution and government, nor even a confederacy." The entire construction would be nonexistent: "But this supremacy is not an absolute supremacy. ... It does not extend beyond the delegated powers—all others being reserved to the States and the people of the States. Beyond these the constitution is as destitute of authority, and as powerless as a blank piece of paper; and the measures of the government mere acts of assumption."[75]

3.5) Common Law and Federalism

The Jeffersonian vision is that of a libertarian federalism. If, in using this term, we emphasize "federalism," we find the idea of a government entrusted with a limited number of functions, and a federal power strictly regulated by a constitutional pact, able to expand its powers only with the consent of the contracting parties (the States). In this view, the rights of local self-government

75 John C. Calhoun, "A Discourse on the Constitution and Government of the United States" (1851), *Works*, vol. 1, pp. 252-53.

circumscribe an agent, the federal government, whose referent is not a single people, but the peoples of the several States. If, on the other hand, we emphasize the adjective "libertarian," we find that natural rights are the supreme political end for which governments have been legitimately constituted among men. Federalism should be *prima facie* nothing other than the form of government most suited to achieving a vital political end of paramount importance; that is, the freedom of individuals to enjoy their own natural rights.

Yet the libertarian view does not fit the Jeffersonian model. The self-government of the States and their supremacy over the federal government have a peculiar and highly distinctive status in Jeffersonian thought; federalism can in no way be relegated to the role of a simple means for achievement of an end, even individual freedom. The federal division of powers is not one of the possible devices to obtain the goal of liberty; rather, it is an end in itself.

The two-year period 1798–1799 was a time during which an underlying political consensus grew up around the era's great questions—a consensus reflecting the Jeffersonian view—under the onslaught of the centralist tendencies embodied by the Federalist Party.[76] If the public debt and the Bank of the United States had been the consensus-building factors of the early 1790s, by the end of the decade the most deeply felt problem was the consolidation of power, the recognition that within the American system the potential despot was the government in Washington and not the governments of the States.

One of the notions most detrimental to states' rights, and a view that pervaded the entire Federalist faction, was that there existed an American common law. The boundaries of this general federal legal system were rather vague, but the claim was made that the rupture of the Revolution had, in some sense, spared

76 The formation of a sort of "Jeffersonian consensus" is witnessed by a number of works, such as George Hay, *An Essay on the Liberty of the Press* (1799) (Richmond, VA: Samuel Pleasant, 1803); Tunis D. Wortman, *A Treatise Concerning Political Enquiry, and the Liberty of the Press* (New York: George Forman, 1800); Madison's Report of 1799, *Virginia Report*, 189-235; and many lesser-known works. On this subject, cf. Levy, *Freedom of Speech and Press*, 267-297, although the author focuses solely on freedom of the press, going as far as defining "libertarian" as "favorable to the utmost freedom of expression."

the English legal tradition, or, alternatively, that the Articles of Confederation and eventually the Constitution itself had reinstated the principles of common law at the federal level. The response to this claim blended the two central aspects of Jefferson's political thought that have been addressed throughout this work. First, in Jefferson's view, the introduction of common law was a rejection of the revolutionary break. It was tantamount to a return to a remote past and a huge step backwards for the American experiment. Reason, not English precedent, should be the foundation of a rightful government among men. Second, the introduction of the English legal tradition into the living body of American laws would lead to an indiscriminate increase in the powers of Congress, of the president, and, above all, of the federal judiciary.

Jefferson's ideas on a common law of the United States can be properly appreciated only in the light of his general theory of federalism. In the third Kentucky resolution, he declared that the First Amendment had removed from the cognizance of the federal courts any issue involving freedom of religion, defamation, or freedom of the press and of speech. This was partly by virtue of the combined provisions of the First and Tenth amendments, whereby the powers not delegated to the union were reserved to the States or the people, so that only the States were empowered to legislate on such issues. Thus, in Jefferson's view, the Bill of Rights was to be taken literally: *Congress shall make no laws* means that the restriction applies specifically to the Congress of the United States, not to the individual States. In other words, the federal courts could only deal with cases falling within the province of federal jurisdiction, as specifically delegated by the Constitution or prohibited by its amendments.

Jefferson rejected the existence of a federal common law. There were as many common law systems as there were states, and these systems were enclosed within their own boundaries, but there existed no American common law. Let us now dwell in greater detail on the arguments put forward in the third resolution, which is frequently underestimated by scholars:

> No power over the freedom of religion, freedom of speech, or freedom of the press being delegated to the United States by the Constitution, nor prohibited by it to the States, all lawful powers respecting the same did of right remain, and were reserved to the States or the people. ... In addition ... another and more special provision has been made by one of the amendments to the Constitution, which expressly declares, that "Congress shall make no law respecting an establishment of religion, or prohibiting the free exercise thereof, or abridging the freedom of speech or of the press" thereby guarding in the same sentence, and under the same words, the freedom of religion, of speech, and of the press: insomuch, that whatever violated either, throws down the sanctuary which covers the others, and that libels, falsehood, and defamation, equally with heresy and false religion, are withheld from the cognizance of federal tribunals.[77]

Jefferson clearly intended the Bill of Rights to act as a limit to federal, but not state, powers.[78] This was by no means a sudden flight of fancy, a phrase dropped almost casually into an official document. On the contrary, it was a crucial point that can be fully apprehended only in relation to Jefferson's federalist principles.

As early as 1799, Jefferson had focused on this issue in extremely general terms in a letter to his friend Edmund Randolph. "Of all the doctrines which have ever been broached by the federal government, the novel one, of the common law being in force & cognizable as an existing law in their courts, is to me the most

77 Jefferson, "Draft of the Kentucky Resolutions," p. 537.

78 Likewise, such a notion was shared by other Jeffersonians: "[During the debate of the Sedition Act, St. George] Tucker and other Republicans recognized that the several States possessed a broad police power and in the absence of a state constitutional provision they could restrict freedom of speech. ... This Republican constitutionalism underscores that the Sedition Act controversy was essentially a question of federalism. Republicans prized liberty, but thought it best secured when power was exercised at the local level," William J.Watkins Jr., *Reclaiming the American Revolution*, pp. 41–42.

formidable."[79] The United States, he added, are a nation "*for special purposes only*."[80] And since the association was strictly limited by the Constitution, the espousal of a common law by the federal power would have wrought upheaval in the system of government "because it would have embraced objects on which this association had no right to form or declare a will."[81] Jefferson concluded with a recommendation and a note in a saddened tone: "I think it will be of great importance ... to portray at full length the consequences of this new doctrine, that the common law is the law of the U.S., & that their courts have, of course, jurisdiction coextensive with that law, that is to say, general over all cases & persons. But, great heavens! Who could have conceived in 1789 that within ten years we should have to combat such windmills."[82]

The most extensive and convincing confutation of the claim that common law had been introduced into the American federal legal system is to be found in the Virginia *Report*.[83] Madison's manner of proceeding is unexceptionable. Starting out from the colonial status of the country, he traced the effects of the Revolution that "converted the colonies into independent States," then went on to analyze the changes brought about by the Articles of Confederation, and finally ended with a reflection on "the Constitution of 1788, which is the oracle that must decide the important question."[84]

During the colonial period, common law "was the separate law of each colony within its respective limits" and had most certainly not been conceived as "a law pervading and operating through the whole, as one society."[85] Could the Revolution have led to a

79 Jefferson to E. Randolph, August 18, 1799, *The Papers of Thomas Jefferson*, vol. 31:p. 168.

80 *Ibid.*, p. 170.

81 *Ibid.*

82 *Ibid.*, pp. 170-171.

83 On the general problem of a federal common law see William B. Stoebuck, "Reception of English Common Law in the American Colonies,"*William and Mary Law Review* 10 (1968), pp. 393-426; Elizabeth Gaspar Brown, *British Statutes in American Law, 1776-1836* (Ann Arbor: University of Michigan Law School, 1964).

84 *Virginia Report*, p. 211.

85 *Ibid.*

change of perspective as far as common law was concerned? Clearly not, since the very essence of the Revolution was that Great Britain had no right to establish laws designed to be valid for the other parts of the empire. "Such being the ground of our Revolution, no support nor colour can be drawn from it, for the doctrine that the common law is binding on these States as one society. The doctrine, on the contrary, is evidently repugnant to the fundamental principle of the Revolution."[86]

Madison did not deny that some parts of common law might be held to be included in the American legal system by virtue of an explicit mention in the Constitution. But this would be the intrusion of an ambiguous English-American common law into the republican legal order. Those who support this position, Madison argued, base their arguments on the provision of Article 3, Section 2: "The judicial power shall extend to all cases *in law and equity*, arising *under this Constitution*, the laws of the United States, and treaties made or which shall be made under their authority." Yet constitutional language by no means allows such an extensive construction, and if it did, the whole of criminal law would in any case remain excluded. Madison also focused attention on a long series of technical/juridical obstacles that foil any such enterprise, namely the determination of the "quantity" and "type" of common law to be introduced in America.[87]

Jefferson and Madison worried that if common law became part of the American federal legal system, Congress would *ipso facto*, by recourse to legal measures, have the ability to revise and integrate the principles of common law, as in the English system, which is a notorious blend of customary law and law enacted by Parliament. If this were to occur, any constitutional limitation to the action of federal power would be swept away. For if "the authority of Congress is co-extensive with the objects of common law [it] would, therefore, be no longer under the limitations marked out in the Constitution. They would be authorized to legislate in all cases whatsoever."[88] If, on the other hand, common law were to

86 *Ibid.*, p. 212.

87 Cf. *Ibid.*, p. 215

88 *Ibid.*

be introduced as a limitation on federal legislative activity, then it would be the judiciary that would have "a discretion little short of a legislative power."[89] Taken together, this would mean that, once common law became established within the American system, nothing would ever be the same again. Change would affect not only the features of the federal government but also the relation between the latter and State governments. In conclusion, common law would become a body of law that could "sap the foundation of the Constitution as a system of limited and specified powers."[90]

In *United States v. Hudson and Goodwin* (1812),[91] Jefferson and his party scored an important victory. The issue was whether the circuit courts of the United States could exercise a common law jurisdiction in criminal cases. The court denied them that authority: "The legislative authority of the Union must first make an act a crime, affix a punishment to it, and declare the court that shall have jurisdiction of the offence."[92] The abolition of common law jurisdiction in 1812 represented a moment when the implications of the Constitution's structure ultimately caught up with experience. It crystallized the recognition—suggested in 1798—that the Constitution and the common law could not coexist and that the American system of government had broken off from its English antecedents more sharply than anyone had appreciated.

Peter DuPonceau, author of an 1824 work on jurisdiction in the early republic, expressed this opinion:

> The revolution has produced a different state of things in this country. Our political institutions no longer depend on uncertain traditions, but on the more solid foundation of express written compacts. ... The common law... is to be considered in the United States in no other light than that of a system of jurisprudence ... [and] no longer the *source* of power or jurisdiction. ... But old habits of thinking

89 *Ibid.*, p. 216.

90 *Ibid.*, p. 217.

91 11 US (7 Cranch) 32 (1812).

92 *Ibid.*, p. 34.

> are not easily laid aside; we might have gone on for many years longer confounding the English with the American common law, if cases had not been brought before the federal Courts, so serious in their nature, and apparently fraught with such dangerous consequences, that hesitation was produced, and the public attention was at last drawn to this important subject.[93]

In spite of the Jeffersonian consensus that was building up around these issues, the nationalists were not inactive. In 1816, Joseph Story stated that "it can hardly be doubted, that the constitution and laws of the United States are predicated upon the existence of the common law." The common law served as an essential ingredient in the "construction and interpretation of federal powers."[94] Story went on to elaborate the types of crimes subsumed under the common law: "All offences against the sovereignty, the public rights, the public justice, the public peace, the public trade and the public police of the United States, are crimes and offences against the United States."[95] Story's seemingly modest desire to provide the fragile United States government power to protect itself against criminals contained illimitable implications. Just as the Jeffersonians had predicted, Story was ready to vest the national government with an indefeasible sovereignty, using federal common law as a Trojan horse.[96]

Behind the dispute on federal common law lies another, which is of even greater significance. Freedom of speech, as we have seen, was in Jefferson's view one of the preeminent natural rights of the individual. Yet he was prepared, theoretically at least, to imagine

93 Peter S. Duponceau, *A Dissertation on the Nature and Extent of the Jurisdiction of the Courts of the United States* (Philadelphia: Abraham Small, 1824), p. 9.

94 Joseph Story's opinion in *United States v. Coolidge* [1816] quoted in Duponceau, *A Dissertation*, p. 237.

95 *Ibid.*, p. 238.

96 However, as late as 1834 the Supreme Court rejected the idea of a federal common law, asserting that "there is no principle which pervades the Union and has the authority of law, that is not embodied in the constitution or laws of the Union. ... It is clear, there can be no common law of the United States." *Wheaton v. Peters* [1834] 33 US (8 Pet.) 591: pp. 657-658.

that the States could occasionally violate it. But never would the federal government be allowed to encroach upon it. Between libertarianism, which implied that any infringement of a sacred and inviolable law is totally disallowed, and federalism, founded on the full self-government of the States and on rigid, precisely defined fields of federal intervention, Jefferson seems to have been almost more inclined to jettison the former in order to go the whole way in pursuing the latter.

At the end of the day, Jefferson was a classical liberal who believed in the people as the best safeguard of freedom and natural rights. What prevented him from assuming the existence of a vast political community denominated United States, or, simply America, devoted to the protection of the natural rights of individuals and complying with majority rule? Why are the States, and not the federal government, "the true barriers of our liberty"? Plainly, in Jefferson's eyes federalism was not merely the manner in which the American republic had historically become structured, but something immeasurably more important; that is, the very essence of the American experiment in self-government. As Kevin Gutzman puts it, "federalism for Jefferson underlay the constitutional vision America's revolution had been fought to vindicate."[97]

Jefferson used the terms monarchic and Anglophiles (actually, *Anglomen*, one of the many terms he introduced into the English language, together with *monocrats*, a word used to indicate exponents of the Federalist Party) to refer to his political opponents. It mattered little that the latter perhaps had no intention of importing a monarch into America. He sought to state the nature of the English model they were trying to impose. The essence of that model, as he saw it, lay in the "parliamentary sovereignty" typical of the English system as it had been produced by the Glorious Revolution. "Parliamentary sovereignty" had permanently supplanted the concept of "popular sovereignty," even though popular sovereignty had been enshrined in a doctrinal formulation worked out by his champions of the Whig tradition. Jefferson was convinced that parliamentary sovereignty was just as

97 Kevin R. C. Gutzman, *Thomas Jefferson, Revolutionary,* p. 55.

dangerous a notion as the concept of monarchy and in many ways indistinguishable from it.

Jefferson had grasped something that eluded many of his contemporaries, namely that the parliament was the true heir of the sovereign, and, in particular, Congress represented the true heir of the English crown. The struggle of political Enlightenment for the disruption of the center of monarchical power risked being reproduced indefinitely if the new sovereign (the legislature) were not bound by a well-defined scope and insurmountable limits. Only in this context can one fully appreciate the significance of his statements on the nonexistence of an American common law and those on the Bill of Rights as a limit applying only to federal power; that is, on the predominance of the States *vis-à-vis* their agent.

What Jefferson feared was the rise of something we might today describe as "legal globalism." It should never be forgotten that if the author of the Declaration is, in a sense, the first *Homo Americanus*—the one who was the first to use the term "Americanism"—he was also very clear on what he meant by "my country." Whenever he used this expression, he always meant Virginia. This is not a case of localism or particularism, coming as it does from one of the greatest exponents of Enlightenment cosmopolitanism. Furthermore, in American political history, the negative connotation of the term "localism" has not gained much ground. The dominating political culture in America, above and beyond the situations shaped in the different historical periods and their resulting general political trends, has always interpreted the relation between localism and freedom as being of the utmost importance.

3.6) The Judge of Last Resort

Stripped to the bone, the essence of the concept delineated in the Kentucky Resolutions was that the States are the ultimate judges of the constitutionality of any federal legislative measure. This undeniably involves a rigorously contractual and voluntary basis for the union. But let us analyze other possible interpretations.

First, the one that ultimately became predominant during the twentieth century, but which could already be glimpsed in the answers to the Resolutions given by the states controlled by the Federalists: The Supreme Court, a branch of the federal government, is the arbiter in conflicts between the States and the federal government itself. In this respect, Jefferson's objection appears rather reasonable. It is the very structure of the Constitution itself that is undermined, since the extent of the powers of a part of the federal system is being adjudicated by the part itself and not by the Constitution. More generally, it is difficult to deny that if the States had been required to comply with any federal law whatsoever, whether in accordance with the Constitution or in flagrant disregard of the latter, then the system of guarantees known as "federalism" would become a mere *flatus vocis*.

The entire Jeffersonian construct of states' rights is grounded is the analogy between relations among men and relations among the States within the federal compact. Thus, there exists no common judge among the parties to the constitutional compact. They are sovereign in establishing the just remedy for a violation of the pact. The ratification of the Constitution notwithstanding, the States find themselves facing one another while still fully endowed with all their natural rights, exactly like individuals in the "state of nature."

As early as the end of the eighteenth century, the Supreme Court began to assume the function of arbiter of conflicts between the States and the federal government, even though this was not authorized by any specific provision of the Constitution. Section 25 of the 1789 Judiciary Act, approved shortly after the new constitution had come into force, allowed the Supreme Court to decide on appeals concerning 1) sentences issued by the courts pertaining to matters regulated by the Constitution, 2) laws approved by Congress 3) and treaties of the United States. One crucial conflict between Jefferson's federal theory and what had, by then, become the approach adopted by the American federal system in that period specifically concerned the powers of the Supreme Court.

While, as we have seen, Rhode Island, Massachusetts, New York, New Hampshire, and Vermont argued that the highest federal office of the judiciary was also the final arbiter of the constitutionality of federal laws, Jefferson and Madison strongly denied this claim. Madison clarified the question in a fairly persuasive manner in his 1799 *Report*: "However true, therefore, it may be, that the judicial department, is, in all questions submitted to it by the forms of the Constitution, to decide in the last resort, this resort must necessarily be deemed the last in relation to the authorities of the other departments of the government; not in relation to the rights of the parties to the constitutional compact, from which the judicial as well as the other departments hold their delegated trusts."[98] When the problem of whether a federal legislative measure did or did not comply with the Constitution was left to the operation of the system of checks and balances, the ultimate judge could in no way be the Supreme Court, which was a creation of the pact itself, inasmuch as it was a department of the federal government. Rather, the ultimate judge was the individual State, as an original party to the constitutional compact.

But according to the most widely held opinion (both today and at the time of Jefferson), a judge of last resort is needed, one who provides a definitive resolution and establishes justice in controversies between the States and the federation once and for all, and who provides the final word on any question. Jefferson's answer concerning the final arbiter is unexceptionable and coherent. In 1823, he wrote to Judge William Johnson regarding the case *Cohens v. The State of Virginia* in which Chief Justice Marshall had maintained that there had to be an ultimate arbiter: "The ultimate arbiter is the people of the Union, assembled by their deputies in convention, at the call of Congress, or of two-thirds of the States.[99] Let them decide to which they mean to give an authority claimed by two of their organs. And it has been the peculiar wisdom and

98 *Virginia Report*, pp. 195-96.

99 Article 5 provides that two-thirds of State assemblies can submit an amendment to the Constitution, but it needs to be approved by the vote of the assemblies or conventions of three-quarters of the States. The true "supermajority" needed to amend the Constitution is thus three-quarters of the States.

felicity of our constitution, to have provided this peaceable appeal, where that of other nations is at once to force."[100]

Thus, the people have the final word—not a metaphysical and constitutionally nonexistent American people, assembled in a single mass—but rather the peoples of the various States represented in purpose-convened conventions with the aim of amending, abolishing, or modifying the government of the union, exactly as prescribed by Article 5 of the Constitution. In a letter to the Virginian judge Spencer Roane, Jefferson denied that the Supreme Court should have any power of interpreting the Constitution of the United States. This was true, he maintained, not just in relation to controversies among States, or between the latter and the federal government, but also among the branches of the federal government itself.[101] For there could be no common judge among the parties of the constitutional compact, neither the Supreme Court, nor, much less, the federal government itself, since the federal government was not the arbiter of the pact but was instead its object.

As mentioned earlier, in a different historical and doctrinal context John Calhoun would take up the Jeffersonian theory, but release it from the conceptual framework of natural law and uphold it purely on the grounds of the sovereignty of the individual federated State. For Jefferson, however, the "natural law model" of Lockean inspiration, once it had been transposed by pure analogy from individuals to the States, was sufficient to allow him to assert the characteristics of the American union. Thus, he never resorted to a theory of "sovereignty" (a term that does not even appear in the Kentucky Resolutions) in order to claim that the States are "free and independent." It is the nature of their bond with each other that makes them such and not their character as original political communities.

This must be the starting point for appreciating the unity and internal coherence of Jeffersonian thought on federalism. It is nonetheless a complex approach, contrasting with much of the

100 Jefferson to W. Johnson, June 12, 1823, in *The Writings of Thomas Jefferson*, vol. 15, p. 451.

101 See Jefferson to S. Roane, September 6, 1819, *The Writings of Thomas Jefferson*, ed. P. L. Ford (New York: Putnam, 1893-99), vol. 10, pp. 140–43.

thought elaborated by subsequent theory, and, most crucially, at variance with the distinction between federation and confederation of States, a distinction as disputable as it was successful. However, the States' rights doctrine was, by the beginning of the century, firmly planted in the political arena of the early Republic, and before it became a purely Southern thing, the New England Federalists were ready to adopt it.

Chapter 4

New England Tried Secession: The Hartford Convention of 1814

> The doctrine of States' Rights was in itself a sound and true doctrine, as a starting point of American history and constitutional law, there is no other which will bear a moment's examination.[1]
>
> –Henry Adams

Plymouth Rock and Jamestown are not two sides of the same coin, but irreducible and antithetical entities, which barely find a possible convergence even today. Yet the Hartford Convention of 1814 reveals a deep link between the two parts of what, at the time, could hardly be considered a nation. New England and the southern states both wished to take advantage of the Union in order to increase the influence of their own sections and, conversely, they desired to abandon the Union when their own area was perceived to be in a losing position.

Thanks to the Jeffersonian revolution of 1800 and the Republicans' thriving in the following years, up to Madison's presidencies, Virginia became the heart of America. The Federalist Party, headquartered in Massachusetts and representing the interests of the North, immediately realized that "Mr. Madison's War" was a deadly attack on their role in the Union. The Hartford Convention was the attempt of a political class, which had always been sectional, to overcome the devastating economic effects of the war.

1 Henry Adams, *John Randolph, A Biography*, Introduction by Robert McColley (Armonk, NY: ME Sharpe, 1996), p. 179.

4.1) Mr. Madison's War

Considered for a long time as only a peripheral theater of the Napoleonic Wars, the conflict of 1812 has been recently enjoying thorough attention, especially in the United States (at times superabundant attention: the related literature gained momentum some years ago due to the bicentennial).[2]

Alan Taylor considers the war a nonevent in terms both of politics and borders,[3] while Gordon Wood calls it "the strangest war in American history."[4] Nevertheless, several scholars have celebrated it as the "second War of Independence," given the fact that the enemy was the same. From a patriotic point of view, it is well known that Francis Scott Key wrote the anthem *Star Spangled Banner* while observing the British bombardment of Baltimore. However, the Hartford Convention was, in fact, an extreme attempt by New England to restate her own irreducible hostility toward a union by then controlled by the Virginian dynasty and the Jeffersonian party.

From the beginning of the War of 1812, Republican policies were the subject of severe criticism in the North. In an oft-quoted sermon, Reverend William Ellery Channing of Boston did not foresee any good coming to his section from the conflict. "We are precipitated into a war, which, I think, cannot be justified—and a war, which promises not a benefit, that I can discover, to this country or to the world." Besides, the war had been caused by deranged commercial restrictions to the detriment of New England: "By this war much of our property is placed beyond our reach—shut up in the ports of our enemy ... in consequence of a severe law of our own government." In brief, it was "a war fraught with ruin to our

---

2 Already several years ago, the historiography was imposing. See Donald R. Hickey, *The War of 1812: Still a Forgotten Conflict? An Historiographical Essay*, in *The Journal of Military History* 65, no. 3, July 2001, pp. 741-769; cf. more recently the debate in *Journal of American History*, no. 2, September 2012, pp. 520-555. There are two journals focusing on the war: *Journal of the War of 1812* and *War of 1812 Magazine*.

3Alan Taylor, *The Civil War of 1812: American Citizens, British Subjects, Irish Rebels, & Indian Allies* (New York: Vintage Books, 2010), p. 11.

4 Gordon S. Wood, *Empire of Liberty. A History of the Early Republic, 1789-1815* (New York: Oxford University Press), p. 659.

property, our morals, our religion, our independence, our dearest rights, whilst its influence on other nations, on the common cause of humanity, is most unhappy."[5]

At first, the Federalists were so wary and cautious that the Republican hope to eliminate their opposition seemed quite possible. In the following months, the opposition to the war increased steadily, and not only in the North:

> By the fall of 1812 Federalists in the middle and southern states had joined their friends in New England to present a united front against the war. ... Talk of supporting the war evaporated when Federalists in Washington saw what kind of war it was to be. Attempts to limit the war to the high seas and to include France in the hostilities had been defeated; the restrictive system had been retained and even expanded; and a tax program had been adopted that discriminated against the North. Under these circumstances Federalists in Congress lost all heart for supporting the war. Instead, they united against it.[6]

John Gardiner of the Trinity Church of Boston delivered a sermon during a day of public fasting against the war, which was proclaimed in Massachusetts on July 23, 1812. The conflict was "the greatest of national calamities," he said, since the United States "have neither army, nor navy, nor money, nor inclination, to flatter us with the remotest probability of success, and which must terminate in the disgrace of our arms, and possibly in the loss of our liberties." Gardiner stated that "as Mr. Madison has declared war, let Mr. Madison carry it on." But his main purpose was to challenge the very idea of the Union, as there is indeed "an essential difference of interest between the southern and eastern

5 William Ellery Channing, *A Sermon Preached in Boston, July 23, 1812*, in *Memoir of William Ellery Channing: With Extracts from His Correspondence and Manuscripts*, vol. 1 (London: Forgotten Books, 1850), pp. 338-9.

6 Donald R. Hickey, *War of 1812: A Forgotten Conflict* (Urbana: University of Illinois Press, 2012), p. 50.

states of the union." History is at such a juncture that you "must either ... cut the connexion, or so far alter the national constitution, as to ensure yourselves a due share in the government. ... The union has long since been virtually dissolved, and it is full time that this portion of the dis-united states should take care of itself."[7]

The Republicans, conversely, considered the risks of the war to be less than the potential benefits, as they expected concessions "from the British [to] vindicate American independence, preserve republican institutions, maintain power, unify their party, and silence the Federalists."[8]

What they foresaw as the consequence of a possible victory was the final demise of their only real opposition in the country, the Federalists, who at the time were located only in New England. The Federalists, on their part, had by then understood "that the Republicans sought to destroy the future prospects of their party. Consequently, most of the Federalists did their best to frustrate a war effort that seemed ideologically driven to ruin them."[9] It was undoubtedly a "party war designed to further the interest of Republicans and to silence the opposition."[10]

For some years, at least since mid-1807, because of the aggressive policy of the European powers, President Jefferson had been considering going to war both against Great Britain and Spain, the latter being allied with Napoleon. In the end, though, he preferred a total embargo on all American exports to Europe in the belief that once deprived of the essential goods they could only obtain from trading with America, the European powers would soon come to an agreement. The embargo, which was enacted by Congress in December 1807, destroyed more than 80 percent of American

7 John S. J. Gardiner, *A Discourse, Delivered at Trinity Church, Boston, July 23, 1812* (Boston: Munroe & Francis, 1812), pp. 3, 17, 18-19, quoted in Daniel Corbett Wewers, *The Specter of Disunion in the Early American Republic*, Ph.D. Dissertation, 2008, pp. 193-194.

8 Donald R. Hickey, *War of 1812*, p. 26.

9 Alan Taylor, "Dual Nationalisms: Legacies of the War of 1812," in *What So Proudly We Hailed: Essays on the Contemporary Meaning of the War of 1812*, eds. Pietro S. Nivola and Peter J. Kastor (Washington DC: Brookings Institution Press, 2012), p. 68.

10 Donald R. Hickey, *War of 1812*, p. 262.

trade, triggering the most severe economic depression since the Revolution. It is clear that during the embargo Massachusetts became the stronghold of the resistance to Jefferson's and then Madison's party.

4.2) From Virginia to Connecticut

Only a couple of years after the Kentucky Resolutions were passed, the position of New England and of its party of choice, the Federalists, had changed considerably. Jefferson's victory, along with the Republican surge, determined a shift of power toward the South and the West. Only then did the idea of abandoning the Union begin to be debated more or less openly. Senator William Plumer of New Hampshire stated that New England would be forced "to establish a separate and independent empire."[11]

Jefferson's purchase of Louisiana in 1803 caused a change of perspective and a realignment of New England with political views that verged on the edge of secession. The fear of northeastern political elites was that their cultural and geographic area—that of the Puritans of pure English lineage—would lose the political weight it had had in 1787 (and which it would regain during and after the Civil War). This threatening situation was caused not only by the Jeffersonian victory and, therefore, the command of a political class deemed incompatible with New England, but also to the enlargement of the Union. On the one hand, the acquisition of French Louisiana (a deal which doubled the territory of the United States) fulfilled Jefferson's vision of supplying Americans with new land, where anyone could escape from poverty and oppression and lead an independent life as a farmer, hunter, or merchant. However, it also brought extremely complex constitutional challenges, as well as rivalries between New England and the South.

In a letter to Richard Peters in 1803, Timothy Pickering talked openly about the formation of "a new confederacy, exempt from the corrupt and corrupting influence and oppression of the aristocratic Democrats of the South." Undoubtedly, "there will be ... a separation. The white and black population will mark the

11 Quoted in Forrest McDonald, *States' Rights and the Union,* p. 61.

boundary. The British Provinces, even with the assent of Britain, will become members of the Northern Confederacy. A continued tyranny of the present ruling sect will precipitate that event."[12]

In 1804 a small group of Federalists, including Timothy Pickering;[13] James Hillhouse, senator of Connecticut; William Plumer, senator and later governor of New Hampshire; Uriah Tracy; and Roger Griswold, decided to form a Northern Confederacy. The 1804 conspiracy was based on a strategy which contemplated the election of Aaron Burr as governor of the State of New York and a subsequent declaration of secession which would launch the secessionist movement. Nevertheless, Burr lost the election, killed Alexander Hamilton in a duel, and became an authentic pariah in America. As Forrest McDonald states, "in all likelihood, the conspiracy would have failed even if Burr had been elected: popular support was limited."[14]

In addition to their ambition to see Burr victorious in the 1804 New York gubernatorial election, they "hoped to elect Federalist majorities to the various state legislatures of New England." Then, "by acts of their state legislatures, New England and New York would remove themselves from the Jeffersonian-tainted Union to form a separate and commercially powerful confederacy, where it was assumed that the Federalist vision of society and polity would dominate."[15] Unfortunately for Pickering and his co-conspirators, the plan failed to generate the expected support among their constituents, the 1804 state elections in New England returned Republican majorities, Burr was defeated in New York, and the conspiracy collapsed as a result.

12 Pickering to Richard Peters, December 23, 1803, in Henry Adams, *Documents Relating to New England Federalism, 1800–1815* (Boston: Little, Brown, 1877), p. 338.

13About the most fervent secessionist of the time see Gerald H. Clarfield, *Timothy Pickering and the American Republic* (Pittsburgh: University of Pittsburgh Press, 1980).

14 Forrest McDonald, *States' Rights and the Union,* p. 61.

15 See Kevin M. Gannon, "Escaping 'Mr. Jefferson's Plan of Destruction': New England Federalists and the Idea of a Northern Confederacy, 1803–1804," *Journal of the Early Republic* 21, no. 3 (Autumn, 2001), p. 414.

Despite the failure in 1804, the idea of a northern confederacy remained intact in the politics of New England, at least until the Hartford Convention of 1814. A few years later, during what is still considered one of the most famous Yankee secessionist speeches, Josiah Quincy warned the whole country that everything was going to change after the Louisiana purchase. "If this bill passes, it is my deliberate opinion that it is virtually a dissolution of the union ... it will free the States from their moral obligation; and that, as it will be the right of all, so it will be the duty of some, to prepare definitely for a separation, amicably if they can, violently if they must."[16]

Nothing, however, put New England and the South under stress more than the embargo and then the war. The Embargo Act of 1807, which totally banned American maritime trade with any foreign country, had disastrous results. New England was now clashing with Republican policies and beginning to adopt the language of states' rights. On January 25, 1809, citizens and political representatives gathered in Faneuil Hall to demonstrate against the embargo. Citizens claimed that "they looked only to the State Legislature, who were competent to devise relief against the unconstitutional acts of the General Government. That your power (say they) is adequate to that object, is evident from the organization of the Confederacy."[17] A few days later, the Massachusetts Assembly in point of fact nullified the embargo, stigmatizing it as "unjust, oppressive, and unconstitutional. While this State maintains its sovereignty and independence, all citizens can find protection against outrage and injustice in the strong arm of state government." The embargo, according to the authorities of Massachusetts, "was not legally binding on the citizens of the state."[18] The Assembly of Connecticut and that of Rhode Island approved similar documents.

---

16 *Annals of Congress*, 11th Congress, January 14, 1811, in Josiah Quincy, *Speeches Delivered in the Congress of the United States 1805–1813*, ed. Edmund Quincy (Boston: Little, Brown, 1874), p. 196.

17 Scott J. Hammond, Kevin R. Hardwick, and Howard Leslie Lubert, eds., *Classics of American Political and Constitutional Thought: Origins through the Civil War* (Indianapolis: Hackett, 2007), p. 999.

18 *Ibid.*

On June 18, 1812, after a vote of the House of Representatives and the Senate, a declaration of war against Great Britain followed: it was rejected by the Federalists but enthusiastically welcomed by the Republicans. Madison's war was perceived by the Federalists as a war against New England, rather than 'old England.' Josiah Quincy stated that the president's war cabinet was "little less than despotic, [and] it was composed by two Virginians and a foreigner."[19] The scene was such that, as a Federalist gazette maintained, "there are not two hostile nations upon earth whose views of the principles and polity of a perfect commonwealth"[20] are more distant. Hence, with the outbreak of the war, New England secessionist feelings reached their apogee.

Impressment was at the core of this calamity, as the Royal Navy recruited American citizens against their will, considering them still British subjects. Such a practice is considered a 'necessary evil' that brought about the mighty Royal Navy.[21]

While the War of 1812 could be considered an impressment crisis, Theodore Dwight, the secretary of the Hartford Convention, was right when he stated that impressment "became ... the only existing cause of war." But if it was the sole cause of war the peace treaty did not "contain the slightest allusion to that subject." In short, "war had been waged to obtain security against impressment, and they had been reduced to the necessity, after a controversy of two years and a half duration for that sole object, to make a peace without obtaining the smallest degree of that security."[22] The opposition to the war was such that "when the federal government came to New England to enlist recruits, those who did enlist were routinely

19 See Edward Payson Powell, Nullification and Secession in the United States (New York, Putnam, 1897), p. 218. It was about Madison, Monroe and Gallatin.

20 *Columbian Centinel*, January 13, 1813, quoted in James H. Ellis, *A Ruinous and Unhappy War: New England and the War of 1812* (New York: Algora, 2009), p. 238.

21 See David Brunsman, *The Evil Necessity: British Naval Impressment in the Eighteenth-Century Atlantic World* (Charlottesville: University of Virginia Press, 2013).

22 Theodore Dwight, *History of the Hartford Convention, with a Review of the Policy of the United States Government Which Led to the War of 1812* (New York and Boston, 1833), pp. 227-228.

arrested on (mostly) fictitious charges of not having paid their debts. The Federalist courts then ruled that, as debtors, these men were the "property" of creditors and therefore could not leave the state."[23]

Shortly after the declaration of war, the Assembly of Connecticut approved a resolution in order to explain their position. After proclaiming Connecticut a "FREE SOVEREIGN and INDEPENDENT State; that the United States are a confederacy of States; that we are a confederated and not a consolidated Republic," the Assembly reminded their governor of his position between the devil and the deep blue sea: "The Governor of this State is under a high and solemn obligation, '*to maintain the lawful rights and privileges thereof, as a sovereign, free and independent State,*' as he is '*to support the Constitution of the United States,*' and the obligation to support the latter imposes an additional obligation to support the former. The building cannot stand, if the pillars upon which it rests, are impaired or destroyed."[24]

4.3) The Hartford Convention

The urge to call a convention developed entirely in Massachusetts: It arose within the municipalities which, during the war and in particular since the beginning of 1814, flooded the State Assembly with documents that sought to unify the efforts "of the commercial states, to obtain such amendments and explanations of the constitution as will secure them from further evil."[25] On February 4, 1814, the Massachusetts House of Representatives and Senate passed a motion about the summons of a *Convention* of delegates from the various New England states in order to adopt "necessary measures"; it also stated, though, that the time had not come yet.[26]

23 Thomas DiLorenzo, "Yankee Confederates: New England Secession Movements Prior to the War Between the States," in *Secession, State & Liberty*, ed. David Gordon (New Brunswick, NJ: Transaction, 1998), p. 146.

24 "Report and Resolutions of Connecticut on the Militia Question," August 25, 1812, in Herman Ames, ed., *State Documents on Federal Relations*, (Philadelphia: University of Pennsylvania, 1906), p. 62.

25 Theodore Dwight, *History of the Hartford Convention*, pp. 341-342.

26 See *Ibid.*

At that point, "New England was practically in rebellion. It had seceded from united national action, and had set up a war confederacy. ... Governor Strong in October called together the legislature, and said to them that the national government had failed to fulfill the terms of the Constitution, to protect Massachusetts from invasion or attack. They must henceforth look to God and themselves. He more than hinted that the time had come for a separate New England alliance. [A Boston paper] ... declared the Union was as good as dissolved."[27]

Military disaster precipitated events: The British occupied a large part of the Maine coast, then entered Chesapeake Bay and chased the federal government off to the capital, after setting Capitol Hill and the White House on fire (August 24, 1814). Furthermore, in the fall of 1814, given the forthcoming bankruptcy, the Swiss-American Secretary of State, Albert Gallatin, had first to impose heavy taxation, and then to ask New England states for loans that were obviously rejected.

On October 5, 1814, a letter of invitation was sent to the other New England governors to send delegates to a convention in order to debate a common defense against the invader and a drastic reform of the Constitutional Pact. Nevertheless, the answer was not the expected one: Vermont and New Hampshire refused to send their delegates, even though two counties of each state sent their representatives. Rhode Island appointed four delegates, Connecticut seven, and the promoting state twelve.

Eventually, 26 delegates coming from the five New England states gathered in Hartford, Connecticut, from December 15, 1814, to January 5 of the following year. Since the call of the convention, the idea of an open declaration of secession by the New England states had spread. Therefore, Vermont and New Hampshire were represented in a rather irregular way—by only a couple of spontaneous counties per state—and the protest on this point continued throughout the three weeks of the convention. The environment was conducive for the moderates to prevail and demand only constitutional changes.

27 Edward Payson Powell, *Nullification and Secession in the United States* (New York: Putnam, 1897), pp. 219-220.

However, a journalist from the *Boston Gazette* used rather inflammatory language, contending that the delegates "can, if they should think proper, take for their example and the basis of their proceedings, the result of the Constitution of 1788 of which the revered Washington was President, and form a new frame of government," which should then "be submitted to the legislatures of the several states, for their approbation and adoption, and as was the case at that time, this new constitution can go into operation as soon as two, three, four, five, or any other number of states that may be named shall have adopted it."[28]

In the Massachusetts delegation, the most prominent figures were George Cabot, Harrison Grey Otis, Nathan Dane, and Timothy Bigelow, probably the most extreme of the group. Connecticut was represented by Chauncey Goodrich from Hartford and James Hillhouse from New Haven. John Treadwell, born in 1745, was the oldest. "With an average age of 52 years, the convention members were a mature, experienced, and respected group. In an era when lawyers were esteemed, it is worth noting 22 of the 26 delegates were attorneys. Nine were jurists."[29] On behalf of the federal government, James Monroe sent Colonel Thomas S. Jesup to monitor the operations.[30]

The moderates prevailed immediately. Even though the participants' motives and purposes have been under debate for two centuries, we can agree with Alison LaCroix:

> These gentlemen believed their project was nothing less than rescuing New England from a desperate, dependent fate as a political and cultural tributary. New England ... had sparked the first flames of the Revolution; New England ... had husbanded the nation's commercial and financial bounty; New

28 *Boston Gazette*, October 31, 1814, quoted in Forrest McDonald, *States' Rights and the Union*, p. 70.

29 James H. Ellis, A Ruinous and Unhappy War: New England and the War of 1812 (New York: Algora, 2009), p. 241.

30 See Jack Alden Clarke, "Thomas Sydney Jesup: Military Observer at the Hartford Convention," *New England Quarterly* 29, no. 3 (1956), pp. 393-399.

> England ... was the conscience of the nation. ... The Federalists believed that their countrymen, led first by Thomas Jefferson and then by James Madison, had betrayed the Republic by abandoning its founding principles of virtue, restraint, and liberty, culminating in a parricidal nightmare war that pitted the United States against the last barrier to Continental tyranny. And so the Federalists decided to act.[31]

Reckoned by most historians, and also by contemporaries, as the "last nail in the coffin of the Federalist party,"[32] the Hartford Convention has an awful reputation in American history. In fact, the protagonists spent the rest of their lives trying to clarify their motivations and to clear themselves from the infamy of traitors of the homeland-in-arms. From Otis's point of view, the meeting was "harmless as a Quaker meeting,"[33] and basically this thought was shared by several authentic secessionists who did not expect much from those who had gathered in the small Connecticut town. Josiah Quincy, perhaps the most determined anti-unionist at the time, was asked by a friend, "What *do* you suppose will be the result of this Convention?" and his witty response was "I can tell you exactly." "Can you indeed?" replied the friend, "Pray tell me what it will be." "A great pamphlet!" snorted Quincy derisively.[34]

Gouverneur Morris, the American founding father who had great expectations from the breakup of the Union, had high hopes with regard to the convention. On December 22, 1814, he wrote to Timothy Pickering: "The traitors and madmen assembled at Hartford will, I believe, if not too tame and timid, be hailed

31 Alison L. LaCroix, "A Singular and Awkward War: The Transatlantic Context of the Hartford Convention," *American Nineteenth Century History* 6, no. 1 (2005), p. 6.

32 Troy Bickham, *The Weight of Vengeance: The United States, the British Empire, and the War of 1812* (New York: Oxford University Press, 2012), p. 199.

33 Harrison Gray Otis, *Otis' Letters in Defence of the Hartford Convention* (Boston: Simon Gardner, 1824), p. IV.

34 Edmund Quincy, *Life of Josiah Quincy of Massachusetts* (Boston, 1868), p. 358, quoted in Kevin Gannon, *Nullification, Secession, or "A Great Pamphlet?": New England Federalism and the Hartford Convention Movement, 1809–1815* (unpublished paper), p. 43.

hereafter as the patriots and sages of their day and generation. May the blessing of God be upon them, to inspire their counsels and prosper their resolutions!"[35] On January 10, 1815, after the moderate tone of the convention became apparent, Morris wrote to Moss Kent, "If, on the other hand, these modest propositions are rejected, I guess that New England, finding her logic of no avail, will resort to the reason of cannon law."[36]

The issue of secession had been extensively debated in Hartford. The delegates wrote, in the document attached to the resolutions, that "if the Union be destined to dissolution, by reason of the multiplied abuses of bad administrations, it should, if possible, be the work of peaceable times, and deliberate consent." Immediately afterwards, realizing that secession had to be an individual act of the single States, they add that possibly "some new form of confederacy should be substituted among those States, which shall intend to maintain a federal relation to each other." It could be possible, the delegates specified, that "the causes of our calamities are deep and permanent" and that these are due "to implacable combinations of individuals, or of States, to monopolize power and office, and to trample without remorse upon the rights and interests of commercial sections of the Union." If so, "a separation by equitable arrangement, will be preferable to an alliance by constraint, among nominal friends, but real enemies, inflamed by mutual hatred and jealousies, and inviting by intestine divisions, contempt, and aggression from abroad. But a severance of the Union by one or more States, against the will of the rest, and especially in a time of war, can be justified only by absolute necessity."[37] Clearly, the times were not favorable, but a countermeasure could be adopted by those who had taken over the Union.

---

35 Henry Adams, *Documents Relating to New England Federalism*, p. 419.

36 Gouverneur Morris to Moss Kent, January 10, 1815, *The Diary and Letters of Gouverneur Morris*, ed. Anne Cary Morris, vol. 2 (New York: Scribners, 1888), p. 579.

37 Public Documents, Proceedings of the Hartford Convention ..., Published by order of the Senate, Boston, 1815, p. 5. (The whole *Report*, as well as the journal and the resolutions of the convention, may be found in Theodore Dwight, *History of the Hartford Convention* [Boston: Russell, 1833], pp. 352-379. A more accessible source is *Great Issues in American History: From the Revolution to the Civil War, 1765-1865*, ed. Richard Hofstadter (New York: Vintage, 1958), vol. 2, pp. 237-241.

Their grievances, indeed, in the first place concerned the system that had taken hold "in some States" in order to make "secure to popular leaders in one section of the Union, the control of publick affairs, in perpetual succession."[38] The two Virginians, who had succeeded one another as presidents, not only were the symptom of the New England misfortunes, but perhaps also the signal that the region was about to become a permanent minority inside the Union.

Clearly, the *Report* continued, the greatest caution had to be used. Nonetheless, what is of crucial importance for present purposes is that the politicians who had met in Hartford were now supporters of the Jeffersonian (and Madisonian) doctrine of "interposition" or state "nullification" of illegitimate federal laws: In the most concise, and accurate, exposition of the Jeffersonian doctrine, the *Report* stated: "In case of deliberate, palpable and dangerous violations of the Constitution, concerning the sovereignty of a State and its people's liberties, the States have a right and are in duty bound to interpose in order to protect the citizens. States which do not have a common judge must be judges themselves and execute their own decisions."[39]

The most evident cause of the break of the constitutional balance was "the admission of new States into the Union, formed at pleasure in the western region, [that] has destroyed the balance of power which existed among the original States, and deeply affected their interest."[40] In addition, the access of naturalized foreigners to the highest positions combined with the support to the French government against Great Britain had broken the balance between the two regions. The Hartford Resolutions demanded precise constitutional changes.

The first request entailed modifying the "unbalanced" federal political representation that had given the slave states enormous weight during the Constitutional Convention, and which had a

38 Proceedings of the Hartford Convention, p. 14.

39 *Ibid.*, p. 9. This passage reproduces almost verbatim Madison's formulation of the *Virginia Resolutions*.

40 Ibid., p. 15.

disruptive effect on the relationship between the two sections of the country. The Hartford conspirators demanded that "Representatives and direct taxes shall be apportioned among the several States which may be included within this union, according to their respective numbers of free persons, including those bound to serve for a term of years, and excluding Indians not taxed, and all other persons."[41] The abolition of over-representation of the slave states would have led to the downsizing of Jefferson and Madison's party. The institution of slavery itself was not under discussion.

The second request was that the admission of new states be subject to the favorable vote of two-thirds of each house of the Congress. The Congress, then, should not have the authority to promulgate embargoes lasting for more than 60 days (a power that was not included in the Constitution) and, only with a two-thirds majority could trade relations of the United States with foreign countries be banned and wars other than purely defensive ones be declared. Moreover, they required that naturalized citizens could not be elected as members of the Senate or of the House of Representatives. The last amendment was thought to be a guarantee against the "Virginia dynasty," which had been prevailing. "The same person shall not be elected President of the United States a second time; nor shall the President be elected from the same State two terms in succession."[42] The conclusion was a quite explicit threat:

> If the application of these States to the government of the United States, recommended in a foregoing Resolution, should be unsuccessful, and peace should not be concluded and the defense of these States should be neglected, as it has been since the commencement of the war, it will in the opinion of this Convention be expedient for the Legislatures of the several States to appoint Delegates to another Convention, to meet at Boston, in the State of

41*Ibid.*, p. 21.

42 *Ibid.*, p. 21.

> Massachusetts, on the third Thursday of June next with such powers and instructions as the exigency of a crisis so momentous may require.[43]

As Peter Parish has noted, these "resolutions ... are in essence a cry of anguish at the dreadful prospect of a Union more and more powerfully dominated by the coalition of South and rapidly growing West."[44] In spite of a tone that was very far from incendiary, "the threat was obvious: give us what we want or we will secede."[45] It is unparalleled in American history that, in the midst of a war, "several states would gather ... even to consider withdrawing from the union and forging a separate peace with the enemy. ... "[46]

As the delegates gathered in Hartford, American and British plenipotentiaries were in Ghent in order to sign a peace treaty; this made the Convention look like a farce, even though some saw a link between the rapid negotiations that led to peace and the convention itself. According to Benjamin Franklin Grady, "the threatening aspect of the proceedings [that] led to the Hartford Convention" pressured Madison to make peace as soon as possible, without even discussing impressment.[47]

On January 31, 1815, Governor Caleb Strong sent Harrison G. Otis, Thomas H. Perkins and William Sullivan on a mission to Washington, D.C., to gather support for the resolutions. The

---

43 *Ibid.*

44 Peter J. Parish, The North and the Nation in the Era of the Civil War, eds. Adam I. P. Smith and Susan-Mary Grant (New York: Fordham University Press, 2003), p. 13.

45 Richard Brookhiser, *James Madison* (New York: Basic Books, 2011), p. 217.

46 Benjamin Wittes and Ritika Singh, "James Madison, Presidential Power, and Civil Liberties in the War of 1812," in What So Proudly We Hailed, p. 103. According to the authors, "Madison even tolerated the open talk about and movement toward secession ... [and] made no effort to stop the Hartford Convention from taking place. The War Department sent a colonel to Hartford to keep an eye on the convention for signs of rebellion or treason," p. 105.

47 Benjamin Franklin Grady, *The Case of the South Against the North* (Raleigh NC: Edwards & Burton, 1899), p. 193.

gentlemen were immediately dubbed "the three Ambassadors."[48] They arrived in Washington, however, the day after the end of the war; given their late action, they were welcomed with general mockery. "All that they had presumed and built on had not occurred. ... The delegates who could in the face of such events obey instructions would only have increased public ridicule. They went home as quietly as possible. The rebels who had so nearly led their States into treasonable conduct were never again heard from; and New England from that day became among the most faithful to the union."[49]

When news of Andrew Jackson's victory in New Orleans arrived in Washington, the government found itself in a strong position vis-à-vis the New England Federalist Party, now considered a group of secessionist traitors. The party was never able to recover and, in fact, died in Hartford. Nevertheless, Troy Bickham is absolutely right in pointing out that its chronology was crucial in this failure. "An entirely different outcome is easy to envisage had the convention met ... a little earlier. ... The threat of a New England secession might very well have compelled divided states, notably New York and Pennsylvania, and those with substantial opposition minorities, such as Maryland and North Carolina, to negotiate."[50] Nobody could have ever imagined so spectacular and sudden an overthrowal: Within two months in early 1815, General Jackson defeated the British army in New Orleans (January 8), and the Senate gave its *placet* to the Ghent treaty (Febuary 15), which concluded the war without any territorial concessions.[51] Hence, the resolutions of the convention were rapidly swept away.

---

48 Cf. Theodore Lyman, A Short Account of the Hartford Convention ... (Boston: Everett, 1823), p.16; Francis F. Beirne, The War of 1812 (New York: Dutton, 1949), p. 332.

49 Edward Payson Powell, *Nullification and Secession in the United States* (New York: Putnam, 1897), pp. 226-227.

50 Troy Bickham, *The Weight of Vengeance: The United States, the British Empire, and the War of 1812* (New York: Oxford University Press, 2012), p. 200.

51 Walter R. Borneman, *1812: The War That Forged a Nation* (New York: Harper Collins, 2004), pp. 269-270.

4.4) Hartford between History and Historiography

The New England leaders at the time gave birth to generations of historians who analyzed their accomplishments. This has been referred to as "family history," which means that grandchildren narrated their grand- and great-grandparents' achievements to American future generations. Henry Adams, William Plumer Jr., Henry Cabot Lodge and Samuel Eliot Morison, for example, recounted their progenitors' political choices, causing a historiographic clash, itself worth analyzing.

In any case, the kinship was not regarded as a problem and, according to Morison, it was even a point of strength: "I may as well confess to my readers at the start that I am a descendant of Harrison Gray Otis, four generations removed. Contrary to general opinion, I believe that a statesman's biography can best be written by a descendant, if he can preserve the natural sympathy that comes from kinship and family tradition, without sacrificing historical judgment and criticism."[52] The volume, which included what was for long considered the most eminent account of the Hartford Convention,[53] supported the classical Federalist theories of the previous century. From Morison's perspective, it was obvious that those who gathered in Connecticut aimed at changing the constitutional *compact*, and that they dared making radical suggestions in such a difficult period for the country; but nobody really took into consideration the possibility of abandoning the Union:

> The Convention showed that it had squarely faced, and rejected, any policy tending toward the dissolution of the union. This decision is greatly to the members' credit. In spite of the influence of Pickering, Morris, and Lowell, in spite of the loud calls of the New England press for extreme measures, in spite of the accumulative provocation of the past

52 Samuel Eliot Morison, *The Life and Letters of Harrison Gray Otis, Federalist, 1765–1848*, vol. 1 (Boston: Houghton Mifflin, 1913), p. ix.

53 Cf. *Ibid.*, pp. 78-200.

> six years, they were able to look into the future and discern that the grievances of New England resulted largely from a temporary state of affairs: the world-wide wars of the Napoleonic era.[54]

By contrast, Henry Adams, grandson of John Quincy Adams, agreed with the theories endorsed by his grandfather, who had abandoned the Federalist Party in 1808 in order to join Jefferson's and Madison's party. He believed there was in fact a large geographical area with substantial political support who wanted to leave the Union in the early nineteenth century. In the late 1820s, he wrote a long essay aimed at demonstrating the anti-unionist nature of the leading Federalist group, whose secessionist project gave birth to the Hartford Convention. His work was published by his grandson almost half a century later, together with other historical political sources.[55]

According to John Quincy Adams, there had been a single major project, which spanned a decade and led to the convention. Most of his argumentation was focused on the fact that the Constitution denies the chance of separate pacts between states, and that Hartford was the only such example in American history.

> This representative convention of several State legislatures was in itself an incipient organization of a new confederacy. The leaders of the party, by whom it had been devised, had been struggling seven years to organize such an assembly. And it was undoubtedly the measure indispensable for effecting the dissolution of the union. The Hartford Convention was to the Northern confederacy precisely what the Congress of 1774 was to the Declaration of Independence. The Convention itself could not be held but by an agreement between two or more States, which is in express violation of the Constitution,—a violation which would have been still

54 *Ibid.*, vol. 2, p.150.

55 See Henry Adams, *Documents Relating to New England Federalism,* pp. 107-329.

> more flagrant, had a second convention been elected according to one of the closing recommendations of that assembly.[56]

Henry Cabot Lodge, another scholar interested in the events also for kinship reasons, held instead an intermediate opinion: he did not deny the widespread secessionist feelings in New England, but came to the bizarre conclusion that the Hartford delegates were political geniuses able to add fuel to the fire and, at the same time, to use "these separatist forces to maintain the union." Their position used the threat of secession just in order to achieve the constitutional changes they desired. Anyway, "the Hartford Convention was not intended to dissolve the union."[57]

In 1970, James M. Banner published the most extensive study of the Convention to date, which seemed to close the debate: "[N] o Convention member ... ever seriously contemplated disunion as an alternative in 1814," but "at bottom ... [they were] profoundly attached to the union."[58] To be sure, the "delegates remained moderate in their attitudes and final resolutions. While opposed to the War of 1812 and all it had visited upon them, they were more concerned with New England's future within the union than outside of it."[59]

It is clear why the debate focuses on the issue of secession: Less than half a century later the South attempted to leave the Union. In doing so, it had to deal with the intransigence and the troops of a president who had been elected only by the North, and was mostly supported by the states that promoted the Hartford Convention in 1814.

---

56 John Quincy Adams, "Reply to the Massachusetts Federalists," in *Documents relating to New England Federalism,* p. 245.

57 Henry Cabot Lodge, *Life and Letters of George Cabot* (Boston: Little, Brown, 1878), pp. 516-519.

58 James M. Banner Jr., *To the Hartford Convention: The Federalists and the Origins of Party Politics in Massachusetts, 1789–1815* (New York: Knopf, 1970), p. 344.

59 Reginald C. Stuart, *Civil-Military Relations during the War of 1812* (Santa Barbara: Praeger Security International, 2009), p. 110.

In fact, the prevailing line of discussion concerning the convention peaked, fifteen years after the events, in what yet remains a memorable debate on the nature of the American union. In January 1830, during the discussion on Samuel Augustus Foot's resolution (Foot wanted Congress to inquire into limiting the sale of public land in the West), the issue of states' rights, already present in all the constitutional debates, became the national political dilemma. This clash is known as the "Hayne-Webster debate on the nature of the union,"[60] and will be discussed at length in the next chapter. Robert Hayne, senator of South Carolina, represented the *states' righters*, whereas Daniel Webster supported the Union. The core of the dispute was whether the latter was founded on a *compact* or not. Webster's purpose was to challenge the Southern leadership and reaffirm New England influence on the confederation.[61]

While in the 1830s New England could dominate the Union through the "national" interpretation, the region had to bear the weight of the secessionist season experienced in war times just fifteen years earlier. Hayne immediately stated that "as soon as the public mind was sufficiently prepared for the measure, the celebrated Hartford Convention was got up; not as the act of a few unauthorized individuals, but by authority of the Legislature of Massachusetts; and ... in accordance with the views and wishes of the party, of which it was the organ." He added: "That convention met, and from their proceedings it appears that their chief object was to keep back the men and money of New England from the service of the union, and to effect radical changes in the Government; changes that can never be effected without a dissolution of the union.[62]

60 *The Webster-Hayne Debate on the Nature of the Union,* ed. Herman Belz (Indianapolis: Liberty Fund, 2000).

61 See Harlow W. Sheidley, "The Webster-Hayne Debate: Recasting New England's Sectionalism," *New England Quarterly* 67 (1994), pp. 5-29.

62 Robert H. Hayne, Senate, January 19, 1830, in *The Webster-Hayne Debate,* pp. 67-68.

In short, the Hartford Convention made rather untenable for many years the claims of New England to be the sole defender of the Union. Even after the end of the Civil War, this episode was recalled in every analysis supporting the southern cause. We can find the essence of these southern objections in the words of Jabez Curry: "One of the most singular illustrations ever presented of the power of literature to conceal and pervert truth, to modify and falsify history, to transfer odium from the guilty to the innocent, is found in the fact that the reproach of disunion has been slipped from the shoulders of the North to those of the South."[63]

Senator and historian Henry Cabot Lodge conceived a rather witty and not entirely unfounded defense strategy to deal with the issue. He absolutely did not deny that at the beginning "when the Constitution was adopted ... there was not a man in the country who regarded the new system as anything but an experiment ... from which each and every state had the right to peaceably withdraw," but with time passing, and especially when "South Carolina began her resistance to the tariff in 1830 ... it was a much more serious thing to threaten the existence of the Federal Government than it had been in 1799, or even in 1814."[64]

In conclusion, New England had been legitimated *post facto* because it moved early; South Carolina decided to question the Union too late. For realist scholars, the lesson that must be learned from the Hartford Convention does nothing but reiterate what is already absolutely clear: The struggle for power is the basis of every political clash, and ideology just supplies it with rhetorical forms. There is, indeed, something deeply ironic—the usual "irony of American history"—in the final defeat of the Federalist Party due to the Hartford Convention.[65] All the leaders of the Party, up to a few years before, had attacked the "Jeffersonian doctrine of 1798."

63 Jabez L. M. Curry, *The Southern States of the American Union* (Richmond, VA: BF Johnson, 1895), p. 121.

64 Henry Cabot Lodge, *Daniel Webster: American Statesman* (Boston: Mifflin, 1883), pp. 176-177.

65 "The Federalist party died behind the closed doors at Hartford." Glenn Tucker, *Poltroons and Patriots: A Popular Account of the War of 1812*, vol. 2 (Indianapolis: Bobbs-Merrill, 1954), p. 651

However, as soon as they lost their control of the federation —that is, after the 1800 revolution which gave power to the Democratic-Republican Party— they adopted the Jeffersonian doctrine of nullification, abandoned any centralist ambition, and started to support a consensual view of the American union. Therefore, the consolidation of the powers within the Congress experienced its nadir exactly in those years.

Chapter 5

John C. Calhoun: Nullification, Concurrent Majority and Secession

> The confederation was formed by the free will of the states. ... If today one of those same states wished to withdraw its name from the contract, it would be hard to prove that it could not do so. In resisting it the federal government would have no obvious source of support either in strength or in right.[1]
>
> —Alexis de Tocqueville

As Vernon Parrington stated in his classic historical study of American ideas, "whatever road one travels comes at last upon the austere figure of Calhoun, commanding every highway of the southern mind."[2] It is extremely difficult to understand the events in the political history prior to the Civil War without an adequate knowledge of the practical and theoretical activity of John C. Calhoun.[3]

---

1 Alexis de Tocqueville, *Democracy in America*, ed. J.P. Mayer (New York: Doubleday & Company, 1969) p. 369.

2 Vernon L. Parrington, *Main Currents in American Thought: The Romantic Revolution in America, 1800–1860* (1927), vol. 2 (New York: Harcourt, Brace, 1954), p. 65.

3 Calhoun is not without detractors, William Freehling sees "his political philosophy [as] hopelessly inconsistent ... [as] he had only a sporadic commitment to an economic interest theory of history," William W. Freehling, "Spoilsmen and Interests in the Thought and Career of John C. Calhoun," *Journal of American History* 52 (1965), p. 25. See also Louis Hartz, *The Liberal Tradition in America: An Interpretation of American Political Thought since the Revolution* (New York: Harcourt, Brace, 1955), pp. 145-177, who labels not only Calhoun and his political doctrine, but the entire political reflections of the South, as a "Reactionary Enlightenment." Obviously, Hartz could not appreciate Calhoun, given that he maintains that the "vast neurotic

However the Carolinian, in spite of the fact that he died eleven years prior to the birth of the Confederate States of America, is often identified with the Confederate epoch, and his expulsion from the "American tradition" goes hand in hand with his depiction as the definitive "symbol of the Lost Cause."[4] This identification started in the aftermath of the Civil War—with the famous Yankee soldier who, according to Walt Whitman, said: "Calhoun's monument ... is the desolated, ruined south; nearly the whole generation of young men between seventeen and thirty destroyed or maim'd; all the old families used up—the rich impoverish'd, the plantations cover'd with weeds, the slaves unloos'd and become the masters, and the name of southerner blacken'd with every shame—all that is Calhoun's real monument."[5]

This identification of the politician and thinker with a nation-region and an epoch serves the larger end of evicting anything "southern" from American orthodoxy, and it was the peculiarly Yankee way of "sanitizing" Calhoun. The author of the *Disquisition* might be of some interest to antiquarians or academics more than subliminally nostalgic about the Old South, not to mention bigots and racists, but history has purged him; he's gone with the wind.

---

fear of what the majority might do" was certainly present in the American tradition, though absolutely without reason, *Ibid.*, p. 128. More recently Sotirios A. Barber, *The Fallacies of States' Rights* (Cambridge, MA: Harvard University Press, 2013) pp. 122-144, discusses Calhoun's 'false' theory of the Union, reiterating a point that is very common in much of the recent scholarship: "Calhoun ... demanded national power in the service of slavery," p. 144. According to another scholar, "he proposed a radically different structure for the United States' republican empire, one that was sufficiently powerful and coherent that it helped inspire white Southerners, including most of all [those] who did not own slaves," James G. Wilson, *The Imperial Republic: A Structural History of American Constitutionalism from the Colonial Era to the Beginning of the Twentieth Century* (Burlington, VT: Ashgate, 2003), p. 207. For a French work that seconds the American obsession with slavery cf. Geŕard Hugues, *Une theórie de l'Etat esclavagiste. John Caldwell Calhoun* (Aix-en-Provence: Publications de l'Universite ́de Provence, 2004).

4 Gerald M. Capers, *John C. Calhoun-Opportunist. A Reappraisal*, (Gainesville: University of Florida Press, 1960), p. VI.

5 Walt Whitman, *Prose Works, Specimen Days, Calhoun's Real Monument*, 95 (Philadelphia: David McKay, 1892), p. 88.

Calhoun was a slaveholder and also a political thinker. While there is a more than abundant literature that analyses the American republic from the point of view of slavery, as well as the odious institution itself,[6] I cannot even hint at the complexity of the Carolinian's relationship with slavery. He clearly championed the South, and slavery came with it. The idea that all his political theories were advanced just to defend slavery has cropped up time and again, but it remains as unconvincing as ever. According to one scholar, "South Carolina's slaveholding politicians not only pioneered in elaborating an ideological defense of racial slavery but also developed the political theories that justified disunion: nullification, state sovereignty, state ownership of national territories, and the constitutional right to secession."[7]

Calhoun defended slavery in the South within his own historical context. He never hinted that it had any universal implications. Southern society was not a creation of the mind of Calhoun; he was merely the most lucid interpreter of that region at a time in which it felt besieged. Though Calhoun advanced the theory of slavery as a positive good, he was not influencing public opinion on that matter, he was merely mirroring it.[8]

In our story, he rises to a quite peculiar stature; Calhoun is in fact the most lucid political thinker of the American resistance to the modern state. His reflections on how an authentic federation should work and how a community should always be thought

6 One of the first radical studies of this kind was Staughton Lynd, *Class Conflict, Slavery, and the United States Constitution*, (Westport, CN: Greenwood, 1980). See also Paul Finkelman, *Slavery and the Founders: Race and Liberty in the Age of Jefferson* (Armonk, M.E. Sharpe, 2001); Eugene D. Genovese, *Roll, Jordan, Roll. The World the Slaves Made* (New York: Pantheon, 1974) and *The Slaveholders' Dilemma: Freedom and Progress in Southern Conservative Thought, 1820-1860* (Columbia: University of South Carolina, 1992); David Brion Davis, *Inhuman Bondage: The Rise and Fall of Slavery in the New World* (New York: Oxford University Press, 2006); and Lacy K. Ford, *Deliver Us from Evil: The Slavery Question in the Old South* (New York, Oxford University Press, 2009).

7 Manisha Sinha, *The Counterrevolution of Slavery. Politics and Ideology in Antebellum South Carolina* (Chapel Hill: University of North Carolina Press, 2000), p. 1.

8 Cf. William Sumner Jenkins, *Pro-Slavery Thought in the Old South* (Chapel Hill: University of North Carolina Press, 1935).

divided at the core, represent the most important theoretical departure from the state mentality in America. The vice president and senator from South Carolina was in fact a nearly unique figure in his time, and his best known work, the *Disquisition on Government* (1851), has carved out an exceptional place for itself, because it is "that rarity in American political thought—a work that explicitly declares itself a theoretical study of politics. A general and comprehensive account of politics places it "in a class of which it is almost the sole example: an American political theory," said Ralph Lerner in 1963.[9] His reflections on constitutional government, "concurrent majority," and "popular sovereignty" and its limits are fully entitled to a place among the great constructions of nineteenth-century political theory, and their importance is not limited just to the American union. But the first myth we have to debunk is that we are in the presence of a modest Marx rooting for the oppressors.

At the beginning of the Cold War, Richard Hofstadter labeled Calhoun "the Marx of the Master Class"—joining together very suggestive political terms at the time detested by ordinary Americans. For Hofstadter, Calhoun was a "reverse Marx" in that he shared with the author of *Das Kapital* the idea of history as an irreducible struggle between various economic interests, but openly chose the side of Southern aristocracy against the oppressed.[10] "The Marx of the Master Class" became a sobriquet at once superficial and ineradicable. Hofstadter was convinced that Calhoun's concepts of nullification and concurrent majority had no more than an antiquarian interest. The Carolinian's real strength was that he understood class dynamics.

> Before Karl Marx published the *Communist Manifesto*, Calhoun laid down an analysis of American politics and

---

9 Ralph Lerner, "Calhoun's New Science of Politics," *American Political Science Quarterly* 47, no. 4, (1963), p. 918.

10 Cf. Richard Hofstadter, *The American Political Tradition and the Men Who Made It*, pp. 67-91. Richard Nelson Current, "John C. Calhoun Philosopher of Reaction," *The Antioch Review*, vol. 3, no. 2 (Summer, 1943), pp. 223-234, was probably the first scholar to suggest this rather awkward analogy.

> the sectional struggle which foreshadowed some of the seminal ideas of Marx's system. A brilliant if narrow dialectician, probably the last American statesman to do any primary political thinking, he placed the central ideas of 'scientific' socialism in an inverted framework of moral values and produced an arresting defense of reaction, a sort of intellectual Black Mass.[11]

The comparison with Marx is today considered implausible,[12] but the reasons why the parallel is scarcely believable are not usually pinpointed. In the first place, Howard L. Cheek is perfectly right in stating that "the oligarchic revolution Hofstadter envisions as the fulfillment of Calhoun's political theory was in reality opposed, not promoted, by the Carolinian."[13] In fact, his political theory is designed to render it impossible for the big interests to compound and become the owners of the governmental apparatus.

Calhoun locates the source of the privileges enjoyed by the "masters" in political power, not in the production of wealth. The true "proprietors" own *not* the means of production but the governmental apparatus. If the notion that Calhoun was a "reverse Marx" is to have any cogency, the reversal must not be understood as a toppling of preferences between the bourgeoisie and the working class, but rather as a palpable inversion of the relation between structure and superstructure. According to Calhoun, conflict does not originate in society, rather it is the government's action that creates two opposite social classes: taxpayers and tax consumers:

> Nothing is more difficult than to equalize the action of the government, in reference to the various and diversified interests of the community; and nothing more easy than to pervert its powers into instruments

[11] Richard Hofstadter, *The American Political Tradition*, p. 69.

12 However, cf. Guy Story Brown, *Calhoun' Philosophy of Politics, A Study of A Disquisition on Government* (Macon: Mercer University Press, 2000), pp. 62-79 for an analysis of the *Disquisition* in relation to the critique of Hegel by the young Marx.

13 H. Lee Cheek, Jr., *Calhoun and Popular Rule. The Political Theory of the Disquisition and Discourse*, Columbia, University of Missouri Press, 2001, p. 19.

> to aggrandize and enrich one or more interests by oppressing and impoverishing the others. ... Nor is this the case in some particular communities only. It is so in all; the small and the great—the poor and the rich—irrespective of pursuits, productions, or degrees of civilization—with, however, this difference, that the more extensive and populous the country, the more diversified the condition and pursuits of its population, and the richer, more luxurious, and dissimilar the people, the more difficult is it to equalize the action of the government—and the more easy for one portion of the community to pervert its powers to oppress, and plunder the other.[14]

Therefore, the government here appears as a kind of committee of affairs representing a section of the bourgeoisie against others. For the Carolinian it is the "right of suffrage" itself which leads "to conflict among ... [the community's] different interests—each striving to obtain possession of its powers, as the means of protecting itself against the others—or of advancing its respective interests, regardless of the interests of others. For this purpose, a struggle will take place between the various interests to obtain a majority, in order to control the government. If no one interest be strong enough, of itself, to obtain it, a combination will be formed between those whose interests are most alike—each conceding something to the others, until a sufficient number is obtained to make a majority."[15]

This does not arise spontaneously in society; it is not the interplay of conflicting interests which gives birth to government, but rather it is politics itself which causes the interests to conflict. And finally, "the community will be divided into two great parties—a major and minor—between which there will be

14 John C. Calhoun, *A Disquisition on Government*, *Works*, vol. 1, p. 16.

15 *Ibid.*, p. 17.

incessant struggles on the one side to retain, and on the other to obtain the majority—and, thereby, the control of the government and the advantages it confers."[16]

Calhoun thinks it is "impossible to equalize the action of the government, so far as its fiscal operation extends." And this derives from the fact that "the agents and employees of the government constitute that portion of the community who are the exclusive recipients of the proceeds of the taxes. Whatever amount is taken from the community, in the form of taxes, if not lost, goes to them in the shape of expenditures or disbursements."[17]

Taxation and public spending generate two conflicting groups fighting for the prize handed out by government. Taxes will be the reward for those who control government and a burden for those who do not. "One portion of the community must pay in taxes more than it receives back in disbursements; while another receives in disbursements more than it pays in taxes." Calhoun clarifies what really causes conflict in society: government. Political power is a primary and autonomous factor, not the consequence of social interaction. While for Thomas Hobbes it was the state of nature and the lack of Leviathan that caused the "bellum omnium contra omnes," Calhoun explains that such a clash happens in society and derives from the very nature of the governmental process: "The unequal fiscal action of the government" regroups society into "two great classes": tax-payers and tax-consumers."[18]

Therefore, Calhoun is not an upside down Marx; he is rather a political thinker who overturns the Marxian relationship between structure and superstructure, making it clear that the masters do not own the means of production, but the mechanism of government.

16 *Ibid.*, p. 18.

17 *Ibid.*, p. 19.

18 *Ibid.*, p. 22.

5.1) Calhoun's Political Principles

The central features of Calhoun's political thought are the theory of the concurrent majority and the concept of the federal compact as founded on an agreement between the States. Of course there are limits in his thought that are largely tied to the time in which he lived, but Calhoun's theories have not lost meaning in contemporary Western societies. In particular, Calhoun's criticism of the concept of the simple numerical majority, which is at the core of his *Disquisition on Government*, emerges intact one hundred and seventy years after its formulation. More than any other penetrating criticism of unlimited democracy, Calhoun reveals how what we might call the *malaise of representation*, which today afflicts all large democratic societies, was already visible at the dawn of democratic institutions in America.

The key to Calhoun's political theory was his defense of the interests of the southern States. In the three decades preceding the Civil War, the South concluded that it was a minority within the Union, oppressed and exploited by the federal government, which by then had become the powerful political lever of the North. Many years ago, Jesse Carpenter analyzed the emergence and growth of the South as a permanent minority, fully aware that it could not break the numerical preponderance of a hostile North that was resolutely placing the financial burden of the federal government on the slave states. The South attempted to defend its society and culture (and of course also slavery) by adopting various political stances. At first, until the Missouri Compromise of March 6, 1820, the self-government guaranteed by the Constitution seemed adequate. Later, in the 1820s, 1830s and 1840s, the South entrusted its defense to the principle of the "concurrent majority." After the admission of California to the Union on September 9, 1850, and until Abraham Lincoln's election on November 6, 1860, the South placed its hopes in constitutional guarantees, and especially in the Supreme Court, until it finally decided to form an independent confederation.[19]

19 Jesse T. Carpenter, *The South as a Conscious Minority, 1789–1861: A Study in Political Thought* (New York: New York University Press, 1930), p. 5. Cf. also Don

Even though Calhoun participated actively only from the end of the 1820s to his death in 1850, he pondered deeply over every possible political and constitutional solution. For many years he sought in the Constitution the defenses against the incursions of the North and the federal government. The most important constitutional provision against the abuse of power by an exceedingly powerful majority was the usual one in modern federalism—a distribution of powers between the States and the federal government. "The powers of the General Government are particularly enumerated and specifically delegated; and all powers not expressly delegated, or which are not necessary and proper to carry into effect those that are so granted, are reserved expressly to the States or the people."[20] The entire Constitution can be interpreted as a system of delegated powers, prescribed and delimited for the purpose of protecting the rights of individuals and those of every State.

The linchpin of all of Calhoun's analysis was the power of the individual State as a contracting party to, and the real *dominus* of, the federal pact. It must be noted that the word "State" is all over the Constitution (it appears 103 times), while the term "nation" does not appear at all. Federal political representation, and not just that of the Senate, is centered on the States: the members of the House of Representatives are elected "by the People of the several States." Regarding eligibility for election, the state-centered character of representation is even more marked: for the House the candidate must be an inhabitant of the State "in which" he or she will be chosen; for the Senate the candidate must be an inhabitant of the State "for which" he or she will be chosen.[21] In sum, for the House a person is chosen as a representative of a State; he or she is never imagined as a delegate of a part of the American

E. Fehrenbacher, *Sectional Crisis and Southern Constitutionalism* (Baton Rouge: Louisiana State University Press, 1980).

20 John C. Calhoun, "South Carolina Exposition (Rough Draft)," November 1828, Calhoun, *Papers*, vol. 10, p. 496.

21 Until the constitutional reform of 1913 (XVII amendment) which introduced popular elections for the Senate, the senators were chosen by state assemblies and were in effect "ambassadors of the States."

people (which simply does not exist from a constitutional point of view), while the senator is in Washington on behalf of her State. The source of political power flows from the States to the federal government, and never *vice-versa*. The Constitution authorizes and prohibits certain actions by the federal government, but to the States nothing is ever permitted, only prohibited. This means that for the federal government an action must be clearly permitted, while State political authorities must check only if a constitutional prohibition exists, in the absence of which they can act freely. A general political capacity is recognized only for the States. The Tenth Amendment ("The powers not delegated to the United States by the Constitution, nor prohibited by it to the States, are reserved to the States respectively, or to the people") is the architrave of American federal polity: It sums up the entire system of permissions and prohibitions in the sense delineated by Calhoun.

Yet many constitutional law scholars assert that the Tenth Amendment contradicts Article VI of the Constitution ("This Constitution, and the Laws of the United States which shall be made in Pursuance thereof; and all Treaties made, or which shall be made, under the Authority of the United States, shall be the supreme Law of the Land"), which established instead a "federal supremacy" clause. These scholars argue that the apparent contradiction between the Tenth Amendment and Article VI created a normative antinomy in the United States legal system. In short, one rule or the other must be chosen: Either the federal supremacy clause applies and hence any State law contrary to the federal law 'vanishes' or the point of view is reversed and a judge decides if a federal law exceeds its delegated competence, in which case the latter ceases.

For Calhoun things were not like this at all: "The clause [in Article VI] is declaratory; ... it vests no newer power whatever in the government, or in any of its departments." In fact,

> [w]here two or more States form a common constitution and government, the authority of these, within the limits of the delegated powers, must, of necessity, be supreme, in reference to their respective

> separate constitutions and governments. Without this, there would be neither a common constitution and government, nor even a confederacy. The whole would be, in fact, a mere nullity. But this supremacy is not an absolute supremacy. It is limited in extent and degree. It does not extend beyond the delegated powers—all others being reserved to the States and the people of the States. Beyond these the constitution is as destitute of authority, and as powerless as a blank piece of paper; and the measures of the government mere acts of assumption.[22]

With the question of the supposed supremacy of the federal government thus resolved, Calhoun turned to dismantling the centralist interpretation of the American Constitution.

The Constitution is a systematic ordering of the ideal of a limited government: The whole document is a long and detailed list of prohibitions and distinctions that reflects the dominant philosophy of the political debate of the Revolutionary generation, which was suspicious of any form of power over people. Nevertheless, the Constitution could be amended to meet the changing needs of the times. No states' rights advocate has ever denied this. Rather, the center of the Constitutional analysis by Calhoun and his followers was precisely the process of Constitutional amendment, which elevated the role of the States. According to Calhoun, the power to amend the Constitution, described in Article V, is the linchpin of state sovereignty and the ultimate proof of its natural place in the American compact. "It shows, conclusively, that the people of the several States still retain that supreme ultimate power, called sovereignty—the power by which they ordained and established the constitution; and which can rightfully create, modify, amend, or abolish it, at its pleasure."[23] The Constitution therefore is not a sort of higher law open to any form of evolution according the spirit of the times, the majority, the political classes in power,

22 John C. Calhoun, *A Discourse on the Government and Constitution of the United States*, Calhoun, *Works*, vol. I, pp. 252-253.

23 *Ibid.*, p. 138.

or the preferences of the justices of the Supreme Court, but a compact between sovereign states, which can be renegotiated only through amendments.

What Calhoun most fiercely opposed was the centralist interpretation of the Constitution, through which, without amending it and without renegotiating the contract with all the member states, the pact was imbued with a different content. Through questionable theories and jurisprudential interpretations, as well as the numerical force of the majority region—the industrial North—the system of guarantees protecting the less populated regions of the Union was collapsing.

Calhoun considered the States to be the sole actors in the Union, as well as in relationships with other territorial entities such as counties and cities. In contrast with Jefferson, who advocated a federal-type relationship between any centers of government, to the point of envisioning the ward-republic (the smallest unit of self-government from which every power is delegated) Calhoun thought there should be a simple administrative relation between a State and local government authorities.

Internally, a State should not be structured in a federal manner, for two reasons. In Calhoun's scientific view of politics, there is no place for an "ethical" conception of the federal relationship (which was sketched out in Jefferson's theory) that should pervade the entire community. And, more importantly, the States are the political entities that contracted the American compact. The federal relationship cannot be wished into existence: Either it exists or it does not. Calhoun was concerned about the rules of the constitutive compact that formed the United States, thus he considered state sovereignty as a simple given fact. As did all proponents of the states' rights school, he was "describing what was, not what ought to be, the nature of the federal Union."[24]

On January 22, 1833—at the end of the Nullification Controversy—Calhoun presented three resolutions to the Senate that exposed the strong conceptual core of his interpretation of the nature of the American Union. First, the peoples of the

24 August O. Spain, *The Political Theory of John C. Calhoun*, p. 197.

several States are part of a constitutional contract, to which each one accedes by the process of ratification as a separate and independent community, and the Union exists as such between the States that have ratified the pact. The general government, constituted for specific purposes, is granted only those powers expressly delegated by the pact, and, when it acts on the basis of non-delegated powers, its acts are without validity and thus null and void. Furthermore, since there is no common judge between the contracting parties, each party is sovereign in establishing the nature of both violations and sanctions. Finally, the assertion that the people of the United States, collectively or individually, were parties to the social contract is false, because it is contrary to the most certain historical evidence; thus all exercise of power by the federal government based on such erroneous conviction is non-existent and inevitably destined to destroy the freedom of the States as parties to the federation.[25]

The question posed by Thomas Jefferson three decades earlier regarding the absence of a common judge among the parties of the constitutional compact appears to be still central, though in a conceptual framework that has no reference to natural law. Rather, in Calhoun's resolutions the federal government itself stands accused of acting as if there were a social contract among the American people. According to Carl Schmitt,

> The theories of Calhoun and Seydel involve essential concepts of constitutional theory for a federation, with the aid of which one should recognize the distinctiveness of certain political formations, and the scholarly value of which persists even if their creators stood on the defeated side.[26]

This is precisely the chief issue. Calhoun, and the entire South with him, believed that the United States was an authentic federation, that the Constitution was an instrument that delegated

25 See *Calhoun, Papers*, Vol. 12, pp. 25-26.

26 Carl Schmitt, *Constitutional Theory*, ed. and trans. Jeffrey Seitzer (Durham, NC: Duke University Press, 2008) p. 391.

the power of amendment to three-quarters of the States, and that the delegation of governmental functions to the superstructure created to manage the common affairs did not substantially alter the contractual and voluntary nature of the association. But history was moving in an entirely different direction.

5.2) The Nullification Crisis

Calhoun's thought on constitutional and political theory developed systematically in the course of his fight against the laws that introduced the tariffs.[27] The problem of tariffs and protectionism had been the subject of extensive debate from the beginning of the Union. The imposition of import duties was one of the few sources of income for the federal government, which had to cope with the national debt derived from assuming the war debts of the individual States. In addition, there had been from the beginning a campaign aimed at convincing the public—quite skeptical on the matter—that American industry, still in its infancy, had to be protected from competition from stronger and more developed foreign enterprises. In 1791 Alexander Hamilton wrote a *Report on Manufactures* in which he supported the necessity of protecting fledgling American industries, encouraging craftsmen to immigrate to America, and promoting inventions and discoveries.

In an environment hostile to government interventionism, Hamilton was perhaps the first to support the idea of an economy strongly subordinated to the national interest, along the lines of a radicalized British model. His ideas met with some success only after the war of 1812, when industry became the primary interest of the North. In 1816 Congress adopted a customs tariff that aimed more at protecting American industry than collecting funds for the

27 Calhoun supported the tariff of 1816, only to strenuously oppose the later ones (and his inconsistency was constantly flung back in his face by his adversaries). In his speech to the Senate against the Force Bill on February 15-16, 1833, he addressed his about-face on the tariff question, maintaining that the 1816 tariff was different from the others: Its goal was to increase federal revenue in order to cover the national debt incurred in the war against Great Britain. Cf. Calhoun, *Papers*, vol. 12, pp. 50-51.

federal treasury. The tariff problem was exacerbated later, when Congress approved in May 1828 such a heavy increase in tariffs that it came to be called the "Tariff of Abominations."

The political debate on the question of the tariff was also transoceanic: William Huskisson, MP from Liverpool, addressed the British House of Commons in favor of a free trade policy, with the purpose of warning the southern States against being exploited by the North. He felt that the tariff would lead to the secession of the southern States in the not too distant future. This speech had a wide resonance in the South, as did other British free trade views. South Carolina Senator George McDuffie artfully propagandized the so-called theory of the "forty bales," also suggested by British free trade proponents. Under this theory, the protective tariff so consistently diminished the English buying power for cotton and increased prices for southern consumers that for every hundred bales of cotton produced, forty ended up directly in the coffers of the industrial North.

In December 1828 Calhoun published (anonymously, since he was then vice president of the United States) the *South Carolina Exposition and Protest*, in which he illustrated the theory of nullification with a wealth of argumentation, and concluded that the southern States might have to abandon the Union.[28] This document divides American political history into a "before" and "after." Prior to the *Exposition* the South lacked the leadership, the "regional awareness," and an articulated constitutional doctrine to defend its political, economic and social place in the Union. From the *Exposition's* publication onward, resentment against the North found expression in a crystal-clear constitutional theory. If "Southern nationalism emerged when sizable numbers of Southerners began to perceive that their own set of shared interests were becoming increasingly incompatible with those of the rest of

28 These were actually two separate documents: the first, the "Exposition" (never formally adopted by the South Carolina legislature, which did, however, publicize it) clarified the reasons for the state's grievances and discussed the appropriate means to remedy it (nullification); the second, "Protest," which can in all likelihood be attributed to Calhoun (though this is not certain), was by contrast a resolution officially adopted by both the South Carolina House and Senate. See "Editorial Note," Calhoun, *Papers*, vol. 10, pp. 442-443.

the Union and were, in fact, being threatened,"[29] this emergence of a sort of "national sentiment" on the part of the South can be traced to the *Exposition*, which lucidly placed on the table every major issue underlying the struggle between the southern States and the federal government. For the first time it clarified the true meaning of nullification and the right of secession, constructing a systematic, logical, and eminently defensible framework in which to anchor the still vague opinions and protests of the southern States regarding issues of commerce and the nature of the Union. The South came to think of itself as an isolated, oppressed, and permanent minority,

From an economic point of view, the arguments of the *Exposition* are a veritable libertarian manifesto. The first part presented the country's budget in strictly economic terms: the South, with a relatively small populace, and the country's principal exporter, was exploited by the North since it had to pay an exorbitant sum on manufactured goods in order to protect New England industry and support the federal government:

> So partial are the effects of the system that its burdens are exclusively on one side and its benefits on the other. It imposes on the agricultural interest of the South, including the South-west, and that portion of the country particularly engaged in commerce and navigation, the burden not only of sustaining the system itself, but that also of the Government.[30]

According to Calhoun, American exports were 53 million dollars annually, to which the southern states contributed around 37 million. The ratio in terms of population, and thus of federal representation, was nearly symmetrically the opposite: the South

29 John McCardell, *The Idea of a Southern Nation: Southern Nationalists and Southern Nationalism, 1830–1860* (New York: Norton, 1979), p. 6.

30 John C. Calhoun, "*South Carolina Exposition (Rough Draft)*," *Papers*, vol. 10, p. 448.

had 76 congressional representatives and the North had 137, and therefore "about one-third of the Union exports more than two-thirds of the domestic products."[31]

This unequal distribution between exported wealth and political representation in turn was the basis of all injustice stemming from federal taxation: "The very acts of Congress, imposing the burdens on them, as consumers, give them the means, through the monopoly which it affords their manufactures in the home market, not only of indemnifying themselves for the increased price on the imported articles which they may consume, but, in a great measure, to command the industry of the rest of the Union." Southern consumers, due to protectionism, paid excessive prices for the goods they consumed. "We are mere consumers, and destitute of all means of transferring the burden from ours to the shoulders of others. We may be assured that the large amount paid into the Treasury under the duties on imports, is really derived from the labor of some portion of our citizens."[32] And, given that the government produced nothing, "Someone must bear the burden of its support. This unequal lot is ours. We are the serfs of the system."[33] In sum, "Our complaint is, that we are not permitted to consume the fruits of our labor; but that, through an artful and complex system, in violation of every principle of justice, they are transferred from us to others."[34]

According to Calhoun's calculations, for every 23 million dollars collected by the federal government, about 16.5 million were produced by southern labor.[35] This imbalance meant a perennial exploitation of the South, in that the financial resources produced did not serve the community, much less the South, but rather protected New England industries. "Our market is the world; and as we cannot imitate their [the northerners'] example by enlarging it for our products, through the exclusion of others, we must

31 *Ibid.*, p. 452.

32 *Ibid.*, p. 456.

33 *Ibid.*, p. 456.

34 *Ibid.*, pp. 464-466.

35 *Ibid.*, pp. 452-454.

decline their advice—which, instead of alleviating, would increase our embarrassments," wrote Calhoun. "We have no monopoly in the supply of our products; one-half of the globe may produce them. Should we reduce our production, others stand ready, by increasing theirs, to take our place; and, instead of raising prices, we would only diminish our share of the supply. We are thus compelled to produce, on the penalty of losing our hold on the general market. Once lost, it may be lost forever—and lose it we must, if we continue to be constrained, as we now are, on the one hand, by the general competition of the world, to sell low; and, on the other, by the Tariff to buy high."[36]

The protectionist system exploited southern producers and consumers, all to the benefit of the manufacturing industry, and represented a forced transfer of resources that would lead to the ruin of an entire section of the country. Calhoun incisively noted that the conflict caused by this redistribution would not limit its pernicious effects just to the South. Following that, it would also turn against northern workers as well, finally giving rise to a class struggle, orchestrated by the federal government.

> No system can be more efficient to rear up a moneyed aristocracy. Its tendency is, to make the poor poorer, and the rich richer. Heretofore, in our country, this tendency has displayed itself principally in its effects, as regards the different sections—but the time will come when it will produce the same results between the several classes in the manufacturing States. After we are exhausted, the contest will be between the capitalists and operatives; for into these two classes it must, ultimately, divide society. The issue of the struggle here must be the same as it has been in Europe.[37]

36 *Ibid.*, p. 474.

37 *Ibid.*, p. 480.

At the heart of the crisis lay a classical liberal protest against the role of government and the "improper intermeddling of the Government with the private pursuits of individuals, who must understand their own interests better than the Government."[38] If the problem was the abuse of power by the manufacturing interests of the North, which caused corruption and threatened the freedom of the entire country, the remedy was to end the government's ability to allow it. Calhoun was perfectly aware that there was a direct relationship between the consolidation of the Union (the total centralization of power so coveted by Hamilton) and the use of the government by northern interests.

The point had already been made by Robert J. Turnbull in a pamphlet in 1827: "The more National, and the less Federal, the Government becomes, the more certainly will the interest of the great majority of the States be promoted, but with the same certainty, will the interests of the South be depressed and destroyed."[39] The collusion between big government and big business, which was crushing the South, could only be thwarted by opposing the creation of a centralized governmental apparatus that could decide the extent of its own powers. Northern interests were solid and legitimate, but if they sought to transform the federal government into a centralized state on the European model, the result would be the destruction of the Union. The power of interposition by the States was the only possible remedy against the abuse of a government that was losing its "federal" character.

In sharp contrast, Alexis de Tocqueville, touring the United States a few years later, did not notice any "material interest [that] one portion of the Union would have, for now, to separate from the others." Rather, for him, all regions got along harmoniously: "The states of the South are nearly exclusively agricultural; the states of the North are particularly manufacturing and commercial; the states of the West are at the same time manufacturing and agricultural. In the South tobacco, rice, cotton and sugar are

38 *Ibid.*, p. 482.

39 Brutus [Robert J. Turnbull], "The Crisis" (1827), in *The Nullification Era: A Documentary Record*, ed. William W. Freehling (New York, 1967), p. 27.

harvested; in the North and in the West, corn and wheat. These are the diverse sources of wealth. But in order to draw upon these sources, there is a means common and equally favorable to all; it is the Union."[40]

Calhoun's case was based instead on recognition of the enormous diversity of interests and political communities that made up the United States (which should have found an impartial mediator in the federal government) and on the clear distinction between governmental power and sovereignty. "The present disordered state of our political system originated in the diversity of interests which exists in the country—a diversity recognized by the Constitution itself, and to which it owes one of its most distinguished and peculiar features—the division of the delegated powers between the State and General Governments."[41] Yet that difference should have been recognized in the Constitution, with its settlement in the federal division of power. The federal government was endowed with certain powers, explicitly enumerated in the Constitution, over which "the States cannot, without violating the constitutional compact, interpose their authority to check, or in any manner to counteract its movements, so long as they are confined to the proper sphere."[42]

But the States, too, should be protected by a total ban on interference in their areas of control: "So, also, the peculiar and local powers reserved to the States are subject to their exclusive control; nor can the General Government interfere, in any manner, with them, without violating the Constitution."[43] The essence of the American compact is contained in this rigid arrangement, based on "striking distinction between Government and Sovereignty."[44] While governmental powers belong on one side to the institutions

40 Alexis de Tocqueville, *Democracy in America: Historical-critical Edition of De la démocratie en Amérique*, vol. 2, ed. Eduardo Nolla (Indianapolis: Liberty Fund, 2010), pp. 594-595.

41 John C. Calhoun, "*South Carolina Exposition (Rough Draft)*", *Papers*, vol. 10, p. 494.

42 *Ibid.*, p. 496.

43 *Ibid.*, p. 496.

44 *Ibid.*, p. 496.

of the States, and on the other to the federal government, "the sovereignty resides in the people of the States respectively."[45] Though Calhoun recognized that the final constitutional authority is in the supermajority of three-quarters of the States "in whom the highest power known to the Constitution actually resides," he immediately added that "not the least portion of this high sovereign authority resides in Congress, or any of the departments of the General Government. They are but the creatures of the Constitution, and are appointed but to execute its provisions; and, therefore, any attempt by all, or any of these departments, to exercise any power which, in its consequences, may alter the nature of the instrument, or change the condition of the parties to it, would be an act of usurpation."[46]

But what means are provided to defend such a perfect system of the division of power, government, and sovereignty? According to Calhoun the federal government equipped itself with a formidable tool against the excesses of the States when Article 25 of the Judiciary Act of 1789 made the Supreme Court of the United States the court of last resort in the country, allowing it to judge if an individual state law violates the prerogative of the federal government or not. Calhoun did not dispute that, but he also added, "by a strange misconception of the nature of our system—and, in fact, of the nature of government,"[47] the bizarre idea developed that the Supreme Court can judge the opposite case as well, namely whether an act of the government or the federal Congress exceeds the rights reserved to the States. "Such a construction of its powers would, in fact, raise one of the departments of the General Government above the parties who created the constitutional compact, and virtually invest it with the authority to alter, at its pleasure, the relative powers of the General and State Governments."[48]

45 *Ibid.*, p. 498.

46 *Ibid.*, p. 498.

47 *Ibid.*, p. 500.

48 *Ibid.*, p. 500.

In Calhoun's view, it was completely irrelevant that the final judicial authority might be considered the repository of the decisions of last resort in all questions submitted to it according to the rules of the Constitution. "However true, therefore, it may be that the Judicial Department is, in all questions submitted to it by the forms of the Constitution, to decide in the last resort, this resort must necessarily be considered the last in relation to the authorities of the other departments of the Government, not in relation to the rights of the parties to the constitutional compact, from which the Judicial and all other departments hold their delegated trusts."[49]

Whereas the Jeffersonian party had adopted the idea of strict construction of the Constitution in order to bring under control the federal government, Calhoun made it crystal clear that no interpretive rule in the text of the Constitution could ever really impose practical restraints on the exercise of power. Such rules are equivalent to an appeal by the minority to a sense of justice and moderation on the majority. As a great political realist, he maintained that historical experience has amply shown that "power can only be restrained by power, and not by reason and justice; and that all restrictions on authority, unsustained by an equal antagonist power, must forever prove wholly inefficient in practice."[50] The States alone could wield this power, and the remedy available to them was the right of interposition, or the right of each individual State to judge if its own rights have been violated by a federal intervention. This is the right to veto on the actions of the federal government and Congress that were considered illegitimate.

After having cited various highly authoritative sources—from Madison and Jefferson to the quite implausible Hamilton[51]—on which to base such an interpretation, Calhoun confronted several possible objections. First, one could argue that the legislative assembly does not represent the sovereignty of the state itself, which

49 *Ibid.*, p. 502.

50 *Ibid.*, p. 504.

51 It must be noted, though, that at the time *Federalist* 51 was believed to be the work of Hamilton.

resides in the people, which would lead to investing a regularly constituted state convention with the power to nullify a federal law. In this case, the right to represent the will of the sovereign people is not subject to discussion by anyone.[52]

The point is essential: Sovereignty belongs always and only to the peoples of the individual States, which cannot cede it to the governments. In a case, such as nullification of a law or action that directly turns on the question of sovereignty, the state legislatures can defend their citizens from such usurpation by "interposing themselves" between the people and the federal government. In the final instance, however, the question must be decided by the people; and conventions, which had already been used to ratify the constitution, seemed best suited to represent the popular will. They are a means of semi-direct democracy in that the delegates to the convention are elected by the people precisely in virtue of their stated positions on the question.

According to others, the right of state interposition, since it is not expressly mentioned in the constitutional text, is based on inference. In any case, it is an evident right, such that one cannot deduce its nonexistence from the fact that it was not stated properly. Thus the *Exposition* continues:

> The omission to enumerate the power of the States to interpose in order to protect their rights—being strictly in accord with the principles on which its framers formed the Constitution, raises not the slightest presumption against its existence. Like all other reserved rights, it is to be inferred from the simple fact that it is not delegate—as is clearly the case in this instance.[53]

Finally, the fact that interposition is sanctioned by a convention, coupled with the deliberate and voluntary slowness of the process, guarantees against a light-hearted recourse to the right of interposition, a point which meets the objections of

52 *Ibid.*, p. 510.

53 *Ibid.*, p. 514.

those who maintain that such a power to impede the authority of the federal government would inevitably tend toward anarchy and chaos. "South Carolina's brand of nullification differed from that of Jefferson and Madison's. ... Calhoun argued that a state's enactment of nullification held full legal bearing unless overturned by a supermajority of three-fourths of all states in the union. In contrast, Jefferson and Madison promoted nullification as a unilateral action that did not involve the other states at all."[54]

The maximum guarantee against a possible abuse of the power of intervention is provided in the fact that the Constitution can be amended only by a majority of at least three-quarters of the States. The power of nullification, then, takes shape as a possibility (and right) of the individual State within the federal compact to appeal to the supermajority: the highest constitutional authority. Nullification is thus entirely within the larger system, but—as we will see—it logically opens the way to a revision of the constitutional pact, thus presenting each state with the dilemma: whether to adhere to the new pact or withdraw from the Union. Calhoun was fully convinced that the mere threat of nullification would lead to a non-traumatic settlement between the parties. In fact, the *Exposition* closed with an appeal to moderation. While recognizing that the seriousness of the problem posed by the protective tariff would justify immediate recourse to intervention, Calhoun, acting out of respect for the other States and for the sake of harmony, urged his fellow South Carolinians to wait for the moves made by the newly elected President Andrew Jackson.

That hope was quickly disappointed. Although Jackson was a candidate from the South who ran on a platform favorable to free trade and states' rights, he soon became a champion of the Union. On April 13, 1830, at a banquet in honor of Thomas Jefferson on his birthday, a significant scene played out between Jackson and Calhoun. Jackson provocatively toasted the health of the Union: "Our federal Union—it must and shall be preserved!" Calhoun's

54 David Benner, *Compact of the Republic. The League of States and the Constitution* (Minneapolis: Life and Liberty, 2015), p. 179.

response was quick and prudent: "The Union, next to our Liberty most dear."[55] Liberty and the Union had become two distinct, if not actually opposed, terms.

5.3) The Webster-Hayne Debate on the Nature of the Union

The press contributed positively to the growing fame of the *Exposition*. Calhoun's ideas quickly fired up the entire country, and Congress had to give them attention. In January 1830 the Senate witnessed the most memorable rhetorical clash in American history. During debate on Foot's resolution,[56] Calhoun's theory gained its widest publicity so far, and the question of states' rights became the nation's foremost political issue. This heated exchange is known as the Webster-Hayne debate on the nature of the Union.[57] Robert Hayne, a South Carolina senator, represented the states' righters, while Senator Daniel Webster argued for the Union. At the heart of the dispute was whether the Union was based on a compact or not.

Hayne's speeches are not particularly innovative, and the influence of his mentor Calhoun is evident in them. Entire phrases are taken almost verbatim from Calhoun's writings. The crucial problem was always who should judge the extent of the powers assigned to the federal government: "If the Federal Government, in all or any of its departments, are to prescribe the limits of its own authority; and the States are bound to submit to the decision,

55 See William M. Meigs, *The Life of John C. Calhoun* (New York, 1917), vol. 2, p. 398.

56 On December 29, 1829, Senator Samuel A. Foot of Connecticut proposed to Congress to consider halting the sale of public lands in the West. Senator Thomas Hart Benton of Missouri immediately denounced the resolution as a shameless attempt by eastern industrialists to prevent common workers from colonizing the flourishing western regions; he appealed to the South to oppose what he considered a threat to the rights of the States.

57 The principal presentations are found in *The Webster-Hayne Debate on the Nature of the Union*, ed. Herman Belz. Haynes' first address was on January 19, 1830; Webster responded on January 20, followed by various rebuttals: Hayne on January 25, Webster the 26th and 27th, and Hayne again the same day. Ten years before, Webster had already developed the general principles of his "nationalism," cf. Daniel Webster, *A Discourse, Delivered at Plymouth, December 22, 1820* (Boston: Wells and Lilly, 1825).

and are not to be allowed to examine and decide for themselves, when the barriers of the Constitution shall be overleaped, this is practically 'a Government without limitation of powers,'" Hayne said. But he assured his listeners that the states' power to interpret the Constitution was the truly conserving principle of the Union: "In all the efforts that have been made by South Carolina to resist the unconstitutional laws which Congress has extended over them, she has kept steadily in view the preservation of the Union, by the only means by which she believes it can be long preserved—a firm, manly, and steady resistance against usurpation." A more general axiom was as stake as well, near and dear to all Anglo-Saxons: "The South is acting on a principle she has always held sound—resistance to unauthorized taxation."[58] The very existence of South Carolina was placed in danger by the effects of the protective tariffs, and the Hayne-Calhoun tenets seemed unassailable in the light of the American tradition.

By this time, it had become evident that the real matter in contention was not the public lands in the West or protective tariffs, but, as Daniel Webster stated, the American institutions. There is a well-founded suspicion that Webster drew Hayne into a controversy on the nature of the Union in order to challenge southern leadership and reinforce New England's influence in the federation.[59] That is, he too held to a sort of "regional nationalism," since his section of the country was by that time dominating the Union. The "nationalist" interpretation, far from being a political weapon for any area, was peculiarly appropriate to cloak the Northeastern interests. Moreover, it is reasonably clear that the purpose of his attacks was to prevent a conjunction of Western and Southern interests. Webster was the real architect of the protectionist economic system against which South Carolina was rebelling. He thus found it necessary to respond, "for personal reasons." But his nationalist vision was not simply a brilliant rhetorical device designed to win a contingent political battle. Webster went to the Senate and girded himself for what is typically

58 Hayne, *The Webster-Hayne Debate*, p. 79.

59 See Harlow W. Sheidley, "The Webster-Hayne Debate: Recasting New England's Sectionalism," *New England Quarterly* 67 (1994), pp. 5-29.

considered by nationalist historians such as Edward Channing as the greatest effort of his life, as well as the greatest American oration—while Calhoun sat impassively in his vice-presidential seat.[60] Webster's defense of the American nation, spread widely through thousands of printed copies, rapidly became the North's *Exposition*.

In his first response, Webster vindicated the term consolidation, abhorred by Southerners:

> Consolidation!—that perpetual cry, both of terror and delusion—consolidation! Sir, when gentlemen speak of the effects of a common fund, belonging to all the States, as having a tendency to consolidation, what do they mean? Do they mean, or can they mean, any thing more than that the Union of the States will be strengthened, by whatever continues or furnishes inducements to the people of the States to hold together? ... I wish to see no new powers drawn to the General Government; but I confess I rejoice in whatever tends to strengthen the bond that unites us, and encourages the hope that our Union may be perpetual.[61]

Hayne had observed, in an earlier exchange with Webster, that Webster viewed consolidation as "the very object for which the Union was formed"—*i.e.*, the very purpose of the Constitution.[62]

In his second response to Hayne, Webster attacked the idea that the Constitution was a compact among the peoples of the various States. Though constitutional limits exist, Webster added, "We look upon the States, not as separated, but as united. ...[T]he States are one. It was the very object of the constitution to create unity of interests, to the extent of the powers of the General Government. In

60 Cf. Edward Channing, *History of the United States*, vol. 5 (New York: Macmillan, 1921), p. 422.

61 Webster, *The Webster-Hayne Debate*, pp. 23-24.

62 *Ibid.*, 51 (Hayne); cf. 110 (Webster).

war and peace, we are one; in commerce, one."[63] Although Webster only set forth a very vague notion of the limits on the actions of the federal government,[64] one cannot conclude that he held a hostile position against the State governments (as did Hamilton). When he stated that "[t]he States are, unquestionably, sovereign, so far as their sovereignty is not affected by this supreme law,"[65] the message to southern politicians was clear: We will not interfere with slavery, but you must remain in the Union, on our terms, and pay the price without calculating the value.[66]

Webster's address unfolds around three nodal points: Revolution, the power of the Supreme Court, and federal supremacy. In the first place, there is the affirmation of a general right to revolution, typical of the political tradition of free peoples, which was equivalent to telling South Carolina that the claim of a constitutional revolution was a figment of their politicians' imagination. Webster's clear warning was: Don't think that we will let you get away with a "constitutional revolution." For Webster, Jefferson's and Madison's Resolutions of 1798, which Southerners considered almost part of the Constitution, were ambiguous. Perhaps they meant to assert that "the States may interfere by complaint and remonstrance; or by proposing to the People an alteration of the Federal Constitution." Perhaps they meant "to assert the general right of revolution, as against all Governments, in cases of intolerable oppression. This no one doubts." On the other hand, it was impossible to believe that they meant to uphold the notion that "a state, under the Constitution, and in conformity with it, could ... annul a law of Congress."[67] Webster continued:

63 *Ibid.*, pp. 98-99.

64 Cf. *Ibid.*, p. 99.

65 *Ibid.*, p. 126

66 Thomas Cooper had argued that it was high time to open a discussion on the value of the Union; "'Value of the Union' Speech," July 2, 1827, in *The Nullification Era*, pp. 48-61. According to William Harper, "They know, too, that all the States have calculated the value of the Union, and although it will always be the most advantageous to the sections where labor and its products are cheaper, yet they are willing to pay the price they have stipulated," William Harper, *The Remedy by State Interposition* ... (September 20, 1830) (Charleston: Van Brust, 1832), p. 18.

67Webster, *The Webster-Hayne Debate*, p. 135.

> We, sir, who oppose the Carolina doctrine, do not deny that the People may, if they choose, throw off any government, when it becomes oppressive and intolerable, and erect a better in its stead. ... But I do not understand the doctrine now contended for to be that which, for the sake of distinctness, we may call the right of revolution. I understand the gentleman to maintain, that, without revolution, without civil commotion, without rebellion, a remedy for supposed abuse and transgression of the powers of the General Government lies in a direct appeal to the interference of the State Governments. ... The great question is, *whose prerogative is it to decide on the constitutionality or unconstitutionality of the laws?...* I do not admit that, under the Constitution, and in conformity with it, there is any mode in which a State Government, as a member of the Union, can interfere and stop the progress of the General Government, by force of her own laws, under any circumstances whatever.[68]

Webster denied the possibility that the States could interpret the Constitution and decried the "absurdity" of considering the federal government "servant of four-and-twenty masters."[69] "If there be no power to settle such questions, independent of either of the States, is not the whole Union a rope of sand?"[70] The

68 *Ibid.*, pp. 124-125.

69 *Ibid.*, p. 126.

70 *Ibid.*, p. 128. During the Philadelphia convention, Judge Oliver Ellsworth, confronted with extremely negative opinions on state governments and the States themselves, reminded the delegates that "without their approbation, your government is nothing more than a rope of sand," Alston Mygatt, *Secret Proceedings and Debates of the Federal Convention* (Louisville: Alston Mygatt, 1844 [first edition published in Albany in 1821]), p. 165. The latter could not have escaped the attention of Webster, who, however, reversed Ellsworth's statement: It was precisely the force retained by the States that risked making the Constitution a rope of sand. Sand and Union were connected together in a very odd manner by Andrew Jackson in a December 25, 1832, letter to Martin Van Buren: "A state cannot come into the union without the consent of Congress, but it can go out when it pleases. Such a Union as this would be like a bag

Supreme Court was obviously that power. The true sovereign of every political organization was the people, not the people of the various States, but rather the people of each State in relation to its own legal system, and the American people as a whole to the Constitution. "We are all agents of the same supreme power, the People. The General Government and the State Governments derive their authority from the same source."[71] With regard to the Constitution, "It is, sir, the People's Constitution, the People's Government; made for the People; made by the People; and answerable to the People. The People of the United States have declared that this Constitution shall be the Supreme Law. We must either admit the proposition, or dispute their authority. The States are, unquestionably, sovereign, so far as their sovereignty is not affected by this supreme law."[72]

This was the crucial point: predicating the existence of a single people that had collectively given rise to the Constitution, Webster, emotionally if not logically, pulled the rug out from under Calhoun and his followers. It was for him necessary to find a source from which the Constitution arose and which was disconnected from the States: This turned out to be "*the People of the United States.*"[73] It was here that Webster masterfully played off the Constitution itself.

It is true that the preamble of the Constitution refers to the peoples of the various States, just as Calhoun's followers maintained, but "the Constitution itself, in its very front, refutes that idea: it declares that it is ordained and established *by the People of the United States.* So far from saying that it is

---

of sand with both ends open—the least pressure and it runs out at both ends," quoted in Richard E. Ellis, *The Union at Risk* (Oxford: Oxford University Press, 1987), p. 87.

71 Webster, *The Webster-Hayne Debate*, p. 126.

72 *Ibid.*, p. 126. My readers will have no doubt noticed the link between Webster's phrase and the famous Gettysburg Address in which Lincoln assured that the war had been fought so that "government of the people, by the people, for the people, shall not perish from the earth," "Address delivered at the dedication of the Cemetery at Gettysburg" in *Collected Works of Abraham Lincoln*, ed. Roy P. Basler (New Brunswick, NJ: Rutgers University Press, 1953), vol. 7, p. 23.

73 Webster, *The Webster-Hayne Debate*, p. 153.

established by the Governments of the several States, it does not even say that it is established by the People *of the several States*; but it pronounces that it is established by the People of the United States, in the aggregate. The gentleman says, it must mean no more than the People of the several States. Doubtless, the People of the several States, taken collectively, constitute the People of the United States; but it is in this, their collective capacity, it is as all the People of the United States, that they establish the Constitution."[74] Thus it was not even necessary to force the historical reality to identify the master over the Constitution. Although the States were completely unaware of it, in Webster's view they acted as a portion of the American people and ratified the Constitution as a part of a collective and aggregate entity. As historically indefensible as it was, this thesis of an American people and its Constitution and Union was gaining ground.

Several classic elements of European public law were evident in Webster's discourse, denying the contractual nature of the Constitution. In effect, if the Constitution is a law and not a treaty between sovereign powers, then by the same reasoning the federal government is not a contract, but a government endowed with full powers.[75] In placing the Constitution well beyond the deliberations of State conventions, from which it had had its origin—that is, denying that it was a compact between the States—Webster had posited the premises for the emergence of a genuinely nationalist school of thought. What Fletcher Webster, eldest son of the senator, wrote to his father after reading his address is highly significant: "I never knew what the constitution really was, before your last short speech. I thought it was a compact between States."[76] In any case, many Americans continued to think it was a compact, even after the senator's brilliant address.

74 *Ibid.*

75 "[I]t is a Constitution (...) [and not] a Confederacy." *Ibid.*, p. 137.

76 Daniel Fletcher Webster to Daniel Webster, March 23, 1830, cited in Irving H. Bartlett, *Daniel Webster* (New York: Norton, 1978), p. 120.

For Webster, the highest good to protect was the Union. If the supreme political goal had always been freedom, it was given very little conceptual autonomy. He insisted on this in his famous closing statement: "Nor those other words of delusion and folly, Liberty first, and Union afterwards—but every where, spread all over in characters of living light, blazing on all its ample folds, as they float over the sea and over the land, and in every wind under the whole Heavens, that other sentiment, dear to every true American heart—Liberty and Union, now and forever, one and inseparable!"[77] The final phrase became first the slogan and then the Union battle cry during the Civil War.

The crucial part of Webster's address, though, was not his new constitutional doctrine on the nature of the Union, but rather the new creed, the new faith in a strong, free and united America. He appealed to the spirit of the Constitution and its evolutionary nature: Born as a compact, it needed to be rethought as something profoundly different. Webster's address marks the beginning of constitutional interpretation on the basis of extra-constitutional principles, an operation at which Abraham Lincoln would later excel. However, in his most famous speech, Webster addressed the theme of constitutional interpretation as part of a much broader reflection on civil and peaceful coexistence. It was necessary to make it very clear to the Southerners that the debate was not about abstract questions or the metaphysics of power: such a course would quickly lead to decisions which were final. He said: "We will take up the existing case of the Tariff law. ... If we do not repeal it, ... [South Carolina] will then apply to the case the remedy of her doctrine. She will ... pass a law of her legislature, declaring the several acts of Congress, usually called the Tariff Laws, null and void. ..." At this point the question would no longer be a subject of mere analysis and political speculation, because contention would arise between federal and state officials in South Carolina. In the

77 Webster, *The Webster-Hayne Debate*, p. 144. The supreme irony was that these words were suggested to Webster in reading Calhoun's address of April 6, 1816, to the House of Representatives, in which he had approved the customs duty: "In his opinion the liberty and the union of this country were inseparably united." Calhoun, *Works*, vol. 2, p. 173; see Charles M. Wiltse, *John C. Calhoun: Nullifier, 1829-1839* (Indianapolis-New York: Bobbs-Merrill, 1949), p. 62.

end, Webster ironically suggested that the "militia of the State will be called out to sustain the nullifying act. They will march, sir, under a very gallant leader"—perhaps Robert Hayne himself, who "commands the militia of that part of the State. He will raise the NULLIFYING ACT on his standard, and spread it out as his banner! ... He will proceed ... to the Customhouse in Charleston. ..." Each party to the contest would appeal to its own laws until Hayne "would be in a dilemma, like that of another great General [Gordius]. He would have a knot before him, which he could not untie. He must cut it with his sword. He must say to his followers, defend yourselves with bayonets; and this is war—civil war."[78]

The Southerners had been warned: The great political questions of the Union were intertwined with those of peace. The constitutional arguments in the debate would soon be exhausted, and the answer would be found in recourse to the extra-constitutional method par excellence: war. The Webster-Hayne debate contributed to defining the opposition between the states' righters, who based all their arguments on the Constitution, and the nationalists who defended the legitimacy of their *meta-constitutional* interpretation. It is clear, though, that Calhoun was the first to ripple the waters. Until the 1830s the North and South did not differ on this matter, and the voluntary and contractual view of the Union was widely shared. The realignment provoked first by the *Exposition* and then by nullification in South Carolina led an entire region, the North, to adopt the organicist theory of the Union set forth by Webster and Joseph Story.[79]

The *National Intelligencer* published tens of thousands of copies of Webster's address, which in short order became the political creed of a large part of the North. This new doctrinal

---

78 Webster, *The Webster-Hayne Debate*, pp. 139-140.

79 Joseph Story published his *Commentaries on the Constitution*, which were also the systematic organization of a series of prior works on the American Constitution, in that timeframe. Story's work was the first to expose all the premises and constitutional interpretations of the term "nationalist." See Joseph Story, *Commentaries on the Constitution of the United States*, 3 vols. (Boston, 1833). On this figure, see James McClellan, *Joseph Story and the American Constitution: A Study in Political and Legal Thought* (Norman: University of Oklahoma Press, 1971).

polarization over the significance of the Union was also a sign that the middle ground that had been reached in the Philadelphia convention, the compromise on sovereignty, was eroding. No common constitutionally supportable position remained between Calhoun and Webster. By then the debate was centered on the federation and the States, between a rigorously organicist position, which considered the Constitution an act of the entire American people, and a consistent contractual view, which held it to be the result of an accord between the various peoples of the States.

In his final constitutional fight, James Madison sought to restore the compromise, upholding that nullification in the extreme version set forth by Calhoun was not admissible, yet at the same time that the Constitution was born as a compact between the peoples of the various States.[80] From the 1830s onward his view was at first isolated, then finally unsustainable.

5.4) Nullification and Secession

When South Carolina made the first attempt to put Calhoun's theory into practice, things nearly came to the point that Webster had predicted. In August 1832 Calhoun sent an open letter to James Hamilton, the governor of South Carolina, in which he submitted "a fuller development of my views ... on the right of a State to defend her reserved powers against the encroachments of the General Government."[81] Restating and expanding the arguments given in the *Exposition*, Calhoun maintained that the right of nullification by a State, contrary to what Webster had argued, was of a peaceful nature and in no way damaged the prerogatives of the national government. Any controversy between a state and the federal government subsequent to the implementation of the right of nullification would be "a legal and constitutional contest—a contest

80 See James Madison, "Notes on Nullification, 1835-36," Madison, *Writings*, vol. 9, pp. 573-606.

81 John C. Calhoun to James Hamilton, Jr., August 28, 1832, in Calhoun, *Papers*, vol. 11, p. 613.

of moral, and not physical force—a trial of constitutional and not military power,—to be decided before the judicial tribunals of the country, and not on the field of battle."[82]

On November 24, 1832, a specially convened South Carolina convention approved the Nullification Ordinance, which declared that the 1828 and 1832 federal tariffs were unconstitutional and not binding on the citizens and officials of South Carolina. The South Carolina representatives declared that not only were the tariffs rejected, but that "any act authorizing the employment of a military or naval force against the State of South Carolina, her constitutional authorities or citizens" would be null and void.[83] If, however, the federal government wanted to act forcefully against the State, such an action would be "inconsistent with the longer continuance of South Carolina in the Union." This response went well beyond Calhoun's views and openly threatened to "proceed to organize a separate government, and do all other acts and things which sovereign and independent States may of right do."[84] In short, the possibility of secession was set forth.

Among the various responses to South Carolina's actions by the other states, responses that were far more copious and articulate than those voiced to the 1798-99 Virginia and Kentucky Resolutions, that of Webster's own state is interesting. The Massachusetts committee did not become sidetracked in analyzing the economic situation in South Carolina or the question of whether the tariff was constitutional or not. That would have been a futile exercise, since South Carolina's measures "propose an unconstitutional and illegal method of obtaining relief from a supposed political grievance."[85] Rather, it seemed clear, "it was not intended in making this arrangement, to maintain the States

---

82 *Ibid.*, p. 628.

83 South Carolina Convention, "An Ordinance. To Nullify Certain Acts of the Congress of the United States ...," November 24, 1832, in *State Papers on Nullification* (Boston: Dutton and Wentworth, 1834), p. 30.

84 *Ibid*, p. 3.

85 Joint Select Committee of the Commonwealth of Massachusetts, Senate, February 15, 1833, in *State Papers on Nullification*, p. 115.

in possession of an absolute political independence."[86] This would be an absurdity comparable to "to interpret one of the clauses in a contract of marriage in such a way as would suppose that it was the intention of the parties to remain single."[87] In short, whatever the situation prior to the passage of the Constitution, the marriage had been consummated. Evoking the eternality of the political pact underlying the Constitution in the marriage metaphor was a clear sign that the ideology of the modern state was gaining ground, at least in the North. But the heart of the argument remained the Supreme Court, which has the task of deciding "whether a law is constitutional, which the Carolina doctrine claims for the States."[88]

In any case, the Massachusetts politicians pointed out to the rebellious State that there were only two methods for righting the (presumed) wrongs: *ballots or bullets*. In fact, "the people cure the evil either by a change in the administration effected in consistency with the forms of the Constitution, or if the case be extreme, by recurring to the natural right of violent resistance to the law."[89] There was no "middle path between these two courses."[90] Northern politicians refused to accept the existence of a right of resistance written into the Constitution itself. Call it whatever you like, but "[e]very attempt to prevent by force, the execution of the laws,—by whatever name it may be called,—is, in its nature, revolutionary."[91]

Some southern states, such as Alabama, openly supported South Carolina's complaints about the protective tariff but were not convinced on the question of nullification. They found it "is unsound in theory and dangerous in practice, that as a remedy it is unconstitutional and essentially revolutionary, leading in its consequences to anarchy and civil discord, and finally to the dissolution of the Union."[92] President

86 *Ibid.*, p. 120.

87 *Id.*, p. 120.

88 *Ibid.*, p. 122.

89 *Ibid.*, p. 123.

90 *Ibid.*, p. 124.

91 *Id*, p. 124.

92 "Senate and House of Representatives of the State of Alabama in General Assembly convened," January 12, 1833, *State Papers on Nullification*, p. 222.

Andrew Jackson, who privately stated that he would have gladly hung Calhoun, also held that "[t]his abominable doctrine [nullification] ... strikes at the root of our Government and the social compact, and reduces every thing to anarchy."[93]

The drama unfolded as Webster had foreseen: Jackson ordered the customs inspector of Charleston to seize all ships bound for the port, and General Scott, the commander over American naval forces, received the order to head for Charleston. On December 10, 1832, Jackson—himself born a South Carolinian—issued a proclamation against his home state, which, though written in a determined and energetic tone, still remained open. Using Webster's tactics and arguments in the proclamation,[94] he attacked the theory of states' rights as "incompatible with the existence of the Union, contradicted expressly by the letter of the Constitution, unauthorized by its spirit, inconsistent with every principle on which it was founded, and destructive of the great object for which it was formed."[95]

> The Constitution of the United States, then, forms a government, not a league, and whether it be formed by compact between the States, or in any other manner, its character is the same. It is a government in which all the people are represented, which operates directly on the people individually, not upon the States; they retained all the power they did not grant. But each State having expressly parted with so many powers as to constitute jointly with the other States a single nation, cannot from that period possess any right

93 Andrew Jackson to Martin Van Buren, December 23, 1832, cited in Richard B. Latner, "The Nullification Crisis and Republican Subversion," *Journal of Southern History* 43, no. 1 (1977), p. 20.

94 Jackson's dependence on Webster is a generally accepted fact among historians. For an analysis of the unionist positions of Webster, John Quincy Adams, and Jackson see Major L. Wilson, "Liberty and Union: An Analysis of Three Concepts Involved in the Nullification Controversy," *Journal of Southern History* 33 (1967), pp. 331-355.

95 Andrew Jackson, *Proclamation of Andrew Jackson, President of The United States, to the People of South Carolina*, December 10, 1832 (Harrisburg: Singerly & Myers, 1864), p. 6.

> to secede, because such secession does not break a league, but destroys the unity of a nation, and any injury to that unity is not only a breach which would result from the contravention of a compact, but it is an offense against the whole Union.[96]

The mobilization of federal troops reinforced the proclamation. In the *Exposition*, his letter to Governor Hamilton, his Fort Hill Address, and his address on the Force Bill, Calhoun explicitly stated that nullification, or even the very threat of enacting it, would be enough to dispose the federal and state governments to compromise. The three great political figures of that time—Clay, Webster, and Calhoun—set themselves to work to avert the danger, and they came to an agreement. The compromise solution on the tariff provided that within ten years it would become a uniform twenty percent tax on all incoming goods. The president, however, insisted that the law reducing the protective tariffs be passed together with the Force Bill, which authorized the federal government to deploy the armed forces to compel states to comply with federal laws. Despite Calhoun's strong opposition, on March 1, 1833, Congress approved both legislative measures. Shortly afterward the South Carolina convention repealed the nullification ordinance.

For Calhoun, the very threat of the use of force was "the most triumphant acknowledgment that nullification is peaceful and efficient, and so deeply intrenched in the principles of our system, that it cannot be assailed but by prostrating the constitution, and substituting the supremacy of military force in lieu of the supremacy of the laws."[97] At the same time, however, the states' rights school had suffered a sharp defeat, since the Force Bill granted the president unlimited power. Recognizing the federal government as the highest sovereign power "by treating the States as a mere lawless mass of individuals—prostrates all the barriers

96 *Ibid.*, p. 10.

97 John C. Calhoun, "Speech on the Force Bill," Senate, February 15-16, 1833, Calhoun, *Papers*, vol. 12, p. 67.

of the constitution," Calhoun wrote.[98] While Senator Felix Grundy had defined the Force Bill as a means for peace, Calhoun stated that "such peace as the wolf gives to the lamb—the kite to the dove! Such peace as Russia gives to Poland, or death to its victim! A peace, by extinguishing the political existence of the State, by awing her into an abandonment of the exercise of every power which constitutes her a sovereign community."[99]

By then the question of secession had arisen, and it became firmly embedded in the American debate. As one of Italy's most important historians emphasized, "No one in the United States, until the eve of the Civil War, held that secession was a crime, much less thought that the federal government would oppose it by the force of arms."[100] The American Constitution was silent on the subject, and the legitimacy or illegitimacy of the right of secession by the States had to be drawn from the nature of the Union. In Calhoun's constitutional doctrine there was a relationship between nullification and secession, and the first attempt to put nullification into practice had made that dramatically clear. As Feldman has rightly noted, "[I]f nullification was thought of as a substitute for the judgment of the Supreme Court ... it appears above all as an alternative to secession."[101]

A true Calhounian theory of secession finds it written implicitly in the Constitution understood as a contract between sovereign parties. Calhoun, in his *Discourse on the Government and Constitution of the United States,* published posthumously and largely incomplete, justified his interpretation of the Constitution as a contract between the states by referring back to the text of the Constitution and the work of the Constitutional Convention. According to Webster's and Story's interpretation, the adoption

---

98 *Ibid.*, p. 68.

99 *Ibid.*, p. 69.

100 *La Guerra Civile Americana*, ed. Raimondo Luraghi (Bologna: il Mulino, 1978), p. 13. The dominant unionist prejudice in Europe, especially among historians, made sure that what in nineteenth century America was called the "War between the States"—and today the "Civil War"—was called the "War of Secession."

101 Jean-Philippe Feldman, *La bataille américaine du fédéralism: John C. Calhoun et l'annulation (1828–1833)* (Paris: Presses Universitaires de France, 2004), p. 265.

of the Constitution had substantively altered the nature of the American federation: Whereas under the Articles of Confederation there existed a simple alliance of sovereign states, the Constitution had established a government endowed with its own autonomous existence. Calhoun's arguments drew instead on the continuous existence of American political institutions. The mere fact that the name "United States" designated both the alliance under the Articles of Confederation and the one which succeeded it gave solid proof that "[t]he retention of the same style, throughout every stage of their existence, affords strong, if not conclusive evidence that the political relation between these States, under their present constitution and government, is substantially the same as under the confederacy and revolutionary government; and what that relation was, we are not left to doubt; as they are declared expressly to be 'free, independent and sovereign States'."[102]

According to Calhoun, the ratification procedure for the Constitution presented the final proof of his thesis: The Constitutional Convention had submitted the text of the Constitution to Congress, as the representative body of the member states "in their confederated character," after which the Constitution had to be ratified by each individual state. The parties to the Constitutional contract had thus participated as sovereign States, demonstrating that the Constitution

> [r]eceived the assent of the States in all the possible modes in which it could be obtained: first—in their confederated character, through its only appropriate organ, the Congress; next, in their individual character, as separate States, through their respective State governments, to which the Congress referred it; and finally, in their high character of independent and sovereign communities, through a convention of the people, called in each State, by the authority of its government.[103]

102 John C. Calhoun, *A Discourse on the Government and Constitution of the United States*, p. 116.

103 *Ibid.*, p. 126.

The interpretation of the Constitution as a compact was supported by Article VII, which established that the ratification of nine out of thirteen States was sufficient for it to enter into force "*between the States so ratifying the Same.*" Thus "the authority which ordained and established the Constitution, was the joint and united authority of the States ratifying it; and among the effects of their ratification, it became a contract between them; and, *as a compact*, binding on them;—but only as such."[104] In brief, while the States created a new system, their ratification of the Constitution had not altered the nature of the pact:

> I have now shown, conclusively, by arguments drawn from the act of ratification, and the constitution itself, that the several States of the Union, acting in their confederated character, ordained and established the constitution; that they ordained and established it for themselves, in the same character; that they ordained and established it for their welfare and safety, in the like character; that they established it as a compact *between* them, and not as a constitution *over* them; and that, as a compact, they are parties to it, in the same character.[105]

He did, however, recognize a significant difference between the system in force under the Articles of Confederation and the one established by the Constitution, but viewed the changes entailed by the Constitution as not in the foundations, but rather in the superstructure of the system. This expanded the role of the common government, but it in no way subverted the contractual nature of the federal system. While under the Articles the federal government could be likened to a "Standing Committee" between the States, the previous semi-diplomatic institutions were replaced by a real and proper system of government institutions, thus actualizing a more perfect union between the states that had consented to it.

---

104 *Ibid.*, pp. 130-131.

105 *Ibid.*, p. 131.

What is important to note is that Calhoun's logical path moves from the contractual theory of the Constitution to arrive at the assertion of the sovereignty of the individual states. For Calhoun, this is always the path by which state sovereignty is revealed: Given the nature of the pact, it could be stipulated only among sovereign parties. The necessary requirement of sovereignty was not what made the Constitution a contract. Rather, American constitutional history made it manifestly clear that it was founded on State sovereignty. The nature of the Constitution provides conclusive proof of the authentic locus of sovereignty in the American system. While we recall the brilliant, though hardly persuasive, definition of Calhoun as a "reverse Marx," from the point of view of public law one could well argue that Calhoun was an "overturned Bodin." Sovereignty is not for him what makes a State a political community, but derives directly from the pact between the States, that is, it is constitutional hermeneutics that definitely proves the *locus* of sovereignty.

While the nature of the American Union is the true subject of Calhoun's investigations, it is clear that the subject of secession must be addressed, first in the restricted area in relation to Constitutional nullification, and then in relation to the nature of the obligations that arise from the federal pact.

In the aforementioned letter to Governor Hamilton, Calhoun delved into the fundamental questions of the problem.[106] Who crafted the Constitution? The individual states, or the "sovereign people"? Only two possibilities existed: Either one must believe in the sovereignty of the entire populace of the American Union, thus considering the Constitution as a creation of the sovereign people—for which it would be absurd to speak about "states' rights" or a "right" of nullification, much less secession—or one must believe that it was the result of the will of the States, as Calhoun argued. A series of logical consequences followed.

106 See John C. Calhoun to James Hamilton, Jr., August 28, 1832, Calhoun, *Papers*, vol. 11, pp. 613-649.

The Constitution was obviously a work of the States, which approved it as distinct political entities, independently from each other. The Union is a union of sovereign States. There is no direct link between citizens and the federal government. Furthermore, a general American citizenship does not exist. Rather, one is a citizen of an individual state, and one obeys the laws in force within it, including federal laws. From the point of view of sovereignty, the Constitution changed nothing. The States had transferred only the exercise of some sovereign powers to the federal government. This is evident from the very structure of the power conferred to a three-quarters majority of the states to amend the Constitution. All sovereignty thus resides in the individual States, while the exercise of sovereign power is shared by means of a pact that delegates a part to the federal government. However, were the simple doctrine of state sovereignty the theoretical basis of secession, the state would be free to withdraw from the pact at any moment, and the Constitution would be indistinguishable from a private contract (which would never have the character of a political pact, even incidentally), a claim that Calhoun never made.

Calhoun instead posited secession as one of the constitutional forms of action that could follow from a nullification decision. The States are joint partners in the federation; the federal government and its political administration were created to manage the common affairs. Secession is thus the act of withdrawing from the Union, of dissolving the partnership. It is crafted as a solution to a conflict between the joint members of the institution that frees the individual partners from any further obligation. Secession has nothing to do with the administrator, that is, the federal government, but rather is a matter involving only the relationship between the States. Nullification is not based on a condition of equality among the members. Rather, it is a notice to the administration that one of its activities is null and without validity because it exceeds the powers conferred upon it. Calhoun clarified the relationship between secession and nullification so effectively that it deserves a long quote.

> One has reference to the parties themselves, and the other to their agents. Secession is a withdrawal from the Union; a separation from partners, and, as far as depends on the member withdrawing, a dissolution of the partnership. ... Nullification, on the contrary, presupposes the relation of principal and agent: the one granting a power to be executed,—the other, appointed by him with authority to execute it; and is simply a declaration on the part of the principal, made in due form, that an act of the agent transcending his power is null and void.[107]

Secession and nullification follow two very different lines of reasoning:

> The object of secession is to free the withdrawing member from the obligation of the association or union, and is applicable to cases where the object of the association or union has failed, either by an abuse of power on the part of its members, or other causes. Its direct and immediate object, as it concerns the withdrawing member, is the dissolution of the association or union, as far as it is concerned. On the contrary, the object of nullification is to confine the agent within the limits of his powers, by arresting his acts transcending them, not with the view of destroying the delegated or trust power, but to preserve it, by compelling the agent to fulfil the object for which the agency or trust was created; and is applicable only to cases where the trust or delegated powers are transcended on the part of the agent.[108]

To understand the role of secession in Calhoun's constitutional doctrine, one must keep in mind the fact that in the system he devised withdrawal from the Union is external, but not foreign, to the constitutional system. By now it should be clear that the right of

107 *Ibid.*, pp. 630-631.

108 *Ibid.*, p. 631.

a State to withdraw from the Union does not derive *sic et simpliciter* from the contractual nature of the Union. Even if the Constitution is and remains a contract, its characteristics are those of a political pact. This in turn creates a series of political obligations that are clearly distinguishable from those of a contractual nature.[109] Calhoun's position can be formulated as follows: The Constitution is of a contractual nature, but, in acceding to the pact, a state implicitly accepts the perpetuity of the Union, and thus its political nature. If the nature of the Union does not change, then it is not permissible to withdraw from the Union itself. Therefore, secession would not be impossible, but would come into play in particular cases of appeal to Heaven Such cases do not arise from the nature of the Union, but from the right of self-government of all communities of free men. In essence, a "pre-political" right of secession exists, which shades into the right of revolution. There are no significant differences on this point between Webster, Calhoun, Jackson, and the entire American tradition. The institutionalization of power does not deprive people of the right to rebel against a despotic government. What matters here is the right of "political" secession, and Calhoun's construction on this point differs markedly from other constitutional doctrines.

What Calhoun could not tolerate in the Webster-Story doctrine was the idea that the Union could "naturally" evolve into something profoundly different without the contracting parties being given an active role in the evolutionary process they had created. In fact, the political obligations that arise from a constitutional pact, such as the American federal pact, cease when the terms of the pact are violated. Only within this conceptual framework can one understand the escalation that leads from the usurpation of a state's right, to nullification, to calling the other co-equal partners into

109 For Carl Schmitt, the alternative is succinctly stated in the classic terms of public law: "If the essence of the federation is that it should be ongoing, the entry into the federation must mean the continual renunciation of the right to secession." Basically, "they must opt either for the perpetuation of the federation, in other words, for neither secession nor nullification, or for the independent political existence of the member states, specifically, for nullification and secession, even if only in the most extreme case. But the concept of a political unity composed of states that is enduring and that, nevertheless, does not abandon its contractual foundation appears as something contradictory in the highest degree," Carl Schmitt, *Constitutional Theory*, p. 391.

a process of constitutional revision, then to possible withdrawal from the Union. The primary function of nullification in Calhoun's system is not the antagonistic use of state power against the federal government. It is rather an appeal to the supreme federal power: the three-quarters majority of the sovereign states. A state signals a de facto alteration in the nature of the Union, and thus of federal powers, by means of nullification. The super-majority has the right to accept a different, more energetic, and powerful agent for managing the common affairs. In the case in which this does not happen, an individual state cannot legitimately secede.[110]

Otherwise, given that the Constitution is no longer the same; two paths are opened for the state that raised the issue of nullification: either accession to the contract as modified, or withdrawal from the Union. One can only speak of Calhoun's theory of secession within these rigorous conditions. Secession is precisely the withdrawal from the political obligations that the states voluntarily imposed on themselves, a withdrawal justified only by the alteration of the constitutional compact.

Nullification, amending power, and "constitutional" secession thus form distinct and independent elements of an indivisible whole. The internal consistency and correspondence of the system to the constitutional text is, as many have recognized, absolutely beyond question. Calhoun's doctrine constructs a splendid ideal type of perfect federation, and it is one of the major theoretical constructions stemming from the American Constitution. His system posits the engine of constitutional change in the amending power retained by the supermajority, not in a five–of–nine majority of Supreme Court Justices, who are neither elected nor represent any state. This jurisdictional method of change was historically

110 Calhoun is adamant on this point: "Nullification may, indeed, be succeeded by secession. In the case stated, should the other members undertake to grant the power nullified, and should the nature of the power be such as to defeat the object of the association or union, at least as far as the member nullifying is concerned, it would then become an abuse of power on the part of the principals, and thus present a case where secession would apply; but in no other could it be justified, except it be for a failure of the association or union to effect the object for which it was created, independent of any abuse of power. ...," John C. Calhoun to James Hamilton, Jr., August 28, 1832, *Papers*, vol. 11, p. 632.

dominant from the earliest years of the republic. Yet the Supreme Court assumed the task that was constitutionally assigned to the states, and for over two hundred years the power to amend the Constitution has been exercised weekly in Washington by narrow juridical majorities.

5.5) The Concurrent Majority

In the last years of his intellectual adventure, Calhoun's theoretical designs became more ambitious. If the South, and each individual State, had veto rights on the essential questions of common legislation, by virtue of the very nature of the American Union—and this was the substance of the idea of limited and constitutional government—then it was necessary to go beyond the American instance to present it in the most general terms possible. The theory of "concurrent majority," fully elaborated in the small posthumous masterpiece of the *Disquisition on Government*, represents the systematic legitimation of the right of veto and the transposition of the American ideal of freedom to the level of general principles of political philosophy.

The expressions "concurrent majority" and "right of concurrent voice" had already appeared in the letter to Governor Hamilton. They became the core of Calhoun's political reflection in later years, and primarily in the *Disquisition*, which is considered one of the most incisive constructions of nineteenth century political theory.[111]

Calhoun began from two axioms regarding the innate qualities of human beings. The first is that people naturally live in a social state, and the second is that for human beings what is directly connected to the self takes precedence over what is connected only indirectly.[112] While the first hypothesis is one of the basic political concepts that have constantly resurfaced in the Western

---

111 Sobei Mogi, *The Problem of Federalism,* vol. 1 (London: Macmillan, 1931), p. 105. John Stuart Mill's judgment reserved for the *Disquisition* is much better known. Calhoun, he wrote, "has displayed powers as a speculative political thinker superior to any who has appeared in American politics since the authors of the 'Federalist'. ... See John Stuart Mill, *Utilitarianism, Liberty and Representative Government* (New York: Dutton, 1950), p. 502.

112 John C. Calhoun, *Disquisition on Government* in Calhoun, *Works*, vol. 1, pp. 1-2.

tradition since Aristotle's *Politics*, the second is directly linked to the "principle of self-preservation," Thomas Hobbes' proposed first natural law. Coupling these two together is unusual: The natural sociability of humanity would seem to stand in opposition to selfishness as the supreme law of human nature. This is true of all living things: "It would, indeed, seem to be essentially connected with the great law of self-preservation which pervades all that feels, from man down to the lowest and most insignificant reptile or insect. In none is it stronger than in man."[113]

The Aristotelian and Hobbesian premises were the foundations from which to launch an attack on the doctrine of natural law, which was the moral philosophy of the founding fathers' generation. Calhoun harshly criticized the hypothesis that, in a natural state, all people are free and equal: "It is, therefore, a great misnomer to call it the state of nature. Instead of being the natural state of man, it is, of all conceivable states, the most opposed to his nature—most repugnant to his feelings, and most incompatible with his wants. His natural state is, the social and political."[114] Within a strongly rationalistic framework Calhoun introduces certain aspects of organicism that would seem to call his theory into question.[115] On this point Louis Hartz contentiously asserted, "What is 'rigorous' about grounding the state in force and Providence after the fashion of Maistre and then creating a set of constitutional gadgets that would have staggered even Sieyès? What is consistent about destroying Locke's state of nature and then evolving a theory of minority rights that actually brings one back there for good?"[116]

113 *Ibid.*, p. 3.

114 *Ibid.*, p. 58.

115 Calhoun's organicism in political thought is highlighted by Spain, *The Political Theory of John C. Calhoun*. But Calhoun does not have an organicist view of society: The permanent conflict between the theory of constitutional government and its corollary of self-interest reveals an understanding of the social fabric that is completely other than organic, such that, "For Calhoun there was no whole transcending its parts," Ralph Lerner, "Calhoun's New Science of Politics," p. 927.

116 Louis Hartz, *The Liberal Tradition in America*, p. 155.

The rejection of natural law is commonly linked to Calhoun's defense of slavery. Indeed, the subversive potential contained in the language of the Declaration of Independence did not escape Calhoun's attention. In any case, the "official" moral philosophy prevalent during the formation of the republic was at its lowest popularity in the mid-nineteenth century. Many southern authors, beginning with Thomas Cooper, denounced the theory of natural law.[117]

The pessimistic anthropological presupposition, far from casting a Hobbesian shadow on Calhoun, is in full accord with all American thought. Both the Federalists and the Antifederalists agreed on the fact that the chief function of government was holding human passions at bay. For example, John Lansing Jr. addressed the New York ratification convention with words nearly identical to those of James Madison in his famous "if men were angels" statement: "[A]rguments will be in vain, checks would be useless, if we were certain our rulers would be good men: but for the virtuous man government is not instituted; its object is to restrain and punish vice; and all free constitutions are formed with two views—to deter the governed from crime, and the governors from tyranny."[118] Calhoun did not seem bothered by people's selfish nature. Rather, he treats it with detachment, reflecting the scientific study of politics that he is about in his treatise.[119]

117 See C. E. Merriam, "The Political Theory of Calhoun," *American Journal of Sociology*, VII, no. 5 (1902), p. 578.

118 Cited in Herbert J. Storing, *What the Anti-federalists Were For*, p. 52.

119 Calhoun strongly believed in "the power of analysis and combination—that power which reduces the most complex idea into its elements, which traces causes to their first principle, and, by the power of generalization and combination, unites the whole in one harmonious system—then, so far from deserving contempt, it is the highest attribute of the human mind. It is the power which raises man above the brute—which distinguishes his faculties from mere sagacity, which he holds in common with inferior animals. It is this power which has raised the astronomer from being a mere gazer at the stars to the high intellectual eminence of a Newton or a La Place; and astronomy itself from a mere observation of insulated facts into that noble science which displays to our admiration the system of the universe. And shall this high power of the mind, which has effected such wonders when directed to the laws which control the material world, be forever prohibited, under a senseless cry of metaphysics, from being applied to the high purpose of political science and legislation? I hold them to be subject to laws as fixed as matter itself, and to be as fit a subject for the application of the highest intellectual power. Denunciation may, indeed, fall upon the philosophical inquirer

Selfishness is an indispensable principle of the individual and social order: "[I]f their feelings and affections were stronger for others than for themselves, or even as strong, the necessary result would seem to be, that all individuality would be lost, and boundless and remediless disorder and confusion would ensue."[120]

Calhoun's criticism of the doctrine of natural law[121] opened the door to the claim that the natural state of humanity is both social and political, and it is perhaps this idea of the natural existence of political society that represents the true break from the American tradition. This Aristotelian presupposition of Calhoun's thought was discussed until the 1850s.[122] However, the statements contained in the first few pages of the *Disquisition* do not provide convincing evidence of a foundation that is truly traceable back to Aristotelian politics. There is but the simple affirmation of the necessity of government for the well-being of society. Furthermore, a government emerges among people to protect society, but it has its basis in the individual right of self-government. Adding

---

into these first principles, as it did upon Galileo and Bacon when they first unfolded the great discoveries which have immortalized their names; but the time will come when truth will prevail in spite of prejudice and denunciation, and when politics and legislation will be considered as much a science as astronomy and chemistry." John C. Calhoun, "Speech on the Force Bill," Senate, February 15-16, 1833, pp. 71-72.

120 John C. Calhoun, *Disquisition on Government*, p. 5.

121 The rejection of the doctrine of natural law must be read in close conjunction with Calhoun's radical epistemological nominalism. His *ordo sunt fratres* became "the federation are the States," since a creator is always greater than the object of his creation. From a political point of view, this transformed into the refusal to treat the numeric majority as "the people"; the term "United States" is a geographical, not political, concept for Calhoun (see *Ibid.*, p. 90). It is also true that the concept of the will of the majority did not refer to the will of the people, but to a particular interest or coalition of interests that prevails over the others. In the same manner, the rights to life, liberty and property, which for the generation of the Revolution were foundational in defining the essence of human beings, exist for Calhoun the nominalist only if recognized by the governments of the societies into which people are born. It is undeniable that the status of the human necessity of society leads to a denial of the political legitimacy of appeals based on the natural rights of humanity, which for Calhoun appear in a chimeric state of nature (see *Ibid.*, pp. 44-45), but the chief *argumentum* against natural law is of an empirical and epistemological nature.

122 See George Fitzhugh, "The Politics and Economics of Aristotle and Mr. Calhoun," *DeBow's Review* 23 (1857), pp. 163-172.

a Lockean proposition that was in perfect harmony with the American tradition, Calhoun stated: "By nature, every individual has the right to govern himself; and governments, whether founded on majorities or minorities, must derive their right from the assent, expressed or implied, of the governed, and be subject to such limitations as they may impose."[123]

It is not at all clear whether Calhoun had really abandoned the traditional view, as exemplified by Tom Paine, of government as a "necessary evil"; while he undoubtedly emphasized the necessity of government among people, there are many passages that recognize the very nature of government as an "evil." For example, in the context of the defense of slavery, he incidentally stated that "there are innumerable things which, regarded in the abstract, are evils, but which it would be madness to attempt to abolish. Thus regarded, government itself is an evil."[124] Calhoun's view remained an empirical observation that primarily served to refute the *Federalist*, which maintained that government was a deliberate choice.

The common thread of the *Disquisition* is a concise but indirect polemic against the authors of the *Federalist* on the nature of humanity and power. Calhoun had to come to grips with the theory of Publius, that government among people can be the result of design and rational choice by individuals rather than of chance and violence (*Federalist* 1). He totally rejected that claim. The Constitution, but not the government, was the result of human design:

> Having its origin in the same principle of our nature, *constitution* stands to *government*, as *government* stands to *society*; and, as the end for which society is ordained, would be defeated without government, so that for which government is ordained would, in a great measure, be defeated without constitution. But they differ in this striking particular. There is no difficulty in forming government. It is not even a

123 John C. Calhoun, "Fort Hill Address", July 26, 1831, *Papers*, vol. 11, p. 417.

124 John C. Calhoun, "Report on the Circulation of the Abolition Petitions," Senate, February 4, 1836, *Calhoun, Works*, vol. 5, p. 203. {Also: *Speeches* (1843), 195.]

> matter of choice, whether there shall be one or not. Like breathing, it is not permitted to depend on our volition. Necessity will force it on all communities in some one form or another. Very different is the case as to constitution. Instead of a matter of necessity, it is one of the most difficult tasks imposed on man to form a constitution worthy of the name; ... Constitution is the contrivance of man, while government is of Divine ordination."[125]

Thus, the real difference between the government and the Constitution is that the former is a necessity, while the latter is the result of human volition.

According to Calhoun, the natural state of human beings is both social and political. Government is a natural fact in the human community, predisposed by God in some way. However, the social tendency that would make government possible is not strong enough to overcome the intrinsic principle of self-preservation that takes priority in living creatures. Consequently, society ever has the tendency to spawn the seeds of its own destruction, and it can create a state of universal antagonism among individuals. An authority is thus necessary that controls the antagonism: Government is then indispensable for preserving society, and society is an indispensable element for the existence of human beings. Government restrains disorder, but at the same time it has the tendency to abuse its authority and become despotic. The causes of the abuse of authority can be attributed to innate qualities in human beings, for whom individual sentiments take priority over social sentiments. This applies to both the governors and the governed. If the authority that must prevent injustice and disorder is not itself adequately controlled, it will end up becoming a means of oppressing the weakest.

August O. Spain writes: "The essential distinction to which checks and balances were to be applied, however, was not, in Calhoun's opinion, between legislative, executive, and judiciary, or between monarchical, aristocratic, and democratic principles of

125 John C. Calhoun, *Disquisition on Government*, pp. 7-8.

control, or even between central and local units of government, but between a majority and a minority differing in economic interest and geographical environment."[126] In particular, for Calhoun there is inherent in power itself a tendency toward despotism; a democratic society does not change this, but, rather, makes it more dangerous. The Constitution of the United States is a restraint that should prevent the transformation of the government into a tyranny. And yet:

> Power can only be resisted by power—and tendency by tendency. Those who exercise power and those subject to its exercise—the rulers and the ruled—stand in antagonistic relations to each other. The same constitution of our nature which leads rulers to oppress the ruled—regardless of the object for which government is ordained—will, with equal strength, lead the ruled to resist, when possessed of the means of making peaceable and effective resistance. Such an organism, then, as will furnish the means by which resistance may be systematically and peaceably made on the part of the ruled, to oppression and abuse of power on the part of the rulers, is the first and indispensable step towards forming a constitutional government.[127]

Calhoun was convinced that the right to vote was not the most important means of guaranteeing that those governed have the potential for mounting a real opposition. While periodic elections are normally adequate to prevent arrogance and arbitrariness by rulers, just exercising the right to vote is not sufficient for the formation of a constitutional government. In fact, "The sum total, then, of its effects, when most successful, is, to make those elected, the true and faithful representatives of those who elected them—instead of irresponsible rulers—as they would be without it."[128]

126 August O. Spain, *Political Theory of Calhoun*, pp. 143-144.

127 John C. Calhoun, *Disquisition on Government*, p. 12.

128 *Ibid.*, p. 14.

The only way to counter the government's tendency toward despotism is the principle of concurrent majority. This is "the adoption of some restriction or limitation, which shall so effectually prevent any one interest, or combination of interests, from obtaining the exclusive control of the government, as to render hopeless all attempts directed to that end."[129] The exclusive control of government is the situation that must be opposed, the one that concurrent or constitutional majority must correct. There is but one way to achieve this: consulting separately each interest group or part of a community that can be unfairly or harmfully affected by a government action, thus spurring the consensus of all interest groups in enacting or enforcing a government action.[130] A right of veto must be granted to each section or to each interest group, either during the formation of the consensus or over the final result. The virtues of concurrent majority are evident when compared to the flaws of a simple numerical majority.

> There is, again, but one mode in which this can be effected; and that is, by taking the sense of each interest or portion of the community, which may be unequally and injuriously affected by the action of the government, separately, through its own majority, or in some other way by which its voice may be fairly expressed; and to require the consent of each interest, either to put or to keep the government in action.[131]

A government based on numerical majority is therefore tyrannical by its nature. Since the theme is that of the tyranny of majority, the comparison with Alexis de Tocqueville is both immediate and recurrent in the scholarly literature. On the other hand, it is not illuminating, given that the tones and premises are totally different. According to Tocqueville, the 1830s see the dispersal of man into the crowd, and the effects of equality on the traditional obstacles to the abuse of power are devastating.

129 *Ibid.*, p. 24.

130 *Ibid.*, p. 25.

131 *Ibid*, p. 28.

Only two protagonists remain, the individual and the state, but power relations are dangerously unbalanced in favor of the latter. In egalitarian societies, despotism comparable to that of ancient Rome is expected to develop. Calhoun, instead, accepts the crucial assumption of modern democracy, in terms of "popular sovereignty," but strives to find constitutional tools to prevent dominant interests from expanding to the others' detriment.

Tocqueville's criticism of the majority theory is less adamant for two reasons: In the first place, there is a total absence of a *pars construens*, i.e., the attempt to solve the problem, which is instead the conceptual core of Calhoun's work. Secondly, Tocqueville's critique of *majoritarianism* shows some elements of strong conservatism and nostalgia for medieval pluralism (while the Carolinian must instead defend a real and threatened territorial pluralism, that of the States in relation to the federal power). The modern state has wiped away all the actors but the individuals and itself, with the state in a strongly favored position, and that is the source of the French aristocrat's concerns. These fears bring him to admit, with great reserve, the democratic theory, while Calhoun derives all his criticism of democracy exactly from popular sovereignty. Thus, it is easy to recognize who of the two is in fact the reactionary.

In an absolutist government, the fundamental principles that preserve power result in violence or oppression of those governed. On the other hand, in a constitutional government, compromise becomes the fundamental principle. The political system proposed by Calhoun presumes a permanent negotiation between the major interests. The contractual and private elements of political obligation tend to be accentuated when an agreement is reached by the consensus of each individual party. Not surprisingly, in a world in which political obligation was taking shape contrary to contractual obligation, Calhoun's proposal met with little success. The *volonté générale* contained in the laws passed by the representative legislatures of the nation were considered the most flexible and effective means for governing people. The system of "permanent negotiation," arising from attributing the right of veto to major groups, effectively distances Calhoun's doctrine from the one that dominated the formation of the modern state. The salvation of a political community, he believed, lies in its ability to think of itself as disjointed, divided, in conflict and, above all, not looking for a "decider." Calhoun was convinced that compromise was the only feasible path in clash arising from conflicts of interest, as the alternative was violence and oppression. His solution to the problem was based on the principles of justice, understood as fairness in the procedures followed in obtaining consensus (the theory of concurrent majority is basically a procedural theory of "just consensus").

The Carolinian anticipated many of the critiques that would be made to his constitutional contrivance over time. Mostly they are based on the notion that conflicting interest groups will not easily reach any kind of agreement, thus organizing the permanent paralysis of the political system. In Calhoun's view, however, two main factors will drive the parties toward the resolution of conflicts. One is "urgent necessity": When a decision absolutely must be reached, it is reasonable to assume that a compromise will be accepted. The second is the "patriotism" that dwells in the heart of the people. Essentially, Calhoun expected people voluntarily to renounce partial and particular interests to avoid dismembering the entire society into factious rivalries, while also guaranteeing well-being and security for themselves.

Calhoun's system was rather vague about the number and importance of the interests involved, leaving commentators with but a single adjective: It should be a *major* interest, which seems quite malleable. Were we in fact to recognize the right of veto to every interest group, the possibility of inefficiency and confusion is far from remote, and that would result in a stalemate. The growth of the number of subjects entitled to the right of veto does not in fact seem in harmony with either the letter or the spirit of Calhoun's theory.

As a matter of fact, the veto undergoes a sort of escalation from a simple constitutional objection to a declaration of nullification and finally to withdrawal from the Union. This is because, in the absence of formidable means of applying pressure, the simple majority would not accept its own fragmentation. If there is no way the system can be dissolved, the expectation of compromise does not, by itself, result in an agreement.

Richard Hofstadter and Daniel Elazar, to mention only two well-known scholars, find Calhoun a thinker who can hardly be situated within American political tradition. The former writes of Calhoun: "Not in the slightest was he concerned with minority rights as they are chiefly of interest to the modern liberal mind";[132] and the latter believes that Calhoun's theory deviated widely from American constitutional traditions.[133] More recently, James Read argued that while "Calhoun's critique of majority rule ... should be taken seriously," his new theory of government through consensus "ultimately fails"—such government being "neither effective nor just."[134]

To the contrary, we should note that, as Howard L. Cheek indicates, Calhoun's political theory was "both original and in accord with the mainstream of the American political tradition,"[135] and also in complete harmony with the entire classical liberal tradition. And his concurrent majority theory of consensus, far from being a failure, is the most sophisticated articulation of the American resistance to the state and its frame of mind.

In Calhoun's thought the tension between democracy, federalism, and liberalism is crystallized in terms of a constitutional conflict, which the dawn of the republic had somewhat obscured. While Thomas Jefferson held the greatest trust in the American experiment in self-government and maintained that the protection of natural rights should be pursued through a federal system of government and popular control of elected officials, subsequent American political history would place democracy and federalism in some tension, if not in an irreducible antagonism. Calhoun proved ready to take up the theoretical challenge posed by the facts.

132 Richard Hofstadter, *The American Political Tradition and the Men Who Made It*, pp. 89-90.

133 Daniel Elazar, *The American Constitutional Tradition* (Lincoln: University of Nebraska Press, 1988), p. 248.

134 James H. Read, *Majority Rule Versus Consensus. The Political Thought of John C. Calhoun* (Lawrence, KS: University Press of Kansas, 2009), p. 3.

135 H. Lee Cheek, *Calhoun and Popular Rule*, p. 78.

For Calhoun, the United States was something more than, and different from, a simple league of States, but the States should never become a centralized democracy subject to the rule of the absolute majority, since "the worst of all possible forms [is] a consolidated Government—swayed by the will of an absolute majority."[136] Letting oneself be governed by majority rule at all levels would mean abandoning all constitutional guarantees. The right of a state as a judge of last resort to interpret the limits posed by the Constitution on the federal government should be defended at all costs. Otherwise the United States would be destroyed, becoming first a modern state and then a dictatorship of the executive branch, as had happened in the past to other republics.

A federal structure does not appear, however, to be in tension with the entire doctrine of democracy, only with its degenerative aspects. "The truth is— the Government of the uncontrolled numerical majority is but the absolute and despotic form of popular governments."[137] Calhoun's version of federalism is then the real check on the tyrannical tendencies of the simple majority, since it would require a concurrent majority on all the major issues. On these vital questions, the will of the majority of the country is worth nothing, unless sanctioned by the majority in each of its constituent parts.

Calhoun's devotion to the principles of self-government and popular sovereignty cannot then be questioned. From a constitutional point of view his place is certainly to be found in the mainstream of the broad American tradition, and the same can be said for his adherence to liberal principles. Contrary to Hofstadter, the degree of authentic liberalism of a thinker should be evaluated according to the position that he takes on the relationship between the state and the market, and on this point Calhoun is adamantly a free market classical liberal.

136 John C. Calhoun to James Hamilton, Jr., August 28, 1832, Calhoun, *Papers*, Vol. 11, p. 642.

137 John C. Calhoun to William Smith, July 3, 1843, Calhoun, *Papers*, Vol. 17, p. 284.

Calhoun saw no difference between those who directed a factory and those who produced agricultural goods. A conflict between the two could arise only when the government abandoned its neutrality and became the tool of one of the groups. His criticism was never directed against manufacturing interests as such, but ever and only against the favors the government reserved for them. The tariff was unjust because it forced others to pay the price of protecting manufacturing. The South—"the seat of the great exporting interests of the country—[was] in a fixed and hopeless minority,"[138] and increasingly backed into a corner by antagonistic Northern economic interests in control of the general government. Calhoun's arguments in defense of his region were structured as a theory of interests that was classically liberal and oriented to free trade in its economics. Calhoun had no complaints about the free market. Rather, all his criticisms were directed against the interests that used the federal government to escape economic competition. This "agrarian Manchesterism"[139] reveals an essential aspect of Calhoun's concept of politics: The source of inequality between people is not the market, but the state. Political power provides the controls that the dominant interests manage to expand to their advantage behind the backs of others.

Calhoun's theory of exploitation cannot be confused with his defense of slavery; it is rather a realistic evaluation of political parasitism. The government, which is necessary for the welfare of society, can violently discipline conflicts of interest, thus making the strongest interest prosper over the others. While the Carolinian accepted this parasitic relationship as natural between Europeans and African slaves in the southern states, he could not tolerate that this would happen between free-men whites in the American federation. From the time he took up the states' rights cause, through the theory of nullification and concurrent majority, his search for

138 John C. Calhoun, "Draft Report on Federal Relations," November 20, 1831? *Calhoun, Papers*, vol. Vol. 11, p. 508.

139 Theodore R. Marmor, "Anti-Industrialism in the Old South: The Agrarian Perspective of John C. Calhoun," *Comparative Studies in Society and History* 9 (1967), p. 379.

the best possible government unfolded as a continuous attempt to find an institutional alchemy able of creating a government that served as a barrier to parasitism rather than as its instrument.

What's more, his crystal-clear explanation of taxation as the linchpin of government action places Calhoun among the vanguard of the contemporary public choice school of thought.[140] As we already noted the very nature of government and taxation, however small or limited, creates two major groups: those who consume and those who produce taxes. An analysis of actual interpersonal exchanges within the shadow of the government and its power to tax is always a prelude to an attempt to devise expedient means to limit power. On this point Calhoun fully demonstrated his understanding of the American political situation and the lessons that could be drawn from it on the virtues and limits of a written constitution:

> A written constitution certainly has many and considerable advantages; but it is a great mistake to suppose that the mere insertion of provisions to restrict and limit the powers of the government, without investing those for whose protection they are inserted with the means of enforcing their observance, will be sufficient to prevent the major and dominant party from abusing its powers.... As the major and dominant party, they will have no need of these restrictions for their protection. The ballot box, of itself, would be ample protection to them.[141]

140 See Peter Aranson, "Calhoun's Constitutional Economics," *Constitutional Political Economy*, Vol. 2, no. 1 (1991), pp. 31-52; Roberta Herzberg, "An Analytic Choice Approach to Concurrent Majorities: The Relevance of John C. Calhoun's Theory of Institutional Design", *Journal of Politics*, vol. 14, 1992, pp. 54-81 and Alexander Tabarrok, Tyler Cowen, "The Public Choice Theory of John C. Calhoun", *Journal of Institutional and Theoretical Economics*, vol.148, 1992, pp. 655-674.

141 *Ibid.*, p. 25.

But it is not just the power of the numerical majority that exceeds every constitutional limit on government action. Any written limit that leaves the government free to interpret the extension of its own powers is destined to fail, opening the way to absolute and de facto unlimited power. This is why the American federal government must be subjected to the control of the States by means of the nullification of federal laws that exceed the delegated power. Calhoun frequently used this as a secondary justification (almost *ad abundantiam*) of the doctrine of nullification, but it reveals how his entire construction was nothing else but an attempt to limit power.

A long-running controversy on the relationship between institutions and virtues has marked Western political thought in the past centuries. From at least Guicciardini and Machiavelli onward, there has been a recurring question of whether a virtuous people constructs just institutions or whether virtuous institutions forge a just people. Calhoun's analysis sides more on the Rousseauian side[142] of this question: It is defective institutions that corrupt people and not dissolute citizens that create imperfect institutions.

In fact, a government of the concurrent majority, the only form that is both classical liberal and constitutional, is manifestly "the product of circumstances,"[143] and this is not due to the intrinsic virtues of the people that have adopted it. In short, the structure of the government is the source of virtue or corruption: a centralized government, created to serve a political community predicated as a single entity, will enable the natural tendency of power to exceed every limit. The state is thus utterly rejected as a model of constitutional government.

142 Rousseau made it clear multiple times that "the most absolute authority is that which penetrates into a man's inmost being, and concerns itself no less with his will than with his actions. It is certain that *all peoples become in the long run what the government makes them*; warriors, citizens, men, when it so pleases: or merely populace and rabble, when it chooses to make them so." Jean-Jacques Rousseau, *Political Economy*, 1755, Charles De Secondat, Baron De Montesquieu and Jean Jacques Rousseau, *The Spirit of Laws; A Discourse on the Origin of Inequality; A Discourse on Political Economy; The Social Contract* (Chicago: Encyclopaedia Britannica, 1952), p. 372 (italics mine).

143 *Ibid.*, p. 79.

A passage in the *Disquisition* is crystal-clear on how political virtue can be the result of institutional design. The destruction of the desire to be part of a true community results from the operation of "a form of government, which periodically stakes all its honors and emoluments, as prizes to be contended for" and thereby splits "the community into two great hostile parties." When government action has polarized society, it is no surprise that "the community should cease to be the common centre of attachment, or that each party should find its reference only in itself." It follows that "the promotion of the interests of party [becomes] more important than the promotion of the common good ..., and its triumph and ascendancy, objects of far greater solicitude, than the safety and prosperity of the community."

These shortcomings are the product of the "numerical majority, [which regards] the community as a unit, and having, as such, the same interests throughout all its parts. ..." The predicated unity of the whole—exactly what the sovereign state is all about—that can never actually be unified "must ... divide it into two hostile parts, waging, under the forms of law, incessant hostilities against one another." Only by ceasing to consider the community as a single artificially united whole can one "unite the most opposite and conflicting interests. ..." If every interest group is granted "the power of self-protection," then "all strife and struggle between them for ascendancy, is prevented." Calhoun continues:

> [Under the] concurrent majority, ... the individual and the social feelings are made to unite in one common devotion to country. Each sees and feels that it can best promote its own prosperity by conciliating the goodwill, and promoting the prosperity of the others. And hence, there will be diffused throughout the whole community kind feelings between its different portions; and, instead of antipathy, a rivalry amongst them to promote the interests of each other, as far as this can be done consistently with the interest of all. And hence, instead of faction, strife, and struggle for party

> ascendency, there would be patriotism, nationality, harmony, and a struggle only for supremacy in promoting the common good of the whole.[144]

We see here a political declaration of default against the modern state and its myth of a unified people. To create true homogeneity it is necessary to abandon the quest for an artificial unity of the political community, thus depriving it of a driving center from which everything emanates and in which everything is decided. Deconstructing the community into its actual opposing interests and providing each with the right of veto is the most certain method for achieving agreement. Harmony emerges from the destruction of the bridge of the ship. Big business is deprived of a big government that it can assail. On American soil the resistance to the modern statist way of thinking, which had been the most important endeavor since Independence (if not earlier), found its most important exponent in the middle of the nineteenth century.

James Madison had maintained that the clash of interest groups in a large republic founded on representation would guarantee the mutual cancellation of their forces. Subsequent history demonstrated that this was not just wishful thinking, as several interest groups joined forces, formed majorities, found the federal government ready to be bent to their own ends. Calhoun warned that the only solution for the survival of the community was to grant a right of veto on the essential questions.

What Madison had thought impossible—the formation of a permanent and well-organized national majority determined to impose its interests to the detriment of southern rights—had clearly happened. Basically, this was a fact of sufficient magnitude to blow the entire Madisonian theoretical edifice sky-high. Lacy Ford has rightly noted, "In Calhoun's view, the founders' argument that large republics were virtually immune to majoritarian tyranny had failed the ultimate empirical test—the test of time."[145] In the

144 *Ibid.*, pp. 48-49.

145 Lacy K. Ford Jr., "Inventing the Concurrent Majority: Madison, Calhoun, and the Problem of Majoritarianism in American Political Thought," *Journal of Southern History* 60, no. 1 (1994), p. 44.

years during which, in Congress after Congress, the majorities that represented northern interests had consolidated to create a bloc that was able to pass any national legislation, Calhoun considered it essential to revise the theory to take into account the historical experience of the first decades of the life of the Union.

While the right of resistance was developed in America as a doctrine of power of the individual state against the encroachments of the federal government into the sphere of competence reserved for it,[146] the theory of the concurrent majority, although a direct descendant of such a concept, was quite new in the panorama of American constitutional doctrines. Both versions of Calhoun's theoretical contributions, nullification and sectional veto, show a very significant shift in perspective. While the theory of concurrent majority had already appeared between 1828 and 1833 in the *Exposition*, the Fort Hill Address, and the letter to Governor Hamilton, in the *Disquisition* it became the linchpin of his entire political analysis. In the first version, the defense of an authentic federal system was adequate and satisfactory: The interests of the South would be preserved through a constitutional interpretation that protected each state from any federal interference. The only way to impose new obligations on the States would be to amend the Constitution. In this phase, Calhoun pointed out the correct interpretation of the Constitution and the true nature of the American Union, a voluntary association that gave rise to a federal system as the agent of the States. His proposals are perhaps at odds with the theories on federal relationships that dominate the present debate, but they are the only methods that would preserve the delicate balance worked out in Philadelphia.

The theory of concurrent majority as the veto power of the minority departs from the Philadelphia design to venture into much more rugged logical and theoretical terrain, which could no longer rely on direct reference to the federal compact. The first result of the theory was to show the emergence of the United States as a

146 See Pauline Maier, "The Road Not Taken: Nullification, John C. Calhoun, and the Revolutionary Tradition in South Carolina," *South Carolina Historical Magazine* 72, no. 1 (1981), pp. 1-19, and Margaret L. Coit, "Calhoun and the Downfall of States' Rights," *Virginia Quarterly Review* 28 (1952), pp. 191-208.

"political community," however imperfect. A distinction suggested by the *Disquisition* is between *perfect* and *imperfect* political communities. In the former, the uniformity of interests is such that a simple majority can be considered a legitimate method of making known one voice, or the political preferences of its citizens. In the latter, where perfect uniformity of interests is lacking, only the concurrent majority can guarantee a just consensus. The States are examples of perfect political communities, while the Union is an imperfect political community.[147] If the interests common to all the States were the grounds for action by the federal government—as a simple agent—and its very *raison d'être*, it is clear that the real problem in creating coalitions among the interest groups is primarily at the federal level.

Naturally, since the veto right of the minority and the consequent Calhounian consensus sourcing from it are relevant at the federal level, the two regions of the country become at this point perfect political communities in which the interest groups can be brought together in any possible way. Nothing precludes the southern and northern states from deciding their respective policies by means of a simple numerical majority. This is because the affinity (always relative) between the interests is such that utilizing the means of the absolute majority would not effectively result in a small tyrannical democracy. Faced with the irresolvable conflict of interests between North and South, Calhoun simplified the federal framework in which the constitutional consensus no longer sees the sovereign States as the real actors. Rather, clusters of States are the new actors.

In the *Disquisition* the entities that wield negative power against the federal government are no longer the States, but the interest groups in conflict. And yet, the interpretation of a compact

---

147 Calhoun was nevertheless aware that a true uniformity of interests is not realistically possible: "That such dissimilarity of interests may exist, it is impossible to doubt. They are to be found in every community, in a greater or less degree, however small or homogeneous; and they constitute, everywhere, the great difficulty of forming and preserving free institutions," John C. Calhoun, "Fort Hill Address," July 26, 1831, p. 417. Again, "the view which considers the community as a unit, and all its parts as having a similar interest, is radically erroneous," John C. Calhoun, "Speech on the Force Bill," Senate, February 15-16, 1833, p. 81.

into which the State has entered, the power to interpret a pact between parties that have no common judge, is the very essence of state sovereignty. But if this power is transferred from the States to geographically and historically determined interest groups, then a federal community does emerge (imperfect because it is based on coalitions of interests and not on individuals), and the construction based on the sovereignty of the individual State evaporates.

Having abandoned the structural bounds of the federal compact, Calhoun's criticism becomes radical. There never was a true constitutional government in America. Though the Constitution had made provisions for rule by concurrent majority, it had historically failed, and only a thorough constitutional revision could recreate the basis for a free government. As he stated in the final pages of the *Discourse,* "the restoration of the government to its federal character, however entire and perfect it may be—will not, of itself, be sufficient to avert the evil alternatives—to the one or the other of which it must tend, as it is now operating."[148]

Only a revised Constitution that unequivocally granted the South the right of veto could save the Union. Though Calhoun trusted the power of amendment, as it was based on the States, he proposed in the end the creation of a dual executive.[149] In laying this out, he attacked the decision to adopt a single executive branch, which he held to be incompatible with the existence of a popular government in a composite community.[150]

In the final pages of the *Discourse*, probably written during the last months of his life, he sharpened his criticism: The federal government was operating by the rule of the absolute majority, thus the real price the Union was freedom.

In these reflections, Calhoun seems to leave the idea of federalism a bit in the background—that is, the American constitutional guarantees, on which he had based his attempt to defend the South inside the Union. In fact, the problem of majority rule, both because

148 John C. Calhoun, *A Discourse*, p. 387.

149 Cf. *Ibid.*, pp. 391-392.

150 Cf. *Ibid.*, p. 392.

of how the Carolinian deals with it, and because of its logic, is intimately connected to the federal structure. Indeed, majority rule generates totally dissimilar issues in a modern state than in a true federation. And this in turn reveals how the majority decision is not a technical, but a purely political theme. The history of the majority principle has never been linear: Having been really problematic until the triumph of modern state, it meets enormous favor during the parliamentary phase, and now finds true resistance only within some federal systems (the United States and Switzerland).

The simple fact that the American federal structure is composed of States, even if somewhat united, made majority rule very dubious, at least in the first century of the republic. With President Abraham Lincoln, a zealous supporter of the strength and rights of the majority, possibly enforced by the persuasion of bayonets, the rule became later quite popular. Desegregation in the 1960s, a political process in which the federal government had the moral upper hand and violated the Constitution in order to protect *minorities* oppressed by the white *majorities* in the southern states, represents a very complex test of majority rule in a federation. It is not by chance that William Riker summed up his very sophisticated analysis in 1964 with these words: "Thus, if in the United States one approves of Southern white racists, then one should approve of American federalism."[151] When slavery, racism, and what really plagued America from the onset are analyzed, we are told, the federal government is always better than the state governments. Federalism, in this view, was the institutional framework that assisted first slavery, then racism, exactly because it put a check on national power.

As it is impossible and futile to combat these intellectual windmills we need to point out the fact that majority rule expresses its whole *potential* in a modern state, not certainly in a federal system. A *simple* democratic system is antithetic to an authentic federation, exactly for the reasons that Calhoun explained so eloquently. Thomas Hobbes made it clear that power can be attributed to a monarch or to an assembly. In the latter case, "if

151 William Riker, *Federalism: Origin, Operation, and Significance*, p. 155.

the Representative consist of many men, the voyce of the greater number, must be considered as the voyce of them all."[152] That is, there must be one voice to speak for Leviathan, be it a King or an assembly. This is the crucial point: The will of the state, which for Hobbes is obviously fictitious, can only exist as determined by a monarch, since nothing transcends individuals, or the sums of their personal interests. The monarch, thus, is a logical need in Hobbes's system, while it is a matter of faith in any other. A single voice is reached in an assembly by seeing which of the conflicting opinions prevails. After all, a single member can express the voice of the whole Parliament—and there is nothing bizarre in it—provided that it is clear that the assembly is sovereign, the King's heir, and the only possible alternative to the Prince that appeared during the history of modern state. Majority rule has nothing to do with the consent of and within the electoral body. Those who govern in democracy are often very far from holding a majority in society—remember that in America, as everywhere else, perhaps a fifth of the citizens' votes are enough to govern at every level—but must, instead, manage to gain it in democratic assembly. In short, the rule is internal to the sovereignty and is aimed at reaching a single voice.

The political issue, then, could be reduced to just one question: Why, in the assemblies of a democratic state, must the greatest number *always* prevail? To which the answer is clear: The assembly succeeds the monarch, does not accept polyphonies, and must speak with a single voice. The human authority holding the ultimate decision in political issues is, thus the assembly, sovereign in itself, i.e., a state that calls itself as a political community thanks to its single voice.

In the state, it is not majority *in* society that is the basis *for* parliamentary majority. Society is only asked to elect a sovereign assembly, which will then have to seek unity. The unitary obsession of the state finds its completion in a rule that allows no exceptions.

152 Thomas Hobbes, *Leviathan* (London: Andrew Crooke, 1651), p. 101.

Without this *pars pro toto* there can be no sovereignty. In short, majority is a synecdoche for modernity in its parliamentary phase; it is predicated of Parliament, not society.

And it is precisely because Calhoun is a modern state enemy that he is obsessed with majority *in the* community, not in the institutions. According to him, and to all the supporters of the states' rights doctrine, the State is nothing but people of the State, not the governmental powers.

The *Disquisition* is one of a few great works of Western thought overcoming the main political currents of the last centuries, those built around the European idea of the state and its compulsive notion of sovereignty. Calhoun does not focus on the categories of public law, but on the possibility of creating human relationships based on the principles of justice and taking interests into account. The Calhounian doctrine—at a time when the state's claim to be the only conceivable political synthesis has definitively entered into a crisis, or at least of exhaustion—could be an antidote to that conceptual tyranny, to an incapacity to think beyond the state, which is perhaps the most hateful intellectual legacy of modern statehood.

Chapter 6

Abraham Lincoln: The Herald of the Modern State

> The growth of Federal power will be unchecked. Its continued manifestation upon a constantly enlarging scale is as inevitable as fate. It is easier, however, to review and analyze the past than to predict the future. We know that the character of our government, as designed by its founders, is already rapidly changing and that we are less prone than heretofore to regard our Constitution as a sacred and inviolable instrument. There is a possibility, with the integrity of the State as an essential unit disappearing, that we may be brought face to face with a one-man, bureaucratic autocracy. There is still further danger of drifting into Socialism, which cannot develop in a republic composed of independent sovereignties, but which will thrive exceedingly under the aegis of a strong centralized government.[1]
>
> —Henry Litchfield West

A few days before his death in 1850 John C. Calhoun wrote to a friend in Virginia:

> The Union is doomed to dissolution, there is no mistaking the signs. I am satisfied in my judgment, even were the questions that now agitate Congress settled to the satisfaction and with the concurrence

1 Henry Litchfield West, *Federal Power: Its Growth and Necessity* (New York: George H. Doran, 1918), pp. VIII-IX.

> of the Southern States, it would not avert, or materially delay, the catastrophe. I fix its probable occurrence within twelve years or three Presidential Terms. ... The mode by which it shall be done, is not so clear. ... But the probability is, it will explode in a Presidential election.[2]

And that is exactly how things went. On November 6, 1860, Abraham Lincoln, the candidate for the Republican party—founded just six years earlier—won the election by taking advantage of the divisions between his opponents Breckinridge, Bell, and Douglas. He won by a very narrow majority, as the three opponents together exceeded Lincoln's 1,866,452 votes by nearly one million votes. But it was clearly an election against the South, a region in which he did not get a single vote.

6.1) The Union as Nation

Between Lincoln's election, his inauguration in March 1861, and the beginning of the Civil War, the South decided that its position could no longer be defended within the Union. What is interesting to note here is the epochal shift that Lincoln effected in American political culture and history. The new president took the cult of the nation to a new level that would have shocked Hamilton and Webster. The animating myth of Northern politics—that protecting the Union was an ultimate end for which it was worth living, fighting, and dying—became reality. Like the great "national" figures of his time in Europe—Cavour, Bismarck—Lincoln must be considered as the one who embodied the decisive, though composite, project of transplanting the modern state into America. As one writer said a quarter of a century ago, "there have been more books written about Abraham Lincoln than any other historical figure, save Jesus Christ and Shakespeare."[3] Given the immense secondary literature

---

2 John C. Calhoun to James M. Mason, March 1850, in Virginia Mason, *The Public Life and Diplomatic Correspondence of James Murray Mason* (Roanoke: Stone, 1903), pp. 72-73.

3 Peter W. Shramm, "Introduction," Lord Charnwood, *Abraham Lincoln. A Biography* (Lanham, MD: Madison Books, 1996), p. 1.

that has been published in recent years, Honest Abe could be by now more famous, and studied, than Shakespeare, John Lennon and Jesus Christ combined.

The states' rights school was routed during the war, though its echo could still be heard until the end of the twentieth century. Federalism and the question of the nature of the American compact, which had been the driving force of the political debate until Lincoln's election, gradually gave way to other themes. In part it was the concept of "sovereignty," which had obsessively been brought onto the scene at least from the time of *South Carolina Exposition* onward, that worked against Calhoun and his followers. It was an extremely difficult concept to manage. Regardless of the prudence one might exercise in using it, using it at all flung the doors open to every European idea of the state as the embodiment of the legal and physical characteristics of the person of the sovereign.

Parallel to this problem, a *Staatstheorie* of German origin was commonly taught in American universities between the mid-nineteenth century and the First World War. While politicians still argued within the classic terms of union, constitution, and states, students began to learn not only that "man cannot be what he ought to be, without the state," but also that "for our existence as human beings the state is a *conditio sine qua non*, and this absolute necessity constitutes the ground on which is founded what is called sovereignty, that is, the self-sufficient power that derives its vital energy from no other, is founded by no superior authority, but imparts it and extends over everything that is requisite in order to obtain the object of the state."[4] Francis Lieber published a textbook in the 1830's reflecting an expansive idolatry of the state, declaring that "law is the direct or indirect, explicit or implied, real or supposed, positive or acquiesced in expression of the will of human society, represented in the state, or, of a part of human society constituted into a state"[5]—a view that would certainly have seemed unusual to

4 Francis Lieber, *Manual of Political Ethics, Designed Chiefly for the Use of Colleges and Students at Law* (1838-39), ed. Theodore D. Woolsey (Philadelphia: Lippincott, 1876), pp. 77, 173.

5 *Ibid.*, p. 101.

the American students of the time. The European concepts of the state, coupled with Lincoln's cult of the nation, finally caused the standard American doctrine of federalism to evaporate.

From his first inaugural address on March 4, 1861, onward, Lincoln made it clear to the States that they were no more than institutional constituents of a true nation. While reassuring southern citizens "that their property, and their peace, and their personal security" were in no way "endangered by the now incoming Administration,"[6] Lincoln warned those who wanted to destroy "our national fabric,"[7] but also calmed them: Continue to obey "our national Constitution, and the Union will endure forever."[8]

The premise of the reasoning underlying the first inaugural address was the nature of the United States as a nation. As we have noted, while the United States *were* for Jefferson a nation "for special purposes only," and for Calhoun an "assemblage of nations,"[9] they *were* instead for Lincoln a nation, without further qualification.

> I hold, that in contemplation of universal law, and of the Constitution, the Union of these States is perpetual. Perpetuity is implied, if not expressed, in the fundamental law of all national governments. It is safe to assert that no government proper, ever had a provision in its organic law for its own termination.[10]

Lincoln's entire argument was based on the historically problematic assumption—however strongly asserted on every page—of the fully "national" character of the government of the United States, from which it directly follows that "no State .... can

6 Abraham Lincoln, "First Inaugural Address," March 4, 1861, *Collected Works*, vol. 4, p. 263.

7 *Ibid.*, p. 266.

8 *Ibid.*, p. 265.

9 Thomas Jefferson to Edmund Randolph, August 18, 1799, in *The Works of Thomas Jefferson*, vol. 9, ed. Paul Lester Ford (New York: G.P. Putnam's Sons, 1905), p. 76; *Speeches of John C. Calhoun* (New York: Harper & Brothers, 1843), p. 480.

10 Abraham Lincoln, "First Inaugural Address," p. 264.

lawfully get out of the Union."[11] While the marriage metaphor had already been used to explain the political pact that united the North and South, for Lincoln, the marriage between the two regions of the country was in fact even more robust than Christian one: "A husband and wife may be divorced ... but the different parts of our country cannot do this."[12]

Three decades earlier Calhoun had thrown down the gauntlet against the confused Madisonian doctrine of "divided sovereignty." In all his speeches he pointed out that only two logical alternatives were possible: Sovereignty resided either in the States or in the federation. Calhoun was convinced that his position could not be attacked either logically or historically. He always presented the "national" alternative as a mere counterpoint and textbook case, since he was certain that it could not be sustained. But he had underestimated the powerful forces that were already driving toward a nationalist solution to the American dilemma. Lincoln accepted the challenge and decisively stated that complete sovereignty resided in the Union/nation. And, though his rational and historical arguments were deficient, he was still a master at referring back to the "bonds of our affection," awaiting a time in which those "mystic chords of memory, stretching from every battle-field, and patriot grave, to every living heart and hearth-stone, all over this broad land, will yet swell the chorus of the Union, when again touched, as surely they will be, by the better angels of our nature."[13] While waiting for that moment, naturally, it was essential to prepare for war.

The Union, far from being the product of the Constitution—Lincoln actually stated that it "is much older than the Constitution"[14]—became a mystical locus of sentiments, a repository of shared memories, and an absolute moral good to be preserved at all costs. In his most successful and final political speech, Lincoln stated that the war had been fought for the nation: "Both parties deprecated war;

11 *Ibid.*, p. 265.

12 *Ibid.*, p. 269.

13 *Ibid.*, p. 271.

14 *Ibid.*, p. 265.

but one of them would make war rather than let the nation survive; and the other would accept war rather than let it perish."[15]

On another point of fundamental importance, however, Lincoln indirectly responded to the two great southern minds, Jefferson and Calhoun. To Jefferson, the real political problem was to ensure that every minority could, at least in theory, become a majority. It was therefore necessary that everyone had the right to vote as well as access to education and information in order to prevent the majority from perpetuating itself. To Calhoun, it was a natural law that the majority and minority tend to reproduce their positions permanently, and he considered it essential to devise constitutional schemes to safeguard the minority.[16] Lincoln, however, recognized no restraints whatsoever: Yes, there are constitutional limits, but otherwise the full and unconditional domination of the majority "is the only true sovereign of a free people. Whoever rejects it, does, of necessity, fly to anarchy or to despotism."[17]

6.2) The Slavery Question

In his second inaugural address, Lincoln said that "these slaves constituted a peculiar and powerful interest. All knew that this interest was, somehow, the cause of the war."[18] In his first inaugural address four years earlier, he reassured the Southerners on the one hand that "I have no purpose, directly or indirectly, to interfere with the institution of slavery in the States where it exists," and on the other hand he promised that the institution could become permanent, as long as the States did not leave the Union: "All the protection which, consistently with the Constitution and the laws, can be given, will be cheerfully given to all the States."[19]

15 Abraham Lincoln, "Second Inaugural Address," March 4, 1865, *Collected Works*, vol. 8, p. 332. On this speech see Ronald C. White, Jr., *Lincoln's Greatest Speech: The Second Inaugural* (New York: Simon & Schuster, 2002).

16 See the previous chapter.

17 Abraham Lincoln, "First Inaugural Address," p. 268.

18 Abraham Lincoln, "Second Inaugural Address," p. 332.

19 Abraham Lincoln, "First Inaugural Address," p. 263.

Almost all Lincoln scholars maintain (and state over and over again in such a manner that at times it sounds like a rehearsed refrain) that the South's bid for independence was prompted by the defense of slavery, and that while the North initially just wanted to save the Union, Lincoln understood later that in order to do that it was indispensable to destroy slavery. Late in the war Lincoln used a very emotional language about slavery and the carnage brought on by the conflict, and his excessively emotive manner has influenced generations of scholars. As James Tackach notes, "As the war dragged on longer than anyone expected and as the casualties mounted, Lincoln was beginning to understand that his nation was passing through a test mandated by God as a punishment for the past sins."[20]

Don E. Fehrenbacher admits that "Lincoln's behavior during his first year in office shows him ... being led by events. ... Lincoln negotiated with abolitionist generals who thought that he was going too slowly and with proslavery generals who threatened to resign if abolition ever became an official war aim. Some states were eager to destroy slavery, whereas others pursued a bitter-end policy to preserve slavery. Most importantly, Lincoln sought to keep both abolitionist and proslavery voters backing the war effort." Later on, he was "forced to shift his strategy and move out in front of emancipation's advancing columns."[21]

As far as slavery is concerned, the most convincing historical explanation is found between these two extreme and indefensible statements—*the war was caused entirely by slavery* and *slavery was not its cause*[22]—which we obviously will not even try to examine here. And yet slavery was a problem that cut across all of American politics from the Revolution to the Civil War.

---

20 James Tackach, *Lincoln's Moral Vision. The Second Inaugural Address* (Jackson, MS: University Press of Mississippi, 2002), pp. 20-121.

21 Don E. Fehrenbacher, *The Slaveholding Republic. An Account of the United States Government's Relation to Slavery*, completed and edited by Ward M. McAfee (New York: Oxford University Press, 2001), p. 314. Some states and some generals were in fact on the side of the Union as they believed, at least in the beginning, that a Northern victory would secure the institution of slavery. Maryland, Delaware, Kentucky and Missouri were slave states that fought on Lincoln's side.

22 Interestingly, John Stuart Mill and Charles Dickens, two well-known Englishmen of that time, presented precisely these two opposing visions in the London newspapers in

During his famous "Speech on Conciliation with the Colonies" in 1775, Edmund Burke had already noted that freedom in the South was subtly connected with the reality of slavery. The spirit of liberty in the South appeared "still more high and haughty than in those to the northward." In the presence of "a vast multitude of slaves," Burke continued, "those who are free are by far the most proud and jealous of their freedom. Freedom for them is "not only an enjoyment, but a kind of rank and privilege."[23]

There is an abundant body of literature which analyzes the whole of American history from the Revolution to the Civil War from the perspective of slavery.[24] While it seems difficult to believe

---

1862. For Dickens, the reasons for the war were clear: "Union means so many millions a year lost to the South; secession means the loss of the same millions to the North. ... [T]he quarrel between the North and South is, as it stands, solely a fiscal quarrel," Charles Dickens, "The Morrill Tariff," *All the Year Round*, December 28, 1862, p. 330. On the contrary, for John Stuart Mill the secessionists wanted to reshape the American continent "from the Potomac to Cape Horn" on the basis of the exploitation of slave labor; John S. Mill, "The Contest in America," *Fraser's Magazine*, February 1862, p. 258. See Charles Adams, *When in the Course of Human Events: Arguing the Case for Southern Secession* (New York: Rowman & Littlefield, 2000), pp. 85-96.

23 Edmund Burke, "Speech on Moving His Resolutions for Conciliation with the Colonies," March 22, 1775, in *Selected Writings and Speeches*, ed. Peek J. Stanlis (Washington DC: Regnery, 1997), p. 192.

24 A typical example is Staughton Lynd, *Class Conflict, Slavery, and the United States Constitution* (Westport, CT: Greenwood, 1980). Manisha Sinha, in *The Counterrevolution of Slavery: Politics and Ideology in Antebellum South Carolina* (Chapel Hill: University of North Carolina Press, 2000), analyzes the political history of the South (and particularly that of its most representative state) as an attempt to build a society free from outside interference in determining its relationship to slavery. Obviously, there are many exhaustive and balanced studies on individual aspects, including Paul Finkelman, *Slavery, Revolutionary America, and the New Nation* (New York: Garland, 1989), Duncan J. Macleod, *Slavery, Race and the American Revolution* (New York: Cambridge University Press, 1974), James Oakes, *The Ruling Race: A History of American Slaveholders* (New York: Knopf, 1982). The greatest scholar on slavery in America is Eugene D. Genovese, whose basic works are *The Political Economy of Slavery: Studies in the Economy and Society of the Slave South* (1965), *Roll, Jordan, Roll: The World the Slaves Made* (New York: Pantheon Books, 1974), and *The Slaveholders' Dilemma: Freedom and Progress in Southern Conservative Thought, 1820–1860* (Columbia: University of South Carolina Press, 1992). The most comprehensive analysis of legislation in the South is Thomas D. Morris, *Southern Slavery and the Law, 1619–1860* (Chapel Hill: University of North Carolina Press, 1996).

that there could be some necessary relationship between owning slaves and conceiving of large plans for freedom and institutional emancipation (for whites), one cannot deny that the two main thinkers of the South, Jefferson and Calhoun, were slave owners and lived in a world strongly shaped by that vicious institution.

Thomas Jefferson addressed the issue, particularly in his *Notes on Virginia* of 1785. As early as 1778 he was given the task of studying and revising the laws governing slavery. At that time he was generally favorable to a gradual emancipation of slaves. He proposed not only prohibiting the importation of new slaves, but also limiting the future condition of slavery in Virginia to just the descendants of actual slaves at that time. The problem of slavery plagued Jefferson throughout his life, and he was never able to settle it, either in public or in private life. In his later years he wrote: "Nothing is more certainly written on the book of fate that this people are to be free. Nor it is less certain that the two races, equally free, cannot live in the same government."[25] In his *Notes on Virginia*, slavery seemed to be an intractable problem that neither reason nor law could resolve. In fact, he was convinced that "deep rooted prejudices entertained by the whites; ten thousand recollections, by the blacks, of the injuries they have sustained ... and many other circumstances will divide us into parties, and produce convulsions, which will probably never end but in the extermination of the one or the other race."[26] On the other hand, he had no doubts on the moral question underlying slavery:

> The whole commerce between master and slave is a perpetual exercise of the most boisterous passions, the most unremitting despotism on the one part, and degrading submissions on the other. ... Indeed I tremble for my country when I reflect that God is just: that his justice cannot sleep forever.[27]

25 Thomas Jefferson, "Autobiography," in *Writings*, ed. Merrill D. Peterson (New York: Literary Classics of the U.S., 1984), p. 44.

26 Thomas Jefferson, *Notes on the State of Virginia* (1787), ed. William Peden (Chapel Hill: University of North Carolina Press, 1955), p. 138.

27 *Ibid.*, pp. 162-163.

Jefferson was first and foremost a pragmatic man of the South, and the rights of slaves had to be commensurate with the interests of whites. The security of the latter took precedence over the freedom of the former. Or, in a more cynical reading, since slaves were a form of property—"for actual property has been lawfully vested in that form, and who can lawfully take it from the possessors?"[28]—the security and property rights of the one conspired against the freedom and rights of the other.

If Jefferson seems to have at least clarified for himself the profound immorality of slavery, the same does not appear true of John Calhoun. Calhoun's obdurate view of slavery can be framed within the historical moment in which he worked, but it remains unacceptable. He openly declared in the Senate that "I hold that in the present state of civilization, where two races of different origin, and distinguished by color, and other physical differences, as well as intellectual, are brought together, the relation now existing in the slaveholding states between the two, is, instead of an evil, a good—a positive good."[29] His defense of slavery as a positive good had a great impact on the two opposing sides of the controversy, since his tone was radically different than the then-existing doctrines (his was essentially a defense based on a theory of power between people, and from this view slavery was considered a "necessary evil"), leading to a much more vigorous debate.[30]

From the time he became the major exponent of political theory in the South, Calhoun found that the two predefined and logically distinct arguments of states' rights and slavery had become inseparable in the defense of southern society. Typically, southern planters cited the theory of the inferiority of the blacks

28 Th. Jefferson to J. Sparks, February 4, 1824, *Writings*, eds. Andrew A. Lipscomb and Albert E. Bergh, vol. 16, p. 10.

29 John C. Calhoun, "Speech on the Reception of Abolition Petitions," Senate, February 6, 1837, in *Calhoun, Papers*, vol. 13, p. 393.

30 See David M. Potter, *The Impending Crisis 1848–1861* (New York: Harper & Row, 1976); William J. Cooper, Jr., *The South and the Politics of Slavery, 1828-1856* (Baton Rouge: Louisiana State University Press, 1978); *The Ideology of Slavery: Proslavery Thought in the Antebellum South, 1830–1860,* ed. Drew G. Faust (Baton Rouge: Louisiana State University Press, 1981).

as an established scientific fact and as the basis of the legitimacy of slavery. It was argued that blacks, beyond a physical and biological inferiority, were afflicted with a cultural backwardness that left them incapable of enjoying the benefits of freedom. Without the guidance of their masters, they would return to the state of savages.[31]

Additionally, a psychological factor underlay the proslavery arguments, and it should never be underestimated, namely, the feeling of genuine terror about the threat of slave rebellion.[32] The most famous slave revolt in America happened in the 1830s. On the night of August 22, 1831, in Southampton County in Virginia, Nat Turner led a violent rebellion. Though the explosion of violence lasted only one day, causing the deaths of around sixty whites, and hundreds of blacks in reprisal, the episode, as recalled by the editor of the most important work on the subject, ended up creating "consequences that touched the entire nation."[33]

The threat and reality of this violence was certainly one of the reasons that impeded Calhoun from even imagining an alternate system to slavery. The slavery problem was reduced to the question of relationship between whites and blacks: The two races could not coexist on an equal basis, thus one of the two must necessarily dominate the other. An exploitative relationship, though manifesting itself in various forms, was indispensable for cultural development and improving living conditions, in all

---

31 The idea of the—at least cultural—inferiority of the black population was shared by religious people who opposed slavery, who rationalized their failure to Christianize the slaves by arguing the inferior educability of the latter. See David B. Davis, *The Problem of Slavery in the Age of Revolution, 1770–1823* (Ithaca, NY: Cornell University Press, 1975), pp. 44-47.

32 The South Carolina populace, as well as that of other Southern states, never concealed its great fear of a slave rebellion: "Let it never be forgotten, that our NEGROES are truly the *Jacobins* of the country; that they are the *anarchists* and the *domestic enemy;* the *common enemy of civilized society*, and the barbarians, who would, IF THEY COULD, become the DESTROYERS of our race" (cited without a source by Robert F. Durden, *The Self-Inflicted Wound: Southern Politics in the Nineteenth Century* [Louisville: Kentucky University Press, 1985], p. 33).

33 Kenneth S. Greenberg, Introduction, *Nat Turner: A Slave Rebellion in History and Memory*, ed. Kenneth S. Greenberg (New York: Oxford University Press, 2003), p. xi.

times and places. The best-known defense of slavery on these grounds was in a speech by James Henry Hammond in the Senate on March 4, 1858:

> In all social systems there must be a class to do the menial duties, to perform the drudgery of life. That is, a class requiring but a low order of intellect and but little skill. Its requisites are vigor, docility, fidelity. Such a class you must have, or you would not have that other class which leads progress, civilization, and refinement. ... Fortunately for the South, she found a race adapted to that purpose to her hand. ...We use them for our purpose, and call them slaves.[34]

This quite extravagant doctrine had been upheld perhaps for the first time many years before by Timothy Ford of Charleston, who stated in 1794 that it was precisely the presence of the slaves that made free people well aware of the value of freedom and ready to fight for it.[35] Throughout all of human history the progress of civilization had been achieved through the substantial exploitation of a working class by a dominant class. Calhoun recognized slavery as a form of exploitation and responded that "there never has yet existed a wealthy and civilized society in which one portion of the community did not, in point of fact, live on the labor of the other."[36] At the same time, he rejected the label of "barbarous" in reference to the form of exploitation of the African slaves, since he held that this was the most humane of exploitative relationships between such different races.

---

34 James H. Hammond, Speech in the Senate, March 4, 1858, *Congressional Globe*, 35th Congress, 1st Session, Appendix, p. 71. For more on this well-discussed figure in South Carolina politics, at one time an ally and later a rival of Calhoun, see Drew Gilpin, *James Henry Hammond and the Old South: A Design for Mastery* (Baton Rouge: Louisiana State University Press, 1982).

35 See Americanus [Timothy Ford], "The Constitutionalist" (Charleston, 1794) in *American Political Writing during the Founding Era, 1760–1805*, eds. Charles S. Hyneman and Donald S. Lutz (Indianapolis: Liberty Press, 1983), p. 904.

36 Calhoun, *Papers*, vol. 13, pp. 395-396.

As irrelevant as they are from a moral point of view—freedom cannot be subordinated to utilitarian arguments—the old southern claims on the proper level of sustenance and housing of slaves compared to salaried Europeans and Americans have been substantiated by many studies. "Evidence recently collected on the heights of British and other European workers confirms the opinion ... that British 'wage slaves' of the early part of the [nineteenth] century were generally more poorly nourished than chattel slaves in the New World." Regarding American urban workers there was a slight nutritional disadvantage compared to the slaves, while the same cannot be said for American farmers, who were at that time the best fed "group of poor people" on the planet. However, "it is now clear that during most of the nineteenth century typical European peasants were as poorly nourished as the typical native-born slaves of the West Indies."[37]

For his part, Abraham Lincoln, as we mentioned, did not maintain a constant view of slavery or of relations between whites and blacks in America.[38] During the debates with Douglas in the 1850s he had strongly supported the idea of the inferiority of blacks:

> I will say then that I am not, nor ever have been in favor of bringing about in any way the social and political equality of the white and black races, that I am not nor ever have been in favor of making voters or jurors of negroes, nor of qualifying them to hold office, nor to intermarry with white people; and I will say in addition to this that there is a physical difference between the white and black races which I believe will forever forbid the two races living together on terms of social and political equality. And inasmuch as they cannot so live, while they do remain together there must be the position of

37 Robert William Fogel, *Without Consent or Contract: The Rise and Fall of American Slavery* (New York: Norton, 1989), p. 395.

38 See *Abraham Lincoln's Changing Views on Slavery*, ed. Robert B. Bruce (St. James, NY: Brandywine Press, 2001).

> superior and inferior, and I as much as any other man am in favor of having the superior position assigned to the white race.[39]

Although Lincoln scholars are obsessed about his views on African Americans, free or in captivity, his "racial attitudes were relatively enlightened for his day,"[40] and he was "no more liberal, and no less, than that of most decent Americans of the day."[41] While he thought slavery an intolerable and abhorrent relationship, a tumor metastasizing throughout American politics that should absolutely be contained, the idea that blacks could inhabit the same land and live on a level equal to whites never occurred to him. In December 1862, shortly before issuing the "Emancipation Proclamation," he reassured Northerners that an invasion of the northern states by emancipated blacks would not happen, as "recolonization" plans (to Africa or elsewhere) were already in place: [42]

---

39 Abraham Lincoln, "Fourth Joint Debate" with Douglas, September 18, 1858, in *Collected Works*, vol. 3, pp. 145-146. The full text of these crucial debates is now collected in *The Lincoln-Douglas Debates: The First Complete Unexpurgated Text*, edited and introduced by Harold Holzer (New York: Harper, 1994). Harry V. Jaffa's interpretation, though strongly biased in favor of Lincoln, is still important. See his *Crisis of the House Divided: An Interpretation of the Issues in the Lincoln-Douglas Debates* (Chicago: University of Chicago Press, 1959). I tend to side with George M. Fredrickson when he states: "Did Lincoln mean the things he said about blacks and race relations ... or was he simply dissembling in order to get himself elected? Neither alternative put him in a very favorable light." *Big Enough to be Inconsistent. Abraham Lincoln Confronts Slavery and Race* (Cambridge: Harvard University Pres, 2008), p. 41.

40 Paul D. Escott, *What Shall We Do With the Negro? Lincoln, White Racism and Civil War America* (Charlottesville: University of Virginia Press, 2009), p. 242.

41 Jan Morris, *Lincoln. A Foreigner's Quest* (New York: Simon & Schuster, 2000), p. 85.

42 Lerone Bennett Jr. forcefully emphasized Lincoln's recolonization plans in an attempt to overturn the image of the president as a friend of the blacks. See *Forced into Glory: Abraham Lincoln's White Dream* (Chicago: Johnson, 2000). According to Bennett, "the 'great emancipator' was one of the major supporters of slavery in the United States for at least fifty-four of his fifty-six years," p. 251. It seems obvious that Lincoln, as well as all whites of his time, very much wanted a country populated by—and welcoming only—people of European origin, but that is a far cry from concluding that Lincoln had a veritable "white dream." Allen C. Guelzo, *Lincoln's Emancipation Proclamation: The End of Slavery in America* (New York: Simon & Schuster, 2004) takes the opposite view, and contends that Lincoln wanted to abolish slavery as soon as he became president.

> Colored people, to some extent, have fled north from bondage; and now, perhaps, from both bondage and destitution. But if gradual emancipation and deportation be adopted, they will have neither to flee from. Their old masters will give them wages at least until new laborers can be procured; and the freed men, in turn, will gladly give their labor for the wages, till new homes can be found for them, in congenial climes, and with people of their own blood and race.[43]

In any case, in this summary exposition of Lincoln's thought it is not possible to address the slavery question in depth. Nor is it necessary to address at any length the matter of the role of slavery in Lincoln's motivation for going to war: the well-known letter to Horace Greeley is the clearest refutation of the idea that Lincoln unleashed war against the South in order to uproot the vile weed of slavery. As he admitted in the clearest terms, his main preoccupation was ever the preservation of the Union. Concern for the plight of the slaves simply had no place in his mission. Lincoln wrote unequivocally that he did not want "to leave any one in doubt" over the reasons that drove him to war.

> I would save the Union. ... My paramount object in this struggle is to save the Union, and is not either to save or to destroy slavery. If I could save the Union without freeing any slave I would do it, and if I could save it by freeing all the slaves I would do it; and if I could save it by freeing some and leaving others alone I would also do that. What I do about slavery, and the colored race, I do because I believe it helps to save the Union; and what I forbear, I forbear because I do not believe it would help to save the Union.[44]

---

43 Abraham Lincoln, "Annual Message to Congress," December 1, 1862, *Collected Works*, vol. 5, pp. 535-536.

44 Abraham Lincoln to Horace Greeley, August 22, 1862, *Collected Works*, vol. 5, p. 388.

Rivers of ink have flowed to cleanse this letter. Michael Burlingame's attempt to make the letter say precisely what it does not say is not atypical: "Those who regard Lincoln's letter to Greeley as a definite statement of his innermost feelings about the war's aims have misunderstood the document. ... [T]he letter was a political statement that aimed to pave the way for the proclamation which he intended to issue soon. ... Lincoln felt obliged somehow to make emancipation acceptable. ... [B]y stressing that emancipation was only a means to help save the Union, Lincoln sought to reduce the strength of the inevitable white backlash that the Proclamation would generate."[45] Since the present writer is not well versed in psychology, it seems better to take Lincoln's words at face value. Also, the least that one can say is that "the man who would later be known as the Great Emancipator first came to power having just accepted a constitutional amendment designed to prevent any attack on slavery in the states where it existed."[46]

As Eric Foner notes, once it became clear to radical Republicans that saving the Union implied the abolition of slavery, abolition ended up being identified with the doctrine of the Union *über alles* and vice versa.[47] Nationalism became mingled with antislavery and thus Lincoln realized that only the abolition of slavery would further his cause. "Lincoln did not invent American nationalism ... [but he] found that he must articulate a systematic vision of the nation for the first time in his long political career, spanning a generation from the Age of Jackson to secession."[48] Nonetheless, as the president spelled out very clearly, for him the Union remained

45 Michael Burlingame, "Lincoln and Race," *Lincoln and Liberty*, edited by Lucas E. Morel (Lexington, KY: University Press of Kentucky, 2014), p. 65.

46 Daniel W. Crofts, *Lincoln and the Politics of Slavery: The Other Thirteenth Amendment and the Struggle to Save the Union* (Chapel Hill, NC: University of North Carolina Press, 2016), p. 236.

47 Cf. Eric Foner, *Free Soil, Free Labor, Free Men: The Ideology of the Republican Party before the Civil War* (Oxford: Oxford University Press, 1995), pp. 72, 224.

48 Mark E. Neely, Jr., *Lincoln and the Triumph of the Nation: Constitutional Conflict in the American Civil War* (Chapel Hill, NC: University of North Carolina Press, 2011), p. 37.

the one and only purpose of the struggle against the South, without slavery figuring even peripherally, at least in the beginning. George Kateb sums it up nicely:

> The great evil of the war was initiated by the South to defend slavery, and waged by the North, whatever Lincoln may have secretly hoped, not to end the greater evil of slavery, but to preserve the Union and with it, slavery in the South and border states, if need be. ... The dissolution of the Union was a greater evil than the perpetuation of slavery. It is grim to say that probably a larger combined number of white troops on both sides in the Civil War died to preserve slavery, directly or indirectly, than to abolish it; to preserve slavery by destroying the Union; or preserve slavery by a possible and desirable compromise that would also preserve the Union.[49]

6.3) Lincoln and the American Constitution

The idea of the Union as an end in itself, not as a means for maintaining the right of self-government, and as the sole institutional structure truly capable of producing "moral good" for Americans was the fundamental defining element that permits one to understand how Lincoln initiated the modern state into America, with the consequent abrupt decline of both classical liberalism and the federal system of government.

Most historians, convinced that the country needed a real "second foundation,"[50] believe that Lincoln uniquely accomplished the mission of making the principles of the Declaration of

---

49 George Kateb, *Lincoln's Political Thought* (Cambridge, MA: Harvard University Press, 2015) p. 120. The author, a political philosopher, is perfectly right in posing the ultimate question on slavery and Union. He asks "whether disunion was a greater evil than slavery, especially if disunion were peacefully accomplished. The moral answer is no, and that answer is supported by the thought that slaves had a right of revolution against the Union and on good Lockean-Jeffersonian grounds, *ibid.*, p. 115.

50 For Charles Beard the Civil War was "the Second American Revolution," in that it produced fundamental changes in social relations that the 1776 revolution had left

Independence available to every American. In past generations, in fact, much of the historiographical debate on the figure of Lincoln was devoted to evaluating if the Republic had emerged unscathed from the tragedy of the Civil War, or if instead it had been radically transformed. For his part, Lincoln always claimed to have followed in the footsteps of Washington and Jefferson, at least on matters pertaining to the *form* of government of the United States. Later on, however, both Lincoln's admirers and a considerable number of historians (the two categories tend to overlap given the general worship of Honest Abe) have maintained that America effectively required a genuine re-founding, thus denying claims of Lincoln's continuity with preceding generations. Supreme Court Justice Thurgood Marshall stated in 1987 that the concepts of liberty, equality, and justice that stemmed from the founding period of the Republic were completely obsolete and praised Lincoln for having saved the Union by destroying the Constitution "for what it was." Marshall candidly stated that "The Union survived the Civil War, not the Constitution." In its place "arose a new, more promising basis for justice and equality, the Fourteenth Amendment."[51]

From this point of view, many current interpretations appear to destroy the old canon of Lincoln's historical continuity. Citing just one among many, in *The Lincoln Persuasion* David Greenstone supported the view that Lincoln had reshaped classic American liberalism, which had until then been too biased in favor of negative liberty, thus giving future generations the salvific concept of positive liberty that prevails today.[52] Indeed, the idea that Lincoln triggered a radical change and forever altered the American political landscape is a commonly accepted statement today. In fact, Lincoln implemented a transformation of the highest order, probably far more profound than most historians are ready to recognize, in

intact. See Charles A. Beard and Mary R. Beard, *The Rise of American Civilization*, vol. 2 (New York: Macmillan, 1930).

51 "Remarks" by Thurgood Marshall, Hawaii, March 6, 1987, cited in Herman Belz, *Abraham Lincoln, Constitutionalism, and Equal Rights in the Civil War Era* (New York: Fordham University Press, 1998), p. 73.

52 See. J. David Greenstone, *The Lincoln Persuasion: Remaking American Liberalism* (Princeton: Princeton University Press, 1993).

that this change destroyed the American Republic as it had existed up to that time and set the course for the definitive migration of European categories on power and the state to America.

At first glance, Lincoln may appear simply as the victorious successor of a series of historical figures, from Alexander Hamilton, to Henry Clay, to Daniel Webster, who sought to create a much stronger and more powerful union than had ever previously existed. However, whether Lincoln consciously knew it or not, his idea of the Union as an end in itself turned out to be the ideal Trojan Horse for bringing the conceptual framework of European statehood onto American soil. That is, in preserving and greatly strengthening the Union (as well as eradicating slavery), Lincoln not only defended a "moral" position, but was interpreting the *Zeitgeist*, becoming in the process the Napoleon of his side of the Atlantic. In fact, Lincoln, like Napoleon (though perhaps with less awareness), acted in complete harmony with the age of the triumph of the state.

A veritable chasm divides the views on power widely held at the beginning of the republic from the doctrine that "tyranny" (variously understood as exploitation, corruption or supremacy) was the natural result of social interaction, and that political power was the answer. For most Americans of the early generations it seemed difficult to believe a true system of coercion existed outside the political sphere. With Abraham Lincoln, the long tradition of suspicion of political power was interrupted.

Broadly speaking, Lincoln denied that his actions were constitutional violations, but in reality what became "Lincoln's Constitution" was a document very different from the one of 1790. Even a cursory reading of the Constitution and the Bill of Rights is enough to show that the generation that made the American Revolution was convinced that the greatest threat to individual freedom came from government and its powers. All the freedoms and rights discussed by the Founding Fathers were intended to protect the individual from the government. As simplistic as it was, this was the *raison d'être* of the preference for a limited government. According to this view, all basic human freedoms must be protected from the actions of one and only one potential aggressor, the government (as we have seen, in the American context this was the federal government rather than the governments of the individual states). However much other individuals might be a practical threat to property and freedom, political power alone could obliterate both property and rights.

Such a point of view is in sharp contrast to the common interpretation of the nature and meaning of social life and of government passed on from Lincoln's time to successive generations of Americans. According to this new political doctrine, actions by public authorities are generally preferable to those of individuals. Furthermore, the federal government is preferable to that of the confederated States, and the autonomy of the executive branch of the federal government should in turn be privileged, as it is already prepared for the required unity of action. This theory's arrival on the American political scene was the most significant step toward the disappearance not only of federalism, but also of liberalism in the form that it had taken in the early republic.

With Lincoln, threats to freedom shifted from the government to the individual. Rather than political authorities, those individuals who avail themselves of their freedom of action with respect to others are the real abusers. Slavery was the quintessential exploitative and oppressive relationship, and, according to the prevailing view in the North, it emerged from excessive individual freedom. Therefore, the government must be tasked with taking the necessary steps to protect individuals from exploitation at the hands of others. This entailed a revolution in thought about government relative to that which had been commonly accepted up to that time. Since the ratification of the Thirteenth Amendment and the triumph of the model of government behind it, the concept of the individual has been viewed with increasing suspicion, while trust in the federal government has continuously increased. On this point, George Fletcher has written a very interestingly-titled work, *Our Secret Constitution: How Lincoln Redefined American Democracy*. According to the author, there are now two Constitutions in the United States. Alongside the original Constitution there is a "secret" one, forged in fact by Lincoln. The two documents are inspired by different values and are irreducibly contradictory. "The first Constitution commits itself to freedom and the second builds both on a preference for equality and the recognition that freedom is often an illusion."[53] While the first Constitution had a deeply rooted distrust of government, the second presupposes complete faith in a strong government as the resolute protector of citizens from their fellow citizens.

By virtue of the profound changes over which Lincoln presided, a new concept of the relationship between the individual and public authority took hold: the same concept that had prevailed, and still prevails, in Europe. The very fabric of the old Constitution was shredded. As Fletcher put it: "The first Constitution plays on the theme of distrust in government. We must secure our freedoms against potentially abusive officials seeking 'rents' by pursuing their own bureaucratic interests. The second constitution presupposes trust in an aggressive government, a watchdog of transactions that might slide into the forbidden territory of 'involuntary servitude.'"[54] One scholar praised in these terms what seemed to him the most enduring change triggered by the Civil War: "Americans now understood that any generation could challenge and enlarge a previous generation's Constitution without violating the original charter."[55] Supporters and opponents of Lincoln can certainly agree on one point: He changed the Constitution forever.

6.4) The Organic Metaphor and the New Nationalism

Without a doubt, Lincoln bent the Constitution to his own ends. The logic underlying the President's abuse of power is fully evident in a significant letter to Albert Hodges. Hodges had accused him of having repeatedly violated the Constitution, for example, in utilizing courts martial to try civilians (who often were simply dissenters). In April 1864 Lincoln responded in the peremptory tone found in all great statesmen.

---

53 George P. Fletcher, *Our Secret Constitution: How Lincoln Redefined American Democracy* (New York: Oxford University Press, 2001), p. 223. The author, a liberal, considers the changes made by Lincoln highly commendable.

54 *Ibid.*, 223.

55 Michael Vorenberg, *Final Freedom: The Civil War, the Abolition of Slavery, and the Thirteenth Amendment* (Cambridge, UK: Cambridge University Press, 2001), p. 250.

> I did understand however, that my oath to preserve the constitution to the best of my ability, imposed upon me the duty of preserving, by every indispensable means, that government—that nation—of which that constitution was the organic law. Was it possible to lose the nation, and yet preserve the constitution? By general law life and limb must be protected; yet often a limb must be amputated to save a life; but a life is never wisely given to save a limb. I felt that measures, otherwise unconstitutional, might become lawful, by becoming indispensable to the preservation of the constitution, through the preservation of the nation. Right or wrong, I assumed this ground.[56]

Lincoln's deep political convictions emerged with great clarity and marked the decline of all the conceptions that had presided over the development of the Republic to that point. Lincoln stated that he held the Constitution to be an "organic law," thus introducing a European idea that had little precedent in America.[57] With this he drew a clear parallel between the human body and the "body" of the entire populace. Within the space of a few phrases we encounter all the constitutive elements of the theory of the modern state, expressed by a man who had probably never heard of Machiavelli, Bodin, or Hobbes, but who nevertheless was following in their footsteps. The Constitution in Lincoln's interpretation was an organic law, in that its purpose was protecting and giving shape to an organic society, through the creation of a state that was in its turn organic. The crucial factor was the conviction that the society—or nation—that the Constitution must protect was far more important than the organic law itself. Consequently, if one is forced to choose between the Constitution and the nation, the latter should take precedence. In Lincoln's view the Constitution had no value apart from its far more important "parent," that is, the Union or the nation. While the prevailing political discourse up

56 Abraham Lincoln to Albert G. Hodges, April 4, 1864, *Collected Works*, vol. 7, p. 281.

57 Lincoln frequently used the term "organic law" as an exact synonym for "Constitution"; for just a few examples, see *Collected Works*, vol. 2, p. 369; vol. 3, pp. 496, 504; vol. 4, pp. 255, 267, 426.

to Lincoln's time had been summarized in the question "whether the union had any meaning apart from the Constitution,"[58] Lincoln reversed the terms. The Union became a mystical object that was an end in itself, which gave or denied meaning to everything attributable to it.

In his final speech, just fourteen years earlier, Calhoun had summarized the commonly held view thusly: If one loves the Union, he "would necessarily be devoted to the Constitution. It made the Union, and to destroy the Constitution would be to destroy the Union."[59] Furthermore, when Lincoln invoked the salvation of the nation-state in order to declare the legitimacy of his actions—clearly unjustified without such an exonerating purpose—he seems nearly a follower of Giovanni Botero and the theorists of the "Reason of State." In the last half of the phrase quoted, "Right or wrong, I assumed this ground," he stated that he was definitively not subject to common morality.

Herman Belz is highly critical of the explanation that sees the Union as the true beacon in Lincoln's political thought. He finds it unpersuasive, because Lincoln's thought was "grounded in the natural rights philosophy of the eighteenth century, if not that of classical natural right."[60] And yet, one cannot find a single scrap of proof to uphold what some scholars maintain that is, that Lincoln was raised in the natural rights tradition. There is no evidence at all to suggest that Lincoln's political doctrine was influenced by any principle derived from natural law, either in its classic or its modern formulation. And were a feeble trace discovered, it would be overwhelmed by Lincoln's ink and voice, which asserted at every turn that the salvation of the Union as Nation was his pole star.

---

58 Richard Gamble, "Rethinking Lincoln," in *The Costs of War: America's Pyrrhic Victories*, ed. John V. Densen (New Brunswick, NJ: Transaction, 1999), p. 141.

59 John C. Calhoun, "Speech on the Slavery Question," March 4, 1850, in Calhoun, *Works*, vol. 4, p. 559.

60 Herman Belz, *Abraham Lincoln, Constitutionalism, and Equal Rights in the Civil War Era* (New York: Fordham University Press, 1998), p. 95.

In addition, Belz, following the lead of Harry Jaffa and other scholars, denied that Lincoln ever violated the Constitution. He stated that "the proper way, following Lincoln's example, is to insist on fidelity to the text, forms, and principles of the framers' Constitution."[61] Without offering any evidence to support his assertion, Belz added that for Lincoln, "American nationality was defined by the Constitution, just as before the war he identified the nation with the ideas of liberty and equality in the Declaration of Independence. In a sense, therefore, the nation was the Constitution."[62] Actually, we just saw that the most valid and reliable source on the question spelled out clearly the opposite argument: The nation was not the Constitution, and Lincoln was willing to break the latter in order to save the former. Without a doubt this is a rather consistent political philosophy. However, it certainly cannot be said that he in any way followed the course laid out by Thomas Jefferson and the Founding Fathers. "Lincoln's devotion to free society was thoroughly nationalist ... universal liberty represented the nation's guiding principle; self-government represented its greatest achievement; free labor represented its prodigious strength; and northern society ... its true character."[63]

Although described as a *moderate* (an adjective that obviously must be assessed within the context of the political spectrum of the Republican party of that time), Lincoln's nationalism was accurately described by Foner as follows:

> That Lincoln's Unionism combined a number of strands of antebellum thought was illustrated by the fact that before his inaugural address he consulted Clay's compromise speech of 1850, Jackson's proclamation against nullification, and Webster's reply to Hayne. Lincoln agreed with the Webster-Clay tradition when he insisted that the Union preceded the Constitution and was a creation of the American

61 *Ibid.*, p. 100.

62 *Ibid.*, p. 98.

63 Graham A. Peck, *Making an Antislavery Nation: Lincoln, Douglas, and the Battle over Freedom* (Champaign: University of Illinois Press, 2017), p.179.

> people, not a compact between states. But to their unqualified devotion to the Union as the paramount end of politics, he added the radical conception of the Union as a means to freedom.[64]

Other scholars have described Lincoln's nationalism in more robust terms. Harold M. Hyman, for example, stated:

> To describe Lincoln as a nationalist is not merely to contrast him with state-oriented secessionists, to say that he was patriotic, or to note that he found convincing inspiration in his constitutional convictions not to haul down the Sumter flag. Lincoln's nationalism was deep, impelling, and systematic. It was a faith, not a slogan. In his apotheosis of the republic the nation took on transcendent virtues.[65]

Yet the aspect of Lincoln's clear statement about the nation and the Constitution that most betrays his intimate convictions is his recourse to an organicist metaphor. The equivalence between a living body and a political community is of prime importance, since it is an essential factor for introducing the categories and terminology of the state into political theory. The state is not simply the marriage between the political and legal orders, or a new way of conceiving of the political community. Rather, it develops within a terminology that induces one to think of the state within the conceptual framework proposed by the statist tradition itself. The establishment of the modern state in Europe went hand in hand with changes in the political lexicon from the sixteenth century onward. The jurists of that time had to imagine the state along the lines of an artificial person, which transcended the person of the prince, and ultimately, his own dynasty, thus ensuring its perpetuation. The new "body politic" had its own life, independent of its subjects and even its sovereign. It represented neither anyone

64 Eric Foner, *Free Soil, Free Labor, Free Men*, p. 225.

65 Harold M. Hyman, *A More Perfect Union: The Impact of the Civil War and Reconstruction on the Constitution* (New York: Knopf, 1973), p. 57.

nor anything, but it simply existed and fed off the myths produced by historians, jurists, theologians and politicians. The foremost of these myths, as we saw in the first chapter, was the myth of having always existed.

A vital component of this intellectual construction, comparable in importance even to the concept of sovereignty, is the general use of the organicist metaphor, or the idea that the sum total of relations between individual human beings constitutes a real and substantive entity, a living organism, that the state, as the artificial person, has the duty to regulate. Above all, this requires that political rule become an inherent element in society; in turn, that society is nothing more than an organism that is inherently political in and of itself. While it is true that analogous metaphors may be found in the political thought of ancient Greece, especially in Plato's *Republic*, it is equally true that they were not commonly accepted prior to the emergence of the modern state.

At this point the problem arises of how it was possible to import this concept into America. As Carl Schmitt observed, the modern state is predicated on a fundamental dogma: the neutralization of all internal conflicts. It is no coincidence that this intellectual construction was imposed in Europe precisely during the era of the wars of religion. Within the borders of the state, all conflicts must be considered an aberration, a temporary inability to distinguish the "real" interests of society and adapt one's actions to them. The very concept of individual interest, that is, of an interest that is different from that of the state as a whole, is suspect or illegitimate. The "political formula" on which the state is based would render all civil war and revolution impossible. Conflicts can never be internal, only international, since a living organism can never be in conflict with itself (unless it is ill), but only with other living beings.

A civil war is the opposite of the dogma of the state: Internal conflict duplicates or multiplies the unity on which the nation-state is predicated. It represents a "house divided" ("A house divided against itself cannot stand")[66] or a sick organism, and such cannot

66 See Abraham Lincoln, "House Divided Speech," June 16, 1858, *Collected Works*, vol. 1, pp. 461-470.

long last. In a modern state, then, adversaries who would tear the bond of unity asunder should be regarded as absolute enemies to be cleansed from the face of the earth, as they threaten unity, the most sacred principle of statehood. From this point of view, if it is correct to consider the Civil War as the advent of the modern state in America, it is difficult to consider it a "useless war," as Thomas DiLorenzo claimed.[67] In contrast with the "rationality" of the modern state, the American republic of Jefferson was such a deformed and monstrous creature that it needed to be destroyed by the most extreme means.

In the short span of a few decades, from roughly 1832 to 1865, America went through a process very similar to what happened in Europe between 1500 and 1815. In Europe the sovereign (first the king, then parliament) was the one that promised to free every individual from the antiquated and tyrannical bonds of Church, city, company, family, and so forth, even though, in fact, these 'bonds' constituted the essential elements of medieval freedom. Americans quickly set out to reenact the same sequence, and what is more, during the triumph of the Nation State. Since their history had no provisions for wars of religion, Americans lived out the tragedy of the modern state during the course of a civil war based on nationalist principles, which represented the *summa* of all possible conflicts. In effect, this was a war waged by the federal government against the States and against the very concept of their existence as free and independent political communities. As one historian noted many years ago:

> Steadily, throughout the war, the President, the swollen bureaucracy, and the representatives of these business interests, battled against States' Rights. In the process they called upon the doctrines of democracy, appealed to a hatred of aristocracy, wept bitter tears over the plight of Southern slaves, and formulated new dogmas to national supremacy. In the end they created a new nation, destroying the

67 See Thomas DiLorenzo, *The Real Lincoln: A New Look at Abraham Lincoln, His Agenda, and an Unnecessary War* (New York: Three Rivers Press, 2003).

> Old Federal Union, and with it the rights of the states. In the process and in the end they destroyed one of the ancient bulwarks of human liberty—the power of the states to protect the people. Perhaps, in the end, there was less liberty in the land than before. It was not, therefore, a War Between the States. It was rather, in its larger aspects, a War Against the States, waged by the national Government on two fronts: against the armed embodiment of States' Rights in the Southern Confederacy, and against the political embodiment of the rights of the states in the North. It ended with the unquestioned supremacy of the Nation over the States.[68]

In this drama, the federal government played the part the sovereign power had played in European history, while the States were forced to assume the role of relics of the past, in a struggle that closely resembled the opposition to political modernity in the twilight of the Middle Ages. The war, then, was truly necessary, since the republic of the Founding Fathers had been constructed on principles that were not so much at odds with the modern state as they were fiercely opposed. Genuine federalism is not a viable option for a modern state. The 'sacred' dogma of unity was already the subject of debate in early America prior to the Southern bid for independence: Such a dogma explains Lincoln's veneration of the concept of the Union, which in preceding decades had aroused but lukewarm devotion, to say the least.

For Lincoln, the Union, understood as a living organism, was the ultimate goal worth fighting for. As proof of Lincoln's concept of the Union and its goals, there is no more important document than his message to Congress of December 1, 1862. His impassioned description of the United States as a living being, as our "national homestead," is the premise on which the President erected his argument for union: "In all its adaptations and aptitudes it

68 William B. Hesseltine, Introduction, *The Tragic Conflict: The Civil War and Reconstruction*, ed. William B. Hesseltine (New York: Braziller, 1962), p. 19.

demands Union and abhors separation. In fact, it would ere long force reunion, however much of blood and treasure the separation might have cost."[69]

In short, the Union, being an article of faith and exempt from rational cost-benefit analysis, had no price. In this foundational speech, Lincoln made clear why it was necessary to prevent the separation by the southern states at any cost: "That portion of the earth's surface which is owned and inhabited by the people of the United States is well adapted to be the home of one national family, and it is not well adapted for two or more. ... [All the resources of this land] are of advantage in this age for one people."[70] Lincoln proceeded by highlighting the demographics of an undivided Union. In 1900 it would have over 100 million people and would be able to launch its attempt at world domination, supplanting a declining Europe.

> We have 2,963,000 square miles. Europe has 3,800,000, with a population averaging 73 1/3 persons to the square mile. Why may not our country at some time average as many? ... Is it inferior to Europe in any natural advantage? If, then, we are at some time to be as populous as Europe, how soon? ... when it will be, if ever, depends much on whether we maintain the Union.[71]

Europe, the center of world power, was the touchstone. America would reach and beat Europe only if it remained united: "If we do not ourselves relinquish the chance by the folly and evils of disunion."[72] Such a feeling of revenge toward Europe frequently accompanied his fervor for the Union, Heather Cox Richardson suggests:

---

69 Abraham Lincoln, "Annual Message to Congress," December 1, 1862, p. 529.

70 *Ibid.*, p. 527.

71 *Ibid.*, pp. 532-533.

72 *Ibid.*, p. 533.

> People focused on the Union rather than individual states, defining their nation against what Republicans deemed a hostile Europe, as well as the secessionist South. Having poured out blood and money in amounts hitherto inconceivable to survive a devastating civil war, and at the end of it finding themselves prosperous as well as successful, Republicans believed in America's unlimited potential. The country was becoming, it seemed, "the greatest nation of the earth."[73]

Lincoln concluded his 1862 message to Congress with his plea:

> "We cannot escape history. ... We know how to save the Union. ... We shall nobly save or meanly lose the last best hope of earth."[74]

In the classic terms of the American debate, Lincoln wanted to save the Union in order to create an empire. This is not at all a different explanation to the perspective of transplanting the conceptual framework of the state. And yet this was not just about dazzling power. The idealistic tones of the President were as sincere as they were relevant. He was convinced that the United States were the "last best hope of humanity," because the glue that held America together was not culture, race, or tradition, but the ideal of "equality." He clearly stated that in 1861 prior to taking the oath of office as President:

> I have often inquired of myself, what great principle or idea it was that kept this Confederacy so long together. It was ... something in that Declaration giving liberty, not alone to the people of this country, but hope to the world for all future time. It was that

73 Heather Cox Richardson, *The Greatest Nation of the Earth: Republican Economic Policies during the Civil War* (Cambridge, MA: Harvard University Press, 1997), p. 255.

74 Abraham Lincoln, "Annual Message to Congress," December 1, 1862, p. 537.

> which gave promise that in due time the weights should be lifted from the shoulders of all men, and that all should have an equal chance.[75]

For Lincoln on this occasion, as on numerous others,[76] freedom and equality seemed to perfectly coincide, so much so that only by starting from the perfect equality of citizens can one begin to speak of freedom. Harry Jaffa, one of the best known scholars on Lincoln, held that the President introduced a new and more complex concept of equality into the American scene. Perfect equality among people, as considered by John Locke and Jefferson, was posited in a hypothetical "state of nature," and civil society was not bound to this state of full equality. Lincoln believed, to the contrary, that civil society should become the means for attaining a state of full, true and effective equality.[77]

Equality among all American citizens was created precisely by the destruction of the principle on which the federation was founded, that of equality among the States. Between 1865 and 1877 the southern states were subject to military occupation and treated as colonies; history has adopted the mild label of "Reconstruction" for those twelve years. This is how Lincoln had understood the horns of the dilemma: The triumph of equality was to be brought about by the annihilation of the States. In the President's view, the Union was naturally the supreme bulwark of the principle of equality.[78]

There is a final element worth noticing in our overview of the outbreak in America of the state concept, that of the "civil religion" that Lincoln held dearly. In the modern era the search for a civil

75 Abraham Lincoln, "Speech in Independence Hall," February 22, 1861, *Collected Works*, vol. 4, p. 240.

76 See Abraham Lincoln, "Speech at a Republican Banquet," December 10, 1856, *Collected Works*, vol. 2, p. 385, and "Fragment: Notes for Speeches," October 1858, *Ibid.*, p. 484.

77 Cf. Harry V. Jaffa, *Crisis of the House Divided*, pp. 330-362.

78 For a quite bizarre view of Lincoln as a "friendly critic of democratic faith," see Patrick J. Deneen, *Democratic Faith* (Princeton, Princeton University Press, 2005), pp. 271-287.

religion capable of displacing Christianity proceeded apace with the intellectual construction of the modern state. One of the secular dogmas of this construction, in effect, consists in asserting that the "mystery of existence" had to be located in this world, and more specifically in the political community, rather than in a heaven above us. Machiavelli, Rousseau and many other thinkers considered the idea of a civil religion as the tool most appropriate to ensure citizens' obedience to political institutions.

Lincoln thought of himself as a good Christian, and many still consider him to be a refined theologian and an exemplary figure of a "classic" faith. Nevertheless, his sole clear reference to the concept of an "American political religion" was distinguished by currents of thought that were decidedly alien to the Christian religion. Talking to the students of Springfield in 1838, Lincoln told them that "a reverence for the Constitution and laws" had to become the supreme virtue of the country. In a tone that even Rousseau himself might have considered excessive, he urged:

> Let every American, every lover of liberty, every well-wisher to his posterity swear by the blood of the Revolution never to violate in the least particular the laws of the country, and never to tolerate their violation by others ... let it be taught in schools, in seminaries, and in colleges ... let it be preached from the pulpit, proclaimed in legislative halls, and enforced in courts of justice. And, in short, let it become the political religion of the nation; and let the old and the young, the rich and the poor, the grave and the gay of all sexes and tongues and colors and conditions, sacrifice unceasingly upon its altars.[79]

What should be done about unjust laws? "[I]f they exist, [they] should be repealed as soon as possible, still, while they continue in force, for the sake of example they should be religiously observed."[80]

---

79 Abraham Lincoln, "Address Before the Young Men's Lyceum of Springfield, Illinois," January 27, 1838, in *Collected Works*, vol. 1, p. 112 (italics mine).

80 *Id.*

It is a matter of some astonishment that the young Lincoln had Rousseau indelibly stamped in the depths of his soul, even though in all likelihood he had never read the Genevan's works.

6.5) Francis Lieber and the German school

Faced with such a complex set of factors (union, nation, organic metaphors, civil religion), all tending toward a single purpose, the regeneration of the American political community in the form of a modern state, the historian of ideas must come to grips with a basic question: Where did all this come from? We know that Lincoln was the most brilliant and talented politician of his time (and, perhaps, in all of American history), but it is obvious as well that he was poorly educated in political philosophy. Appealing to the *Zeitgeist* to explain how this self-taught lawyer may have incorporated the basic ideas and concepts of the constructs of the European state is a reasonable, but unsatisfactory, response.[81]

If we begin researching the specifics, the question becomes even more tangled, as Lincoln never cited sources or texts from which he drew inspiration, if there were any. What we might broadly define a "national sentiment" had begun to assert itself with increasing force in American culture. "God designs that each country should wear a peculiar ideal physiognomy," wrote the famous nationalist Thomas Starr King in 1851. "The breakup of the Union into two or more confederacies would degrade God's handwork–this was the moral King and his fellow nationalists did not hesitate to draw".[82]

---

81 From this point of view, for example, John L. Thomas argues that Lincoln's ideas were formed by the democratic forces of his time, and that he drew the themes and vocabulary that he would use from "the edges of the popular mind.'" Thomas further that "the search for the political culture from which Lincoln emerged leads out of the halls of state into the American heartland of popular assumptions and aspirations where programs give way to persuasions, platforms to preferences, ideology to *mentalité*," John L. Thomas, Introduction, *Abraham Lincoln and the American Political Tradition*, ed. John L. Thomas (Amherst: University of Massachusetts Press, 1986), p. 4.

82 Merle Curti, *The Growth of American Thought* (New York: Harper & Brothers, 1951), p. 393.

Just as in Europe, the importance attributed to the national community was predicated on a common historical heritage. "Among the sentimental elements in the pattern of nationalism and patriotism the reverence for and idealization of the nation's past was of much moment."

The works of Francis Lieber (who in 1827 was one of the first German academics to arrive in America) may have contributed to shaping Lincoln's thought in various ways, or at least contributed to the cultural climate in which it formed. Lieber's role was crucial in bringing together the German, English and American political cultures. It should be added as well that the enormous number of Germanic immigrants to America in the 1830s and 1840s offered fertile ground for the spread of nationalistic ideals. This is particularly true of the many "liberals" who fled from the German states after the failure of the nationalist revolution in 1848-49. A considerable number of these young, idealistic intellectuals, who were thoroughly steeped in the idea of the national state and the unity of the nation as a supreme political goal, made careers in journalism or gave themselves to political activism,[83] ultimately contributing by these means to the promulgation of the assumptions and the terminology of the nation-state throughout America.

The strong Germanic element in several northern states also contributed to accelerating the demise of the concept of states' rights, a notion completely alien to the traditions of their homelands. "The principle of states' rights ... did not appeal to the intelligent Germans, who had seen the evils of particularism at home, but the great body of German immigrants did not understand the question, nor did they bother about it until it became a leading issue that forced itself upon them."[84]

If we turn our gaze upon the academy, it becomes difficult to underestimate Lieber's influence in transplanting the modern state outlook into the New World. After having taught in South Carolina

83 See Albert Faust Bernhardt, *The German Element in the United States with Special Reference to Its Political, Moral Social, and Educational Influence* (Boston: Houghton Mifflin Company, 1909), vol. 1, pp. 583-589.

84 *Ibid.*, vol. 2, p. 127.

for over twenty years, Lieber held the first American chair of History and Political Science at Columbia College in New York. Though less significant than he himself believed—he compared his work to that of Aristotle, Thomas More, Hobbes, Hugo Grotius, and Pufendorf[85]—his academic importance was considerable. As two historians of German cultural influences in the United States noted:

> His contributions to political theory marked the beginning of a new era in American ideas on the nature of the state. There had been anticipatory statements of the theory he advanced, but these had been fragmentary and unsystematic as compared with the organic system presented in his learned treatises. The publication between 1838 and 1853 of his three books on political ethics, on legal and political hermeneutics, and on civil liberty and self-government put him at the head of the new school of political thought, at the same time putting the then regnant theory of natural law to rout.[86]

From its inception by Francis Lieber and for many decades afterward, American political science followed the course set by German *Staatstheorie*, which is predicated on concepts such as the cult of the state, "the state whose origin is in history, whose nature is organic, whose essence is unity, whose function is the exercise of its sovereign will in law, and whose ultimate end is the moral perfection of mankind."[87] In Lieber's own words from one of his most significant works:

---

85 Quoted in Frank Freidel, *Francis Lieber: Nineteenth Century Liberal* (Baton Rouge: Louisiana State University Press, 1947), pp. 164-165; see also James Farr, "Francis Lieber and the Interpretation of American Political Science," *Journal of Politics* 52, no. 4 (1990), pp. 1027-1049.

86 Henry A. Pochmann and Arthur R. Schultz, *German Culture in America, 1600–1900: Philosophical and Literary Influences* (Madison: University of Wisconsin Press, 1957), p. 125.

87 Sylvia D. Fries, "Staatstheorie and the New American Science of Politics," *Journal of the History of Ideas* 34, no. 3 (1973), p. 391.

> The state is aboriginal with man; it is no voluntary association; no contrivance of art, or invention of suffering; no company of shareholders; no machine, no work of contract by individuals who lived previously out of it; no necessary evil, no ill of humanity which will be cured in time and by civilization; no accidental thing, no institution above and separate from society; no instrument for one or a few; no effect of coercion, or force of the powerful or weak; no mystery founded on something beyond comprehension, or on an extra-human base; the state is a form and faculty of mankind to lead the species towards greater perfection—it is the glory of man.[88]

As noted by Vernon Parrington, Lieber's doctrine is "a prophetic conception, from the doctrine of states' rights to the principle of an evolving state that draws all lesser sovereignties into its orbit by the law of attraction."[89] Lieber offered a "philosophical basis" for Supreme Court Justice Joseph Story's legal theories: "Under the combined legal and philosophical attack the compact theory found its philosophical breastworks leveled, its natural rights theory undermined, and its commanding position effectively turned."[90] Alan Grimes places Lieber at the center of the transition between "the constitutional and legal approach to an understanding of the nature of the American Union, and the rise of the organic concept of nation."[91]

The important role Lieber played in shaping the ideas that Lincoln would outstandingly exploit has also been noted by other historians. In effect, Lieber "had indeed argued before the war that the original Constitution was insufficient to the needs of the Nation." In the 1830s and 1840s Lieber's name had become well known in both the North and South "by attacking the idea of a fixed Constitution." A staunch defender of the growth of federal power,

88 Francis Lieber, *Manual of Political Ethics*, vol. 2, p. 162.

89 Vernon L. Parrington, *Main Currents in American Political Thought*, vol 2, p. 89.

90 *Id.*

91 Alan Pendleton Grimes, *American Political Thought* (New York: Holt, 1960), p. 283.

he held "that federal power should expand slowly and organically—and thus constitutionally—as the nation grew. ... [He believed] that the war would solidify the Union and thus fulfill his dream, nurtured during his school years in Germany, of living in a modern nation-state."[92]

Lieber became well-known during the Civil War, writing dozens of articles and pamphlets. The southern uprising was the beginning of the final removal of all limits to federal power. In a letter written in 1863, after having stated that "the South do [sic] not fight for independence ... for the very simple reason that the South never was dependent,"[93] Lieber sharply criticized those who, even in the North, continued to believe that the war was illegitimate, and had a shaky legal foundation. The matter should have been expressed in these terms: Did the South have a right to secede or not?

> Either the South had a perfect right to secede, or it had no such right. If the latter, we are of course right in fighting for our Government, for Law, and Country; and if the South had a right to secede, why then they constitute a sovereign nation, and we, being a sovereign nation too, have, according to all law [sic] of nations, the right of conquering another sovereign nation.[94]

Lieber became also the true organizer of the new nationalism:

> Is there anything nobler to behold in our own times than the struggle of the Italians for a united Italy, after centuries of longing. ... Is there anything more fervent than the yearning of the Germans for one undivided Germany, at any cost, disregarding all the long-sustained but diminutive sovereignties,

92 Michael Vorenberg, *Final Freedom*, p. 64.

93 Francis Lieber, *The Arguments of Secessionists: Letter to the Union Meeting, New York, September 30, 1863* (New York: Holman, 1863), p. 4.

94 *Ibid.*, p. 5.

> knowing that the sovereign source of political right, above all assumed sovereignties, is the conscious desire of a great people to be a nation?[95]

All the classic elements of nineteenth-century European nationalism are distilled into Lieber's work, including the organic unity of the population, the idea of the nation as hierarchically superior to the Constitution, and the identification of the national missions and its highest "moral and civil" achievements.

> Of all the theoretical writers on nationalistic doctrine none was more original or more influential than Francis Lieber. ... In his mind "nation" implied a homogeneous population living in a coherent territory, a population possessing a common language, literature, institutions, traditions. The nation was an organic unity. Lieber also preached the doctrine of the world mission of the national state in general and of the American nation in particular.[96]

Though one of its most important proponents, he was not alone in propagating this concept of the nation. St. Louis educator William T. Harris, one of the early Hegelians in America, and John W. Burgess, who, after completing his studies in Germany, inherited the chair held by Lieber at Columbia College, joined the cause of making the new nationalist dogma familiar to their fellow citizens. Without a doubt the Civil War was the turning point. "During and after the Civil War, Northern intellectuals developed the incipient organic theory, which at first did not reach the rank and file even in the North."[97]

---

95 Francis Lieber, *Two Lectures on the Constitution of the United States: Concluding a course on the Modern State, Delivered in The Law School Of Columbia College, (1860–1861) with an Address on Secession (1851)*, New York, Printed by Direction of the Board of Trustees, 1861, p. 13.

96 Merle Curti, *Growth of American Thought*, pp. 482-483.

97 Merle Curti, *The Roots of American Loyalty* (New York: Columbia University Press, 1946), p. 175. Curti adds that "in America the doctrine of organic nationalism lay back of many of the words and acts of public men: at times Lincoln himself came close to it; and Wade, Julian, Stevens, and Sumner thought and acted within its general outlines.

As this new nationalist dogma became widespread it led to the abandonment of the quasi-innocent "love of country" of early America—frequently simply a peculiar attachment to one's own state: Jefferson, for example, though he created the term "Americanism," never thought of himself as other than a Virginian. The transformation is of paramount importance:

> The nation was also thought of as a living organism, not a contractual relationship: a personality and an entity, composed of body, mind, and soul, not a mere voluntary association of political communities. ... In almost all the writings on the subject no idea enlisted more enthusiastic support than the concept of the nation as a living organism with moral will and purpose.[98]

This new way of understanding the nation radically changed the old American federal theory. The debates over state sovereignty, whether federal or divided—Madison's and Calhoun's legacy that had dominated the public and intellectual scene until the outbreak of the Civil War—had had their day. The Constitution was no longer at the center of every political discussion, in that sovereignty no longer found its source in the Constitutional pact, but rather from the "national spirit." In the historical process lasting well over a decade that brought about these changes, leading to the final demise of classic liberalism in America, the figure of Abraham Lincoln stood above all others.

> Since the turn of the century, Marshall, Webster, and Story had given classic expression to nationalist

In his widely heard lecture, 'Are We a Nation?' (1867), Charles Sumner moved from his antebellum emphasis on the limited powers of the national government to an essentially organic theory of nationalism. The doctrine also influenced a group of political theorists, academicians, lawyers, clergymen, and educators. Of these, the most outstanding were John C. Hurd, Sidney Fisher, Elisha Mulford, Francis Lieber, William T. Harris, Robert Ellis Thompson, and John W. Burgess. Not all the ideas making up the organic theory were avowed by each of these men, but their writings as a whole presented the doctrine fully." *Ibid.*, pp. 175-176.

98 *Ibid.*, p. 176.

doctrines. In the early weeks of 1861, Francis Lieber was advising law students at Columbia College that the Constitution's most important element "is its prominent and distinct nationality," and, at Harvard, law professor Washburn echoed the theme. Like theirs, Lincoln's nationalist idiom was quiet rather than flamboyant. It tied together the nation, Constitution, and liberty in a trinity that he argued was inseparable. Together they made free government possible and worthwhile.[99]

6.6) The Consequences of the Civil War

According to Karl Marx, the Civil War was a "world-transforming ... revolutionary movement."[100] Although that conclusion was not especially difficult to draw, it is clear that the war wrought unprecedented changes in the entire American political landscape. The first—and definitely desired—consequence of the war was the complete centralization of political power. Representative George W. Julian of Indiana, expressing his opposition to a bill that would have restored the self-government of the southern states, which were still subject to military occupation, warned that withdrawing the army would "fatally hedge up the way of justice and equality. ... What these regions need, above all things, is not an easy and quick return to their forfeited rights in the Union, but government, the strong arm of power, outstretched from the central authority here in Washington, making it safe for the freedmen of the South."[101] This appeal for the centralization of power had few precedents in American politics, but in those days it was common currency and became the most enduring legacy of the war.

99 Harold M. Hyman, *A More Perfect Union*, p. 57.

100 Karl Marx to Friedrich Engels (October 29–November 17, 1862), in *Karl Marx on America and the Civil War*, ed. Saul K. Padover (New York: McGraw-Hill, 1972), p. 263.

101 *Congressional Globe*, 39 Cong., 2nd Session (January 28th, 1867), p. 78, cited in James M. McPherson, *Abraham Lincoln and the Second American Revolution* (New York: Oxford University Press, 1992), p. 131.

In recent scholarship, the war has been interpreted as the epitome of federalism, not the rejection of it. According to Stephen Engle, "the fighting had demonstrated that there was indeed a North, and its existence amplified federalism's resiliency. In the face of Southern dissolution and antagonism to the Republican Party, Northern mobilization had reflected the popular desire to save the Union. Governors had established a partnership with Lincoln that demonstrated the powerful bond between the nation and the states. The war had proven that the republic the Founding Fathers engineered decades before had matured into a more perfect Union of states."[102] With all due respect, nothing could be further from the truth.

After the war the prevailing idea of the States was now their perpetual and not exactly voluntary place in Union, accompanied by the conviction that they were nothing more than mere provinces in a vast empire. The three Constitutional amendments adopted after the war established the States in this new position beyond any reasonable doubt. The Twelfth Amendment abolished slavery. The Thirteenth redefined American citizenship, which from then forward would be conferred by federal rather than state authority. The Fourteenth guaranteed the right to vote to every citizen, independently of any consideration of race, skin color, or previous condition of slavery. The first ten amendments, which constitute the Bill of Rights, were anchored (directly or indirectly) to the usual formula "Congress shall not." The Fourteenth Amendment contains the words "No State shall..." This was a change of the highest order. The Bill of Rights had always been considered the unassailable fortress that sheltered all Americans from the abuse of power by the federal government. After the Fourteenth Amendment, its significance became that of a shield protecting minorities from oppression by an internal majority within any state. This shift in emphasis in understanding the Bill of Rights underwent a very rapid acceleration in the second half of the twentieth century. In

---

102 Stephen D. Engle, *Gathering to Save a Nation: Lincoln and the Union's War Governors* (Civil War America series) (Chapel Hill, NC: University of North Carolina Press, 2016), p. 477.

all three of these amendments, the power to enforce their terms is explicitly assigned to the Congress of the United States.

As we have seen, the crisis between the North and South developed from 1828 onward, resulting in the attempt by the South to obtain its independence on the basis of two interrelated matters: the interpretation of the Constitution and the protectionist import duties. The northern victory was absolute on both fronts. The Constitution was altered by the post-war amendments, and its interpretation was delegated *in toto* to the Supreme Court, while the States as such were denied any role in the process. From that time on, the Constitution became one of the typical matters under federal jurisdiction.

Similarly, at the end of the war the dominance of the federal government over the economy became nearly absolute. The system of federally authorized national banks made obsolete the great fight against the establishment of a national Bank of the United States. If the fight by Thomas Jefferson's followers could be summed up as a battle for a limited government and a gold-based currency, by the end of the 1870s a nearly omnipotent federal government was issuing script currency.

> The Supreme Court, under Chase ... upheld the constitutionality of the legal tender act. Before the end of Reconstruction, Greenbackers were clamoring for more paper money. Few citizens before the war had contributed directly to the treasury. By the war's close everyone and everything was taxed.[103]

Lincoln's presidency (even though he had stated that "the principles of Jefferson are the definitions and axioms of free society")[104] decided the fate of the American experiment in self-government and limited government. As we have seen, one of the most important consequences of the meta-Constitutional theory of the Union as an end in itself—and of considering its dissolution

103 James A. Rawley, *The Politics of Union: Northern Politics during the Civil War* (Lincoln: University of Nebraska Press, 1980), p. 184.

104 Abraham Lincoln to H.L. Pierce et al., April 6, 1859, in *Collected Works*, vol. 2, p. 375.

a "moral catastrophe"—was in making American political thought more open to the adoption of European theories. To mention just one example, toward the end of the nineteenth century John W. Burgess defined sovereignty in terms of that "original, absolute, unlimited, universal power over the individual subject and over all associations of subjects" and described the state as "the source of all titles to land and of all powers over it."[105]

America proceeded toward a gradual convergence with Europe; that process reached its apex in the twentieth century. Lincoln must be considered the man who "normalized" America, thus opening the door to the Americanization of the world. In fact, the President took America into the realm of political modernity and, at least from a purely intellectual point of view, he succeeded because by then the rules of the game had completely changed from the original ones. The natural law tradition that had dominated the early days of the Republic gave way to an intellectual construction based on the dogma of sovereignty (albeit in a vastly more elastic sense than that elaborated by European jurists). The battle was between defenders of the sovereignty of the individual States and champions of federal sovereignty. The term "sovereignty," which was never mentioned in Jefferson's Kentucky Resolutions, made a first modest appearance in the Hartford Convention of 1814 and ended up taking center stage in the controversy caused by South Carolina's nullification ordinance of 1832. In a similar context, the constitutional theory espoused by Madison in the *Federalist*—that is, a divided sovereignty between the States and the federation—was no longer applicable.

The decline of the natural law tradition over the course of the nineteenth century was not an exclusively American phenomenon, but, in the context of the United States, this process brought about truly peculiar and complex problems, if for no other reason than that America at its founding was based on natural law. Its disappearance threw open the doors to a concept of the government that was only limited on paper.

---

105 John W. Burgess, *Political Science and Comparative Constitutional Law,* vol. 1 (Boston: Ginn, 1891), pp. 47, 52.

Regarding the specific federalist Constitutional form taken by early American liberalism, as interpreted by Jefferson and his followers, it was precisely its success that caused its decline: Once untethered to natural law, American federalism was increasingly transformed into a means of ideological conflict between the two halves of the country, which over time had become two distinct nations.

Above all the war meant that the southern states were permanently excluded from the American mainstream. The entire interpretation of the South as "other" with respect to the rest of the country stems from its defeat in the war: "For as long as the lower reaches of the North American continent have been commonly referred to as 'the South'—this obstreperous section of the United States has been a puzzle, a preoccupation, and problem to the nation and to itself."[106] Ninety years ago, Ulrich Phillips held that, all told, the South presented a certain uniformity. It was "a land with a unity despite its diversity, with a people having common joys and common sorrows, and, above all, as to the white folk a people with a common resolve indomitably maintained—that it shall be and remain a white man's country."[107]

While one of the principal characteristics of southern society was doubtless in having had slavery, which created a "black and white" society with particular relationships between the two groups, it is equally true that at one time the South was America. It was only after the Civil War that the Plymouth Plantation and New England became more important than Virginia and Jamestown, Puritanism was declared the founding religion, and the American past was reconstructed based on New England as the norm, with respect to which the southern states were but an aberration. One example will suffice, which has all the symbolic force needed to illustrate the point. Before the war, America had only two national holidays, both of which were connected to its independence: July

106 John Egerton, "The End of the South as an American Problem," in *The South as an American Problem*, eds. Larry J. Griffin and Don H. Doyle (Athens: University of Georgia Press, 1995), p. 259.

107 Ulrich B. Phillips, "The Central Theme of Southern History," *American Historical Review* 34 (1928), p. 31.

4, obviously, and February 22, George Washington's birthday. Thanksgiving, a Puritan holiday that today has become the chief celebration of the American "civil religion," was not nationally observed. In 1846 Sarah Josepha Hale began a campaign to make Thanksgiving the national American holiday, and in following years "wrote impassioned editorials in the nationally read magazines; she wrote thousands of letters to all the state governors, to members of Congress, to presidents, urging them not merely to revive an old custom but to create a focus of loyalty to the nation by reminding the American people of a common, heroic past." But the southern states saw it as a Yankee holiday, "hence the crusade met with only partial success." It was only in "the midst of the Civil War [that] Mrs. Hale succeeded in persuading President Lincoln to proclaim the first national Thanksgiving."[108]

In short, the South has been expunged from the country's memory. Some of its major figures have been "domesticated" and incorporated into the American iconography, while others have simply been forgotten.[109] After the war the South appeared as an 'absolute elsewhere,' which then became an 'American problem' over the course of the twentieth century. On the road to modernity New England set itself apart as a perfect society, the very model or the 'should be' for even the remotest corner of the rest of the country, while the South's task has been to play the contrarian, sometimes absolutely irreconcilable, role of 'not me.'

---

108 Merle Curti, *Roots of American Loyalty*, pp. 135-136.

109 Jefferson could not be obscured; to the contrary, he became such an iconic figure (as corrected by Yankees, of course) that much of the literature presents him as someone who idolized the Union and the Constitution. The same was not true of Calhoun: He could simply be ignored. To cite just two examples: In his classic *The Jacksonian Persuasion: Politics and Belief* (New York: Vintage, 1957), Marvin Meyers felt no need either to mention John Calhoun, the real giant of political thought of the Jacksonian period, or list him in the bibliography. But it seems even more indicative that a well-received anthology of the 1950s, *Social Theories of Jacksonian Democracy: Representative Writings of the Period 1825–1850*, ed. Joseph L. Blau (New York: Bobbs-Merrill, 1954), which presented the greatness of twenty-six thinkers (politicians, economists, and 'sociologists') of that time, lacks any mention of the great Carolinian.

And things have not completely changed today. While at one time the identification between New England and America in the minds of those south of the Mason-Dixon line left at least some gap between the two, now the attack on the southern past is integrated with a continuous process of 'cultural re-education' to which southern citizens are subjected from infancy. The symbols, ideas, and heritage of the South are constantly attacked. Raimondo Luraghi, a scholar who dedicated his entire life to the study of the American South, stated: "We must conclude that a massive operation is underway, orchestrated in the North and headed up chiefly by Black Muslims, ideologues of political correctness and other extremists that is designed to rob the South of its own history."[110]

In conclusion, we must turn our gaze once again to the American professors of *Staatstheorie*. While it is true that their dominance vanished after the First World War, and the cause of their failure lay in the fact that they were "unable to apply the German idea of the state to the American political tradition,"[111] that judgment is only valid from the point of view of intellectual history. Lincoln was not interested in such a complex enterprise. He did not have go so far as to make the two traditions compatible. Rather, for him it was sufficient to burn all bridges that led back to the old American concept of a dichotomy between freedom and government. It should be noted that Lincoln did not need to win an academic debate. To make his view of freedom and the state prevail, he could fall back on far more convincing weapons than those available to the professors. His armies forced every American citizen, whether in the North or South, to assimilate the idea that there is a commonality of interests between the individual and the state (identified now as the nation or Union).

110 Raimondo Luraghi, *La spada e le magnolie. Il Sud nella storia degli Stati Uniti* (Rome: Donzelli, 2007), pp. 191-192; cf. also *Cinque lezioni sulla guerra civile americana*, 1861–1865 (Naples: La città del sole, 1997). It must be noted that Luraghi was himself a communist, one of those very serious historians of Marxist persuasion of the past century, just like Eugene Genovese.

111 Sylvia D. Fries, "*Staatstheorie* and the New American Science of Politics," p. 403.

Lincoln destroyed the roots of an old classical liberal notion of a hostility between individual freedom and the power of the state. While eradicating that idea, dear to the revolutionary generation, he rendered devoid of all meaning a Constitution founded exactly on a dichotomy between freedom and government. In so doing, he brought about the providential, collateral, unplanned effect of eliminating slavery.

Conclusion

In America there is still a tradition, impervious to all criticism, that considers the whole vocabulary of the state as foreign, essentially ambiguous, and at the very least inappropriate to describe the reality of governmental institutions. One could argue that there is a strain of thought in the British roots of modernity that does not sit well with the state. When Jean Bodin's legacy was the talk of the day all over Europe, Edward Coke and other common law jurists were very suspicious of the concept of sovereignty in itself. Similarly, John Dewey, by far the most influential American philosopher and the public intellectual par excellence of the last century, held that the concept of the state should be rejected because "the moment we utter the words 'The State' a score of intellectual ghosts rise to obscure our vision."[1]

The American past and present should rather be analyzed within the paradigms produced by school of "pluralism," the major exponents of which were first Arthur Bentley and later Robert Dahl. For Bentley, governing is a "process" that wends its way through competing groups, all of which act on the basis of well-identified interests. "The very nature of the group process (which our government shows in a fairly well-developed form) is this, that groups are freely combining, dissolving, and recombining in accord with their interest lines."[2] Such a theory reached a near-definitive formulation with Dahl. According to this well-known political theorist,

> Instead of a single center of sovereign power there must be multiple centers of power, none of which is or can be wholly sovereign. ... The theory and practise of American pluralism tends to assume ... that the existence of multiple centers of power,

1 John Dewey, *The Public and Its Problems* (London: Allen & Unwin, 1927), pp. 8-9.

2 Arthur F. Bentley, *The Process of Government: A Study of Social Pressures* (Chicago: University of Chicago Press, 1908) p. 359.

> none of which is wholly sovereign, will help ... to tame power, to secure the consent of all, and to settle conflicts peacefully. Because one center of power is set against another, power itself will be tamed, civilized, controlled, and limited to decent human purposes, while coercion, the most evil form of power, will be reduced to a minimum. ... Because constant negotiations among different centers of power are necessary in order to make decisions, citizens and leaders will perfect the precious art of dealing peacefully with their conflicts, and not merely to the benefit of one partisan but to the mutual benefit of all the parties to a conflict.[3]

Dahl makes it crystal clear that pluralism is not simply a way to interpret social reality, it is rather a normative political statement. The more we view society as producing a plethora of power centers, the less we need to succumb to the doctrine of sovereignty. Politics is (or should be) a relational game between pressure groups in a perennial fight among themselves, with veto power far more widespread than the power to impose solutions. There is no place in this analysis for the idea of an over-arching center determining the outcomes at the end of the struggle. It could look like a quasi Calhounian multiverse, or an extended Madisonian republic, were it not for the fact that today these groups occupy a social space that has no territorial basis.

While the American empiricist tradition reconstructed the world through a series of analytically observable and separable facts, its political counterpart held that everything could be traced back to the logic of groups: Political institutions were at the service of a much broader social reality dominated by aggregations of individuals. In this view the role of the state is greatly reduced, and power is diffused among myriad social relations. David Easton also flatly denied the role of a center or state as a fundamental synthesis of political power from which society takes its directions. Rather,

3 Robert A. Dahl, *Pluralist Democracy in the United States: Conflict and Consent* (Chicago: Rand McNally, 1967), p. 24.

directions issue from within society itself thorough an independent network of evaluation and decision-making.[4]

This "pluralist" view has robust antecedents within European thought, which in the first part of the twentieth century opposed the "monistic" ideas of the state. Léon Duguit, Harold J. Laski, and Hugo Krabbe, to name just the best-known scholars, began a broad intellectual movement that opposed the nineteenth-century German concepts of the state, beginning with the fictitious nature of the personality of the state. Society, and not the legal system, became the locus of the analysis of rights, duties and laws.[5] In America, Roscoe Pound's school of thought held similar ideas: The law, which arises from the interaction between interest groups present in society, is a product of society itself, and it is observed as long as the public favors it.[6]

These few examples are offered only to illustrate that there are many traditions of thought critical of the ordinary European conception of the state, as they do not fully accept the dogma of sovereignty, and ultimately tend to place society 'above' the state.

Obviously, the themes of pluralism and 'realism' have been parsed and interpreted in highly original ways within the European tradition—consider not just the elitists (Gaetano Mosca, Vilfredo Pareto and Robert Michels) but Maurice Hauriou's and Santi Romano's institutionalism, or Antonio De Viti De Marco's Italian school of finance—and yet in America the doctrine of pluralism has achieved a unique status. It is not a theory in conflict with others in the marketplace of ideas and representations. Rather, it has become a semi-official explanation of how American society operates.

4 Cf. David Easton, *The Political System: An Inquiry into the State of Political Science* (New York: Knopf, 1953).

5 See Léon Duguit, *Souveraineté et liberté: Leçons faites à l'Université Columbia (New York) 1920–1921* (Paris: Alcan, 1922); Harold J. Laski, *The Foundations of Sovereignty and Other Essays* (New York: Harcourt, Brace and Company, 1921); Hugo Krabbe, *The Modern Idea of the State* (1919), trans. George H. Sabine and Walter J. Shepard (New York: Appleton, 1922).

6 Cf. Roscoe Pound, *An Introduction to the Philosophy of Law* (New Haven, CT: Yale University Press, 1922).

In any case, for the theory of American political pluralism, the European doctrine of the state is quite objectionable. Generally speaking, in the twentieth-century view of American pluralism, interest groups tend to become the engine of politics, relegating the state to the role of an "honest mediator" between the various and conflicting demands of the different organized groups. The state, then, has no more authority than the sum of the fragmented groups within its territory. Thus the idea of a state that is completely independent of the political system, in the European sense, cannot exist because the state is essentially the political system itself. Sovereignty is ideally located in the people, but, given that the populace is divided into a plethora of minorities and special interest groups, it can never be transferred directly to any given center of power. This makes the assumption of state sovereignty factually impossible in a healthy democracy. And democracy in turn is the art of creating an artificial majority that acts in the name of the whole community, funneling all political representation in the country to the government.

Marxists like Wright Mills and his disciples labeled this notion of a majority that acts in the name of the community a "romantic pluralism,"[7] a typical middle-class delusion. Mills argued to the contrary that the economy, politics, and the military are firmly controlled by an American elite. In the post-war debate between pluralists and elitists, the European concept of the state is quite clearly absent. The analyses of freedom, democracy, polyarchy, and power all take place within the imagined space of American society and its empirically identifiable groups, and no one feels a real need to postulate the existence of a sovereign state that guides society (or a republic of republics).

The persistence of these sorts of analyses in the American political culture provides a clear indication that, at least intellectually, the implantation of the modern state must be considered a

7 See C. Wright Mills, *The Power Elite* (New York: Oxford University Press, 1956) and Leonard Silk and Mark Silk, *The American Establishment* (New York: Basic Books, 1980).

Pyrrhic victory. Though Lincoln wrought a profound change in the conceptual categories on and of American politics during the Civil War, the transplant did not fully succeed.

In the age of totalitarianism the resistance to the European idea of the state was no longer centered on the federalist theory of the first century of the Republic, but rather the theory of a "polyarchical" power distributed among the various groups that make up American society. The States, reduced to decentralized political and administrative units, no longer interacted with the federal government. Instead, various corporatist organizations channeled the interests of American society to the government. At least in scholarly interpretations (or imagination), twentieth-century politics did not leave Washington as a sole and uncontested actor. Rather, the federal government, though freed from any localized counterweight, had to deal with corporations, unions, and pressure groups of all sorts.

Later in the century, at least from the 1960s onward, federalism has had a marked resurgence in James Buchanan and the public choice school of thought. Integrating the state structure into economic analysis, public choice theory shows how references to the general interest actually conceal the interests of the people who comprise the public agencies. If the rulers provide public goods in exchange for votes, voters will behave as rational consumers. It is thus necessary to seek new constitutional limitations on the freedom of action by politicians. It is in this sense that the federal option is being rediscovered as the most convincing. Public choice economists have developed a "competitive federalism" model that sources from theoretical research on how to contain the government and placate its unquenchable thirst for the wealth and lives of its citizens.

In any case, though there are very interesting exceptions, the theory of pluralism represents the mainstream of the twentieth century. Comparing nineteenth-century federalism with twentieth-century pluralism, the conclusion can be drawn that, in terms of the size of the government, the balance is quite different. The American republican government contracted between the Revolution and the Civil War when federalism was at the heart of all political and constitutional debate. Over the course of the twentieth century, the political doctrine of pluralism was the backdrop to the largest growth of government activity in history. This of course does not mean that pluralism was the cause of that growth; pluralism is simply a model of reality—a figment of the scholarly imagination—while federalism was both a way of thinking and an "institutional fact."

Most Americans would be amazed to find out that Lincoln inherited a federal government that was in fact weaker in many ways than the one inaugurated by George Washington seventy years earlier.[8] As two economic historians point out,

> By calling for a balanced budget amendment, Jefferson anticipated by 200 years the fiscal views of Ronald Reagan and his followers. But unlike them, he and his followers, even without constitutional backing, were able to keep the federal government small and to reduce the public debt. The next 60 years would be a period of low government expenditures and debt reduction.[9]

The parallel with President Reagan (1981-1988) is not coincidental. Having achieved the presidency on a classical liberal platform, with the slogan "farewell welfare" and backed by a huge nationwide consensus, Reagan nevertheless left the federal government far larger and far more indebted than he had found it. This was not caused by ill will or incompetence, but because, once a government has reached a certain critical mass, it does not seem possible to restrict centralization and reduce the weight of bureaucracy. The secret of Jefferson's success and Reagan's failure

8 A work that conclusively demonstrates the substantial stagnation of the federal government during its first eighty years of history is Peter Zavodnyik, *The Age of Strict Construction: A History of the Growth of Federal Power, 1789–1861* (Washington, DC: Catholic University Press, 2007).

9 Donald R. Stabile and Jeffrey A. Cantor, *The Public Debt of the United States: An Historical Perspective, 1775–1990* (Westport, CT: Praeger, 1991), p. 29.

lies in the fact that the former was the president of a genuine federation, the second was not. The latter, despite the dominance of pluralist thought, reigned over an imperial and modern state.

The public debt is clearly a litmus test for the size of the federal government. The growth of the debt has not been constant: "Before the Civil War, the debt remained small and constant, rising during wars and declining after them. The debt remained small because the government's scale of operations and its budget remained small."[10]

Certainly, the antebellum South was paying a disproportionate share for the maintenance of the federation, but overall government expenditure was low in both relative and absolute terms with respect to the wealth produced. Gripped in a web of suspicion and jealousy produced by the States, entangled in the contractual doctrine of the Union, and unable directly to tax citizens' income (which was only guaranteed by a constitutional amendment in 1913, frequently considered the last nail in the coffin of American federalism), the federal government did not grow. The job that Grover Norquist, president of Americans for Tax Reform, the downsizing of the federal government, would be fulfilled much more effectively by the States if we were living in a genuine federation.

Whatever else might be said regarding the states' rights tradition, one thing is certain: Over the course of the modern era it has shown itself to be the most potent intellectual restraint on the growth of Leviathan. This is due to a simple reason that the entire tradition we have analyzed knew perfectly well. The Constitution is not enough: The modern state, because it is self-regulating and judge of the extent of its own power, inevitably creates an absolute monopoly. In contrast, in an authentic federal system the government is subject to controls by other governmental powers. The institutional history of America, at least in the time frame we discussed, can be clearly seen as a large laboratory in which Calhoun's refrain is clearly corroborated: *Power can only be resisted by power*.

10 *Ibid.*, p. 208.

Primary Sources

ADAMS, Henry, ed., *Documents Relating to New England Federalism, 1800–1815* (Boston: Little, Brown, 1877).

ADAMS, John, *The Works of John Adams,* ed. Charles F. Adams, 10 vols. (Boston: Little, Brown, 1860–1865).

AMES, Herman V. ed., *State Documents on Federal Relations,* (Philadelphia: University of Pennsylvania Press, 1900).

ARISTOTELE, *Politica,* Italian translation, ed. Renato Laurenti (Bari: Laterza, 1972).

ARISTOTLE, *Politics,* Benjamin Jowett trans., Introduction by Max Lerner (New York: Random House, 1943).

BLAU, Joseph L., ed., *Social Theories of Jacksonian Democracy: Representative Writings of the Period 1825–1850* (New York: Bobbs-Merrill, 1954).

BODIN, Jean, *The Six Books of a Commonwealth* (1576), ed. K. D. MacRae (Cambridge, MA: Harvard University Press, 1962).

BRADFORD, Alden, ed., *Speeches of the governors of Massachusetts, from 1765 to 1775 ...* (Boston: Russell & Gardner, 1818).

BURKE, Edmund, *On the American Revolution: Selected Speeches and Letters*, ed. Elliott R. Barkan (New York: Harper, 1966).

BURKE, Edmund, *Selected Writings and Speeches*, ed. Peek J. Stanlis (Washington, DC: Regnery, 1997).

BURKE, Edmund, *The Portable Burke*, ed. Isaac Kramnik, (London: Penguin, 1999).

CALHOUN, John C., *The Works of John C. Calhoun*, ed. Richard K. Crallé, 6 vols. (New York: Appleton, 1851-1855).

CALHOUN, John C., *Speeches of John C. Calhoun. Delivered in the Congress of the United States from 1811 to the present time* (New York: Harper & Brothers, 1843).

CALHOUN, John C., *The Papers of John C. Calhoun*, eds. Clyde N. Wilson et al., 27 vols. (Columbia: South Carolina University Press, 1959-2003).

COOPER, Thomas, *Consolidation: An Account of Parties in the United States, from the Convention of 1787 to the Present Period* (Columbia, SC: Black & Sweeny, 1824).

ELLIOT, Jonathan, ed., *The Debates in the Several State Conventions on the Adoption of the Federal Constitution*, 5 vols. (Philadelphia: J. B. Lippincott, 1836).

ELLIOT, Jonathan, ed., *The Virginia and Kentucky Resolutions of 1798 and '99* ... (Washington, DC: Jonathan Elliot, 1832).

FARRAND, Max, ed., *The Records of the Federal Convention of 1787*, 3 vols. (New Haven, CT: Yale University Press, 1911).

FREEHLING, William, ed., *The Nullification Era: A Documentary Record* (New York: Harper Torchbooks, 1967).

FROHNEN, Bruce, ed., *The Anti-Federalists: Selected Writings and Speeches* (Washington, DC: Regnery, 1999).

GARDINER, John S. J., *A Discourse, Delivered at Trinity Church, Boston, July 23, 1812* (Boston: Munroe & Francis, 1812).

HAMILTON, Alexander, Madison James, Jay John, *The Federalist: With the Letters of "Brutus*, Terence Ball ed. (New York: Cambridge University Press, 2003).

HAMILTON, Alexander, The *Papers of Alexander Hamilton*, eds. H.C. Syrett, *et al.*, 27 vols. (New York: Columbia University Press 1961-1987).

HARPER, William, *The Remedy by State Interposition, or Nullification: Explained and Advocated by Chancellor Harper, in His Speech at Columbia, (S. C.) on the 20th September, 1830* (Charleston, SC: Van Brust, 1832).

HAY, George, *An Essay on the Liberty of the Press* (1799) (Richmond, VA: Samuel Pleasant, 1803).

HEGEL, G. W. F., *Lectures on the Philosophy of World History*, vol. 1, 1822-1823, ed. and trans. Robert F. Brown and Peter C. Hodgson, with the assistance of G. Geuss (Oxford: Oxford University Press, 2011).

HEGEL, G. W. F., *Vorlesungen über die Philosophie der Weltgeschichte* (Berlin, 1822/23), eds. K. H. Ilting, K. Brehmer and H. N. Seelman (Hamburg: Felix Meiner, 1996).

HYNEMAN, Charles S. and Lutz Donald S., eds., *American Political Writing during the Founding Era, 1760–1805* (Indianapolis: Liberty Press, 1983).

JACKSON, Andrew, *Proclamation of Andrew Jackson, President of The United States, to the People of South Carolina*, December 10, 1832 (Harrisburg, PA: Singerly & Myers, 1864).

JEFFERSON, Thomas, *A Summary View of the Rights of British America,* with an Introduction by Thomas P. Abernethy (New York: Park Av., 1943).

JEFFERSON, Thomas, *Notes on the State of Virginia* (1787), ed. William Peden (Chapel Hill: University of North Carolina Press, 1955).

JEFFERSON, Thomas, *Writings*, ed. Merrill D. Peterson (New York: Literary Classics of the U.S., 1984).

JEFFERSON, Thomas, John and Abigail Adams, *The Adams-Jefferson Letters, The Complete Correspondence Between Thomas Jefferson and Abigail and John Adams*, (1959), ed. Lester J. Cappon (Chapel Hill: The University of North Carolina Press, 1988).

JEFFERSON, Thomas, *The Papers of Thomas Jefferson*, eds. Julian P. Boyd et al., 43 vols. (Princeton: Princeton University Press, 1950-).

JEFFERSON, Thomas, *The Works of Thomas Jefferson*, ed. Paul Lester Ford, 9 vols. (New York: Putnam, 1905).

JEFFERSON, Thomas, *The Writings of Thomas Jefferson,* eds. Andrew A. Lipscomb and Albert E. Bergh (Washington, DC: Thomas Jefferson Memorial Association, 1904-1907)

JENSEN, Merrill, John P. Kaminski, Gaspare J. Saladino, eds., *Documentary History of the Ratification of the Constitution*, (Madison: State Historical Society of Wisconsin, 29 vols. (1976–2017).

KANT, Immanuel, *Political Writings*, trans. H. B. Nisbet, ed. Hans Reiss (Cambridge, UK: Cambridge University Press, 1970).

KETCHAM, Ralph, ed., *The Antifederalist Papers and the Constitutional Debates*, (New York: Mentor, 1986).

LIEBER, Francis, *The Arguments of Secessionists* (New York: Holman, 1863).

LIEBER, Francis, *Manual of Political Ethics* (1838-39), ed. Woolsey Theodore D. (Philadelphia: Lippincott, 1876).

LIEBER, Francis, *Two Lectures on the Constitution of the United States* (New York: Printed by Direction of the Board of Trustees, 1861).

LINCOLN, Abraham, Stephen Douglas,*The Lincoln-Douglas Debates: The First Complete Unexpurgated Text* ed. Harold Holzer (New York: Harper, 1994).

LINCOLN, Abraham, *The Collected Works of Abraham Lincoln*, ed. Roy P. Basler, 7 vols. (New Brunswick, NJ: Rutgers University Press, 1953).

LIVINGSTON, William, *Examen du gouvernement d'Angleterre, comparé aux Constitutions des États-Unis* (Paris: Froullé, 1789).

LODGE, Henry Cabot, *Life and Letters of George Cabot* (Boston: Little, Brown, 1878).

LYMAN, Theodore, *A Short Account of the Hartford Convention* (Boston: Everett, 1823).

MADISON, James, *The Papers of James Madison*, eds. William Hutchinson et al., 17 vols. (Chicago: University of Chicago Press, 1962-1991).

MADISON, James, *Notes of Debates in the Federal Convention of 1787* (1840), ed. Adrienne Koch (Athens: Ohio University Press, 1966).

MARX, Karl and Friedrich Engels, *German Ideology*, in *Collected Works*, vol. 5 (London: Lawrence and Wishart, 1976).

MASON, Virginia, *The Public Life and Diplomatic Correspondence of James Murray Mason* (Roanoke: Stone, 1903).

MILL, John Stuart, "The Contest in America," (Boston: Little, Brown and Company, 1862).

MILL, John Stuart, *Utilitarianism, Liberty and Representative Government* (New York: Dutton, 1950).

MORRIS, Anne Cary, ed., *The Diary and Letters of Gouverneur Morris*, 2 vols. (New York: Scribners, 1888).

MORTON, Borden, ed., *The Antifederalist Papers* (East Lansing: Michigan State University Press, 1965).

MYGATT, Alston, *Secret Proceedings and Debates of the Federal Convention* (1821) (Louisville: Alston Mygatt, 1844).

PAINE, Thomas, *The Complete Writings of Thomas Paine,* ed. Philip S. Foner (New York: Citadel Press, 1945).

Proceedings of the Hartford Convention (Boston: Published by order of the Senate, 1815.

QUINCY Josiah, *Speeches Delivered in the Congress of the United States 1805–1813*, ed. Edmund Quincy (Boston: Little, Brown, 1874).

RAMSAY, Allan, *Thoughts on the Origin and Nature of Government* (London: T. Becket & P.A. de Hondt, 1769).

RANDOLPH, J. W., ed., *The Virginia Report of 1799–1800* (Richmond: J. W. Randolph, 1850).

SEYDEL, Max von, *Commentar zur Verfassungs-Urkunde für das Deusche Reich* (Freiburg-Leipzig: Mohr, 1897).

SEYDEL, Max von, *Staatsrechtliche und politische Abhandlungen* (Freiburg-Leipzig: Mohr, 1893).

SHEENAN, C. A., McDowell G. L., eds., *Friends of the Constitution: Writings of the "Other" Federalists, 1787–1788* (Indianapolis: Liberty Fund, 1998).

State Papers on Nullification (Boston: Dutton and Wentworth, 1834).

STORING, Herbert J., ed., with the assistance of Murray Dry, *The Complete Anti-Federalist*, 7 vols. (Chicago: Chicago University Press, 1981).

STORY, Joseph, *Commentaries on the Constitution of the United States*, 3 vols. (Boston: Hillard, Gray and Company, 1833).

TAYLOR, John, *New Views on the Constitution of the United States* (Washington City: Way and Gideon, 1823).

TOCQUEVILLE, Alexis de, *Democracy in America: Historical-critical Edition of De la démocratie en Amérique*, Vol. 2, ed. Eduardo Nolla, 4 vols. (Indianapolis: Liberty Fund, 2010).

WEBSTER, Daniel and Robert Hayne, *The Webster-Hayne Debate on the Nature of the Union*, ed. Belz Herman (Indianapolis: Liberty Fund, 2000).

WORTMAN, Tunis D., *A Treatise Concerning Political Enquiry, and the Liberty of the Press* (New York: George Forman, 1800).

SECONDARY SOURCES

ADAIR, Douglass, *Fame and the Founding Father: Essays by Douglass Adair*, ed. Trevor Colbourn (Indianapolis: Liberty Press, 1998)

ADAMS, Charles, *When in the Course of Human Events: Arguing the Case for Southern Secession* (New York: Rowman & Littlefield, 2000).

ADAMS, Henry, *John Randolph, A Biography*, Introduction by Robert McColley (Armonk, NY: ME Sharpe, 1996).

ALDRICH, John H. and GRANT Ruth W., "The Antifederalists, the First Congress, and the First Parties," *Journal of Politics* 55, no. 2 (1993), pp. 295-326.

ALLIS, JR. Frederick S., *Government Through Opposition, Party Politics in the 1790s* (New York: Macmillan, 1963).

AMES, Herman, ed., *State Documents on Federal Relations* (Philadelphia: Univ. of Pennsylvania, 1906).

ANDERSON, Frank M., "Contemporary Opinion of the Virginia and Kentucky Resolutions. Part II," *American Historical Review* 5, no. 2 (December 1899), pp. 225-252.

ANDREWS, Charles M., *Colonial Background of the American Revolution: Four Essays in American Colonial History* (1924) (New Haven: Yale University Press, 1958).

ARANSON, Peter, "Calhoun's Constitutional Economics," *Constitutional Political Economy* 2, no. 1 (1991), pp. 31-52.

ARENDT, Hannah, *On Revolution* (New York: Viking Press, 1965).

ASSMANN, Jan, *The Mind of Egypt: History and Meaning in the Time of the Pharaohs* (1996), trans. Andrew Jenkins (Cambridge, MA-London: Harvard University Press, 2003).

BAECHLER, Jean, *Le capitalisme, tome I. Les origins* (Paris: Gallimard, 1995).

BAECHLER, Jean, *The Origins of Capitalism* (1971) (Oxford: Basil Blackwell, 1975).

BANNER, JR. James M., *To the Hartford Convention: The Federalists and the Origins of Party Politics in Massachusetts, 1789–1815* (New York: Knopf, 1970).

BANNING, Lance, "Republican Ideology and the Triumph of the Constitution, 1789 to 1793," *William & Mary Quarterly*, 3rd series, 31, no. 2 (1974), pp. 167-188.

BANNING, Lance, *The Sacred Fire of Liberty: James Madison and the Founding of the Federal Republic* (Ithaca: Cornell University Press, 1995).

BARBER Sotirios A., *The Fallacies of States' Rights* (Cambridge, MA: Harvard University Press, 2013).

BARROW, Clyde W., "The Miliband-Poulantzas Debate: An Intellectual History," in *Paradigm Lost. State Theory Reconsidered*, eds. Stanley Aronowitz and Peter Bratsis (Minneapolis: University of Minnesota Press, 2002), pp. 3-52.

BARROW, Clyde W., *Critical Theories of the State: Marxist, Neo-Marxist, Post-Marxist* (Madison: University of Wisconsin Press, 1993).

BARTELSON, Jens, *The Critique of the State* (Cambridge, UK: Cambridge University Press, 2001).

BARTLETT, Irving H., *Daniel Webster* (New York: Norton, 1978).

BARZEL, Yoram, *A Theory of the State* (New York: Cambridge University Press, 2002).

BASSANI, Luigi Marco, *Liberty, State & Union: The Political Theory of Thomas Jefferson* (Macon, GA: Mercer University Press, 2010).

BAYLIN, Bernard, *The Ordeal of Thomas Hutchinson* (Cambridge, MA: Harvard University Press, 1974).

BEARD, Charles A. and BEARD Mary R., *The Rise of American Civilization*, 2 vols. (New York: Macmillan, 1930).

BEARD, Charles A., *An Economic Interpretation of the Constitution of the United States* (New York: Macmillan, 1913).

BEARD, Charles A., *Economic Origins of Jeffersonian Democracy* (New York: Macmillan, 1915).

BEAUD, Olivier, *La puissance de l'Etat* (Paris: PUF, 1994).

BEEMAN, Richard, *Plain, Honest Men: The Making of the American Constitution* (New York: Random House, 2009).

BEER, Samuel H., *To Make a Nation: The Rediscovery of American Freedom* (Cambridge, MA: Harvard University Press, 1993).

BEIRNE, Francis F., *The War of 1812* (New York: Dutton, 1949).

BELZ, Herman, *Abraham Lincoln, Constitutionalism, and Equal Rights in the Civil War Era* (New York: Fordham University Press, 1998).

BENNER, David, *Compact of the Republic. The League of States and the Constitution* (Minneapolis: Life and Liberty, 2015).

BENNETT, JR. Lerone, *Forced into Glory: Abraham Lincoln's White Dream* (Chicago: Johnson, 2000).

BENTLEY, Arthur F., *The Process of Government: A Study of Social Pressures* (Chicago: University of Chicago Press, 1908).

BERNSTEIN, R.B., "Thomas Jefferson and Constitutionalism," in *A Companion to Thomas Jefferson*, ed. Francis D. Cogliano (Malden, MA: Wiley-Blackwell, 2012), pp. 419-438.

BERNSTEIN, Richard B., *Thomas Jefferson* (New York: Oxford University Press, 2003).

BICKHAM, Troy, *The Weight of Vengeance: The United States, the British Empire, and the War of 1812* (New York: Oxford University Press, 2012).

BILDER, Mary S., *Madison's Hand: Revising the Constitutional Convention* (Cambridge, MA: Harvard University Press, 2015).

Bird, Wendell, "New Light on the Sedition Act of 1798: The Missing Half of the Prosecutions," *Law and History Review*, Vol. 34, No. 3 (August 2016), pp. 541-614.

Bird, Wendell, *Criminal Dissent: Prosecutions Under the Alien and Sedition Acts of 1798* (Cambridge, MA: Harvard University Press, 2020).

Blumenberg, Hans, *The Legitimacy of the Modern Age*, trans. Robert M. Wallace (Cambridge, MA: MIT Press, 1983).

Bobbio, Norberto, *Stato, governo, società. Per una teoria generale della politica* (1978) (Turin: Einaudi, 1985).

Böckenförde, Ernst-Wolfgang, *Diritto e secolarizzazione. Dallo Stato moderno all'Europa unita*, ed. Geminello Preterossi (Rome, Laterza, 2007)

Bognetti, Giovanni, "Federalismo," *Digesto* (Turin: UTET, 1991), Vol. 6.

Bognetti, Giovanni, "Il *Federalist* e lo Stato federale liberale," in *Il Federalista: 200 anni dopo*, ed. Guglielmo Negri (Bologna: il Mulino, 1988), pp. 169-218.

Boorstin, Daniel J., *The Genius of American Politics* (Chicago: University of Chicago Press, 1953).

Borden, Morton, Introduction, *The Antifederalist Papers* (East Lansing: Michigan State University Press, 1965).

Borneman, Walter R., *1812: The War That Forged a Nation* (New York: Harper Collins, 2004).

Bourdin, Bernard, *The Theological-Political Origins of the Modern State: The Controversy Between James I of England and Cardinal Bellarmine* (2004) trans. Susan Pickford (Washington DC: Catholic University of America Press, 2010).

Bowen, Catherine D., *Miracle at Philadelphia* (Boston: Little, Brown, 1966).

Boyd, Steven R., *The Politics of Opposition: Antifederalists and the Acceptance of the Constitution* (Millwood, NY: KTO, 1979).

Brewster, Leonard, “The Impossibility of the State,” *Journal of Libertarian Studies* 16 (Summer 2002), pp. 19-34.

Broadwater, Jeff, *Jefferson, Madison, and the Making of the Constitution* (Chapel Hill, NC: University of North Carolina Press, 2019).

Brookhiser, Richard, *Alexander Hamilton, American* (New York: Free Press, 1999).

Brown, Elizabeth Gaspar, *British Statutes in American Law, 1776-1836* (Ann Arbor: University of Michigan Law School, 1964).

Brown, Kate E., “Rethinking “People v. Croswell”: Alexander Hamilton and the Nature and Scope of "Common Law" in the Early Republic,” *Law and History Review*, Vol. 32, No. 3 (August 2014), pp. 611-645.

Bruce, Robert B., ed., *Abraham Lincoln's Changing Views on Slavery* (St. James, NY: Brandywine Press, 2001).

Brunner, Otto, *Land and Lordship: Structures of Governance in Medieval Austria*, eds. Howard Kaminsky and James Van Horn Melton (Philadelphia: University of Pennsylvania Press, 1992).

Brunner, Otto, *Land und Herrschaft* (Vienna: Rudolf M. Rohrer Verlag, 1939).

Bull, Hedley, *The Anarchical Society: A Study of Order in World Politics* (London: Macmillan, 1977).

Burgess, John W., *Political Science and Comparative Constitutional Law,* 2 vols. (Boston: Ginn, 1891).

Cabot Lodge, Henry, *Daniel Webster: American Statesman* (Boston: Mifflin, 1883).

Carey, George W., *In Defense of the Constitution*, revised and expanded edition (Indianapolis: Liberty Fund, 1995).

CARNEIRO, Robert L., "A Theory of the Origin of the State: Traditional Theories of State Origins Are Considered and Rejected in Favor of a New Ecological Hypothesis" (1970), in *The State: Critical Concepts*, ed. John A. Hall (New York: Routledge, 1994), pp. 433-445.

CARPENTER, Jesse T., *The South as a Conscious Minority, 1789–1861: A Study in Political Thought* (New York: New York University Press, 1930).

CAVANAUGH, William T., "Killing for the Phone Company: Why the Nation-State Is Not the Keeper of the Common Good," *Modern Theology* 20 (April 2004), pp. 246-260.

CHANNING, William Ellery, *A Sermon Preached in Boston, July 23, 1812,* in *Memoir of William Ellery Channing: With Extracts from His Correspondence and Manuscripts,* Vol. 1 (London: Forgotten Books, 1850).

CLARFIELD, Gerald H., *Timothy Pickering and the American Republic* (Pittsburgh: University of Pittsburgh Press, 1980).

CLARKE, Jack Alden, "Thomas Sydney Jesup: Military Observer at the Hartford Convention," *New England Quarterly* 29, no. 3 (1956), pp. 393-399.

COFRANCESCO, Dino, *La democrazia liberale (e le altre)* (Soveria Mannelli: Rubbettino, 2003).

COGLIANO Francis D., ed., *A Companion to Thomas Jefferson* (Malden, MA: Wiley-Blackwell, 2012).

COIT, Margaret L., "Calhoun and the Downfall of States' Rights,"*Virginia Quarterly Review* 28 (1952), pp. 191-208.

COLBOURN, H. Trevor, *Fame and the Founding Fathers* (New York: W.W. Norton, 1974).

COLLINS, James B., *The State in Early Modern France* (1995) (New York: Cambridge University Press, 2009).

COOPER JR., William J., *The South and the Politics of Slavery, 1828-1856* (Baton Rouge: Louisiana State University Press, 1978).

CORNELL, Saul, *The Other Founders: Anti-federalism and the Dissenting Tradition in America, 1788-1828* (Chapel Hill: University of North Carolina Press, 1999).

COX RICHARDSON, Heather, T*he Greatest Nation of the Earth: Republican Economic Policies during the Civil War* (Cambridge, MA: Harvard University Press, 1997).

CUNNINGHAM JR., Noble E., *The Jeffersonian Republicans: The Formation of Party Organization 1789–1801* (Chapel Hill: University of North Carolina Press, 1957).

CUNNINGHAM, Noble E., *The Jeffersonian Republicans. The Formation of Party Organization, 1789-1801* (Chapel Hill: University of North Carolina Press for the Institute of Early American History and Culture, 1963).

CURRY, Jabez L. M., *The Southern States of The American Union Considered in Their Relations to the Constitution of the United States and to the Resulting Union* (Richmond, VA: Johnson, 1895).

CURTI, Merle, *The Growth of American Thought* (New York: Harper & Brothers, 1951).

CURTI, Merle, *The Roots of American Loyalty* (New York: Columbia University Press, 1946).

DAHL, Robert A., "James Madison: Republican or Democrat?," *Perspectives on Politics* 3, no. 3 (2005), pp. 439-448.

DAHL, Robert A., *A Preface to Democratic Theory* (Chicago: University of Chicago Press, 1956).

DAHL, Robert A., *Pluralist Democracy in the United States: Conflict and Consent* (Chicago: Rand McNally, 1967).

DAVIES, John K., "On the Non-Usability of the Concept of 'Sovereignty' in an Ancient Greek Context," in *Federazioni e federalismo nell'Europa antica* (Milan: Vita e Pensiero, 1994), Vol. 1, pp. 51-65.

DAVIS, David Brion, *Inhuman Bondage: The Rise and Fall of Slavery in the New World* (New York: Oxford University Press, 2006).

Davis, David Brion, *The Problem of Slavery in the Age of Revolution, 1770–1823* (Ithaca: Cornell University Press, 1975).

Davis, S. Rufus, *The Federal Principle: A Journey through Time in Quest of a Meaning* (Berkeley: University of California Press, 1978).

De Mattei, Roberto, *La sovranità necessaria* (Rome: Il Minotauro, 2001).

Deudney, Daniel, "Binding Sovereigns: Authorities, Structures, and Geopolitics in the Philadelphian System," in *State Sovereignty as Social Construct*, ed. Thomas J. Biersteker and Cynthia Weber (Cambridge, Melbourne: Cambridge University Press, 1996), pp. 190-239.

Dewey, John, *The Public and Its Problems* (London: Allen & Unwin, 1927).

Diamond, Jared, *Guns, Germs and Steel: The Fates of Human Societies* (New York: Norton, 1997).

Dickens, Charles, "The Morrill Tariff," *All the Year Round*, December 28, 1862.

Dietze, Gottfried, *The Federalist: A Classic of Federalism and Free Government* (Baltimore: Johns Hopkins Press, 1960).

DiLorenzo, Thomas, "Yankee Confederates: New England Secession Movements Prior to the War Between the States," in *Secession, State & Liberty*, ed. David Gordon (New Brunswick, NJ: Transaction, 1998), pp. 135-153.

DiLorenzo, Thomas, *The Real Lincoln: A New Look at Abraham Lincoln, His Agenda, and an Unnecessary War* (New York: Three Rivers Press, 2003).

Dollinger, Philippe, *The German Hansa* (Stanford: Stanford University Press, 1970).

Donovan, Frank, *Mr. Madison's Constitution: The Story Behind the Constitutional Convention* (New York: Dodd, Mead, 1965).

Dorpalen, Andreas, *Heinrich von Treitschke* (New Haven, CT: Yale University Press, 1957).

DRAPER, Theodore, "Hume & Madison: The Secrets of Federalist Paper N. 10," *Encounter* 58 (1982), pp. 34–47.

DUGUIT, Léon, *Souveraineté et liberté: Leçons faites à l'Université Columbia (New York) en 1920–1921* (Paris: Alcan, 1922).

DUMOLYN, Jan, "The Political and Symbolic Economy of State Feudalism: The Case of Late-Medieval Flanders," *Historical Materialism* 15 (2007), pp. 105-131.

DUNCAN, Christopher M., "Men of a Different Faith: The Anti-Federalist Ideal in Early American Political Thought," *Polity* 26, no. 3 (Spring 1994), pp.387-415.

DUNCAN, Christopher M., *The Antifederalists and Early American Political Thought* (DeKalb: Northern Illinois University Press: 1995).

DUPONCEAU, Peter S., *A Dissertation on the Nature and Extent of the Jurisdiction of the Courts of the United States* (Philadelphia: Abraham Small, 1824).

DUPONCEAU, Peter S., *A Dissertation on the Nature and Extent of the Jurisdiction of the Courts of the United States* (Philadelphia:
DURDEN, Robert F., *The Self-Inflicted Wound: Southern Politics in the Nineteenth Century* (Louisville: Kentucky University Press, 1985).

DUREY, Michael, "Thomas Paine's Apostles: Radical Emigres and the Triumph of Jeffersonian Republicanism," *William and Mary Quarterly* 3rd series, Vol. 44, no 4 (October 1987), pp. 661-688.

DWIGHT, Theodore, *History of the Hartford Convention, with a Review of the Policy of the United States Government Which Led to the War of 1812* (New York-Boston: Russel, 1833).

EASTON, David, *The Political System: An Inquiry into the State of Political Science* (New York: Knopf, 1953).

EDLING, Max M., *A Revolution in Favor of Government: Origins of the U.S. Constitution and the Making of the American State* (New York: Oxford University Press, 2003).

Egerton, John, "The End of the South as an American Problem," in *The South as an American Problem*, eds. Larry J. Griffin and Don H. Doyle (Athens: University of Georgia Press, 1995), pp. 259-74.

Einhorn, Robin L., "Patrick Henry's Case against the Constitution: The Structural Problem with Slavery," *Journal of the Early Republic* 22, no. 4 (2002), pp. 549-573.

Eksterowicz, Anthony J. and Cline Paul C., "Ratification of the Constitution: The Great Debate as Portrayed in American Government Textbooks," *PS: Political Science and Politics* 24, no. 2 (1991), pp. 211-215.

Elazar, Daniel J., "Confederation and Federal Liberty," *Publius* 12, no. 4 (1982), pp. 1-14.

Elazar, Daniel J., *Exploring Federalism* (Tuscaloosa: University of Alabama Press, 1987).

Elazar, Daniel, *The American Constitutional Tradition* (Lincoln: University of Nebraska Press, 1988).

Ellis, James H., *A Ruinous and Unhappy War: New England and the War of 1812* (New York: Algora, 2009).

Ellis, Richard E., "The Persistence of Antifederalism after 1789," in *Beyond Confederation: Origins of the Constitution and American National Identity*, eds. Richard Beeman, Stephen Botein and Edward C. Carter (Chapel Hill: North Carolina University Press, 1987), pp. 295-314.

Ellis, Richard E., *The Union at Risk* (Oxford: Oxford University Press, 1987).

Farr, James, "Francis Lieber and the Interpretation of American Political Science," *Journal of Politics* 52, no. 4 (1990), pp. 1027-1049.

Faust, Albert Bernhardt, *The German Element in the United States with Special Reference to Its Political, Moral Social, and Educational Influence. In two volumes* (Boston-New York: Houghton Mifflin Company, 1909).

Faust, Drew G., *The Ideology of Slavery: Proslavery Thought in the Antebellum South, 1830–1860* (Baton Rouge: Louisiana State University Press, 1981).

FELDMAN, Jean-Philippe, *La bataille américaine du fédéralism: John C. Calhoun et l'annulation (1828–1833)* (Paris: Presses Universitaires de France, 2004).

FERLING, John, *Adams v. Jefferson: The Tumultuous Election of 1800* (New York: Oxford University Press, 2004).

FINKELMAN Paul, "Turning Losers into Winners: What Can We Learn, If Anything, From the Antifederalists?" *Texas Law Review* 79 (2001), pp. 849-94.

FINKELMAN, Paul, *Slavery, Revolutionary America, and the New Nation* (New York: Garland, 1989).

FIORAVANTI, Maurizio, "Stato e costituzione," in *Lo Stato moderno in Europa: Istituzioni e diritto* (2002), ed. Maurizio Fioravanti (Rome: Laterza, 2004).

FISKE, John, *The Critical Period of American History*, 1783–1789 (Boston: Houghton Mifflin, 1888).

FITZHUGH, George, "The Politics and Economics of Aristotle and Mr. Calhoun," *DeBow's Review* 23 (1857), pp. 163-172.

FLAUMENHAFT, Harvey, *The Effective Republic: Administration and Constitution in the Thought of Alexander Hamilton* (Durham: Duke University Press, 1992).

FLETCHER, George P., *Our Secret Constitution: How Lincoln Redefined American Democracy* (New York: Oxford University Press, 2001).

FOGEL, Robert William, *Without Consent or Contract: The Rise and Fall of American Slavery* (New York: Norton, 1989).

FONER, Eric, *Free Soil, Free Labor, Free Men: The Ideology of the Republican Party before the Civil War* (Oxford: Oxford University Press, 1995).

FORD, Lacy K., "Inventing the Concurrent Majority: Madison, Calhoun, and the Problem of Majoritarianism in American Political Thought," *Journal of Southern History* 60, no. 1 (1994), pp. 19-58.

FORD, Lacy K., *Deliver Us from Evil: The Slavery Question in the Old South* (New York: Oxford University Press, 2009).

FRANGIPANE, Marcella, *La nascita dello Stato nel vicino Oriente* (Rome: Laterza, 1996).

FREEHLING, William W., "Spoilsmen and Interests in the Thought and Career of John C. Calhoun," *Journal of American History* 52 (1965), pp. 25-42.

FREIDEL, Frank, *Francis Lieber: Nineteenth Century Liberal* (Baton Rouge: Louisiana State University Press, 1947).

FRIED, Morton H., "Tribe to State or State to Tribe in Ancient China?" in *The Origins of Chinese Civilization*, ed. David N. Keightley (Berkeley: University of California Press, 1983), pp. 467-94.

FRIEDRICH, Carl J., *Trends of Federalism in Theory and Practice* (New York: Praeger, 1968).

FRIES, Sylvia D., "Staatstheorie and the New American Science of Politics," *Journal of the History of Ideas* 34, no. 3 (1973), pp. 391-404.

GAMBLE, Richard, "Rethinking Lincoln," in *The Costs of War: America's Pyrrhic Victories*, ed. John V. Densen (New Brunswick, NJ: Transaction, 1999).

GANNON, Kevin M., "Escaping 'Mr. Jefferson's Plan of Destruction': New England Federalists and the Idea of a Northern Confederacy, 1803–1804," *Journal of the Early Republic* 21, no. 3 (Autumn, 2001), pp. 413-443.

GANNON, Kevin, *Nullification, Secession, or "A Great Pamphlet?": New England Federalism and the Hartford Convention Movement, 1809–1815* (manuscript).

GENOVESE, Eugene D., *Roll, Jordan, Roll: The World the Slaves Made* (New York: Pantheon Books, 1974).

GENOVESE, Eugene D., *The Political Economy of Slavery: Studies in the Economy and Society of the Slave South* (New York: Pantheon Books, 1965).

GENOVESE, Eugene D., *The Slaveholders' Dilemma: Freedom and Progress in Southern Conservative Thought, 1820–1860* (Columbia: University of South Carolina Press, 1992).

GIBSON, Alan, "Inventing the Extended Republic: The Debate over the Role of Madison's Theory in the Creation of the Constitution," in *James Madison: Philosopher, Founder, and Statesman*, eds. John R. Vile, William D. Pederson, and Frank J. Williams (Athens: Ohio University Press, 2008), pp. 63-87.

GIBSON, Alan, "The Madisonian Madison and the Question of Consistency: The Significance and Challenge of Recent Research," *Review of Politics* 64, no. 2 (2002), pp. 311-338.

GIDDENS, Anthony, *The Nation State and Violence* (Cambridge, UK: Polity, 1985).

GIERKE, Otto von, *Johannes Althusius und die entwicklung der naturrechtlichen staatstheorien: zugleich ein beitrag zur geschichte der rechtssystematik* (Breslau: Verlag von Wilhem Koebner, 1880).

GIERKE, Otto von, *The Development of Political Theory*, by Bernard Freyd (New York: W. W. Norton, 1939).

GILPIN, Drew, *James Henry Hammond and the Old South: A Design for Mastery* (Baton Rouge: Louisiana State University Press, 1982).

GIPSON, Lawrence H., *The British Empire before the American Revolution*, 15 vols. (New York: Knopf, 1936-1970).

GRADY, Benjamin Franklin, *The Case of the South Against the North* (Raleigh, NC: Edwards & Burton, 1899).

GREENBERG, Kenneth S., Introduction, *Nat Turner: A Slave Rebellion in History and Memory*, ed. Kenneth S. Greenberg (New York: Oxford University Press, 2003), pp. xi-xix.

GREENSTONE, J. David, *The Lincoln Persuasion: Remaking American Liberalism* (Princeton: Princeton University Press, 1993).

GRIMES, Alan Pendleton, *American Political Thought* (New York: Holt, 1960).

Gross, David, "Temporality and the Modern State," *Theory and Society* 4, 1 (1985), pp. 53-82.

Grossi, Paolo, "Modernità politica e ordine giuridico," *Quaderni fiorentini* 28 (1998), pp. 13-39.

Grossi, Paolo, "Un diritto senza Stato," *Quaderni fiorentini* 25 (1996), pp. 267-284.

Grossi, Paolo, *Mitologie giuridiche della modernità* (Milan: Giuffrè, 2007).

Gumplowicz, Ludwig, *The Outlines of Sociology* (Philadelphia: American Academy of Political and Social Science, 1899).

Gutzman, Kevin R., "A Troublesome Legacy: James Madison and The Principles of '98," *Journal of the Early Republic*, Vol. 15, No. 4 (Winter, 1995), pp. 569-589.

Gutzman, Kevin R., *Thomas Jefferson, Revolutionary: A Radical's Struggle to Remake America* (New York: St. Martin's Press, 2017).

Hammond, Bray, *Banks and Politics in America from the Revolution to the Civil War* (Princeton: Princeton University Press, 1957).

Hammond, Scott J., Kevin R. Hardwick, and Howard Leslie Lubert, eds., *Classics of American Political and Constitutional Thought: Origins through the Civil War* (Indianapolis: Hackett, 2007).

Hardin, Russell, *Liberalism, Constitutionalism, and Democracy* (Oxford: Oxford University Press, 1999).

Hartz, Louis, *The Liberal Tradition in America. An Interpretation of American Political Thought since the Revolution* (New York: Harcourt Brace, 1955).

Heer, Friedrich, *Intellectual History of Europe* (1953) (New York: World Publishing, 1966).

Heideking, Jürgen, "The Pattern of American Modernity from the Revolution to the Civil War," *Daedalus* 129, 1 (2000), pp. 219-247.

Hesseltine, William B., Introduction, *The Tragic Conflict: The Civil War and Reconstruction*, ed. William B. Hesseltine (New York: Braziller, 1962).

HICKEY, Donald R., *The War of 1812: Still a Forgotten Conflict? An Historiographical Essay, The Journal of Military History* 65, no. 3, July 2001: 741-769.

HICKEY, Donald R., *War of 1812: A Forgotten Conflict* (Urbana: University of Illinois Press, 2012).

HICKOK, JR. Eugene W., ed., *The Bill of Rights: Original Meaning and Current Understanding* (Charlottesville: University Press of Virginia, 1991).

Higham, John, "The Cult of the 'American Consensus': Homogenizing Our History," Commentary, XXVII, February 1959: 93-100.

HINSLEY, Harry, *Sovereignty* (1966) (Cambridge, UK-New York-Melbourne: Cambridge University Press, 1986).

HOADLEY, John F., *Origins of American Political Parties, 1789-1803* (Lexington: University Press of Kentucky, 1986).

HOFFERT, Richard and Robert W., *A Politics of Tensions: The Articles of Confederation and American Political Ideas* (Niwot: University Press of Colorado, 1992).

HOFFMAN, John, *Beyond the State: An Introductory Critique* (Cambridge, UK: Polity Press, 1995).

HOFFMAN, Ronald, ALBERT Peter J., eds., *The Bill of Rights: Government Proscribed* (Charlottesville: University Press of Virginia, 1997).

HOFSTADTER, Richard, ed., *Great Issues in American History: From the Revolution to the Civil War, 1765-1865* (New York: Vintage, 1958).

HOFSTADTER, Richard, *The American Political Tradition and the Men Who Made It* (New York: Norton, 1948).

HOFSTADTER, Richard, *The Progressive Historians. Turner, Beard, Parrington* (New York: Knopf, 1968).

HYMAN, Harold M., *A More Perfect Union: The Impact of the Civil War and Reconstruction on the Constitution* (New York: Knopf, 1973).

JACKSON, Robert, *Sovereignty. The Evolution of an Idea* (Cambridge, UK: Polity Pres, 2007).

JAFFA, Harry V., *Crisis of the House Divided: An Interpretation of the Issues in the Lincoln-Douglas Debates* (Chicago: University of Chicago Press, 1959).

JENSEN, Merrill, *The Articles of Confederation: An Interpretation of the Social-Constitutional History of the American Revolution, 1774–1781* (Madison: University of Wisconsin Press, 1940).

JOHNSON, Curtis N., *Aristotle's Theory of the State* (New York: St. Martin, 1990).

JOHNSON, Joel A., "Disposed to Seek Their True Interests: Representation and Responsibility in Anti-Federalist Thought," *Review of Politics* 64, no. 4 (2004), pp. 649-674.

JOUVENEL, Bertrand de, *Sovereignty: An Inquiry into the Political Good* (1955), trans. J. F. Huntington, Preface by Daniel J. Mahoney and David Des Rosiers (Indianapolis: Liberty Fund, 1997).

KANTOROWICZ, Ernst, *The King's Two Bodies: A Study in Medieval Political Theology* (Princeton: Princeton University Press, 1957).

KELSEN, Hans, *Die Gleichheit vor dem Gesetz* (Berlin: de Gruyter, 1927).

KELSEN, Hans, *Reine Rechtslehere* (1934) *Introduction to the Problems of Legal Theory,* trans. Bonnie L. Paulson and Stanley L. Paulson (Oxford: Clarendon Press, 1992).

KENYON, Cecelia M., "Men of Little Faith: The Anti-Federalists on the Nature of Representative Government," *William and Mary Quarterly*, 3rd series, 12, no. 1 (1955), pp. 3-46.

KETCHAM, Ralph, "Antifederalist Essays and Speeches, 1787–1788," in *Roots of the Republic: American Founding Documents Interpreted,* ed. Stephen Schechter (Lanham, MD: Madison House, 1990), pp. 381-422.

KHAZANOV, Anatolii M., "Some Theoretical Problems of the Study of the Early State," in *The Early State*, eds. Henri J. M. Claessen and Peter Skalník (The Hague: Mouton, 1978), pp. 77-92.

KING, Preston, *Federalism and Federation* (Baltimore: Johns Hopkins University Press, 1982).

KIRK, Russell, *Le radici dell'ordine americano*, ed. Marco Respinti (Milan: Mondadori, 1996).

KIRK, Russell, *The Roots of American Order*, 3rd ed. (Washington, DC: Regnery 1991).

KLARMAN, Michael J., *The Framers' Coup: The Making of the United States Constitution* (New York: Oxford University Press, 2016).

KLUBES, Benjamin B., "The First Federal Congress and the First National Bank: A Case Study in Constitutional Interpretation," *Journal of the Early Republic* 10, no. 1 (Spring 1990), pp. 19–41.

KOCH, Adrienne and AMMON Harry, "The Virginia and Kentucky Resolutions: An Episode in Jefferson's and Madison's Defense of Civil Liberties," *William and Mary Quarterly,* 3rd series, Vol. 5, no. 2 (April 1948), pp. 145-176.

KOCH, Adrienne and AMMON Harry, "The Virginia and Kentucky Resolutions," The William and Mary Quarterly, Vol. 5, No. 2 (Apr., 1948), pp. 145-176.

KOEBNER, Richard, *Empire* (Cambridge, UK: Cambridge University Press, 1961).

KOHN, Hans, *Introduction* to Heinrich von Treitschke, *Politics* (New York: Macmillan Company, 1963).

KOLKO, Gabriel, *Century of War* (New York: New Press, 1994).

KORITANSKY, John C., "Alexander Hamilton's Philosophy of Government and Administration," *Publius* 9, no. 2 (Spring 1979), pp. 99-122.

KRADER, Lawrence, *Formation of the State* (Englewood Cliffs, NJ: Prentice Hall, 1968).

KRAMER, Larry D., "Madison's Audience," *Harvard Law Review* 112, no. 3 (1999), pp. 611-679.

KRASNER, Stephen D., "Sovereignty: An Institutional Perspective," in *The Elusive State: International and Comparative Perspectives*, ed. James A. Caporaso (Newbury Park, CA: Sage, 1989), pp. 69-96.

KRAUS, Michael and JOYCE Davis D., *The Writing of American History* (1953) (Norman: University of Oklahoma Press, 1990).

KUPERSMITH, Abraham, "Montesquieu and the Ideological Strain in Antifederalist Thought," in *The Federalists, the Antifederalists, and the American Political Tradition*, eds. Wilson Carey McWilliams and Michael T. Gibbons (New York: Greenwood Press, 1992), pp. 47-75.

KURTZ, Donald V., *Political Anthropology: Power and Paradigms* (Boulder, CO: Westview, 2001).

LA PERGOLA, Antonio, *Residui "contrattualistici" e struttura federale nell'ordinamento degli Stati Uniti* (Milan: Giuffrè, 1969).

LACROIX, Alison L., "A Singular and Awkward War: The Transatlantic Context of the Hartford Convention," *American Nineteenth Century History* 6, no. 1 (2005), pp. 3-32.

LACROIX, Alison L., *The Ideological Origins of American Federalism* (Cambridge, MA: Harvard University Press, 2010).

LARSEN, Jacob A. O., *Greek Federal States* (Oxford: Clarendon Press, 1968).

LASKI, Harold J., *The Foundations of Sovereignty and Other Essays*; Hugo Krabbe, *The Modern Idea of the State* (1919), trans. George H. Sabine and Walter J. Shepard (New York: Appleton, 1922).

LATNER, Richard B., "The Nullification Crisis and Republican Subversion," *Journal of Southern History* 43, no. 1 (1977), pp. 19-38.

LE FUR, Louis, *État fédéral et Confédération d'états* (Paris: Marchanal et Billard, 1896).

LEE CHEEK, H., *Calhoun and Popular Rule: The Political Theory of the Disquisition and Discourse* (Columbia: University of Missouri Press, 2001).

LERNER, Ralph, "Calhoun's New Science of Politics," The *American Political Science Review, 57* (4), 1963, pp. 918-932.

LEVI, Lucio, "La Federazione: costituzionalismo e democrazia oltre i confini nazionali," introduction to A. Hamilton, J. Jay, J. Madison, *Il Federalista* (Bologna: Il Mulino, 1988), pp. 9-110.

LEVY, Leonard W., *Freedom of Speech and Press in Early American History: Legacy of Suppression* (New York: Harper & Row, 1963).

LIENISCH, Michael, *New Order of the Ages. Time, the Constitution, and the Making of Modern American Political Thought* (Princeton: Princeton University Press, 1988).

LIPSET, Seymour Martin, *American Exceptionalism: A Double-Edged Sword* (New York: Norton, 1996).

LIVERANI, Mario, *Myth and Politics in Ancient Near Eastern Historiography*, edited and introduced by Zainab Bahrani and Marc Van De Mieroop (Ithaca: Cornell University Press, 2004).

LIVERANI, Mario, *Uruk: La prima città* (Bari-Rome, Laterza, 1998).

LOCKHART, Charles, *The Roots of American Exceptionalism: History, Institutions, and Culture* (New York: Macmillan, 2003).

LORD ACTON, *History of Freedom and Other Essays* (London: McMillan, 1907).

LOWI, Theodore J., "Why Is There No Socialism in the United States?," *International Political Science Review* 5, no. 4 (1984), pp. 369-380.

LUBASZ, Heinz, ed., *The Development of the Modern State* (New York: Macmillan, 1964).

LUCATELLO, Guido, *Lo Stato federale* (Padua: Cedam, 1939).

LUHMANN, Niklas and DE GIORGI Raffaele, *Teoria della Società* (Milan: Angeli, 1992).

LULL, Vincente, MICÓ Rafael, *Archaeology of the Origin of the State: The Theories* (New York: Oxford University Press, 2011).

LURAGHI, Raimondo, *Cinque lezioni sulla guerra civile americana*, 1861–1865 (Naples: La città del sole, 1997).

LURAGHI, Raimondo, ed., *La Guerra Civile Americana* (Bologna: il Mulino, 1978).

Luraghi, Raimondo, *La spada e le magnolie. Il Sud nella storia degli Stati Uniti* (Rome: Donzelli, 2007).

Lutz, Donald S., "The Articles of Confederation as the Background to the Federal Republic," *Publius* 20, no. 1 (1990), pp. 55-70.

Lutz, Donald S., *Popular Consent and Popular Control* (Baton Rouge: Louisiana State University Press, 1980).

Lutz, Donald S., *The Origins of American Constitutionalism* (Baton Rouge: Louisiana State University Press, 1988).

Lynd, Staughton, *Class Conflict, Slavery, and the United States Constitution* (Westport, CT: Greenwood, 1980).

Macleod, Duncan J., *Slavery, Race and the American Revolution* (New York: Cambridge University Press, 1974).

Maier, Pauline, "The Road Not Taken: Nullification, John C. Calhoun, and the Revolutionary Tradition in South Carolina," *South Carolina Historical Magazine* 72, no. 1 (1981), pp. 1-19.

Maitland, Frederic W., Introduction to Otto F. von Gierke, *Political Theories of the Middle Ages* (Cambridge-New York: Cambridge University Press, 1900).

Malandrino, Corrado, *Federalismo: Storia, idee, modelli* (Rome: Carocci, 1998).

Malone, Dumas, *Jefferson and His Time*, 6 vols. (Boston: Little, Brown, 1948–1981).

Malone, Dumas, *Jefferson and the Ordeal of Liberty* (Boston: Little, Brown, 1962).

Maravall, José Antonio, *Stato moderno e mentalità sociale*, 2 vols. (Bologna: il Mulino, 1991 [1972]).

Marmor, Theodore R., "Anti-Industrialism in the Old South: The Agrarian Perspective of John C. Calhoun," *Comparative Studies in Society and History* 9 (1967), pp. 377-406.

MATSON, Cathy D. and ONUF Peter S., *A Union of Interest: Political and Economic Thought in Revolutionary America* (Lawrence: University Press of Kansas, 1990).

MATTEUCCI, Nicola, *Lo Stato moderno. Lessico e percorsi* (Bologna: il Mulino, 1993).

MAYER, David N., *The Constitutional Thought of Thomas Jefferson* (Charlottesville: University Press of Virginia, 1994).

MCCARDELL, John, *The Idea of a Southern Nation: Southern Nationalists and Southern Nationalism, 1830–1860* (New York: Norton, 1979).

MCCLELLAN, James, *Joseph Story and the American Constitution: A Study in Political and Legal Thought* (Norman: University of Oklahoma Press, 1971).

MCCOY, Drew R., *The Last of the Fathers: James Madison and the Republican Legacy* (New York: Cambridge University Press, 1989).

MCDONALD, Forrest, *Alexander Hamilton: A Biography* (New York: Norton, 1979).

MCDONALD, Forrest, *Novus Ordo Seclorum: The Intellectual Origins of the Constitution* (Lawrence: University Press of Kansas, 1985).

MCDONALD, Forrest, *States' Rights and the Union: Imperium in Imperio 1776-1876* (Lawrence: University Press of Kansas, 2000).

MCDOWELL, Gary L., "Federalism and Civic Virtue: The Antifederalists and the Constitution," in *How Federal is the Constitution?*, eds. Robert A. Goldwin and William A. Schambra (Washington, American Enterprise Institute, 1987), pp. 122-144.

MCILWAIN, Charles H., *The Growth of Political Thought in the West* (New York: McMillan, 1932).

MCPHERSON, James M., *Abraham Lincoln and the Second American Revolution* (New York: Oxford University Press, 1992).

MEIGS, William M., *The Life of John C. Calhoun* (New York: Neale Publishing Company 1917)

MERRIAM, C. E., "The Political Theory of Calhoun," *American Journal of Sociology* 7, no. 5 (1902), pp. 577-594.

MERRIAM, Charles E., *History of American Political Theories* (New York: Macmillan, 1903).

MIGLIO, Gianfranco, "Genesi e trasformazioni del termine-concetto 'Stato'" (1981), in *Le regolarità della politica* (Milan: Giuffrè, 1988), vol. II, pp. 801-32.

MIGLIO, Gianfranco, "L'unità fondamentale di svolgimento dell'esperienza politica occidentale" (1957), in *Le regolarità della politica* (Milan: Giuffrè, 1988), vol. II, pp. 325-350.

MILIBAND, Ralph, *The State in Capitalist Society* (New York: Basic Books, 1969).

MILLICAN, Edward, *One United People: The Federalist Papers and the National Idea* (Lexington: University Press of Kentucky, 1990).

MILLS, C. Wright, *The Power Elite* (New York: Oxford University Press, 1956).

MOGI, Sobei, *The Problem of Federalism,* Vol. 1 (London: Macmillan, 1931).

MORISON, Samuel Eliot, *The Life and Letters Harrison Gray Otis, Federalist, 1765–1848,* 2 vols. (Boston: Houghton Mifflin, 1913).

MORLEY, Felix, *Freedom and Federalism* (Chicago: Regnery, 1959).

MORRIS, Richard B., *Forging the Union*, 1781–1789 (New York: Harper & Row, 1987).

MORRIS, Thomas D., *Southern Slavery and the Law, 1619–1860* (Chapel Hill: University of North Carolina Press, 1996).

MURRAY, Joseph A., *Alexander Hamilton: America's Forgotten Founder* (New York: Algora, 2007).

NAGEL, Robert F., *The Implosion of American Federalism* (New York: Oxford University Press, 2002).

NEDELSKY, Jennifer, *Private Property and the Limits of American Constitutionalism, The Madisonian Framework and Its Legacy* (Chicago-London, The University of Chicago Press, 1990).

NISBET, Robert A., *Social Change and History: Aspects of the Western Theory of Development* (New York: Oxford University Press, 1969).

OAKES, James, *The Ruling Race: A History of American Slaveholders* (New York: Knopf, 1982).

ONUF, Peter S., *Jefferson's Empire: The Language of American Nationhood* (Charlottesville: University Press of Virginia, 2000).

OPPENHEIMER, Franz, *The State* (1908), trans. John Gitterman (San Francisco: Fox & Wilkes, 1997).

OPPENHEIMER, Martin, *The State in Modern Society* (Amherst, NY: Humanity Books, 2000).

OSTROM, Vincent, *The Political Theory of a Compound Republic: Designing the American Experiment* (Lincoln: University of Nebraska Press, 1987).

OTIS, Harrison Gray, *Otis' Letters in Defence of the Hartford Convention* (Boston: Simon Gardner, 1824).

PADOVER, Saul K., ed., *Karl Marx on America and the Civil War* (New York: McGraw-Hill, 1972).

PARISH, Peter J., *The North and the Nation in the Era of the Civil War,* eds. Adam I. P. Smith and Susan-Mary Grant (New York: Fordham University Press, 2003).

PARRINGTON, Vernon L., *Main Currents in American Political Thought: An Interpretation of American Literature from the Beginnings to 1920: The Beginnings of Critical Realism in America, 1860–1920*, Vol. 3 (New York: Harcourt Brace, 1930).

PARRINGTON, Vernon L., *Main Currents in American Thought: An Interpretation of American Literature from the Beginnings to 1920: The Romantic Revolution in America, 1800–1860* (1927), Vol. 2 (New York: Harcourt, Brace, 1954).

PETERSON, Merrill D., *Thomas Jefferson and the New Nation: A Biography* (New York: Oxford University Press, 1970).

PHILLIPS, Ulrich B., "The Central Theme of Southern History," *American Historical Review* 34 (1928), pp. 30-43.

PIERSON, Christopher, *The Modern State* (New York: Routledge, 1996).

POCHMANN, Henry A. and SCHULTZ Arthur R., *German Culture in America, 1600–1900: Philosophical and Literary Influences* (Madison: University of Wisconsin Press, 1957).

POGGI, Gianfranco, *The Development of the Modern State: A Sociological Introduction* (Stanford: Stanford University Press, 1978).

PORTINARO, Pier Paolo, *Il labirinto delle istituzioni nella storia europea* (Bologna: il Mulino, 2007).

POTTER, David M., *The Impending Crisis 1848–1861* (New York: Harper and Row, 1976).

POULANTZAS, Nicos, *Pouvoir politique et classes sociales de l'état capitaliste* (Paris: Maspéro, 1968).

POUND, Roscoe, *An Introduction to the Philosophy of Law* (New Haven: Yale University Press, 1922).

POWELL, Edward Payson, *Nullification and Secession in the United States* (New York: Putnam, 1897).

POWELL, H. Jefferson, "The Principles of '98: An Essay in Historical Retrieval," *Virginia Law Review*, Vol. 80, No. 3 (April 1994), pp. 689-743.

QUAGLIONI, Diego, *La sovranità* (Rome: Laterza, 2004).

RAKOVE, Jack, "The Legacy of the Articles of Confederation," *Publius* 12, no. 4 (1982), pp. 45-66.

RAWLEY, James A., *The Politics of Union: Northern Politics during the Civil War* (Lincoln: University of Nebraska Press, 1980).

READ, James H., *Majority Rule Versus Consensus. The Political Thought of John C. Calhoun* (Lawrence, KS: University Press of Kansas, 2009).

REINHARD, Wolfgang, *Geschichte der Staatsgewalt: Eine vergleichende Verfassungsgeschichte Europas von den Anfängen bis zur Gegenwart* (München: C.H. Beck, 1999).

Reinhard, Wolfgang, *Storia del potere politico in Europa* (Bologna: il Mulino, 2001).

Riker, William, *Federalism: Origin, Operation, and Significance* (Boston: Little Brown, 1964).

Rogow, Arnold A., *A Fatal Friendship: Alexander Hamilton and Aaron Burr* (New York: Hill & Wang, 1999).

Rosen, Gary, *American Compact: James Madison and the Problem of Founding* (Lawrence: University Press of Kansas, 1999).

Rutland, Robert A., *The Ordeal of the Constitution: The Antifederalists and the Ratification Struggle of 1787–1788* (1966) (Boston: Northeastern University Press, 1983).

Salvadori, Massimo L., *Potere e libertà nel mondo modern: John C. Calhoun, un genio imbarazzante* (Bari-Rome Laterza, 1996).

Sandoz, Ellis, *Republicanism, Religion, and the Soul of America* (Columbia: University of Missouri Press, 2006).

Sartori, Giovanni, "Liberty and Law," in *The Politicization of Society*, ed. Kenneth S. Templeton (Indianapolis: Liberty Press, 1979), pp. 251-311.

Schiera, Pierangelo, Introduction to Otto Brunner, *Terra e potere. Strutture pre-statuali e pre-moderne nella storia costituzionale dell'Austria medievale*, Pierangelo Schiera ed. (Milan: Giuffrè, 1983).

Schmitt, Carl, "Staatliche Souveränität und freies Meer: Über den Gegensatz von Land und See im Völkerrecht der Neuzeit," in *Das Reich und Europa*, ed. Fritz Hartung (Leipzig: Köhler und Ameland, 1941).

Schmitt, Carl, "The Constitutional Theory of Federation," in *Telos* 91 (Spring 1992) pp. 26-56.

Schmitt, Carl, *Constitutional Theory*, ed. and trans. Jeffrey Seitzer (Durham, NC: Duke University Press, 2008).

Schmitt, Carl, *The Concept of the Political* (1932) ed. George Schwab (Chicago: University of Chicago Press, 1996).

Schmitt, Carl, *Verfassungslehere* (1928) (Berlin: Dunker & Humbolt, 2017).

Sheidley, Harlow W., "The Webster-Hayne Debate: Recasting New England's Sectionalism," *New England Quarterly* 67 (1994), pp. 5-29.

Sicker, Martin, *The Genesis of the State* (New York: Praeger, 1991).

Sidgwick, Henry, *The Elements of Politics* (London-New York: Macmillan, 1891).

Sidjanski, Dusan, *Fédéralisme Amphictyonique: éléments de système et tendance international* (Lausanne: Rouge, 1956).

Siemers, David J., *The Antifederalists: Men of Great Faith and Forbearance* (Lanham, MD: Rowman & Littlefield, 2003).

Silk, Leonard and Silk Mark, *The American Establishment* (New York: Basic Books, 1980).

Sinha, Manisha, *The Counterrevolution of Slaver: Politics and Ideology in Antebellum South Carolina* (Chapel Hill: University of North Carolina Press, 2000).

Sinopoli, Richard C., "Liberalism and Political Allegiance in Anti-Federalist Political Thought," *Publius*, Vol. 22, No. 2 (Spring 1992), pp. 123-139.

Sinopoli, Richard C., *The Foundations of American Citizenship: Liberalism, the Constitution, and Civic Virtue* (New York: Oxford University Press, 1992).

Skowronek, Stephen, *Building a New American State. The Expansion of National Administrative Capacities, 1877-1920* (New York: Cambridge University Press, 1982).

Sombart, Werner, *Warum gibt es in den Vereinigten Staaten keinen Sozialismus?* (Tübingen: Mohr, 1906),*Why is there no Socialism in the United States*, translated and edited with an Introductory essay by C.T. Husbands, foreword by Michael Harrington (White Plains, NY: Sharpe, 1976).

Spain, August O., *The Political Theory of John C. Calhoun* (New York: Bookman Associates, 1951).

Spero, Patrick and Zuckerman Michael eds., *The American Revolution Reborn* (Philadelphia: University of Pennsylvania Press, 2016).

Stabile, Donald R. and Cantor Jeffrey A., *The Public Debt of the United States: An Historical Perspective, 1775–1990* (Westport, CT: Praeger, 1991).

Sternsher, Bernard, *Consensus, Conflict, and American Historians* (Bloomington: Indiana University Press, 1975).

Stoebuck, William B., "Reception of English Common Law in the American Colonies," *William and Mary Law Review*, 10 (1968), pp. 393-426.

Strayer, Joseph R., *On the Medieval Origins of the Modern State* (Princeton: Princeton University Press, 1970).

Stuart, Reginald C., *Civil-Military Relations during the War of 1812* (Santa Barbara, CA: Praeger Security International, 2009).

Taylor, Alan, "Dual Nationalisms: Legacies of the War of 1812," in *What So Proudly We Hailed: Essays on the Contemporary Meaning of the War of 1812*, eds. Pietro S. Nivola and Peter J. Kastor (Washington. DC: Brookings Institution Press, 2012), pp. 67-96.

Taylor, Alan, *The Civil War of 1812: American Citizens, British Subjects, Irish Rebels, & Indian Allies* (New York: Vintage Books, 2010).

Terni, Massimo, *La pianta della sovranità: teologia e politica tra Medioevo ed età moderna* (Rome-Bari: Laterza, 1995).

Teschke, Benno, *The Myth of 1648. Class, Geopolitics, and the Making of Modern International Relations* (London: Verso, 2003).

Thomas, John L., Introduction, *Abraham Lincoln and the American Political Tradition*, ed. John L. Thomas (Amherst: University of Massachusetts Press, 1986).

Thomson, Janice E., *Mercenaries, Pirates, and Sovereigns: State-Building and Extraterritorial Violence in Early Modern Europe* (Princeton: Princeton University Press, 1994).

TILLY, Charles, "Reflections on the History of European State-making," in *The Formation of National States in Western Europe* (Princeton: Princeton University Press, 1975), pp. 3-83.

TILLY, Charles, "War Making and State Making as Organized Crime," in *Bringing the State Back In*, ed. Peter B. EVANS, Dietrich Rueschemeyer, and Theda Skocpol (Cambridge, UK: Cambridge University Press, 1985), pp. 169-191.

TILLY, Charles, *Coercion, Capital, and European States, AD 990-1990* (Oxford: Basil Blackwell, 1990).

TURNER MAIN, Jackson, *The Antifederalists: Critics of the Constitution, 1781-1788* (New York: Norton, 1961).

TWOMEY, Richard J., *Jacobins and Jeffersonians: Anglo-American Radicalism in the United States, 1790–1820* (New York: Garland, 1989).

UPSHUR, Abel P., *A Brief Enquiry Into the True Nature and Character of our Federal Government: Being a Review of Judge Story's Commentaries on the Constitution of the United States* (1840) (Philadelphia: John Campbell, 1863).

VAN CREVELD, Martin, *The Rise and Decline of the State* (Cambridge: Cambridge University Press, 2004).

VORENBERG, Michael, *Final Freedom: The Civil War, the Abolition of Slavery, and the Thirteenth Amendment* (Cambridge: Cambridge University Press, 2001).

WAITZ, Georg, "Das Wesen des Bundesstaates," in *Allgemeine Kieler Monatsschrift für Wissenschaft und Literatur* (Berlin, 1853), pp. 495-530.

WALLING, Karl-Friedrich, *Republican Empire: Alexander Hamilton on War and Free Government* (Lawrence: University Press of Kansas, 1999).

WARFIELD, Ethelbert Dudley, *The Kentucky Resolutions of 1798: An Historical Study* (New York: G.P. Putnam's Sons, 1887).

WATKINS, Jr. William J., *Reclaiming the American Revolution: The Kentucky and Virginia Resolutions and Their Legacy* (New York: Palgrave, 2004).

WEBER, Max, *Economy and Society*, eds. Guenther Roth and Claus Wittich (New York: Bedminster Press, 1968).

WEBER, Max, *Essays in Sociology* (1919), trans. and ed. H. H. Gerth and C. Wright Mills (New York: Oxford University Press, 1958).

WEBER, Max, *The Protestant Ethic and the Spirit of Capitalism* (1905), trans. Talcott Parsons (New York: Scribner's, 1930).

WEBSTER, Daniel, *A Discourse, Delivered at Plymouth, December 22, 1820* (Boston: Wells and Lilly, 1825).

WEST, Henry Litchfield, *Federal Power: Its Growth and Necessity* (New York: George H. Doran, 1918).

WESTERKAMP, Justus B., *Staatenbund und Bundesstaat: Untersuchungen über die Praxis und das Recht der mordenen Bunde* (Leipzig: Brockhaus, 1892).

WEWERS, Daniel Corbett, *The Specter of Disunion in the Early American Republic*, Ph.D. Dissertation, 2008.

WHITE JR., Ronald C., *Lincoln's Greatest Speech: The Second Inaugural* (New York: Simon & Schuster, 2002).

WILHELMSEN, Frederick D., "Donoso Cortés and the Meaning of Political Power," *Intercollegiate Review* 3 (January-February 1967), pp. 109-127.

WILL, George F., *Restoration: Congress, Term Limits, and the Recovery of Deliberative Democracy* (New York: Free Press, 1992).

WILSON, Major L., "Liberty and Union: An Analysis of Three Concepts Involved in the Nullification Controversy," *Journal of Southern History* 33 (1967), pp. 331-355.

Wiltse, Charles M., “From Compact to National State in American Political Thought” in *Essays in Political Theory. Presented to George H. Sabine*, eds. M. R. Konvitz and A. E. Murphy (Ithaca, NY: Cornell University Press, 1948), pp. 153-78.

Wiltse, Charles M., *John C. Calhoun: Nullifier, 1829-1839* (Indianapolis-New York: Bobbs-Merrill, 1949).

Wittfogel, Karl A., *Oriental Despotism: A Comparative Study of Total Power* (New Haven, CT: Yale University Press, 1957).

Wood, Gordon S., *Empire of Liberty. A History of the Early Republic, 1789-1815* (New York: Oxford University Press).

Worster, Donald, *Rivers of Empire: Water, Aridity and the Growth of the American West* (New York: Pantheon, 1985).

Yoffee, Norman, *Myths of the Archaic State. Evolution of the Earliest Cities, States, and Civilizations* (Cambridge: Cambridge University Press, 2005).

Young, Alfred F. and Nobles Gregory H., *Whose American Revolution Was It? Historians Interpret the Founding* (New York: New York University Press, 2011).

Young, James P., *Reconsidering American Liberalism: The Troubled Odyssey of the Liberal Idea* (Boulder, CO: Westview Press, 1996).

Zavodnyik, Peter, *The Age of Strict Construction: A History of the Growth of Federal Power, 1789–1861* (Washington, DC: Catholic University Press, 2007).

Zellar, Ronald C., *A Brave Man Stands Firm: The Historic Battles between Chief Justice John Marshall and President Thomas Jefferson* (New York: Algora, 2011).

INDEX

A

B

C

D

E

F

G

H

N

O

P

Q

R

About The Author

LUIGI MARCO BASSANI, born in Chicago in 1963 and educated in Italy and the United States, is Full Professor of the History of Political Thought in the Department of International, Legal, Political, and Historical Studies at the University of Milan. He earned his Ph.D. in Political Science in 1995 at the University of Pisa, writing a dissertation on the political theory of John C. Calhoun. His paramount research interest is on American political thought from the Revolution to the Civil War, but he has published widely on other subjects, ranging from revolutionary syndicalism to libertarian theory and Classical Liberalism. Most of his works are in Italian, but his book *Liberty, State, and Union: The Political Theory of Thomas Jefferson* was published by Mercer University Press in 2010. He has received numerous fellowships and awards from various institutions, including the International Center for Jeffersonian Studies, Monticello, Virginia. He has also been awarded positions as a visiting scholar at Duke University (2015), Florida Atlantic University (2018) and Faulkner University (2020).

Patrons of *Chaining Down Leviathan*

Chris "Chip" Beeker Jr.

Steven Berger

Norman Black

Angela and Roger Box

Catharine Savage Brosman

William E. Craver III

James Garner GA Tech EE73

Bradley G. Green

Joseph Johnston Jr.

Gregory and Susan Kent

James E. Klutz

Stephen Winn Linton

Rev. Daniel Morse

Kirkpatrick Sale

Bert Schwitters

William E. Shofner

Gregory James Tisdale

Gary Via

William J. Watkins Jr.

Richard W. Wilcke

Douglas G. Wilkerson

Kerry S. Williams SFC US Army (Ret.)

William A. Winston

Available From the Abbeville Institute Press

James Everett Kibler
The Classical Origins of Southern Literature

Twenty Abbeville Institute Scholars
Exploring the Southern Tradition

D. Jonathan White, ed.
Northern Opposition to Mr. Lincoln's War

Abbeville Institute Press